Peter Asher

Peter Asher

A Life in Music

David Jacks

Backbeat
Books
Essex, Connecticut

An imprint of Globe Pequot, the trade division of
The Rowman & Littlefield Publishing Group, Inc.
4501 Forbes Blvd., Ste. 200
Lanham, MD 20706
www.rowman.com

Distributed by NATIONAL BOOK NETWORK

British Library Cataloguing in Publication Information available

Library of Congress Cataloging-in-Publication Data

Names: Jacks, David, author.
Title: Peter Asher : a life in music / David Jacks.
Description: Essex, Connecticut : Backbeat, 2022. | Includes index.
Identifiers: LCCN 2022011575 (print) | LCCN 2022011576 (ebook) | ISBN
  9781493061211 (cloth) | ISBN 9781493061228 (epub)
Subjects: LCSH: Asher, Peter, 1944- | Peter and Gordon. | Singers—United
  States—Biography. | Sound recording executives and producers—United
  States—Biography. | Singers—England—Biography. | Sound recording
  executives and producers—England—Biography. | Popular music—History
  and criticism.
Classification: LCC ML420.A9185 J33 2022 (print) | LCC ML420.A9185
  (ebook) | DDC 782.42164092 [B]—dc23/eng/20220310
LC record available at https://lccn.loc.gov/2022011575
LC ebook record available at https://lccn.loc.gov/2022011576

To Kathleen

CONTENTS

INTRODUCTION

"Are you alone?" the voice on the other end of the line asked. "Can you speak freely?"

Peter Asher was surprised at the sudden cloak-and-dagger twist in what had begun as a casual conversation. When the phone call from the Los Angeles British consulate general's office came near the end of 2014, he assumed they once again needed his help for an upcoming cultural event—something in which the British-born Asher would always enthusiastically participate.

Cautiously, he answered: "Uhhh, yes?"

"Well," the voice announced, "I'm happy to inform you that Her Majesty the Queen has decided to offer you the rank of Commander of the Most Excellent Order of the British Empire."

"I was amazed," Peter admitted to me when we spoke a few months later. The CBE ranking is only one notch below a knighthood.

But if anyone deserves such an honor for their contributions to music and culture, it would be Peter Asher. In a career spanning over sixty years, "he's done it all," singer Raul Malo enthused. "He's been an artist; he's been a manager; he's been a producer. . . . To me, he embodies what a person in the music business should be about."

Beginning with Peter and Gordon's first record, "A World Without Love," a worldwide smash in 1964 that Peter (though uncredited) had a big hand in producing, on through the seventies with a string of hits for both James Taylor and Linda Ronstadt (earning Peter two Grammy Awards for Producer of the Year), and into his seventies working with young artists like Ed Sheeran and Esperanza Spalding—while somehow finding time to add his touch to Broadway musicals and blockbuster movie soundtracks—he has succeeded in almost every aspect of the music business. His influence is everywhere (the look of Austin Powers, anyone?), even influencing The Beatles during their most creative phase. He has discovered, managed, and mentored legends, *plus* was one of the first producers to use samples on a pop single. And

1

though the blinding red hair of his youth has faded to a grayish gold (and somewhat receded), his overriding love of music has remained firmly intact.

"He has such a deep passion for music," insisted Malo, whose atmospheric 2006 release *You're Only Lonely* Asher lovingly produced. "That was one thing that was inspiring being around him—how much he loves music. He's not in it for the money or this and that—I mean, the money's nice, you know? And he's made a lot of money in his life . . . but I think, deep down, he would do it for free, if he had to."

Steely Dan's Donald Fagen, who was once managed by Peter, hit on another reason his friend stands apart in the industry: "He doesn't lie—which is very unusual in the music business." Singer David Crosby, another old friend, agreed: "Don't ask him if you don't wanna hear what he really thinks, 'cause he probably will tell you! That makes a lot of people *very* uncomfortable. 'Cause they'll go into a meeting expecting a shine job, and he'll say"—now Crosby affected a low-key British accent—"'You know, this is really crap, actually.'"

There's another personal quality, also rare, that Peter regularly displays: "As you get older," said composer Randy Newman, whose musical masterpiece *Faust* was produced by Peter, "you realize people mean well, but relatively few of them—including myself—do what they say they'll do. He's a *guarantee*. If he says he'll do something, he'll do it. I can count 'em on . . . one hand, *maybe*, the people I know that are like that. And he is."

And don't forget intelligence: When his friend Robin Williams accepted the Best Comedy Album Grammy Award for his Asher-produced release *Live 2002*, he gave special thanks to Peter, calling him "DJ Mensa" (Mensa being the society for those with the highest of IQs, of which Peter is a longtime member). Amid laughs, Williams explained: "He's English; he knows more than we do." And Newman concurred: "He's *very* intelligent. For regular people, he's in the 95th percentile, but for this business he's, you know, ninety-nine and a half."

"He's almost *too smart* to be in show business."

But show business is where Peter has made—and continues to make—his mark. How, though, did this bookish, reserved Englishman rise to the top of his profession? Determination? Talent? Was luck involved?

It always is: "Obviously, a great deal of everything is luck—except there's no such thing," confided Peter, who prefers to call it "happenstance—what happens to happen." The skill in his case or anyone's, Peter explained, is in "taking advantage of what does come your way."

In 2003, I had a chance encounter with Peter Asher. That bit of happenstance has produced this book: a look at a singular life and unbelievable career spanning over sixty years of modern music and culture. Having acquired Peter's first hit record at the tender age of eight (thanks, Mom), I continued to admire his production work through the years and always wondered how these works of art came to be. In this book I try to tell the stories behind the songs and the albums that have captivated, not just me, but millions of fans the world over.

Alongside Peter's own recollections, over two hundred of Peter's friends, collaborators, and colleagues comment on their experiences creating music with him. Most thought it about time his story was told.

However, when I first broached the idea of a biography to Peter, his surprised response was: "Who's going to want to read it? It's only me . . ."

His late friend Andrew Gold told me never to bet against Peter because he was "hardly ever wrong." As you're holding this book in your hands, I suppose even a genius can be mistaken . . .

1

THE CARROTS OF WIMPOLE STREET

On April 3, 1912, just a week before the *Titanic* set sail on her only voyage, the fourth of Louise and the Reverend Felix Asher's five children was born in Nottingham. Richard Alan John Asher certainly inherited his mother's love of music, and though he did not follow his father into the clergy, Richard always loved the hymns of the church; his mind easily grasped the workings of harmony and thrilled to voices raised in song—a love he passed on to his future children. "My father used to make us all sing in a little harmony group at home," Peter Asher remembered. "He would sing bass. We sang a lot as kids, my sisters and I."

After attending Lancing College, Richard enrolled at the London Hospital, where he got his qualifications in 1935. In 1942, Dr. Asher was appointed physician at Central Middlesex Hospital—not a particularly prestigious hospital at the time. Though a new World War was raging, Richard was deemed unfit for the armed forces. "He had some problem with his toes, some disease where they were all kind of bunched up," Peter recalled. "But I think doctors got pretty much of a pass anyway because they needed them. He was a pacifist by the end of the war," Peter confided, smiling, "so *that* would have been an issue!" Dr. Asher excelled as a general physician, where his eccentricity began to show itself—mastering how to sign his name upside down (to save time, he said) and bicycling through the hospital corridors as he went from ward to ward, seeing scores of patients on his rounds.

On July 27, 1943, Richard married red-haired twenty-nine-year-old Margaret Augusta Eliot—like his mother, a talented musician and teacher. Margaret could trace her ancestry back past William the Conqueror and other members of the British peerage, eventually arriving at distant relative Arnulf of Metz, a seventh-century Frankish bishop and saint. The newlyweds soon moved into a flat at 2 Seaford Court on Great Portland Street, where Margaret gave private music lessons, supplementing her income as a teacher at the prestigious Royal Academy of Music. She also began to play concerts around England, which helped boost morale during wartime: "One day playing in a canteen, where the noise of the till drowned the music," she later recalled, "and another day playing trios at the bottom of a coal mine."[1] A woman in an orchestra was then quite rare, but with many of the men off fighting Hitler, they were welcomed—somewhat: "I remember my mother telling me," said Peter, "they were instructed that when they walked onto the stage to walk behind the men to make themselves invisible."

Not long after he arrived at Central Middlesex, Dr. Asher was given the task of overseeing the Mental Observation Ward. He was not formally trained in psychiatry but had amazing powers of observation, noting how mental disease often had a physical cause. He also began to write, with many articles appearing in *The Lancet*—one of the oldest and most-respected medical journals in the world. "He was known for his succinct way of writing, rather than the medical tradition of verbosity and confusion," Peter noted.

One early piece, published in 1947 in the *British Medical Journal*, was "The Dangers of Going to Bed." With skill and wit, and quite ahead of his time, he made the case for getting patients up and moving much quicker than was then customary. But of all his writings, many gathered in two volumes after his death (*Talking Sense* and *A Sense of Asher*), he is best known for "Munchausen syndrome."

Now an accepted mental condition known even by the general public, Munchausen syndrome involves a person who fabricates or elaborates an illness to get attention. After observing several patients who were admitted numerous times with different "illnesses" and wildly varying stories to explain their need for treatment, Dr. Asher wrote his paper (published in *The Lancet*, February 1951), naming the condition after the wild and fictitious exploits of Baron von Munchausen. "Whereas most Doctors would name a disease after themselves," Peter observed, "it was my father's nature that he would name it after Baron Munchausen, of whose adventures he was an avid reader." Today, a related condition named "Munchausen syndrome by proxy" is well-documented, in which a parent, for example, concocts a story regarding their child's supposed illness and revels in the attention.

On June 22, 1944, the Ashers welcomed their first child—the thirty-ninth great-grandson of mighty Saint Arnulf. No long fancy name—simply Peter Asher. "My father believed in simplicity," Peter recalled, "especially when many forms and ration books required the use of full names. He decided, correctly, that it would be a convenience in life (both to him and later to us) to give minimalist names." Margaret, encouraged by Dr. Asher, was determined to feed Peter herself, "so it was a choice between staying at home or taking the baby with me to work," she later recalled. Accordingly, baby Peter began to accompany Margaret to her concerts. "I often think," she stated, "that he did more for morale of the troops than the classical concerts they heard. When I came off the platform, I invariably found some soldier had picked

1. Margaret Asher quote from "The War, Music and Baby": SWWEC LEEWW.2001.1401 Asher, M (courtesy of The Second World War Experience Centre).

him up." One experience, though, proved quite alarming: "I played in a Town Hall and was advised to leave my baby and the carrycot in the Mayor's parlour. When I went to collect him, no baby and no carrycot. An earnest social worker had taken him as she thought he was abandoned," Margaret remembered. "But of course, all was well in the end."[2]

Sister Jane joined the family two years later, with another sister, Clare, arriving two years after that—all sporting their mother's flaming red hair. While juggling the raising of her growing brood, Margaret continued tutoring music students, including a young man who, while serving in the Fleet Air Arm during the war, had befriended a professor of piano at the Guildhall School of Music.

"When I came out of the services, he asked me to come and see him," Sir George Martin recalled. "He said, 'You know, you *really* should take up music.' And I said, 'I can't! I've never had a music lesson in my life!' And he said, 'Yes you can! If you apply yourself, you *can* do it. And, if you agree, I'll arrange for you to have an audition with the principal of the Guildhall School of Music and Drama. Play him all the things you played me, and he will decide then whether you should be taken on as a student. *If* you're taken on as a student, I'd like to remind you that you're an ex-serviceman and you will get a government grant to live on.' Which hadn't occurred to me. The principal liked what I'd done and said, 'Okay, we'll take you on as a student of composition and orchestration and conducting. But you'll have to take up a second instrument.' So I went into the Guildhall, studied for three years, and I took up the oboe as my second instrument. Never played it before."

Why the oboe? "Very practical reasons." Martin laughed. "There weren't many of them around, compared with a violin or a piano. And they're much smaller to carry than a harp."

He soon gravitated to Margaret Asher. "She took me on as a pupil, and she was terrific . . . a jolly good teacher," Martin enthused. "Her musicianship did rub off on me—there's no doubt about that.

"Efficient is the best way I can describe her, in teaching, and very, very musical. By that I mean she wasn't just a 'nuts and bolts' person telling you how to handle a bit of wood; she had tremendous understanding of music. And if she hadn't been an oboe player, whatever it was she played, she would have been a great musician. I mean, music was her life. And I enjoyed being taught by her." The future Beatles producer would work with Margaret toward perfecting his tone, then with his oboe packed away, bump into various carrot-topped children as he exited the house.

With their combined income, the Ashers moved from Great Portland Street to a bigger and posher Georgian townhouse in London's West End. 57 Wimpole Street was mere steps from where the famed Barretts of Wimpole Street had once lived. With their bright orange hair, neighbors took to calling the Asher children "The *Carrots* of Wimpole Street."

---

2. Margaret Asher quotes from "The War, Music and Baby": SWWEC LEEWW.2001.1401 Asher, M (courtesy of The Second World War Experience Centre).

One basement room became Margaret's music study. Bookshelves were crammed with sheet music, and along with a chair and sofa, there was just enough room for an upright piano. An amateur musician himself, Dr. Asher loved games, puzzles, and other intellectual pursuits. These passions were passed on to Peter and his siblings, as was an appreciation for all the fine arts. The Ashers were very much like the Darlings in Barrie's *Peter Pan*—two gifted parents and their three adoring children growing up in the middle of London, all playful, inquisitive, and full of life. But life was not that easy.

Though England was still, in many ways, Blake's "green and pleasant land," the fifties seemed black and white to many Britons as they tried to recover from the war's destruction. "The place was full of bombsites," Peter remembered. "We still had rationing—when I was a kid you couldn't get sweets without, you know, stamps in your ration book. And even though we won the war—with a little bit of help, it must be admitted—we still had this nagging feeling that maybe the 'Age of the British Empire' and 'Britain Triumphant' might be kind of over."

A friend of Margaret Asher's, upon seeing how adorable and precocious the three Asher children were, suggested she try to get them in front of the cameras. Valery Glynne Progressive Management was, at that time, the premier children's theatrical agency in Britain, and Peter, Jane, and Clare were signed up immediately. "The three of us got signed because all of us looked cute and graded in size," Peter said, bringing his hands down to indicate their height, "but actually, we never did do anything, all three of us together."

Peter found work almost immediately, acting as the young son of parents Claudette Colbert and Jack Hawkins in the black-and-white 1952 film *The Planter's Wife*

Peter and Claudette Colbert in
The Planter's Wife (1952).

(released in the United States as *Outpost in Malaya*). The film focused on plucky white farmers attempting to keep communist native insurgents from driving them off their rubber-tree farmland, while Colbert's character yearns to return home to both protect her child and save her marriage. Peter, only age seven during production, holds his own opposite the Academy Award–winning actress. Peter has fond memories of Colbert, once commenting: "I remember her smelling delicious!"

Peter's second film that year was a period piece set in the Victorian era of the early 1900s entitled *Isn't Life Wonderful!*, a gentle tale of a proper English family and their problems—specifically a ne'er-do-well relative and a son's possible marriage—all told through the eyes of young Charlie, Peter's character. He was certainly proving to be a good actor for his young age.

In between acting jobs, Peter continued to study music—honing his harmony skills as a boy soprano, performing at various competitions around Britain. "You would be on a little stage," Peter recalled, "singing some soprano thing with just a pianist behind you, judges or somebody sitting at a table in front of you. I remember doing a few of those and being quite terrified. In terms of stage fright, compared to that, walking out with a band is *nothing!*"

He was taking oboe lessons from Margaret and absorbing a lot of classical music, but certain pop records began to catch Peter's ear. Leroy Anderson was an early favorite—his "Blue Tango" (1952) and "The Typewriter" (1953) were both spun numerous times by Peter on the Ashers' hand-cranked gramophone.

Then came Peter's third film role, *Escapade* (1955)—an interesting combination of family drama and antiwar film. Sir John Mills's character becomes so consumed with advocating for world peace he neglects his wife and ignores the trouble his sons are encountering at school. Eventually his boys, one of whom Peter portrays, take off on a dangerous mission for world peace on their own.

A film that could never have been made, let alone released, in the States during that Cold War period, *Escapade*'s producer was US filmmaker and activist Hannah Weinstein. Fleeing the McCarthy anticommunist hysteria of early fifties America and moving to England, Weinstein set up a production company called Sapphire Films, and within a few years had a hit on her hands with the television series *The Adventures of Robin Hood*. The swashbuckling show starring Richard Greene was popular not only in Britain but also in the States—one of the first independently made syndicated programs of its kind and incredibly popular with American children. Weinstein remembered Peter from *Escapade* and began using him in *Robin Hood* episodes. "They were very much aiming at America. We had to say 'castle' instead of '*cästle*,'" Peter recalled, repeating the word with a more British pronunciation, "because they said Americans wouldn't understand."

Americans certainly wouldn't have understood, in those Red-baiting days, the hiring of blacklisted writers to bang out the show's scripts. Using pseudonyms, pros like Ring Lardner Jr. and Waldo Salt helped to keep the quality of the stories high for a low-budget show and also inserted subtexts that were lost on the kids but gave their parents food for thought.

Peter enjoyed himself, learning archery, riding horses, and engaging in feats of derring-do for the cameras. He had a recurring role for a time as young Prince Arthur, but one memorable 1956 episode featured both Peter and Jane as brother and sister. The show's producers normally didn't cast siblings, thinking they'd waste time quarreling, but they needn't have worried with the professional Ashers. The episode, entitled "Children of the Greenwood," had the pair trapped in a castle by an evil lord, their father falsely accused of murder. You can already tell, at this early stage, why Jane continued on to a successful acting career—she's simply very good.

Peter continued with appearances in other British television series, including *Sword of Freedom* (another Weinstein-produced swashbuckler) and *Col. March of Scotland Yard*—a detective series starring Boris Karloff. Peter was even named one of the "Most Promising Youngsters" in a yearly survey by Britain's *Picturegoer Magazine*. But he had also become a student at one of the oldest and most illustrious of London's public schools, Westminster. "That's the English gift for irony," Peter observed, "because 'public' schools in England are not public at all—they're actually quite private and exclusive and hard to get into."

Queen Elizabeth I established Westminster School in 1560. All-boys until 1967, its ivy-covered classrooms and dormitories sit in the shadow of Westminster Abbey. "It was a hard school," according to Peter, "and they don't let you off for stuff." It became increasingly difficult for Peter to abandon his studies for auditions, "and once you start saying 'no,'" he said, "they rapidly lose interest."

Before all interest was lost, though, Peter was cast in his final film role—the youngest member of a family of thieves in the film comedy *The Big Money*. The distinguished actor Ian Carmichael starred as Peter's older brother, and a very comely Jill Ireland filled the big sister role quite nicely. Ireland "was extremely hot," Peter remembered, "and the fantasies circulating in my young brain were in no way fraternal in nature." Noting the famous movie tough guy she would later marry, Peter remarked: "Good thing Charles Bronson never found out!"

BBC Radio programs were easier to say "yes" to—there was no need for makeup or costume fittings, no need to memorize stage direction—or even lines, for that matter. "There was so much," Peter remembered, "and each thing was only a day." One of his last regular acting engagements was as a recurring character on the Children's Hour radio serial *Jennings at School* (also a series of popular novels by Anthony Buckeridge). Aimed at adolescents, the light drama—concerning the adventures of Jennings and his boarding school classmates—was a good, steady gig for a young actor. David Schutte, a Jennings expert, noted that the series' listening audience was huge, with close to thirty thousand children requesting it each month. It ran, with various casts, for sixteen years.

Peter actually had the lead role for the first three episodes of 1957, but deciding that voices were sounding too similar, the producers moved Peter to the role of classmate Darbishire, which was fine by him: "Darbishire had all the best lines," Peter was quick to note. "'*Fossilized fishhooks!*' and all these bizarre exclamations."

Andy Irvine, a pioneer of British folk-rock from his days in both Sweeney's Men in the sixties and Planxty in the seventies, was, like Peter, also a child actor

Valery Glynne Progressive Management casting photos of the Asher family, 1956.

in fifties London. "I do remember we did a lot of radio together," Irvine recalled, including *Jennings*, where Andy played schoolmate Temple, and friend and fellow actor Nigel Anthony was Venables. Peter, Andy, and Nigel became a tight unit almost immediately.

"We discovered that we all had an interest in music," Irvine continued. "We'd all got a plastic ukulele, which was *the* Christmas present of the year, but I had also been learning classical guitar for a couple of years. So, we went to Peter's flat"—most likely Margaret's basement music room—"and we started to play skiffle."

Skiffle was an early British do-it-yourself music craze that was popular in the mid-fifties, before rock'n'roll began to overtake it. It was based around American folk songs like "Rock Island Line," and its most popular performer was the exuberant Lonnie Donegan. Kids across Britain turned their mums' washtubs upside down, attached broom handles with a long string, and played it like an upright bass. As drums were hard to come by, rubbing thimbled fingers quickly across a washboard provided the rhythm. Thousands of British lads formed skiffle bands, including a young John Lennon with his group, The Quarrymen. With Nigel scraping the washboard and Andy and Peter singing and playing guitars, The A 1 Skiffle Group was quickly formed.

Around this time, Peter began to show an early interest in tape recorders. He would spend hours playing with his Fi-Cord, one of the first portable reel-to-reel recorders available commercially in Britain. Whether experimenting with tape loops, slowing things down, speeding things up, or screaming gibberish into the mic and playing it backward, the properties of sound and how it could be manipulated began to fascinate Peter.

The three friends soon discovered Woody Guthrie, Leadbelly, and Cisco Houston, and The A 1 Skiffle Group became The Red River Folk Group. Rehearsals continued in the Asher basement. "I have a recording of the two of us, from about 1958," Andy told me, confessing: "It's not very good!"

"We used to go to the hoot nights Saturday nights in Soho Square to sing," Peter recalled, but they were denied their chance due to the policy of hoot ringmaster and British folk heavyweight Ewan McColl. "He didn't approve of people singing music other than their own culture. We couldn't, as two English lads, get up and sing American folk songs." Interesting, given the fact that Celtic music had a massive influence on the American folk tradition. Nonetheless, these evenings in Soho proved educational as Peter became enthralled with the twelve-string guitar playing of blues singer Long John Baldry. "Part of the beginning of my love for twelve-string guitars," Peter fondly recalled. "He had gigantic hands and could play things nobody else could."

Though stunned upon hearing Elvis's "Heartbreak Hotel," the first rock'n'roll record Peter bought was 1956's "Rock With the Caveman," by England's homegrown rocker, Tommy Steele. "Rock Around The Clock," by Bill Haley and His Comets, also made quite an impression on young Peter, as did witnessing Haley onstage in London—his first rock concert.

In 1957, a young doctor named Stephen Lock applied for a job at Central Middlesex Hospital, wanting more general medical experience. There were four jobs available, and he landed one: Dr. Asher's houseman, or intern. "I must say, the attitude of the establishment was that I'd possibly got the worst job in the hospital. It's very interesting; he didn't really sort of 'fit in' with the medical establishment at all."

Certainly, due to "Munchausen syndrome" and all his other writings, the hospital had gained a higher profile. But still, according to Lock: "They were frightened of him." Asher's honesty could be startling: "He would say of the hematologist in the hospital, 'Of course, Dr. Discomb is talking utter nonsense.' And he'd say that out, you know, to a collection of students and interns and everyone else. That wasn't done in those days . . . and Dr. Discomb didn't like it very much!" And though Dr. Asher wore the black jacket and striped trousers befitting a London specialist, he had a flamboyant nature: "It was just at the beginning of our Jamaican immigrants coming to Britain," Lock remembered. "And we had one patient who was dressed absolutely wonderfully—sort of purples and reds, scarlets, and everything else." Dazzled, Dr. Asher confessed to Lock: "Oh, I *wish* I could wear clothes like that!"

As the fifties came to a close, Jane's career continued to blossom, with better roles in film, radio, and television. Concurrently, Clare landed a part on the British radio soap opera *Mrs. Dale's Diary*, the first significant BBC Radio drama. Its oft-used line, "I'm awfully worried about Jim," eventually became a national catchphrase.

But unfortunately, despite his early promise, their brother's acting career was basically over.

One factor often overlooked when discussing the British beat boom of the sixties is the end of conscription in October 1960. Until that time, young Englishmen could be routinely called up for two years of military duty. Peter had already made his choice: "I would have joined the RAF 'cause we'd all read Biggles"—referring to the adventure novels of W.E. Johns that feature Captain Bigglesworth, Spitfire pilot. "Of course, having gone to public school, I would have been an officer"—he laughed—"'cause if you were upper-class, you were officer material automatically!" (All Biggles-type fantasies would have evaporated had an actual war, like Vietnam, been Britain's fate: "We didn't have to run away to Canada or wherever, but we would have"—he laughed—"in no time!") During conscription, it would have been extremely difficult for any artist to build a career, or a group to form and tighten, when the momentum could be interrupted with national service. With that no longer a threat, thousands of young British boys could follow their muse, taking up guitars and drumsticks instead of rifles—and many did just that.

For the majority of British youth (and, for that matter, American youth), singing and playing music was one way out of the dull future that seemed to lie in store for those in the lower and working classes. "When you come from where I come from," explained the UK singer known as Lulu, "you either have to be a boxer, a thief, a footballer, or you can do music." She said that last word with a sense of magical hopefulness. "Not that I wanted to get out, but that was the drive, I suppose."

The tale of how a small girl in a working-class port in the northern British Isles fell in love with American blues and soul is strikingly similar to hundreds of other UK acts, including The Beatles: "In Glasgow," Lulu said, speaking of her hometown, "when you live in a city like that, people have hard times—day to day. It's fighting to survive. So, what they do after work is they drink, and they play music." Not only did American sailors bring in music to this bustling port, but American airmen stationed outside the city also shared the latest rock'n'roll and rhythm-and-blues records with their Scottish friends.

"And my father used to sing," Lulu continued. "Everybody—for recreation, they'd drink and have parties at home and sing! They didn't stand around with glasses of wine saying"—here she changed to a very posh voice—"'*Dahhling, HOW is the economy?*' It was gritty!" And when little Marie Lawrie (her given name) began to sing at parties, she was encouraged. "You get a lot of attention, and it's very flattering," she said. "All I ever wanted to do was sing—that's all I ever cared about. I didn't care about anything else. Not even boys—well, maybe boys a *little* bit!"

Peter Asher, by contrast, was a well-educated, upper-class lad with practically every career possibility open to him. Music for Peter was not a way out of a dreary existence—it was in his DNA. He was enthralled with music in all its permutations and played whenever time allowed. He wasn't yearning for fame or fortune—it was simply fun.

Now falling under the thrall of artists like Charlie Parker and Miles Davis, Peter turned his attention to jazz. England was going through a period when traditional Dixieland-style jazz music became hugely popular, and artists such as Chris Barber, Acker Bilk, Kenny Ball, and Bob Wallis were selling records and packing clubs throughout Britain. Peter began playing standup bass, and pal Nigel Anthony graduated from washboard to actual drums. Andy Irvine, though, knew his heart was in folk music and soon went his own way.

Peter honed his musical chops by taking part in jam sessions with various acquaintances joining in, including one of Nigel's friends: Richard Hewson, a guitarist, trumpeter, and student at the Guildhall School. The three soon formed a jazz trio, never getting proper paying gigs but playing a lot of parties. Hewson, though, remembered that Peter was already thinking about pop music: "One day he came 'round and said, 'Do you want to write a song?' And I didn't know *anything* about pop songs!" The resulting tune was, Hewson said laughing, "complete crap!"

And how good a jazz bassist was Peter? "Oh, he was *good*," Adrian Lyne said of Peter's musical chops. "I wouldn't say he was the 'best in the world,' but nor was I!"

Lyne, who went on to direct such memorable hit films as *Flashdance* and *Fatal Attraction*, was focused on a music career during the trad jazz period. "I sort of played 'semi-pro' with different bands, playing the trumpet. And I wasn't very good, really—it was more passion than technique.

"I had my own band, with the dubious name of The Neolithic Jazz Men!" He laughed heartily. "We were quite popular, even with that daft name! We played riverboats and pubs and a lot of workingmen's clubs in North London." Peter would play with Lyne's band when their regular bassist was unavailable. "I can see him doing it," Lyne said, thinking back to those nights when jazz ruled the London club scene. And Peter, Lyne remembered, "was such a sweet man. I just liked him enormously."

Though a highly successful filmmaker, Lyne misses his days making music: "I just loved it. If I'd been any *good*—if I could have played like Clark Terry or Chet Baker— I'd still be doing it *now*. In my late twenties I started directing, and then eight years later I started directing films. But I've never felt quite the same way. If I played a good solo, trumpet solo . . ." Lyne paused, recalling his satisfying nights on the bandstand: "It's the best thing on earth! I've never felt that good since, you know?"

Peter, encouraged by his friends and music-loving parents, denied having any thoughts that jazz was his forte: "I was nowhere nearly good enough to play the be-bop that I loved . . . and I didn't practice nearly hard enough either, it must be admitted." But he was beginning to wonder if music might eventually be more than just a hobby. He got his answer when a fellow student at Westminster entered his life.

2

GORDON AND PETER

Gordon Trueman Riviere Waller's father, like Peter's, was also a doctor—an ear, nose, and throat surgeon—with the family residence upstairs from his medical office in the village of Pinner. And, like the Ashers, the Wallers enjoyed music together, though the atmosphere was slightly different: "My father was a brilliant tenor," Gordon said. "And one of my sisters is a great pianist. So, when the family got together and Dad got drunk and my sister got drunk and I got drunk, my sister would play the piano and he would sing. And I would try to!

"I was always in trouble. I was always in fights. I think I was probably a big worry to my parents. And I didn't give a shit about school, except sport." But there came a fateful day in 1957 that changed his life forever.

"I remember the afternoon, absolutely clear as a bell," Gordon recalled. "The people next door, who had a huge garden with a field at the end of it, used to have, like, a garden party every year." As Gordon passed by his neighbor's party, one particular record stopped him in his tracks. "About the third time it came on, I said, 'Who's that?' 'Well, that's Elvis!' I said, 'Elvis? Who's Elvis?' They said, '*That's* Elvis!' And so, I stayed there all night with them, 'cos I just loved it! Playing these old 78s over and over and over and over again."

Gordon's parents, realizing their son was becoming almost obsessed with this new music, bought Gordon a guitar for Christmas. He immediately began to teach himself chords, learning over a half-dozen songs that first day. Soon he was taking the guitar with him to parties, where he learned a fact all young men with guitars quickly realize: "If you're playing guitar, you've got twenty times more chance of pulling the girls than the guys who aren't playing!"

Then came Gordon's first paying gig, earning ten pounds to play at a party given by a rich schoolmate: "*Fuckin' 'ell, ten quid?* That would keep me drunk and in cigarettes for three weeks!" Gordon talked his mother into buying him an electric guitar, borrowed an amp from a friend, and showed up ready to rock. In the midst of his first hip-shakin' number, he managed to catch the attention of an "unbelievable, angelic, sexy, nymphomaniac Swedish chick," according to Gordon, and that did it. "I thought, '*This* has got to be the way to go!'"

At the dawn of the 1960s, performing at one of his father's Christmas parties, he was approached by a guest who worked at EMI asking if he was interested in auditioning for one of the biggest record labels in the world. Gordon couldn't believe his good fortune, but his father had a decidedly different response: "My dad was furious with this guy! He wanted me to carry on at school. But"—Gordon laughed—"I was waaaay past academics by then! I'd had a taste of blood, and I wasn't goin' back." He auditioned and was offered a contract, but he would have to leave school. His parents steadfastly refused to allow *that* to happen. EMI, though, left the door open: "Well," Gordon remembered them saying, "when you finish school, get back to us."

Around this time, Gordon met fourteen-year-old Jennifer Dunbar. "It was 'first love' for both of us," she confessed. She adoringly witnessed some of Gordon's early gigs, where all his hours of Elvis practice became evident, unleashing a perfected snarling lip to the delight of the assembled youngsters. "The way that Elvis had burst onto the world music scene was absolutely full of '*Fuck You*,'" Roderick Peters recalled, adding: "Gordon had that in spades."

Dr. Roderick Peters, now a respected psychotherapist and author, was a young lad at Westminster School when he met Gordon: "He came over to the house where I was boarding one evening," Peters remembered, "and came into my study. And his way of getting to know me is actually very characteristic of Gordon, which was very confrontational—kind of, 'Right. I'm here. What are you going to do about it?' You always had a feeling as if he was semi-spoiling for a fight—if not physical, then at least a conflict of wills. Or testosterone.

"The whole way that he walked around school and dressed was full of that challenging confrontational individuality," Peters recalled. Take the gray suit, which, he noted, all the boys were required to wear: "He had his altered, so they were sort of 'drainpipe' trousers. He *had* to wear a tie, otherwise he would've been required to leave the school, but he had it knotted halfway down his chest with the top button opened. And his hair was like Elvis . . . brushed back in a great wave."

Gordon's confrontational nature had its origins at home: "I got to know his father quite well," Peters said, remembering Dr. Waller. "He could be kind and pleasant, and then he could be really cutting and unpleasant and quite cruel to Gordon, especially." Many times, while staying at the Wallers', "it would get quite uncomfortable 'round the table," recalled Peters. "It was difficult for me going there because, in the way that parents sometimes do, he chose to set me as the sort of example of what his son *should* have been . . . I hated it. As did Gordon."

Despite what Dr. Waller thought his son "should" be, the moment that solidified what he *would* be happened sometime early in 1961. Gordon overheard guitar playing, including some rather advanced finger-work, coming from one of Westminster's

Westminster School, Liddell House, 1961. (Gordon: top row, 2nd from right; Peter: third row, 2nd from right.) *Reproduced by kind assistance of the Governing Body of Westminster School.*

rooms, and he crept in to listen. When the playing finally stopped, Gordon said, "That's good."

"Thank you," Peter Asher replied.

Until that moment, their paths had not crossed. Gordon, winning medals with his athletic activities, was not part of Peter's circle—young intellectuals busy with academics and working on the school magazine. Gordon's strong antiauthoritarian attitudes would have precluded him from joining groups such as the school's debate team, for example, or theatrical productions—two activities at which Peter excelled. Dr. Peters, watching the two of them interact, remembered the stark contrast: "Peter was deathly white, and his hair was like a flame at that time. He was so still and calm . . . almost like frozen water. Gordon," Peters recalled, "was at odds with the whole world." Or, as Gordon frankly told me: "Peter was a human being; I was just an animal."

But they certainly learned from each other: "There was a lot of rock'n'roll that he introduced me to," Peter explained. "And, if anything, I think what we started off trying to do was combining both our interests. When we started singing, first we would do a number of folk songs that I would often introduce into the mixture, and a number of rock'n'roll songs and Buddy Holly songs that *he* would introduce into the mixture, and our 'style,' such as it was, grew out of that. Of course, a lot of our style grew out of trying to sound as much like The Everly Brothers as possible, which is what everybody did."

"I have never met anybody who can sing harmony like him," said Gordon. "He'll probably hate me for saying this, but Peter's a fuckin' lousy singer on his own. He really is. I mean he is not a 'singer' as such. But—he's the most *fantastic* harmonizer! If my voice is 'whipped cream,' Peter's voice is 'skimmed milk.' It is just pure."

Their first public performance together, though, had no singing involved. Peter and Gordon teamed up with friend Christopher Garmany to debut at the Westminster School's chamber music competition, performing for those assembled a competent guitar trio arrangement of the instrumental "Apache" by the popular British band The Shadows. "Having read the rules of the chamber music competition, we realized we were eligible. It said, 'six or less instruments playing an existing piece' or whatever," Peter recalled. "It *didn't* say, 'they cannot be electric guitars.'" Music instructor Mr. Harvey felt it was unfair to judge their performance alongside a Beethoven Trio, which took top honors that day, so Asher, Waller, and Garmany were given "honorable mention." "That was in the spirit of Westminster," Peter explained. "Other schools might have tried to stop us—the same way I got to read 'Howl' at the school poetry competition and nobody stopped me. That's Westminster at its best."

Peter, a year ahead of Gordon, left Westminster for King's College, majoring in philosophy, not music. Peter explained why: "I think because it was about the vaguest thing I could think of. I had no idea what I wanted to do for a career. I didn't know much about philosophy, but it sounded kind of interestingly intellectual and rather vague, which it turned out to be." Peter puts himself squarely in the logical positivist camp along with fellow Englishman Bertrand Russell, though suspects he might be a Wittgensteinian. "But," Peter confessed, "that's if I could really understand it."

Though now at different schools, the two friends continued to practice together. Folk songs such as "500 Miles" and rockers such as "Lucille" started sounding very good indeed when Gordon's rich baritone ran alongside Peter's strong tenor. The singing duo of Gordon and Peter (as they were then billed) began by playing various pubs at lunchtime for free food and beer.

Gordon's girlfriend, Jennifer Dunbar, had moved recently with her family from Pinner to the Marylebone section of London, just a few blocks from the Asher residence. Peter became friendly with Jennifer's brother, John Dunbar, a fine arts major at Cambridge. The two well-read lads hit it off immediately with shared interests in film, art, science, and, of course, books. "We both read a lot," John Dunbar said. "He was sort of amongst the few people that one could talk with about other subjects in that kind of milieu—that music lot." Eventually, Dunbar would play an important role, both in Peter's life and in the history of sixties pop culture.

Peter took time from his philosophy studies in 1962, undertaking a final appearance on the London stage as part of the Royal Shakespeare Company's production of Giles Cooper's *Everything in the Garden*, starring Geraldine McEwan. "It was about urban housewives who start a brothel to make money on the side," Peter recalled. He began the show as understudy but ended the run playing the part of McEwan's son, Roger, the most morally grounded member of the family.

In 1963, Jane Asher, after her big break onscreen in *The Greengage Summer*, became a semi-regular on the very popular Saturday night BBC TV show *Juke Box Jury*, where a panel of four judges made up of show business cognoscenti listen to new records and decide if they'll "hit" or "miss." Tuning in one evening and seeing the quite photogenic Miss Asher, Len Black thought to himself: "If that girl sings as good as she looks, we could make some hit records!"

Len Black had been working for a time as a song-plugger for music publishers, providing tunes by under-contract songwriters to artists and record labels. He called Jane's agent and arranged for her to meet him and an accompanist for an audition. After a song or two, it was clear: "She didn't have it," Black recalled, thinking she had a "squeaky voice." But as she was leaving, Jane mentioned: "I have a brother who plays and sings." Politely, Black agreed to see Peter and his friend but was not too impressed when he heard them. "I said go away and come back in six months—you're not quite ready." As Gordon and Peter continued to polish their act, Jane made another acquaintance who would ultimately prove more important to Peter's career.

In April 1963, Jane was asked by the magazine *Radio Times* to review a concert by a promising beat group that had managed to get their second single, "Please Please Me," to the number-one spot. The Beatles were to appear on April 18th at the Royal Albert Hall with the BBC broadcasting the second half of the show for a radio special. This was quite a prestigious venue, and Beatles producer George Martin was also in attendance.

Backstage, as introductions were being made, Martin suddenly recognized the red-haired young woman in front of him as the little "carrot top" he knew when taking oboe lessons from her mother. "And I made the most smart-assed remark I've ever made in my life," Martin said, "which I *immediately* regretted—it was the most stupid thing to say. I was introduced: 'This is Jane Asher, this is George Martin.' I said, 'Last time I saw you, you were in the bath.' And she looked at me, astonished."

Though everyone laughed, Martin said he felt the daggers coming from Jane's eyes. Still embarrassed decades later, he shook his head: "What a gauche thing to say."

Jane met the band and then spent hours chatting with Paul McCartney. He was cute, clever, and charming, quoting Chaucer to her. She was attractive, educated, artistic, and understood the ins and outs of show business. They hit it off immediately.

A young man named Andrew Loog Oldham had been hired by Brian Epstein's company NEMS to help publicize both "Please Please Me" and The Beatles' brand-new single, "From Me to You." Oldham was fully submerged in the London pop culture of fashion and music. His right-hand man at this time was Peter Meaden, a "face" in the burgeoning mod scene. The mods were stylish, unlike their leather-clad detractors called "rockers," who still revered Gene Vincent and Eddie Cochran. Mods embraced pop art and Carnaby Street fashions, while musically preferring American R&B and Jamaican ska. Both Oldham and Meaden were ambitious, but Meaden's head was a little too much in the clouds for Oldham, who had just become manager for The Rolling Stones. Oldham "had fingers in every pie," Philip Townsend recalled.

Townsend was a photographer who had met Oldham while snapping celebrities in the south of France for the magazine *Tatler*. Townsend was now booking music acts on the side for the debutant parties and private dances around London he was hired to shoot. Oldham phoned one day, telling him that Meaden was coming over. "He wanted to get rid of him," Townsend said. "Andrew is very persuasive! He just said, 'He's coming along to help *you* out.'" The Townsend-Meaden Agency was formed and set up shop on Brompton Road in Kensington. And, along with pushing Meaden on Townsend, Oldham also suggested that they look into booking Gordon and Peter for their parties. Oldham had booked them once himself and sensed the duo would be perfect for the debutant crowd.

"Because they were just starting out, they didn't have a band to back them," Brian Parker remembered. Parker was a guitarist in an R&B trio called The Renegades, another act in the Townsend-Meaden stable, and on the more up-tempo numbers The Renegades would add sonic support for the acoustic duo, becoming the pair's first backing band. Gordon still yearned to be a rocker, so he and Townsend invented "Aubyn St. Claire," and his services would be provided along with Gordon and Peter—"Two acts for the price of one," Townsend said, laughing. For the "Aubyn" set, Gordon combed his hair up, took his suit jacket off, and would sing a half-dozen rock and R&B numbers backed by The Renegades, who were mining the same sonic vein as The Rolling Stones. He would then go backstage, change his clothes, comb his hair down, grab his acoustic guitar, and come back out with Peter. The debutants witnessing this, at the Chelsea Town Hall or at private parties in millionaires' mansions along Totteridge Lane, were none the wiser.

Len Black, in the meantime, had been hired by composer John Barry to manage his company based in Denmark Street. Gordon and Peter found his new office and came to see him, as six months had passed. All their gigs for Townsend-Meaden had helped: "They were better; they were tighter," Black recalled. "I said, 'Okay, let me try and do something with you.'"

Pickwick Room newspaper ad.

Black and boss John Barry would leave their Denmark Street offices at lunchtime and head to a new two-story restaurant/bar called The Pickwick Club. "We'd go in every day," Black recalled, "so I got to know the manager quite well. One day he said to me, 'I'm looking for a piano player for the restaurant.' I said, 'I have an idea—I have a couple of boys who play guitar. Why don't you have them in? They can move from upstairs to downstairs, as opposed to a piano player that's stuck in one place.' And he said, 'Okay.'"

The Pickwick, located on a street filled with show-business offices, had quickly become something of a private dining club. Rising stars like Michael Caine and Terrence Stamp and British showbiz royalty like *Goon Show* comedian Harry Secombe would drink, dine, and close deals. Gordon's sweetheart, Jennifer Dunbar; twin sister, Margaret; and Roderick Peters all attended Gordon and Peter's debut performance at the club. The pair performed on two stools with no amplifiers or microphones, performing their repertoire and taking requests. Jennifer Dunbar recalled that, as the weeks went by, the lines to get in to catch this new acoustic duo dramatically increased.

Meanwhile, Paul McCartney had become quite close to the Asher family. He was still living in Liverpool when he first met Jane, but as the year progressed and The Beatles continued to become more and more successful, it made sense for them all to move to London. In August 1963, the band members began sharing a flat in Mayfair, but Paul was yearning for something more—something that provided the comfortable feelings of family and home that he was missing now in London. He was spending more and more of his downtime at the Wimpole Street townhouse, and one evening Margaret simply suggested that he move into their spare room, which was next to Peter's on the top floor. It was an opportunity too good to pass up. McCartney's biographer and longtime friend, Barry Miles, explained it was "not just for the convenience of living with his girlfriend—which, of course, was obviously very nice—but also the Asher household provided him with a home away from home. Margaret Asher was very, very kind to him, and very much a mother substitute. Paul's own mother had died when he was fourteen, so he loved that—the fact that he could come in and, you know, she was always making him food, and his clothes and everything were taken care of."

An interesting situation—sleeping just steps away from your sweetheart. But before you jump to conclusions, dear reader: "There's no hanky-panky in the house," Peter emphasized. "It was conducted in the proper way an English house would be conducted; Paul definitely lived in his room." Peter described his parents as "generally, I suppose, liberal and progressive in their attitudes, but still basically good English white Tories, you know?"

Paul began using Margaret's basement music room as a space for songwriting sessions with John Lennon. Peter remembered one October day in particular when England's hottest hitmakers got down to business: After only a couple of hours, "Paul called up to my bedroom and asked me if I wanted to hear a new song that he and John had just written, which they clearly thought was quite good. I came down to the basement where they sat side by side at the piano and sang 'I Want to Hold Your Hand' for the first time to an audience." His verdict? "I was overwhelmed."

Also, in October 1963, Paul and John had been cajoled by Andrew Oldham to give The Rolling Stones the first crack at recording "I Wanna Be Your Man"—becoming the Stones' second single when released the following month. But before either the Stones' or The Beatles' own recordings of the song were released, clubgoers at The Pickwick heard it first. "I learned the song from Paul," Peter recalled. "I said, 'Would you mind if we sang this? It's a great song!' And he said, 'Yes.'" Working up a nice two-part harmony version with Gordon, the duo sang it for a couple of weeks at their Pickwick gigs, mentioning the Lennon and McCartney authorship and upcoming Stones release, thereby creating some anticipation for the record among their burgeoning fans. The situation would be different today, with cameras in every audience member's pocket and an instantaneous online upload threatening a release's exclusivity, but in 1963, permission was casually given and "I Wanna Be Your Man" became Peter and Gordon's first brand-new Lennon and McCartney cover.

Peter meeting Gordon, Paul meeting Jane, Len Black suggesting an unknown guitar act for The Pickwick Club—each a significant bit of luck in Peter's life, or, as he might say, "happenstance." One November evening at The Pickwick, the next great bit of happenstance came in the form of EMI executive Norman Newell.

3

A WORLD WITHOUT LOVE

Norman Newell began his career selling sheet music and writing songs for one of London's many publishing houses. He eventually caught the eye of EMI and was hired in 1949 to head their Columbia label. Initially relying on the licensing of American hits, he began to build a roster of British acts, including signing a teen-age Petula Clark. He also continued to have success as a songwriter, providing the lyrics to the ballads "More" and "A Portrait of My Love"—big hits on both sides of the Atlantic. In the postwar years, he was as powerful as you could get in Britain's music industry. "The epitome of EMI," said guitarist "Big" Jim Sullivan. "Very tall and well-educated."

"Norman was one of the great British lyricists . . . a very interesting man," artist manager Alex Armitage explained. "He was pretty well the first accepted—what we would call 'out'—homosexual in the music industry. The fact that he was openly gay was absolutely astonishing." Remember: In the early sixties, many in society thought of homosexuals as mentally ill, criminals, or both. Most gay men in the business, including Beatles manager Brian Epstein, kept it a closely guarded secret.

The advent of rock'n'roll was quickly changing the industry, and though EMI had success with Cliff Richard, Johnny Kidd, and now The Beatles, this sort of "music" was still not taken very seriously. The powers-that-be at EMI thought their commercial acts were inconsequential but necessary to make the company money, thereby financing their *much* more important business: classical recordings. Newell's expertise was more in the world of musical theater than the rock'n'roll realm, but he was always on the lookout for commercial talent.

One evening near the end of 1963, Newell caught Gordon and Peter's act at The Pickwick Club. What transpired sounds like the biggest of showbiz clichés: The well-dressed Newell (whom Gordon, recalling the meeting, called "Mr. Glitter" because of all the rings he wore) summoned the boys over. Peter remembered he "sat us down at his table, bought us a drink," and asked, "Have you boys ever made a record? Would you come and audition?" They didn't say no. Gordon especially didn't want to pass up a *second* chance at an EMI contract.

In this era of music streaming, file sharing, and software such as ProTools and GarageBand, we seem light-years away from the realities of struggling musicians only a generation ago. "Back then, unless you had access to a real recording studio, there was no way to make any sort of a record," Peter recalled. The duo nervously arrived at EMI's studios at Abbey Road and auditioned with, among other songs, Hedy West's "500 Miles," which fit with Newell's plans. "Norman was imagining us as an English version of Peter, Paul and Mary or The Kingston Trio," Peter explained. "We were going to be England's answer to the 'folk boom' that was happening in America."

Newell offered them a contract. "A terrible record deal. The big record companies screwed everyone back then," Peter laughed.

"I think it was a penny per single," he recalled. "And, of course, the killer was it was half royalties overseas! Like a lot of contracts were, and are, to this day." Obviously, when they signed, no one could foresee the British Invasion only months away, which meant that any million-selling single Peter and Gordon later achieved in the States meant a "massive" payday of . . . approximately $5,000. This was simply EMI's standard starting contract—even The Beatles had to toil under these rates for years. But, unlike modern contracts, nothing was "recouped" to cover the label's costs, according to Peter: "You *did* get paid."

Newell, like any good producer, began to wonder: What would be the single? "500 Miles" was a strong contender—it had not been a hit before in the UK, and their performance was very good—but still not quite what he had in mind. A commercial song that was not a cover was needed. Could the pair come up with one? Peter thought he knew whom to ask.

McCartney had recently played Peter an unfinished song that he originally thought might make a good Beatles track. The idea had come to Paul years earlier, and periodically he would bring the song to John Lennon's attention during their writing sessions. But he was never able to get past the first line with the phrase "*lock me away.*" Lennon's savage wit would then be unleashed, letting Paul know he *needed* locking away for using that daft line. Eventually Paul gave up, accepting the fact that The Beatles would never record it.

Now, needing a song for himself, Peter asked his new housemate if he and Gordon could have a crack at the orphaned song. Paul happily agreed. "He wrote out the words and the chords for us to learn," Peter remembered, with Paul even providing a recording featuring simple guitar strums and a one-minute rendition of the tune. But only days before the session was scheduled, it was still unfinished—two promising verses, but no bridge (sometimes called a "middle-eight," referring to the eight bars that help a song's structure by bridging a chorus, say, to a verse).

Gordon recalled, "He didn't have a middle-eight for it, and we kept asking him to do it, and he didn't. We said, 'Come on, Paul, we're desperate!' So he went into his bedroom and came back about two minutes later." Paul, guitar in hand, said, "Right.

What do you think of this?" He then sang them the lilting, melancholy missing piece, beginning with the words "*So I wait*" and finishing with "*Baby, until then*," dovetailing nicely back into the verse.

Remembered Gordon: "We said, 'GREAT!'" They immediately picked up the phone, called Norman Newell, and excitedly proclaimed, "We got a song!" Today, Peter still retains both the demo tape and the pages with Paul's scribbled verses and last-minute bridge, proclaiming, "When things get really bad, I'm off to Sotheby's in a minute!"

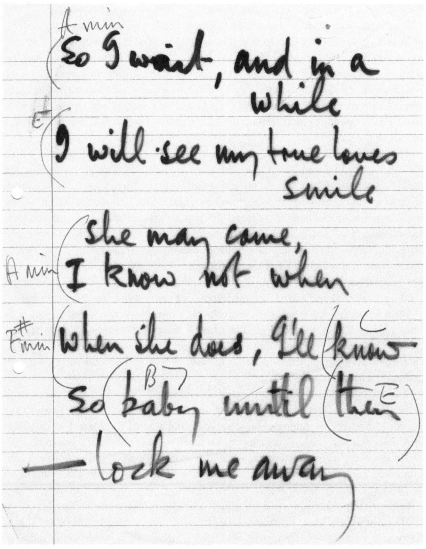

McCartney's last-minute bridge. See credit on copyright page.

Tuesday, January 21, 1964, was a bright, clear day in London. Blanketed in snow the week before, the sun had returned to the city, and on this crisp winter morning, Peter and Gordon began their recording career at EMI's Abbey Road Studio Two. The session began with Peter, playing acoustic guitar, running through "A World Without Love" for bassist Eric Ford and drummer Dougie Wright. "There was no music written," Wright remembered, and as they came up with the structure, music director Geoff Love took notes to make sure the arrangement remained tight. Love had arranged many sessions for Newell over the years, including tracks for Shirley Bassey, one of EMI's most successful artists.

Peter wanted a particular drum sound, which Wright was able to come up with on his brand-new American Gretsch kit, doubling up the floor tom with the kickdrum: BOM—BOM BOM . . . BOM—BOM BOM. "I kept it very cool; there was no point in being clever," Wright said. "We were just there to put the carpet down for everybody to rest on." Later in the day, a second session commenced for the overdubs and vocals. The guitarist hired was Vic Flick, one of London's leading studio musicians. Flick's ominous guitar lead on the "James Bond Theme" was one of *the* iconic sounds of the sixties.

The guitarist remembered the session well: "That was one of the few times I used the electric twelve-string," Flick said, referring to the bulky Vox guitar used as the record's lead instrument, specifically requested by Peter. Keyboardist Harold Smart played a massive Hammond B-3 organ, which had to be carried into the studio by four construction workers hired off the street. Flick and the other musicians each received, according to "Big" Jim Sullivan, "£7 for the session and ten shillings for carriage—to carry your amp and guitar in." The exchange rate in 1964 translated to about twenty dollars, "which was a quite lot of money back then," Flick recalled, "but, of course, we were terribly exploited." (Unfortunately the exploitation went on, as Flick's old guitar leads were sampled and mixed into modern recordings without any compensation.)

Clem Cattini, a legendary session drummer from that era, referred to London's small cadre of studio musicians as "The Musical Navvies" (*navvy* being a nineteenth-century Irish term meaning "laborer"). Dougie Wright defined the term thusly: "Someone who gets pulled from pillar to post, gets kicked around rotten, but still comes up with the answers."

With definite ideas about how the song should sound, Newell let Peter get on with it with hardly any interference. And Peter was thrilled with the process: "I loved the studio, I loved the technology," he remarked, "and I loved the idea of having great musicians that you could make suggestions to or, indeed, tell them what to do.

"That was a thrilling idea to me—the idea of taking a song and sculpting it into something other than what it was." A definite seed was planted in Peter's mind on this very first day at Abbey Road.

Peter's first production attempt, albeit uncredited, the record was released on EMI's Columbia label on February 28th. The first time I visited Peter's office, almost thirty-nine years to the day of that first single's release, there were no platinum albums on his wall, and neither of his two Grammy Awards for "Producer of the Year" were in sight. But there, on a small table next to his desk, sat his 1964 Gold Disc award for "A World Without Love."

"Obviously, the fact that we had a fantastic, brand-new song to record was incredible," Peter recalled, "and allowed us to have a hit straightaway, which is unique."

Norman Newell not only advised them to change their billing to "Peter and Gordon" (as he thought it sounded better), but he steered them toward signing with his own manager, Richard Armitage. Len Black, the man who had gotten them their break at The Pickwick Club, had unfortunately been too slow in securing a management deal with the duo. "I thought, 'I'd better sign these boys up.' But I was too late—Norman Newell came in one night, snatched them up, and I was fucked."

Manager Richard Armitage was born into show business, as his father, Reginald, was a songwriter of many popular English tunes in the 1920s and '30s, with four of his musical revues running in the West End simultaneously (a feat not achieved again until the days of Andrew Lloyd Webber). Reginald wrote under the name Noel Gay, and his son Richard formed Noel Gay Artists in the fifties to manage performers and supply songs under their copyright to various acts.

"Norman was a client with this company for over fifty years," said Alex Armitage, one of Richard's sons and now CEO of the still-thriving Noel Gay Artists. "Norman was one for an easy life and wanted people that he produced to be properly represented. Noel Gay was a really, really good agency and management company in those days—it was very successful and *very* honorable." I had brought up with Alex a claim Gordon made to me—that Norman Newell got five percent of what Noel Gay Artists earned from managing Peter and Gordon as a kickback for steering them his father's way. Newell, Alex Armitage assured me, "would have introduced people to Richard Armitage 'cause he wanted those people to be properly, professionally, *honestly* represented.

"My father, God love 'im, was as straight as a die," Armitage continued. "Nothing would have embarrassed him more than *any* suggestion of that ilk." John Burgess, Newell's friend and fellow EMI producer, flatly stated: "If that's what Gordon thinks, then he didn't know Norman Newell or Richard Armitage very well."

As "A World Without Love" began its rise up the charts, Peter and Gordon commenced the seemingly endless series of TV, radio, and concert appearances needed to establish themselves in the public's eyes and ears. Their new manager realized a solid group was needed to go on the road with them to help fill out their folksy sound.

As a youngster, Eddie King began his education on the piano with lessons from his mother, a music teacher. "My whole life was practice, practice, practice, practice, practice. I hated it." But all the lessons left King with the ability to sight-read any music and grasp arrangements fairly quickly. Then in the late fifties, King recalled, "The whole world exploded. It was Presley and it was Gene Vincent and it was Buddy Holly." He traded the piano for a guitar and, of course, formed a band.

With none of the members blessed with a good rock voice, the group's drummer (with the wonderful *nom de plume* "Basher" Bailey) recruited Bill Green, a friend from work. To sound more authentic, taking his cue from American heartthrobs and motorcars, Green became "Ricky Ford." Though Green fronted the combo, Eddie King was the band's maestro because "he had perfect pitch," according to Green. "He was a great musician."

The band, dubbed Ricky Ford & The Cyclones, was a hard-driving professional unit, working almost every night. Many of the London singing stars playing the Bristol area—Terry Dean, Vince Eager, Billy Fury—got solid backing from The Cyclones. With their good reputation, a call came for the band to back Peter and Gordon. When the group arrived in the afternoon for their rehearsal and sound-check, King got his first look at the pair. "They were like very well-spoken upper-class folkies," he recalled, somewhat appalled at their stage presence, or lack thereof: "They did the whole show sittin' on *stools!*"

The rehearsal went so well an offer was made: "Their management said, 'Would you go out on the road with them and back them?' So we said, 'Yeah, but *get off the stools*, for God sakes!'" The sedentary singers did from that day onward.

The sessions for Peter and Gordon's first album took place that March at EMI's studios at Abbey Road, with Norman Newell again using arranger Geoff Love to flesh out the sound. Guitarist "Big" Jim Sullivan, who played on many of these early sessions, remembers Love providing charts for everyone with solos written out note for note, though "there was always suggestions flying about" from the musicians, who do their job—driving when needed ("Lucille," "Leave My Woman Alone"), subdued when necessary ("500 Miles," "Pretty Mary"). The duo's vocals, recorded together on one mic, were double-tracked (meaning recorded twice), and reverb was added for fullness—standard practice for the time. The album was a good snapshot of their live repertoire, combining the boys' love of fifties rock with the folk songs they'd learned off records by, among others, Joan Baez (whom Gordon idolized). Their own early attempts at songwriting, though not close to Lennon and McCartney standards, showed promise.

With the album sessions completed, on March 27th Peter had dinner with good mate John Dunbar and his new girlfriend, Marianne Faithfull. Dunbar and Faithfull had met at Cambridge, fallen in love, and would eventually marry, with Peter standing as best man. That evening (and thanks to Bill Wyman for confirming the date), Andrew Oldham was throwing a party to celebrate the sixteenth birthday of singer and actress Adrienne Posta. Peter, who was going to attend, talked John and Marianne into coming along, which, Peter now says, "may have been a mistake." It was at this party that Marianne Faithfull was introduced to Mick Jagger, who would soon not only write the song that would kick-start her music career ("As Tears Go By") but would also infamously become her lover. Peter later remarked he was a "full-service best man from hell! I get you both married *and* divorced . . ."

That very week in March, "A World Without Love" had climbed to #21 in the *New Musical Express* singles chart. Just behind it at #22, a new record appeared, "My Boy Lollipop," sung by a pretty, effervescent Jamaican singer named Millie Small. The song was an infectious slice of "blue beat" (a term that was used at the time to refer to Jamaican music in general), and Millie was billed as "The Blue Beat Girl." Produced by Island Records founder, Chris Blackwell, who brought her to England, its offbeat ska rhythm, catchy harmonica break by Peter Hogman, and, above all, Millie's dynamite delivery, thrilled the record-buying public.

Back at Adrienne Posta's party, Peter was introduced to Millie. Intrigued, he began to see her regularly over at Chris Blackwell's apartment. "He had a flat on the Cromwell Road and Millie had the flat opposite. She would hang around at his flat with a lot of other Jamaican émigrés," Peter recalled, adding: "There was a lot of dominoes playing and a lot of dope smoking—both of which they do faster and better than anyone else in the world." Millie was unlike any other girl he had ever met, and a romance began to blossom. With both Millie and Peter out promoting their first records, they saw a lot of each other—taping *Top of the Pops* episodes together in London and appearing on the same bill in concert halls across the UK.

In 1964, Britain was certainly not a utopia when it came to race relations—the first legislation to outlaw discriminatory practices wouldn't come for another year. So the relationship did run into some obstacles from time to time, but not from Peter's family. "He liked Millie," Peter said, speaking of his father. "Obviously, going out with a black girl then was odder than it would be now . . . he certainly had nothing against it, that's for sure." How could anyone not like her? "She was full of energy," Peter's friend Barry Miles remembered. "Very bouncy and ebullient . . . a really beautiful little girl." Dr. Asher was certainly intrigued with the genetic possibilities in store. Surrounded for years with a household full of red-haired relatives, Dr. Asher once watched Peter and Millie together and remarked, according to Miles, that getting some West Indian blood in the gene pool would not only strengthen it but "get rid of those wretched red hair genes."

After the break to record their album, touring continued through April, performing at workingmen's clubs and small halls that had been booked many weeks in advance. Now that their first single was a hit, the gigs were pandemonium. Ricky Ford would front The Cyclones for a thirty-minute opening set, and then Peter and Gordon would take the stage to screams that were becoming louder with each appearance. Despite now being an act with a huge buzz and a Top Ten record in the charts, they honored every engagement, no matter how small, which, to Bill Green, was a lesson in professionalism. He recalled: "You would have thought they were at the Albert Hall, you know, at every gig. And I was always impressed with that."

In early April, Jane Asher was once again on TV's *Juke Box Jury*, listening to new records and judging their hit potential, when suddenly the opening chords to "A World Without Love" began to echo through the studio. The show's host and her fellow panelists began to smile and laugh as all eyes fell on Jane, listening to a disc written by her boyfriend and sung by her brother. After it finished playing, the seventeen-year-old actress confidently said, "It's going to be number-one, I know it is!"

By April 25th, their debut single *had* reached number-one on the UK charts, knocking The Beatles' "Can't Buy Me Love" out of the top position. "If you have to be knocked off the number-one spot," McCartney told a reporter, "it's nice to know it's your own song." Bill Green remembered the thrilling moment while on tour, driving into Buxton: "We pulled up in the van—it must've been very early in the morning—and I ran and got the *Melody Maker* and the *New Musical Express*. And their faces, their mugshots, were all over the front, you know?

"It was an exciting experience," Green marveled, "witnessing firsthand the hysteria that was going on there. It was absolutely *crazy*." Green recalled many occasions when he and the band had to fight their way through the adoring throngs to enter their hotels.

The headliners, though, did not let it all go to their heads. "Gordon," Green recalled, "was a very, very friendly guy . . . such a nice fellow. And Peter I always found an absolute gentleman." He remembered an incident that showed the young singer's kindness and generosity: "Peter had this black overcoat, which had this lovely sort of high Tudor collar . . . I just loved this coat. And I think it was the night before I left, he actually gave it to me. So I treasured that for quite a time—wore it out in the end." The next day, Eddie King and the rest of The Cyclones were asked to stay for the upcoming tour, but not Green. Understanding what a great opportunity this was for the band, he left with no hard feelings. Though never making it big, Green wouldn't stop rockin'—still billed as Ricky Ford, he continues to perform today.

For almost all of 1963, "Beatlemania" had Britain by the throat. Puzzlingly, EMI's American subsidiary, Capitol Records, kept passing on releasing Beatles records in the States, forcing manager Brian Epstein to license the recordings to smaller independent labels, like Chicago-based Vee-Jay. Without major promotion, the discs, not surprisingly, went nowhere. Perhaps one should pause for a moment and recall what America was listening to in 1963 while England was awash in Merseybeat:

- "Sugar Shack" (Jimmy Gilmer and The Fireballs)
- "The End of the World" (Skeeter Davis)
- "Rhythm of the Rain" (The Cascades)
- "Blue Velvet" (Bobby Vinton)
- "Hey Paula" (Paul and Paula)
- "Can't Get Used to Losing You" (Andy Williams)
- "Sukiyaki" (Kyu Sakamoto)
- "I'm Leaving It Up to You" (Dale and Grace)
- "I Will Follow Him" (Little Peggy March)
- "Blame It on the Bossa Nova" (Eydie Gormé)

American rock'n'roll was certainly in the doldrums by 1963. The original white-hot flame that had fired the imagination of British youth had, for the most part, been stamped out in the country that sparked the explosion. Of the "dangerous" originators, Buddy Holly was dead, Jerry Lee Lewis was disgraced, Chuck Berry was in jail, Little Richard was in church, and Elvis Presley was in Hollywood. Yes, Motown was beginning its rise, Phil Spector was producing magical pop symphonies in the studio, and surf music promised teens an endless summer, but mostly it was safe, controlled Frankies and Bobbys on the radio. With Kennedy's assassination that November, America could not have been more ready for a breath of fresh air.

The day after Christmas, Capitol Records finally woke up to the undeniable future and released "I Want to Hold Your Hand," The Beatles' fifth single, onto the American airwaves. The group landed in New York on February 7, 1964, and two days later, after performing on *The Ed Sullivan Show*, The Beatles conquered America. It was a complete and total sea change, musically and culturally. Anything associated with Lennon and McCartney was assured to get airplay, and Peter and Gordon were certainly poised to take advantage of this situation.

Though not remembered by most, at the exact same time that Capitol Records released Peter and Gordon's debut single, "A World Without Love" was also released in the United States by Philadelphia crooner Bobby Rydell on the Parkway label. He had toured England in December 1963, sharing the stage with The Beatles on a few dates. According to Rydell, his manager had befriended Brian Epstein, who offered the song with the pledge that it was unrecorded—which, at that time, was correct. Peter, though, is doubtful: "My understanding was he'd heard our version and immediately covered it. You see, if Brian had a version, it couldn't have had a bridge. That bridge really was written shortly before the session." Adding to Peter's suspicion is the fact that Parkway's owner, Allen Klein, had copies of England's Top Ten hits sent to his office weekly. Rydell performed the song May 10, 1964, on *The Ed Sullivan Show*, but Peter and Gordon's version was quickly overtaking Rydell's as, almost overnight, the scrubbed, Brylcreemed crowd had been deemed passé. Ironically, Rydell's last hit—the prophetically entitled "Forget Him"—inspired Lennon and McCartney to write "She Loves You."

By May 16th, "A World Without Love" had reached number-one in the United States, making the duo the first British group after The Beatles to top the charts on both sides of the Atlantic. Peter and Gordon had now become worldwide pop stars. Gordon couldn't wait to claim this mantle, Westminster be damned. Peter, well into his studies at King's College, went to have a talk with his tutor, the esteemed Professor Vesey: "I explained to him what we'd been doing and what had happened, and I said, 'Now it's number-one in America, and they really want us to go over there and do *The Ed Sullivan Show* and tour and everything, and I'd really like to do it; it sounds like fun. And would you consider giving me a year's leave of absence?' To pursue this, you know, foolishness. And he did. I'm not sure what I would have done if he'd said 'No.'" He pondered this for a moment: "Hmmm . . . 'Cause I'd done two years of philosophy—I didn't want to waste it!" Students at English universities stayed in school until their coursework was finished; leaving for a spell was simply not done. But kindly Professor Vesey agreed to bend the rules for Peter: "He said, 'Okay, come back within a year and you can take up where you left off.' But tragically, he's still awaiting my return."

Dr. Waller gave Gordon even less time: "My father said, 'You've got six months, then. Otherwise, you're gonna go back and you're gonna get your A levels and you're gonna go to university.' 'Okay, Dad, fine.' Well, six months later I was, like, buying him a Rolls Royce."

Noel Gay Artists got to work promoting their new clients. One of Armitage's early deals was to put Peter and Gordon into a quickie musical film to capitalize on their chart-topping success. *Just For You* was basically a series of music clips introduced by British actor and radio DJ Sam Costa. His comments, all delivered from bed, are painfully unfunny, and the musical acts—save for Peter and Gordon, Millie Small, and Freddie and The Dreamers—are completely forgettable (though future Yes vocalist Jon Anderson can be spotted as a member of The Warriors). With their Lennon and McCartney–penned hit being too costly to license, Peter and Gordon instead performed two of their own compositions ("Soft as the Dawn" and "Leave Me Alone"), which, unfortunately, are also fairly forgettable. To help get the most out of this low-budget production, producer Jacques De Lane Lea recycled the Peter and Gordon footage almost two years later in an American release entitled *Disk-O-Tek Holiday*—equally bad, though it at least tried to have a plot.

The last week of May saw the pair, backed again by The Cyclones, second-billed on a Rolling Stones tour. Gordon saw a kindred spirit in Brian Jones (then the Stones' driving force), whose taste for hellraising and womanizing was on par with his own. The two became close, with Brian giving Gordon some blues harmonica tips and eventually inviting both him and Peter to Rolling Stones' recording sessions.

Only a week after their debut disc hit number-one, Peter and Gordon rushed back into Abbey Road to cut their second single, "Nobody I Know." McCartney, pleased with getting "A World Without Love" to the top of the charts, wanted first crack at the follow-up and presented the song to the duo "without any delays or nagging," Peter recalled. With harmony heroes The Everly Brothers firmly in mind, McCartney crafted a melody easy to stick in the head of every youngster who heard it, including the descending guitar riff that punctuated the track. As with "A World Without Love," McCartney smoothly switches from a major key in the verse to a minor key for the bridge—all told, a perfect little pop confection. (And, as with "A World Without Love," due to a longstanding agreement, "Nobody I Know" was credited once again to Lennon and McCartney, though Lennon really had no hand in either song's creation.) As Richard Armitage finalized plans for Peter and Gordon's initial trip to the United States, Columbia released the single on May 29th. Their American label, Capitol, quickly put promotional copies of the new record into the hands of DJs around the country in preparation for the tour and rushed it into stores on June 15th, along with the pair's first American album.

For Peter and Gordon, The Beatles, and every other British act, America was, as the title of one of Chuck Berry's songs proclaimed, "The Promised Land." "America was the country we all idolized," Peter recalled, remembering the Yanks that Britons were introduced to in the postwar years. "They had these perfect teeth and huge cars and gigantic refrigerators and great clothes. And, of course, they had rock'n'roll, which is the music we all loved." Lennon idolized Elvis and Chuck Berry, McCart-

Pictorial Press Ltd / Alamy Stock Photo.

ney worshiped Little Richard and Buddy Holly, The Rolling Stones were besotted by Howlin' Wolf and Muddy Waters, and Peter and Gordon adored The Everly Brothers. "The English music scene was *entirely* based on our admiration for American music and how great it was," Peter admitted. "But it seemed terribly far away. America was another world . . ."

Peter Asher and Gordon Waller descended into "The Promised Land" on June 22, 1964, landing at JFK Airport in New York City. They immediately headed over to the studios of WINS and Murray the K's radio show. The next day, before appearing on B. Mitchell Reed's popular program on WMCA, they stopped at Manny's—a legendary music store near Times Square. McCartney had told Peter of the great instrument emporium, as The Beatles had shopped there when in town the previous February. Its walls were famously lined with scores of signed photographs—everyone from Gene Krupa and Nat King Cole to Buddy Holly and now, of course, The Beatles. As he waited in line to pay for his guitar strings, Peter realized the customer standing next to him was Gene Krupa himself! For the self-professed "jazz snob," the trip to America was already worthwhile.

Rehearsals for the tour commenced that second afternoon in Manhattan. Gordon was a big fan of the instrumental "Scratchy" by Memphis-based guitarist Travis Wammack. At Gordon's urging, Armitage had arranged for Wammack's trio to support Peter and Gordon on their monthlong trek across the country. Gordon was over the moon to have an authentic band from Elvis country backing him.

Beginning on June 25th, they began a five-day engagement at the New York World's Fair, which had opened two months previously out at Flushing Meadows, Queens. Being one of the first British acts to arrive in the United States on the heels of The Beatles, and with both their singles now in the US charts, the reaction of young girls witnessing their performances was bound to be chaotic.

The performance pavilion was designed with a water barrier of about twenty feet separating the audience from the stage. Peter and Gordon were introduced, and they launched into their first set on American soil. "Imagine our ineffable joy when, during the show, the first screaming girl jumped into the moat and swam across it in order to throw her dripping self upon us," Peter recalled to music industry commentator Bob Lefsetz. All hell broke loose as more and more girls knocked down what security remained and dove in, all determined to reach the two adorable male sirens standing just out of reach. Playing an electric guitar, Wammack saw trouble coming: "I didn't need to be holding on to my instrument when they came up there wet, so I automatically unplugged my guitar." The two main targets, though, reacted a bit slower, and not only did the boys receive a shock, but the audience got one, too: "Gordon's favorite word was 'fuck,'" recalled Wammack, "and you just didn't hardly hear that word back then. But when they grabbed him, he yelled it out over the microphone and you could hear a pin drop!"

Despite the electrical hazards, the intensity of their female fans was thrilling to the quiet, reserved Peter and still brings a smile to his face: "Oh, it was wonderful! It was great! No, I recommend it. Having screaming girls calling your name and trying to tear your clothes off is excellent, especially at that age, but I'm sure It would be wonderful even now. Unaccountably," he mused, "it hasn't happened lately . . ."

In 1964, Al Coury was working as Capitol Records' head of Sales and Promotion for the northeastern United States. The home office in Hollywood trusted Coury to supervise while the boys were in New England. As the tour made its way to Rochester, New York, he went to the Civic Auditorium to check things out.

Coury recalled, "The first thing that I noticed when I got to the place was something that was absolutely wrong: They had the stage where these guys were gonna perform right in the middle of the arena! In the *round*, you know? And I immediately knew from my experience—working with The Beatles when they came through in Boston—is that's bad! Because you can get 'em on stage, but you're never gonna be able to get 'em *off* stage!"

Coury huddled with members of the Rochester Police to work out a plan: "We're gonna have to have police on both sides, in the front, push these young kids back, and I'll be with them—I'll get 'em off stage and we'll sort-of have like a human ramrod to get through these hundreds and hundreds of kids." The police quickly hustled the boys through the crowd of ten thousand fans, and they began their set on a stage more suited to a boxing match. And, as expected, the performance was almost too much for the youngsters surrounding the two troubadours; the screams and flashbulbs were both deafening and dazzling. "They drove the audience crazy," Coury remembered. "I mean it was pandemonium."

Coury had been told what the final song would be and was at the side of the stage, ready. Peter was first to come off, and as Coury threw his arm around the singer's neck, he pulled Peter close and shouted, "GO!" As Gordon followed on their heels, the tight ball of pop stars and police moved through the crowd faster and faster. "I saw girls stick their hand in, grab Peter Asher's hair, and pull it out!" Coury laughed. "I saw hair go flying by me! You know? I mean they were literally attacked!"

As Peter tried to keep his head down, Coury had him in a near headlock with the police continuing to push from behind, heading for the tunnels that would lead to the dressing rooms and a waiting limo. "And when we got in and through to the tunnel, you had to go right or left—you couldn't go straight 'cause that's a cement wall!" Coury laughed again. "We went right into the wall with Peter's head. I couldn't stop the guys behind me!" Dazed and bruised, Peter and a very amused Gordon made their escape, leaving the screams (and tufts of red hair) behind them.

When hearing Coury's tale, his poor head smashing into cement, Peter smiled and said, "Well, that explains a lot!" But amazingly, he said he never really felt in danger from fans. "It was almost like everyone was acting a part—the girls knew what they were supposed to do, and they did it, and so did we. So, we'd prance around and smile and wave, and they'd go crazy and try to grab us. But I never really felt in danger. The Beatles probably did because it just got so HUGE. But in our case, it was *intense* but never huge enough to feel life-threatening."

By Independence Day, "Nobody I Know" had become a Top Twenty hit across America, Top Ten in the UK. That same week the duo flew to Hawaii for a three-night stand with The Beach Boys, Jan and Dean, The Kingsmen, The Rivingtons, and others, billed as "The Million Dollar Party," presented by radio station KPOI. DJ Tom Moffatt called his old friend Hal Blaine, then well on his way to becoming the top session drummer in Los Angeles, to help put the backing band together for the shows. To play lead guitar, Blaine recruited Glen Campbell—already well-known in LA's recording studios years before making hits under his own name. And for bass guitar, the job fell to seventeen-year-old Phil Sloan. "It was the first time I'd ever played bass," Sloan confided.

"Jan Berry from Jan and Dean was using Glen and Hal on all of his records, and I was singing background," Sloan recalled. "I was basically a guitar and piano guy." But with youthful fearlessness, Sloan decided, "I'd watched people play bass, I'd listened to bass on records, so I figured I'd do it. Yeah, it was fairly easy." To make the situation even more incredible, Sloan had only played in studios up until then—this would be his first live show.

Sloan, Blaine, and Campbell flew into Honolulu a day early, arrived at the brand-new International Center Arena, and began rehearsing with all the acts that needed musical support, including Peter and Gordon. "I was amazed at how well they played guitar," Sloan said. "They played all the riffs exactly as was on the record." Gordon, used to the straightforward drumming on their recordings, became annoyed with Blaine, Peter recalled. Though Blaine was a world-class drummer at the top of his game, Gordon told him to tone down his flashy drum style.

Sloan also recalled the fear that older session musicians felt as this musical British Invasion got underway: "They felt that all the British groups were self-contained; therefore, there's not gonna be any need for musicians." But as both record and instrument sales exploded in the wake of The Beatles' success, music became more important in people's lives, and the sixties proved to be the golden age of the session musician. As proof, Blaine himself played on every Grammy-winning Record of the Year six years running—from 1966's "A Taste of Honey" to 1971's "Bridge Over Troubled Water."

A late addition to the lineup was Screamin' Jay Hawkins, one of the original wild men of rock. The Rivingtons carried his coffin from the back of the auditorium through the anticipating crowd, placing it onstage as Sloan, Campbell, and Blaine riffed ominously. Moffatt observed, as Screamin' Jay jumped out and began his set, that Peter and The Beach Boys were getting into the spooky swing of things backstage: As Peter stood absolutely still, The Beach Boys circled around him with rolls of toilet paper, turning the smiling singer into a mummy for a few macabre minutes.

Rejoining Wammack and his trio, the tour stopped in Chicago, where scores of girls hid in various rooms and closets throughout the floor where Peter and Gordon were staying, all in a bid to meet their idols. Art Roberts, a top DJ for Chicago's mighty WLS, called the hotel to speak with neither Peter nor Gordon, but their guitarist. Roberts told Wammack to make sure he performed "Scratchy" at that evening's show. It turned out that Roberts was such a fan of Wammack's instrumental, spinning it so often, that "A World Without Love" was number two on the station's playlist, and Wammack's record had the top spot!

More crowd hysteria followed them as they continued, playing one, two, and sometimes three nights in Cleveland, San Francisco, Dallas, Houston, and other cities. In Birmingham and Montgomery, they shared the stage with rock legend Jerry

Lee Lewis. Lewis was amazed at the size of the crowd: eighteen thousand people—the biggest crowd he'd played for in years, thanks to Peter and Gordon's popularity. Gordon himself was amazed watching Lewis's set; having worshiped the Mississippian for years, now he had achieved top billing over one of rock's founding fathers. Only meeting "The King" himself could top this.

When the tour came through Memphis, Peter stayed as a guest in Travis Wammack's home. Both he and Gordon got to hear some of the young guitarist's recent tracks and were so taken by them, they decided to record two for their next album. Taking a chance one evening, Gordon couldn't resist and went to Graceland hoping to meet his idol. Though Elvis wasn't home, his father, Vernon Presley, invited Gordon in to have dinner. Later, speaking to *New Musical Express* reporter Keith Altham, Peter remarked on Elvis: "He has removed himself from the glare of personal publicity. No one knows what he is like. I think this marvelous." This is somewhat similar to what Peter himself has attempted for most of his career.

The radio station promoting their appearance in Los Angeles noted that Peter had celebrated his twentieth birthday while on tour. DJs encouraged fans to make up for this by sending the station birthday cakes. Hundreds of cakes began arriving at the local station, which then shipped them over to Peter and Gordon's hotel; two more large adjoining suites had to be booked just for the cakes, all with the intention of donating them to a local children's hospital. Returning to the hotel after that night's show, the band decided to have a small party and sample a few. "Gordon," Wammack remembered, "goes down to the lounge and brings these two hookers up."

When Gordon eventually propositioned one of the ladies, she playfully pretended to be shocked and replied, "I should hit you with this cake!" In response, Gordon picked up an entire cake and smashed it into her face. That was all it took: "Everybody got into it; we had the derndest cake fight you ever seen." Wammack laughed. "I was throwin' cakes out the window! After an hour, there wasn't a cake left, and there was probably four inches of cake on the carpet." Even the usually reserved Peter joined in, but it was his "birthday," after all.

At times, Gordon's behavior threatened to ground the entire entourage. Wammack remembered more than one occasion when flight crews threatened to land the plane and throw them all off due to Gordon harassing the stewardesses.

In Atlanta, a crowd numbering over one hundred greeted them at the airport, even though it was just a temporary stopover. They got off the plane and waved to the crowd, who screamed their names and waved their records, hoping they could score an autograph. Peter noticed a petite black girl near the front of the crowd holding flowers. As he came toward her, he quickly realized she was blind. Taking the flowers and thanking her, he gave her a quick kiss on the cheek.

Suddenly, the mostly white crowd changed from cheering to jeering the two singers. Peter was completely caught off-guard, as he had no experience with the racial etiquette of the Deep South. Less than a year after Martin Luther King, Jr.'s March on Washington, segregationist sentiment was still the norm in this part of the country. Gordon, not caring about his image as a fresh-scrubbed pop idol, simply sneered back at the booing crowd. "Oh, fuck off," he said loudly as they turned back to the plane.

Peter later spoke to Ren Grevatt of England's *Melody Maker*, saying: "They still have signs for white and colored on washroom and waiting room doors. It's a bit unbelievable. I like their Southern accents, but I don't like their customs."

The tired pair finally made it home July 28th, returning as conquering pop heroes, much as their friends The Beatles had. They didn't have much time to rest, as there were TV appearances to do, a new single and album to record, a tour of Sweden the next month, and a tour of Australia coming up in September, followed by *more* American dates. They had jumped on the modern pop star merry-go-round, enjoying the ride but starting to wonder just how long it all could last.

4

I GO TO PIECES

In 1964, Andy Irvine was busking around Ireland, sleeping in barns, and playing in pubs for "10 bob a night"—basically one or two dollars (if he was lucky). He hadn't seen his old mate Peter in over a year. One day, glancing at a copy of the music paper *Melody Maker*, he saw the names "Peter and Gordon." "I thought, well, who do I know called Peter and Gordon?" Andy remembered putting two and two together: "But I thought, '*How* did he *do* it?' I mean between 1963 and '64, he suddenly became . . . this pop star! And with his rather feeble little voice!"

What Irvine remembered as a "feeble little voice" from The A 1 Skiffle Group was now a more mature and confident voice, honed through years of practice, strengthened by touring, polished in the studio, and encouraged by the top artists of the day. Peter was also learning other facets of the business, especially the process of record production: "I was interested all along," he told me. "I mean, I really loved the studio process right from the beginning. I found it fascinating, and I knew that was something I wanted to do." Said EMI producer John Burgess: "Peter was a budding producer. You could tell, straightaway."

Peter and Gordon spent the month of August concentrating on recording their second album, as they knew the rest of the year would be consumed with touring the world. The two had been working on original material and sprinkled the album with good Asher/Waller compositions like "I Don't Care What They Say" and the bluesy "Love Me Baby" (which featured, according to guitarist Eddie King, backing from Paul McCartney on guitar and Brian Jones on harmonica). Two solid numbers came from the pen of nineteen-year-old Travis Wammack, the guitarist on their American tour. But the obvious choice for their third single was "I Don't Want to See You Again," another McCartney-penned track—atypical for a song of heartbreak in its bouncy major key and, typically from McCartney, catchy as hell. Peter suggested an oboe duet for the instrumental break—an obvious homage to his mum.

Both Peter and Gordon realized how valuable Cyclones guitarist King could be for them—not just on the road, but in the studio. Beginning with their second album, Eddie played guitar on almost every Peter and Gordon session for the next two years. As other producers and arrangers became aware of King's talents, he played on many hits, including Dusty Springfield's "I Only Want To Be With You." "I used to rock up at Abbey Road at 10 a.m. and do three sessions a day and finish at 10 p.m.," King remembered. "We'd go downstairs—little lady behind a window—and you'd sign this little chitty and she'd give you a brown envelope with money in it" (referring to their Musician's Union payments).

"It was a very strict regime, you know? You went into Abbey Road and you had to have a tie on and it was guys on the door with uniforms and the sound engineer had a white coat on!" King laughed at the memory of the buttoned-down conservative attitudes in the midst of the creative musicmaking that would influence not just his generation, but generations to come.

"I've often likened it to chucking a pebble in a pond, you know. . . . If you're in the middle, you don't actually see the ripples at the edge. I don't think any of us realized where the ripple was reaching.

"We didn't set out to be significant"—King laughed—"we just set out to do the *job*, you know?"

It seems every ten or fifteen years, a new generation of musicians grab an aural slice of the sixties and call it theirs—whether it's Oasis aping the late-period Beatles or Amy Winehouse echoing Ronnie Spector's style. What is it about that era's music that is so captivating and inspiring decades later? Certainly there's the explosion of creativity that was happening on a weekly basis when new vinyl hit both the shops and airwaves. The decade was about discarding outmoded ways of thinking—social, political, and artistic—and it seemed *anything* was possible. What musician today wouldn't respond to that freedom?

But there's something else apparent in the grooves of those old records—an energy that's unmistakable and, unfortunately, missing from today's Top 40 hits. And it all stems from how those sixties tracks were recorded. "There's an immediacy about them," composer and arranger John Cameron explained. Cameron, who famously did the orchestrations for *Les Misérables* for both the original London and New York stage productions, was an in-demand arranger at London's recording studios during the sixties. "What you came into the studio with had to work," he said, recalling all the preplanning that would go into selecting the right instruments to have on hand, be it oboe or harpsichord, and which musician should play them. Then, on the day of the session, singers and musicians would be in the *same room*, working together to find the right feel—the groove—to make the track work. And either you accomplished this in the three hours that had been allotted by the label . . . or you'd blown it.

"It's not like now where, if the bass doesn't work you bring somebody back in, you re-create the drums, you put it all in ProTools and put everybody in tune," Cameron said. "Now, you have so much scope to go back and 'get it right' you are at risk of

John Lennon, George Harrison, Peter Asher, and George Martin listen to a playback of The Beatles' "Baby's In Black" at Abbey Road, August 11, 1964. © *Beatles Book Photo Library.*

losing that *frisson of danger*, you know?" Peter Asher agreed that the feel in the studio is incredibly important, as is a good foundation of preproduction work: "Certainly some of what I've applied as a producer, in terms of being prepared, comes from that era."

As Peter learned the art of record making and Jane continued to have success in the acting world, Dr. Asher faced a professional crisis: Central Middlesex Hospital had decided to relieve him from his oversight of the Mental Observation Ward. During the war, there weren't enough psychiatrists around, but now with the rise of medical specialists, plus the rules and regulations inherent with the National Health Service, it was no longer possible for Dr. Asher to retain that post. "Supposing you were doing surgery and you had no surgery qualifications," his old friend and colleague Dr. Lock explained. "The potential risks and the sort of public relations aspect to it. I think he managed to keep his place in the Mental Observation Ward for so long because, although people would say, 'Well, you haven't had any formal training,' he would probably use sarcasm and wit and win the day."

But now it was a battle he could not win, and it shook him to the core. "He'd lost his raison d'être," Dr. Lock continued. "He resigned *all* his posts in the health service, and he resigned from all his London memberships—things like the Royal Society of Medicine. And he was discovered, I believe, one night about three o'clock in the morning in the long corridor in the hospital putting up a stained-glass window that said: '*To the memory of the glorious National Ill-health Service.*'"

A day later, Lock said, it had disappeared.

In Britain, the trad-jazz scene had also been shunted aside; until the arrival of The Beatles, this genre had been incredibly popular with young and old alike. Keith Avison had been a trombonist with Acker Bilk's band in the late fifties, later moving over to Bob Wallis's ensemble. Gigs, though, were now drying up. "We were in the London Palladium for seven months in 1963," Avison happily recalled, but by 1964, "we were only doing two or three gigs a week." With a wife and twins to support, Avison began to look for another job. One day Wallis asked him: "How'd you like to work for a rock'n'roll band?"

"I said, 'No, thank you very much. They're takin' all our bloody work!'" Despite harboring some resentment, Avison and Wallis went together to Noel Gay Artists to see what this job might entail. "It was a matter of looking after the two lads," Avison learned, "seeing that they had everything that they wanted, traveling with them." Passing the interview, Avison was told to come along on the next two Peter and Gordon gigs taking place the following weekend in northern England. Having been in the business for years, Avison proved adept at anticipating the needs of his young charges, changing broken strings, and responsibly handling the evening's receipts. But he more importantly proved to Gordon he could handle both fast cars and hard liquor, and in short order "Avo" (as Gordon called him) became their road manager for the next three years. "They were lovely guys," he recalled, "and I got on with each one of them. Quite a lot of the time," Avison admitted, "they were looking after me, because I liked to have a drink and things."

Peter and Gordon's third single, "I Don't Want to See You Again," was released in the UK on September 9th, as the pair, accompanied by Avo and Eddie King, embarked on promoter Harry Miller's "Starlift '64"—a tour of New Zealand and Australia with fellow Englishmen The Searchers and Eden Kane (originally born Richard Sarstedt in India), New Zealand sensation Dinah Lee, and American singer Del Shannon. Bassist Frank Allen, who had joined The Searchers earlier that year, re-membered having a bite to eat with Peter on their layover in Hawaii: "He was a very easy guy to talk to and to be with, as intelligent and sophisticated as I was gauche and ignorant. I admired that degree of maturity in one so young.

"Gordon, too, was a nice guy but the opposite coin to Peter, preferring to accept enthusiastically the temptations of free-flowing drink, women, and partying. It was certainly Peter's company I was happier in," Allen mused, "probably because I always tend to head for an oasis of normality and moderation in a world of overcharged testosterone and crazy living that is more the rule of thumb than the exception in the environment of the average pop group."

The Searchers were self-contained, but the other artists needed backing. For the weeklong New Zealand trek, the task fell to The Dynamics, a Christchurch band that Dinah Lee recommended. The band was asked to choose between being men-tioned in the tour advertising or being paid. Bassist Peter Hansen recalled the obvi-ous decision: "We said, 'The money!'"

The Dynamics got together all the latest hit records from the tour's artists and learned the parts, Hansen remembered, "because we didn't know what the hell we were gonna be doing." They had a quick four-hour rehearsal with the artists, locked down the set lists, and they were off.

As artists from Buddy Holly to Rick Nelson learned, traveling via chartered plane can turn from pleasant to horrible in an instant. As the tour made its way from Dunedin to Christchurch, the small plane hit some *very* bad weather. Dynamics guitarist Paul Muggleston remembered it vividly: "Mike Pinder, who was the lead guitarist/vocalist for The Searchers, just happened to be my eye contact on that flight, and he's going, 'Oh, SHIT!' And I'm going, 'Oh, FUCK!' And there's *lightning outside the bloody windows*, and everybody's crapping themselves!" Muggleston laughs now at his memory of terror and helplessness but remembered thinking that despite his nonexistent billing on the tour, they were all equals now: "Don't matter *how* much money you got up there, only God's gonna get you down!" The plane eventually landed safely to the great relief of all aboard. The mob of screaming fans waiting for them at the airport had no clue how close to a premature end their idols had just come.

Dinah Lee was a hot new sensation Down Under with her recent chart-topping cover of Huey "Piano" Smith's "Don't You Know Yockomo." She was an energetic performer whose hair, makeup, and clothes were the latest London styles. "This was a very exciting and crazy time for all of us," she remembered. "It was very difficult to go out in public, as fans always seemed to be there at any time, day or night. Plus the touring schedule was always full on—each day a different city, a different venue." As happens with performers cooped up together, sharing the heightened experiences of crowd adulation (not to mention a brush with death), Dinah and Peter became quite close. "I loved his look—very Mod, very British," she told me. "And I, too, with my Mod look—we just seemed to click. I loved his intelligence and wit. We really enjoyed each other's company." This pairing came as a surprise to Dinah's friends in The Dynamics; they had made an obviously mistaken assumption about the soft-spoken, bookish Brit, as Muggleston sheepishly admitted: "We thought Peter was gay."

Also on the tour was Del Shannon, who'd had a smash hit in 1961 with "Runaway" and more recently "Keep Searchin'." He'd discovered an R&B singer in Detroit named Lloyd Brown and had written a song called "I Go To Pieces" specifically to showcase Brown's talents, but the record got nowhere. Shannon recorded it himself and had no better luck. Relaxing one afternoon between shows, Shannon pulled out his Martin acoustic and played the song for a couple of The Searchers, hoping they might record it. They listened politely and said no, thanks; but Peter and Gordon, sitting nearby, definitely heard something they could sink their teeth into.

They recorded the song October 28th with their new producer, John Burgess. Rock'n'roll was never Norman Newell's forte, and the EMI brass tapped Burgess to take over. Originally Newell's assistant, and long a staff producer for the company, Burgess oversaw a string of hits for fifties British rocker Adam Faith and helmed more recent smashes for Manfred Mann ("Do Wah Diddy Diddy") and Freddie and The Dreamers ("You Were Made for Me").

"He wasn't musical. I mean, he couldn't read music and he couldn't write music," engineer Geoff Emerick said when we spoke about Burgess. "His claim to fame was picking a song." Later gaining fame himself when tapped by George Martin to engineer The Beatles' later works (including *Revolver, Sgt. Pepper,* and *Abbey Road*), Emerick was assistant engineer on many Peter and Gordon sessions, which took place mostly in Studio Two at EMI's Abbey Road facility—at that time "probably the best studio in the world," Burgess told me proudly.

Mike Vickers, a member of Manfred Mann, agreed with Emerick's assessment of Burgess: "John was not knowledgeable at all—certainly compared to George Martin, who was musically very literate. And he could be very frustrating to work with because he couldn't really discuss things in a musical way. But he certainly knew hits and he certainly had a good ear for them." Additionally, Vickers suggested that many other producers of that era were not terribly musical, either. "I'd say quite a high percentage of them."

EMI expected tracks to be recorded quickly and efficiently. "There *was* a budget," Emerick says. "If it was a Peter and Gordon session, yeah, John probably had to record two or three songs in a session. And then, probably, the overdubs and the vocals in the evening, and then the next day you'd be mixing it." "For albums," Burgess recalled, "you could spend a *little* bit more time, but not a lot. You had to sort of get cracking."

The speed of their sessions, as opposed to the more 'popular' bands of the day, still rankled Gordon decades later: "We were sheep! The Rolling Stones did what the hell they wanted. The Beatles? Hah! They had George Martin on their side . . . George Martin, who would say to EMI"—and he adopted a low-key upper-class accent here—"'Uh, no, we're not—We're not ready yet. We'll probably have that track ready in, let's say, two weeks. Give us three to be on the safe side.'

"Right?" Gordon asked, his voice on edge. "But with *us*, it was, 'Oh yeah, we'll get another three tracks done on Thursday and they should be ready, ohhh, 'bout four o'clock Thursday afternoon.' And so, CHOOM! CHOOM! CHOOM! Track, track, track! 'That's another one! That's half an album!' No listening to it and really going away and thinking about it EVER went on!"

To make matters worse, the care that might have gone into sequencing their UK albums was completely ignored by their American label, Capitol. Just as they did with The Beatles' albums, Capitol would re-sequence the running order, drop tracks, add one or both sides of a single, and even sonically change them—tweaking the highs and lows or adding more reverb. *In Touch with Peter and Gordon*, their second LP, was released in the UK on December 4th with fourteen tracks. A week later, Capitol released an eleven-track album called *I Don't Want to See You Again*. Four of the dropped UK tracks would never see release stateside.

Despite all this, their records were selling and people were listening, and listening closely. "One of the most interesting and flattering things that happened to me," Peter said, "was David Crosby told me that when he and [fellow future Byrds member] Chris Hillman started singing together, they were trying to sound like *us!*"

"Yeah, we were listening," Crosby laughed. "There's no question!" David Crosby, one of the great harmony singers of the rock era, recalled: "We were monitoring anybody that could sing good harmony. I would always notice if somebody was good at it—the same way I noticed Nash when he was singing that top part on 'King Midas In Reverse'"—one of The Hollies' latter hits during Graham Nash's tenure with the band, before he joined forces with Crosby and Stephen Stills. "I noticed Peter's harmonies, and they were good! He was a *very good* singer."

He continued by trying to explain how their approaches to harmony were similar: "The Byrds were really good because we were mostly two-part," Crosby said, speaking of two voices—one singing the main melody line, one singing in harmony along with it. And with Crosby as the third voice, "that let me change the interval between the melody and harmony constantly and be non-parallel. It's a very emotional tool if you can move from the third to the fifth to the fourth to the seventh and back to the third," he explained, referring to the notes that make up any chord occurring in a song. "If you have all that room to move around in, you can create a lot of emotional tension that way."

Peter and Gordon's recordings were, obviously, a lot of two-part harmony singing, "which meant that Peter had that liberty also, and he took advantage of it." When I pressed Crosby to name the best harmony singers of rock's formative years, he first named The Everly Brothers' Phil Everly ("They wrote the book"); second, his former singing partner, Graham Nash; third, Paul Simon's foil, Art Garfunkel; ". . . and I'm not too far out to put Peter in that league," he concluded.

Before departing for their second US tour, Peter and Gordon filmed their segment for another movie meant to capitalize on the British beat boom. Entitled *Pop Gear* (and released in the United States as *Go Go Mania*), the film was, again, a compendium of acts mostly lip-synching to their hits on a soundstage. More professionally done (and with bigger talent) than the dismal *Just For You*, the film certainly looked impressive due to the participation of cinematographer Geoffrey Unsworth. Unsworth, who coincidentally shot Peter's first film, *The Planter's Wife*, would go on to shoot such classics as *2001: A Space Odyssey* and *Cabaret*.

Jimmy Savile, a popular DJ and host of Britain's hit TV program *Top of the Pops*, introduced the film's segments. It is now believed Savile used his celebrity status to molest hundreds of people, mostly young girls, for decades. "Did we know he was molesting young girls? No," Peter stated. "But it is true to say that there was a different vibe then. Not, God help us, in terms of children—but young, teenaged girls were considered fair game, to an extent. One never wants to go on record justifying anything illegal; there is a difference, *clearly*, between molesting eight- or nine-year-olds and molesting fifteen-year-olds who look hot." And with the thousands of young girls throwing themselves at Peter and Gordon, they certainly weren't paying attention to what Savile was doing. "Nor," Peter admitted, "did we always ask for a birth certificate.

"In any context, not taking 'no' for an answer is evil, and abusing your position is evil."

Though what became known as "Rock Journalism" was still years away, American teenagers could get fairly good inside information about their English idols through the pages of periodicals like *16 Magazine*, a twenty-five-cent newsstand staple since it began in the fifties with Elvis on its first cover. By 1964, the editor was Gloria Stavers, who seemed to have an instinctive grasp on the desires of young female music fans for accurate information and, of course, color pinups of their "fave raves" (as Stavers would say).

Peter became friends with Stavers over the years and said, "She was beautiful, she was talented, she took this magazine and created something unheard of!" Not only did Stavers keep teen girls up-to-date on Herman's Hermits and The Monkees, "she got Bob Dylan and Lenny Bruce in *16 Magazine*," Peter exclaimed. "She was being deliberately subversive."

On the eve of their November tour, *16 Magazine* published a typical article, entitled "Peter and Gordon Reveal Their Hates & Loves!" There you could find out important facts to help make the singing duo that had been coming out of seemingly every radio for six months seem more knowable and human, such as Peter's distaste for cucumbers and smoke-filled rooms, along with his love of jazz singer Annie Ross and "way out custom-made clothes."

Looking at the magazine today, Peter smiled and said, "Yeah, this is generally still true, isn't it?" Gordon declared his love of chocolate cake, his silver MG-B convertible, and sleeping very late, "sometimes 'til three in the afternoon."

"All true," Peter mused. He then read out loud his old partner's claim: "I HATE cold, logical people." "That's Gordon," Peter laughed, and in mock wonder, asked: "Who could he *mean?*"

Their second American tour began November 8, 1964, and, once again, Travis Wammack's band provided the accompaniment. On the 15th, they made their first appearance on *The Ed Sullivan Show*, performing their latest Top Twenty hit, "I Don't Want to See You Again" along with their old chestnut, "500 Miles." Sullivan, happy with the duo's performance, waved the pair over to stand with him as the crowd cheered—an "honor" he didn't always bestow. Another high point occurred while in Memphis, spending the day at Stax Records' recording studio and observing artists like Rufus Thomas cut takes of hot Southern soul. The pair were journeying through America for only the second time, but the novelty was already wearing off.

"Our American experience was grim," Peter said, "because we loved America and we wanted it to be great, but it was always a muddle." A big part of the problem was management. Not only were Richard Armitage's main clients (such as television writer and host David Frost) not pop stars, but he also had a fear of flying. So the difference between what had been anticipated in London to the realities of the situation in the States was as wide at the Atlantic Ocean.

"He had a real grasp of the English television world," according to Peter. "He was really good at *that* stuff. But putting an American tour together? Showing up in America *himself?* None of that he had the faintest clue about. He was utterly hopeless." Security certainly needed rethinking, for by tour's end the list of missing items was huge: a guitar, a stage outfit, two pairs of boots, and three pairs of Peter's glasses, among many other items—all taken by adoring, albeit larcenist, fans.

The tour ended in mid-December, but before heading back to England, the pair spent some time in Los Angeles. At a taping of ABC's *Shindig!* they ran into Jerry Naylor, who had taken over as lead singer for The Crickets after Buddy Holly's untimely death. The band was nearing its end, and Naylor was beginning to plan his future as a solo artist. "I told 'em we were getting ready to record," Naylor recalled, "and 'would you come and sing with me?' And in those days, we all did that, you know? 'Come hang out with us and sing.' And literally, it would be nothing more planned than that."

The session for Naylor's single "I Found You" took place at Capitol's studios in Hollywood under the direction of Mike Curb. Also on hand was guitarist Glen Campbell, who had cowritten the song with Naylor. Peter and Gordon enjoyed providing backing vocals on the Buddy Holly–styled number and experiencing the somewhat more laid-back feel of an American recording studio. With a new level of confidence after a year of sessions, impressed with the assembled musicians and with some studio time remaining, Peter and Gordon suggested Naylor take a crack at recording "Leave Me In The Rain"—the final song on their recent UK album.

Norman Newell's production of the original version was nice enough, but the LA track is bursting with energy. Naylor takes the lead vocal, but with Peter and Gordon's harmonies mixed to the front, it basically becomes their track. Gordon wails on harmonica, and the crack studio musicians (including Carol Kaye on bass and Larry Knechtel on piano) are in fifth gear from the start; no wonder guitar legend Davie Allan, who plays on the track along with Campbell, called it "one of my favorite sessions."

Mike Curb, reached by phone, was clear on who should take credit for the track: "The guy that was producing the record in terms of making all the creative decisions was Peter Asher." Curb, today an amazingly successful music mogul and entrepreneur, said he gained much just watching Peter work: "I think I learned a lot about the 'groove' of a record by watching producers like Peter Asher," Curb said. "His whole idea was gettin' the feel right.

"You know, we never, ever broke Jerry through with the kind of record he deserved," Curb said regretfully. "I think I tried to copy a Holly record too much with 'I Found You.' What I should have done was ask Peter to coproduce that record. Or I should have left the studio and let him take over!" Curb laughed. "I always thought I missed a big opportunity there." So did Naylor's label, Mercury Records, which never bothered to release that hot "Leave Me In The Rain" remake. Today, no one knows where the master tape is.

The new single "I Go To Pieces" was released in the UK on November 20th and in the United States on December 28th. It became a Top Ten smash in the States, but like their last single, it completely sank in England. Peter and Gordon were not alone in this, as other British Invasion acts found themselves having more success in America than in their homeland—Chad and Jeremy and The Dave Clark Five, among others. Peter seemed at a loss to explain this phenomenon when speaking in January 1965 to *Melody Maker* reporter Bob Dawbarn: "The situation is certainly strange. We have been thinking hard what sort of record by us would go in Britain—whatever we do in the States seems to sell."

They not only were selling records in the States but tickets, too. By the end of 1964, the US booking agency GAC named them one of the top three British concert acts, just behind The Beatles and The Dave Clark Five. But the duo needed an idea to get them back in the UK charts, and Peter recalled their producer, John Burgess, suggesting Buddy Holly's "True Love Ways."

Holly was much beloved in the UK and immensely influential—not just with Peter and Gordon but with just about every other British band (the name "Beatles" itself was a play on Holly's band, The Crickets). Holly's original recording of the song—one of the last sessions he completed before his untimely death—was pretty, but Gordon wanted to take the song to a higher emotional level. "I think this song meant a lot to him," Peter once remarked.

For chart success, the production, arrangement, and performance needed to be outstanding, and in this they succeeded; Geoff Love's arrangement was gorgeous, incorporating Peter's idea of a big crescendo. Gordon's soulful delivery was brilliant, and Peter's harmony choices were equally thrilling. They went into the studio March 4th and, within four tries, had the master take. It was mixed, mastered, and in the shops three weeks later.

Rumors began circulating—probably because of their recent poor chart showings—that Peter and Gordon were either splitting up or permanently moving to the States. Peter denied them in the UK music papers, saying: "Just because we're there quite a bit doesn't mean we're going to live there. I wouldn't dream of becoming an American citizen." (A longtime California resident, Peter today holds dual citizenships as a matter of convenience.) And as to talk of a breakup, he said: "There is absolutely no truth to that." Folks tuning in to see the pair perform on a local television show broadcast near Carlisle the following week would have thought differently as, instead of Peter and Gordon singing "True Love Ways," they saw only Peter—gamely miming alone to a playback of the new single. Gordon's car had broken down en route on the M1 near Rugby. Even though British Railways stopped an express train to pick him up, he arrived too late to appear.

Their music instincts, though, were perfect—by May 22nd, Peter and Gordon were back in the UK Top Five for the first time in almost a year.

5

THE MORNING'S CALLING

On April 19, 1965, Peter and Gordon, accompanied by guitarist Eddie King and road manager "Avo" Avison, traveled to Japan for a week of live dates and television appearances. With today's more global culture, it might be difficult to imagine the complete and utter strangeness these four Englishmen were faced with when they arrived. "We all know what Japan is *now*," King said, "but in 1965, Japan was like a fuckin' weird place, you know? Nobody knew anything about anything." The only other comparable Western acts to go before them were The Ventures (the US instrumental combo who were hugely influential to the Japanese bands at the time) and British blues rockers The Animals.

Promoter Tatsu Nagashima, who would also bring The Beatles over during their final world tour in 1966, arranged to have an up-and-coming band called The Spiders provide the backing for the tour. Guitarist/vocalist and founding member Hiroshi "Monsieur" Kamayatsu remembered coming up with the band's name with his musician father: "My father was thinking that in those days the beat groups had animal or bug names," Kamayatsu said by phone through a translator. "I also wanted to have a bug name and was thinking about the spider's net capturing the whole world!"

At the first rehearsal with The Spiders, King, the tour's musical director, got a big surprise: "Not one of 'em spoke English." The day went slowly as King took the band through the set list. "They kept bowing at me and doing all that," he recalled. "Really strange."

Even stranger to King is the fact that he has a Top Five hit in Japan. Peter and Gordon had produced a record of King performing his original composition "Always At A Distance," which Columbia released in the UK with no promotion and, accordingly, it failed to chart. But in Japan, it was a hit—just a few notches below Peter and Gordon in the charts. "I was made a big fuss of," King recalled, "taken to the record company, given lunch and all that." Toshiba-Odeon, EMI's Japanese label, also presented King with a transistor radio as a gift.

It should be noted, for those too young to remember, that back in the fifties and early sixties, the transistor radio introduced the concept of a pocket-sized device that would allow you to listen to music everywhere—four decades before Apple introduced the iPod. It was not programmable, of course—you listened to what a local disc jockey wanted to play—but it helped to solidify the importance of music in everyday life for millions of young people.

The short tour hit Tokyo, Nagoya, Kyoto, and Osaka, with the four Englishmen traveling by train, separately from The Spiders. Peter and Gordon were received quite enthusiastically, even in normally reserved Japan. Immediately preceding the headliners, Eddie King performed three or four numbers, including his surprise hit. The Spiders, who opened the show with their own set, got quite a strong reaction with their dance steps and R&B–based beats. Within the year, The Spiders released their first album and are now considered one of Japan's best bands from the sixties, with a string of hit records and successful movies to their credit.

Kamayatsu remembered the tour with great fondness: "It was a learning experience, this music from England. They were wearing black suits, black ties—very sophisticated and with great manners. And their harmonies were so beautiful and very new to me. We were familiar with The Everly Brothers, but this was different." Kamayatsu concluded his reminiscences by saying: "The tour is a really fascinating memory in my heart." Now revered as an elder rock statesman in Japan, Monsieur Kamayatsu continues to record and perform.

Eddie King and Peter traveling in Japan, 1965.

On the way back to the UK, Peter and Gordon stopped in Los Angeles to tape an episode of NBC's musical variety show *Hullabaloo*. "TV shows were great to do in America," Peter remembered. "The most fun were the ones where you got to sing and play live. A lot of them, like Dick Clark (which was very important), you were just lip-syncing to your record. We actually enjoyed singing and playing live with real musicians—those were our favorites. There was, of course, the legendary *Shindig!*, which was great—they had a great band. But actually, the one that was my favorite even more than *Shindig!* was *Hullabaloo*. You'd do your own song, but then they'd put people together—they'd pick a song and say, 'Okay, you're all doing *this*.'" On this particular episode, after performing their current hit, "True Love Ways," Peter and Gordon teamed up with The Supremes, Sam the Sham and the Pharaohs, and that week's host Frankie Avalon to perform The Beatles' current hit, "Eight Days a Week." Here was where Peter first met Diana Ross, whom he would produce quite successfully years later.

After returning home, the duo went into the studio to get their next single and album out of the way before leaving for another extensive tour of America. Their producer, John Burgess, gave the pair a much fuller and punchier sound than Norman Newell had, and Geoff Love's arrangements were oftentimes full of drama—an apt description for their treatment of Phil Spector's "To Know You Is to Love You," chosen as their next single. Though Spector's original version (recorded in 1958 with his trio The Teddy Bears) was fairly subdued, Peter suggested a British version of Spector's later "Wall of Sound" technique.

The track was recorded, for a change, in Abbey Road's cavernous Studio One to accommodate the large orchestra and backup singers brought in for the occasion. UK jazz great Kenny Clare was behind the drums, and the backing singers used on the session were known as The Breakaways, as they had "broken away" from Liverpool-based early sixties hit makers The Vernons Girls to mainly focus on session work, singing on Petula Clark's "Downtown" and Cilla Black's "You're My World," among countless other British hits. Breakaways member Margo Quantrell remembered arranger Love was "always smiling," and though they were given sheet music to sing from, he was not opposed to them suggesting their own ideas "if it improved the track."

The song was recorded live May 31st in one three-hour session. Two months later, it was a UK Top Five smash.

The Asher/Waller songwriting team was improving, bringing solid numbers like "Don't Pity Me" to the sessions (which would be released as a single in the States— their first self-composed A-side). Gordon decided they should try Elvis's "All Shook Up" in a slowed-down arrangement, which simmered wonderfully. Other tracks recorded that month were two that featured solo performances from the pair. Gordon turned in a great, gritty, soulful take on Smokey Robinson's "Who's Lovin' You," and though certainly not as soulful as Smokey, Gordon displayed the edginess of John Lennon in his vocal performance. Peter's solo number was Burt Bacharach and Bob Hilliard's "Any Day Now (My Wild Beautiful Bird)," a hit for Chuck Jackson in

1962. "In retrospect, it takes absurd balls," Peter recalled, smiling. "Who does this white kid think he is? You know? But I love the song. I look at it this way: If another few people heard the song that didn't know it, and maybe even went back to explore where it came from, so much the better."

As sessions continued for their album, Peter and Gordon oversaw the production of a second single for Eddie King. The duo had heard the Jeff Barry/Ellie Greenwich song "I Wanna Love Him So Bad" (performed by The Jelly Beans) when first touring the United States the previous summer. Feeling it could be a Top Ten hit in the UK as it was in the States, they produced a gender-changed version for King. The Break-aways provided excellent background vocals, as always, and Eddie remembered one of the session musicians very well: "This kid walks in with a Fender bass . . . younger than us, very young. His name was John Paul Jones." Jones had begun his career as a session player only a year earlier and would end up doing hundreds of sessions like this one, as both musician and arranger, until joining Led Zeppelin in 1968. The record's flipside, a previously unrecorded Asher/Waller composition entitled "If All You Need," had actually been recorded in Tokyo while they were touring there earlier in the year, with a few of The Spiders lending a hand. Unfortunately, as with King's first UK release, it sank without a trace.

King would at times stay in the Asher household when in London and occasionally help out fellow houseguest Paul McCartney, who never learned to read or write musical notation. He would turn McCartney's songs into notes on a page so that he could present them to Beatles producer George Martin and "appear adept and confident," according to King. Other times, King would be the first to hear a new McCartney composition. Once, the obviously excited Beatle woke him up at five in the morning: "Hey! Listen to this! What d'ya think of this?" McCartney was unsure if the tune—which came to him in a dream—was completely original, and the lyrics certainly weren't finished, but King became the first person to hear McCartney's "Yesterday," one of the most popular songs of the twentieth century.

But despite the phenomenal success and global influence of England's pop scene in the first half of the 1960s, UK's youth movement had still not found its footing. The music that seemed to be blasting out of every transistor radio in the free world—made in Merrie England—was not played on British radio, or at least not on the "official" stations. Though the country had a swinging Mary Quant and James Bond image overseas, old men in gray suits still seemed to control everything. With a few exceptions—poets reading their verse at jazz clubs, for example—the arts were fairly separated: Actors stayed within their cliques, and musicians generally hung with other players.

It should be noted, though, that England's art schools provided the perfect milieu for creative folk of all stripes to meet. "You could spend a few years on a government grant," said Barry Miles. "In those days, they *paid* you to go to college—it's not like now, where they charge you some staggering amount of tuition. Then it was all free. So it was a way of not having to go to work for a few years." An enormous amount of British creativity marinated there, including some of the future gods of sixties rock—John Lennon, Keith Richards, Eric Clapton, Pete Townshend, and Ray Davies, to name just a few. "Very few people came out of art school and finished up as painters," Miles, the former art student turned successful author, admitted.

The art school scene had perhaps lit the match for a youthful creative explosion, but the bomb finally went off on June 11, 1965, when a group of American Beat poets, including Allen Ginsberg and Lawrence Ferlinghetti, gave a reading at Albert Hall entitled "Poets of the World/Poets of Our Time," attracting about seven thousand people—art students, musicians, filmmakers, and poets. Miles, then a bookstore manager and the evening's organizer, realized that everyone there "suddenly recognized each other as a sort of constituency—that they were all involved in some kind of creative activity." Finally the barriers began to break: "Dress designers could hang with people making films," Miles remembered, "and rock musicians could write poetry and do paintings." Almost immediately, the cultural atmosphere switched from black and white to color, and the British underground began in earnest. In a few months, Peter himself would make a significant contribution to the scene.

With the next album in the can, Peter and Gordon embarked on a tour that would give them a view of America unlike any they had experienced before. Dick Clark, host of TV's cultural phenomenon *American Bandstand*, had been capitalizing on his fame as a musical tastemaker since the late fifties by promoting what he dubbed the "Caravan of Stars"—a handful of big-name acts along with some promising up-and-comers crisscrossing the United States in a large bus, performing at theaters and town halls from coast to coast.

"The wisest thing about Dick Clark," Walt Parazaider told me, "was he had a canny knack of knowing that an act was going to be big." Clark would sign them up for a tour while their price was still low, "knowing that by the time that tour came around," Parazaider said, "they'd be able to put butts in the seats."

Sax-player Parazaider had been hired to join Jimmy Ford and the Executives, a professional show band out of Chicago. Ford's band had the job of backing all the acts for the tour (other than those, like The Turtles, who were a self-contained unit). Parazaider insisted that they also hire his best friend, guitarist Terry Kath. "I had met Terry when we were teenagers, and we made a pact never to leave each other," Parazaider recalled. "I said, 'I'm not gonna do it unless we go together.'" The Executives already had a guitarist but not a bass player. So Kath bought a Hofner bass (McCartney's instrument of choice), and with their '56 hearse loaded with gear, the two friends drove out to California for the rehearsals.

A ballroom at the Hollywood Plaza Hotel served as the rehearsal space. Parazaider learned how a professional show was run: "The Drifters would come in, set down charts for trumpet and tenor sax and charts for everybody else, and we'd run through their stuff." This would be repeated for each act—Ronnie Dove, Billy Joe Royal, Brian Hyland, The Shirelles, and Peter and Gordon—all had arrangements written out for the musicians. "That's what Dick wanted," according to Parazaider.

"He insisted on professionalism." Ronnie Dove equated the tightness of the band to those who would back up the artists on their records—plus, this one band had to change from rock to soul to pop constantly. "The sound was wonderful," Billy Joe Royal agreed. "They had the hard job, and they really didn't get the recognition they should."

When Peter and Gordon flew into Los Angeles to prepare for the tour, they were met by Ken Mansfield, Capitol's new West Coast promotions manager. Mansfield had previously been a member of the folk group The Town Criers and had managed a nightclub near San Diego called The Land of Oden, named after the old folk song covered by, among others, Peter and Gordon.

"I picked 'em up at the airport and stayed with them the whole time," Mansfield said, stopping to correct himself—"stayed with *Gordon* the whole time; Peter would go back to the hotel at a decent hour and read or rest." Gordon, though, was something else, as Mansfield recalled: "The only time I've ever gotten thrown out of a strip club with someone being . . . what's the word? 'Lewd.'" Mansfield laughed. "They kicked us out for his offensive language . . . in a strip club! *That's* how bad Gordon was.

"He was crazy," Mansfield said, shaking his head. "He'd take the rental car and go right down the middle of the Sunset Strip at about seventy miles an hour . . . I thought we were gonna be killed. Just *roaring* right down the middle at one o'clock in the morning."

The Caravan of Stars kicked off at the beautiful, historic Avalon Ballroom on Catalina Island July 2nd and ended up in Miami on the other side of the continent. For the next eleven weeks, the tour stopped in almost each state in between, playing practically every evening—and on some days a show in the afternoon, as well. Singer Mel Carter ("Hold Me, Thrill Me, Kiss Me") remembered Clark conserving money by having the acts stay in motels every *other* night. The rest of the time, after finishing a show, the acts would board the bus for an all-night trip to the next gig. "It was like a 'death march,'" singer Billy Joe Royal joked. "But you're young. And I was just excited about being there."

Some of the acts, such as Peter and Gordon, The Shirelles, and Billy Joe Royal, were on board from start to finish. Others joined the tour as it made its way across the country as schedules permitted (and popularity rose). One was singer and songwriter Jackie DeShannon, who, during her time on the bus, made a lasting impression on Gordon. DeShannon, who already had her compositions covered by The Byrds and The Searchers, among others, gave Gordon some good advice: "You know, you should really write some stuff that comes from here," she said, pointing to her heart. In an effort to write more about his feelings and experiences, Gordon (with help from Peter) penned "The Morning's Calling" while spending a night on the bus—"*running from a life that isn't real*," the lyrics went. Gordon thought this smart, cool blonde was irresistible, and the two were quite an item during DeShannon's time on the bus. Billy Joe Royal laughingly remembered that DeShannon referred to Gordon's penis as "Wendell."

Promoting the Caravan of Stars as they made their way into Western Pennsylvania.

Halfway through the tour, Tom Jones came on board. As headliners, Peter and Gordon had been closing the show. Jones, with his virile voice and sexy moves, was the British answer to Elvis. With his first big hit, "It's Not Unusual," climbing the US charts, Jones's manager demanded his charge should become the new show closer. "Who tops the show, who closes, was a big deal," Royal remembered. "They worked out a deal—one would close the first half before intermission, one would close the other." The two acts would alternate this way for the rest of the tour.

Another act undertaking their first US tour was The Turtles. The group was fresh out of high school and promoting their first hit, a cover of Dylan's "It Ain't Me Babe," when they were signed to do Clark's Caravan of Stars. They soon learned there was a hierarchy when it came to sleeping arrangements on the bus. Mark Volman, one of the group's lead singers, recalled: "There were no bunks to sleep on. Basically it was like old people going to a casino—sit-up time.

"So, everybody sort of paired up." Gordon Waller graciously shared his spot on the bus with The Turtles' other lead vocalist, Howard Kaylan. Tom Jones, sitting behind Gordon, paired up with Volman, and the two teenaged neophytes felt privileged to be invited to share these double seats with two big British acts as the bus began to cross the continent . . . until the first all-nighter. At that point, Volman recalled: "Gordon would have the top seat—both seats—and Howard would be forced to the floor." Laughing, he continued: "Tom would get the two seats, and I was forced to the floor! Yeah! It was just, 'Oh! You don't know? That's the way it works . . .'

"Once you knew the routine, you knew how to get comfortable underneath the seats." But it got hot being close to the constantly churning wheels, or as Volman put it: "Sticky!" During their time together, Gordon showed The Turtles a song he was working on, "Wrong from the Start." The Turtles later recorded it during the sessions for their second album—the first time an Asher/Waller composition was covered by another act.

Britisher Ian Whitcomb, in the States to promote his Top Ten smash, "You Turn Me On," hopped on the bus in El Paso. Peter and Gordon had actually inspired Whitcomb to try for pop stardom when he saw the duo on vacation in Seattle during the summer of 1964. Thinking, "If these guys can do it, so can I," Whitcomb turned to his girlfriend and proclaimed: "*I'm* going to be a rock star!" Now, one year later, here he was on tour with them! Being a product of exclusive British "public" schools, as Peter and Gordon were, Whitcomb thought they'd have something in common and fast friendships would be quickly formed. "But it took a long time to get friendly," Ian remembered, as Peter thought his hit "set pop back decades!" Remember that Peter was sharing his home with one of pop music's top songwriters—his critical bar was set fairly high as McCartney, along with Burt Bacharach, Brian Wilson, and others, continued to bring a sophistication and intelligence to pop and rock music (which Ian's hit, to be fair, clearly lacked).

Whitcomb, who was working toward a history degree from Trinity College, Dublin, had brought his textbooks along with him in hopes of getting some studying done for his upcoming final exams—books on Karl Marx, working-class movements, and capitalism. Peter, Whitcomb remembered, would read them, "and then he would summarize them for me." Once, while discussing Marx, singer Ronnie Dove approached the pair, deeply suspicious, and asked if they were communists. Horrified, Peter replied, "Certainly not!"

Brian Hyland ("Sealed with a Kiss") recalled that girls would usually chase young men with long hair in the vicinity of a Caravan venue, but they weren't satisfied with just anyone. "One afternoon," Hyland recalled, "Billy Joe Royal and I were walking back to the auditorium when we were spotted by a group of teenagers who began to chase us and caught up with us after a couple of blocks, asking questions while we continued running! They abruptly stopped when we answered them, and we heard them say, 'Oh, they're not English!'" Laughing, the two American singers watched the disappointed girls walk away.

There were no days off. "We are on the move the whole time," Peter remarked to a reporter at the time. "We finish at midnight, get up at seven, and by three o'clock we're doing another show. It's a good way to kill yourself." Dick Clark, above all else, was an astute businessman and knew how to get the most out of his business ventures—or, as Ian Whitcomb put it a bit more bluntly: "Dick Clark was a cheapskate."

Clark, to his credit, always had an integrated roster on his Caravan tours, and this tour was no different. But this was the summer of both Selma, Alabama, and the Watts riots in Los Angeles. Racial tensions in the country were high, to put it mildly. Peter was no stranger to the ugliness of racial prejudice, remembering "For Rent" signs back in London that would sometimes state: "No Blacks, No Irish." But he didn't quite get the realities of day-to-day life for African Americans in the southern United States.

He had struck up a close friendship with The Shirelles' Doris Coley (lead singer on their hit, "Dedicated To The One I Love") and recalled accompanying her into a truck stop and naively suggesting they share a booth. "She said, 'This is not a good idea,'" Peter remembered. "I was going, 'Oh, nothing will happen.' Of course, she knew the reality of what *had* happened." He laughed. "I was being all nonchalant and English, and she was going, 'No, you don't understand—my people *live* this . . . we know what these people are capable of.'"

Whitcomb recalled stopping to use the facilities at various southern roadside stores and seeing racist postcards on display. At one shop, Whitcomb (ever the musicologist) bought a recording of the Ku Klux Klan's fight song, "Stand Up and Be Counted," and could even sing me a stanza four decades later.

"Peter and I were sort of stunned and—I shouldn't say mildly amused—by these things," said Whitcomb. One incident that wasn't so amusing happened in Alabama one evening as some of the acts, hoping to grab a bite, walked over to the restaurant adjacent to their motel. In the parking lot, the group was verbally abused with comments like, "Look at those guys with that hair! They look like little girls!"—all standard for the time. The group continued walking to the entrance, trying to ignore them. One of the hecklers stuck his foot out to trip singer Mel Carter, who decided to turn around and stand up for both the group and himself—just as a police car drove up. The officer grabbed Carter—the only African American male at the scene—and, after handcuffing him, threw him in the back of the car, despite protests from Tom Jones and the others, who were threatened with arrest themselves if they didn't back up.

"After I was arrested, I was trying to explain what was happening," Carter remembered. One officer—white, of course—turned around and drew his gun on the singer, saying, "Shut up." "And I kept on going. And he took the gun and put it inside my mouth, and he said, 'I said shut up. If you say another word, I'll blow your brains out.'"

"I have to tell you: Mel Carter's a class act and a hell of a singer," Walt Parazaider recalled. "We were outraged about that. But you know what? We were in their world." That may have been so, but after Carter was released without charge, the Caravan acts began to stage their own civil rights protests. Beverly Lee, another of The Shirelles, remembered that when they entered motel lobbies, "we all mixed, black and white, male and female, because, at the time, they didn't want blacks staying in some of the hotels. When we got into the lobby to check in, we sat, you know, like an integrated couple." She smiled. "Just to mess with the people!"

Finally, after over sixty days rumbling across the continent, the final show ended in Miami on September 6th. Dick Clark then threw a big party for all the participants in the Caravan. "At the end of the tour," Billy Joe Royal recalled, "we'd been together so long that everybody knew everybody's act." So for one night only, a bizarre, alternate Caravan of Stars unfolded for a select few. "Billy Joe Royal, Peter Asher, Tom Jones, and Mel Carter dressed as The Shirelles," recounted Beverly Lee. "And we dressed the guys in our outfits, and we put the makeup on them and everything. And they looked wonderful!" Tom Jones in a chiffon dress and beehive wig singing "Will You Love Me Tomorrow" must've been a sight to behold. Later in the evening, Shirelles Doris Coley and Beverly Lee came out as Peter and Gordon, wearing their suits. "But I'll never forget," said Lee of the drag Shirelles, "how wonderful they looked."

Perhaps. Walt Parazaider had a different take: "You know, as guys they were acceptable. As ladies"—he laughed—"not so much. It was hilarious. In fact, it was very hard to play trying to back 'em 'cause you were laughing so much. Everybody was just havin' a ball."

The members of the Caravan began to go their separate ways after that final evening. But for Walt Parazaider, this show band experience pointed the way toward his future. "It was a benchmark in my life, I have to tell you. That was the impetus that got me thinking about putting a band together." In his living room less than two years later, along with his good friend Terry Kath, Parazaider formed his dream band, which became one of the most successful rock groups in history—Chicago.

6

WOMAN

There was no rest for Peter and Gordon following the grueling Caravan of Stars—they immediately made their way from Florida north to New Jersey for a booking in Atlantic City. The Steel Pier, along the Boardwalk, was called "The Showplace of the Nation," and since 1898, its Marine Ballroom had played host to everyone from John Philip Sousa to Frank Sinatra. The pier had become a carnival midway with roller coasters and ferris wheels, chickens dancing for change on cramped, airless stages, and beautiful girls riding horses that would leap from high platforms and plunge into small pools of water—all to the delight of sunburned tourists.

Peter and Gordon shared their bill with the American band Sam the Sham and the Pharaohs, whose 1964 smash "Wooly Bully" was the biggest-selling hit of any American group during that peak British Invasion year. Peter and Gordon kept crossing paths with Sam and his Pharaohs in 1965—first at their memorable *Hullabaloo* taping in May, then when Sam and his band briefly joined up with Dick Clark's Caravan of Stars during the summer.

Sam Samudio's upbringing couldn't have been more different from Peter's. He was born of Mexican American parents in Dallas, but his mother died when he was young, and his father was gone much of the time to find work. Poverty and prejudice took its toll as he grew: "I wasn't a particularly nice guy. I had come up through a bunch of blues bars and crap like that, so I was just"—Samudio laughed—"like a street dog! You know? Ready to growl if somebody'd step on my tail! But it goes with the territory and, you know, we all mature—hopefully—or we mellow out." Samudio paused and then stated, coolly: "Mellow is a code word for senility.

"But I always remember Peter as a gentleman—always. He was just quiet . . . and him being quiet, I knew those wheels were turnin' up there! I know that there was a lot more goin' on behind that forehead than people knew." When Peter and Sam crossed paths again in a few years, their relationship would be quite different.

In front of an adoring audience during their tour of Japan.

While performing those dates at the Steel Pier, the young woman handling publicity for Mal Braverman, Sam's press agent, came in from New York to check on things and see the show. Betsy Doster, like many youngsters at that time enamored with the folk music scene, had moved from Omaha to Greenwich Village in New York. "I ran away and was a waitress at the coffeehouses. It was a wonderful, wonderful time to be there." There weren't just singers like Bob Dylan, Dave Van Ronk, and Tim Hardin performing nightly, but young comedians like Richard Pryor. From someone who had only read about this life from the liner notes of Kingston Trio records, now being in the midst of it was incredible—but also a struggle. "I realized at a certain point that there really wasn't much of a future with waitressing and I should get a day job, probably." Someone at the newly opened Café au Go Go mentioned they needed someone in the daytime to do publicity, to which Betsy replied, "Great, I'll do that."

"And I called up one reporter," Betsy recalled, "and said, 'Lenny Bruce is opening.' And he said, 'Great—send me a press release.' I said, 'Okay. What's a press release?'" Eventually, she went to work for Mal Braverman, "an actual old-style," according to Betsy, "straight-out-of-the-movies kind of Broadway press agent." Braverman had established clients like Tony Bennett and Bobby Vinton but was starting to sign rock'n'roll acts like The Animals and Sam the Sham and the Pharaohs.

Things were in full swing when Betsy arrived in Atlantic City. "The contestants were piling in for the Miss America contest," Betsy remembered, with the pageant to be held the following week. As if all those beautiful girls weren't enough to distract Gordon, he had become quite taken with Lynne Jordan, the woman who sat astride the Steel Pier's famous jumping horse. While he was chasing after her, according to Betsy, "her husband was running around chasing Gordon!"

Amid this spectacle, Betsy found herself caught up in a "corny old dressing room romance," as she later put it. But she wasn't completely caught off-guard: "From working in publicity and reading those teen magazines and all, I knew that Peter had a reputation for being smart and came from a good family, so I knew what he was before I went there, and I hoped that he would like me.

"What he and I shared originally," recalled Betsy, "was that he was a folk music fan, was a Woody Guthrie fan. So we shared that in common to start with." But she was also impressed at Peter's amazing musicality: "You could give him the most complicated time signature ever and he could count it out, you know?"

Peter and Betsy got together in New York after the Atlantic City engagement, and the two of them tried to maintain a long-distance relationship as Peter returned to the UK and another round of television, radio, and recording dates. A new single was needed, and this time "Baby I'm Yours" was chosen for the British market. The song, a favorite of Peter and Gordon's while on the Caravan of Stars, had already been a hit in the States over the summer, performed by Barbara Lewis, so Capitol Records passed on issuing it. This was the third cover song in a row for the duo, and Peter thought they should try for something more original for the next release.

Peter's friend John Dunbar had been toying with the idea of starting an experimental art gallery. Concurrently, Barry Miles, who had recently staged the "Poets of the World/Poets of Our Time" reading at the Albert Hall in June, had left his bookseller's job at Better Books and wanted to open his own shop. The two were introduced and decided one evening, over dinner, to work together and try to combine the two projects into one. "It seemed a very good idea," Miles said, "'cause I was bringing in all these Fluxus boxes and Yoko Ono's *Grapefruit*. A lot of the work that I was selling at Better Books was very visually oriented and to do with this crossover between literature and art."

It was a heady time of ideas and plans. Peter, Miles, and oftentimes Paul McCartney would kick back and brainstorm at John and Marianne's Knightsbridge flat, listening to music and smoking hash. "We smoked it *all* the time," Marianne Faithfull told me. "It's unfortunate, really, but the sixties went by without much communication." She laughed. "The trouble with hash in London—and I'm sure Peter will back me up on this—is that it rendered you practically speechless." "I don't remember it being unproductive. It may have ended up that way," Peter suggested. "I didn't smoke as much as they did. One of my problems with hash is half the time they'd smoke it with tobacco, which I couldn't tolerate. But yes—the hash was quite strong, and if you smoked too much, you'd get lethargic." But despite the strength of the substances ingested, creative ideas certainly *did* flow, and writers like Terry Southern and musicians like Donovan and John Mayall stopped by often—to listen

Peter Asher, Barry Miles, and John Dunbar. *Photo by Graham Keen/TopFoto.*

to experimental music and discuss poetry and art. It was a point when anything and everything seemed possible.

After suggesting and discarding many names, the name "Indica" was deemed perfect for the art gallery/bookshop. The name, of course, comes from *Cannabis indica*—a rather potent strain familiar to hash smokers.

On the cusp between beatniks and hippies, neither John nor Miles was rich, by any means. After finding a suitable spot in Mason's Yard to set up their art gallery, an influx of cash was needed to secure it and refurbish the space. "Unfortunately, Marianne wouldn't give us any money," Miles recalled. "Clever girl." He laughed. "But Peter had some money. And he was prepared to lend John and I £700 each and then he himself put in £700." So on October 20, 1965, Barry Miles, Peter Asher, and John Dunbar began their partnership formally and, using their initials, named it MAD, Ltd.

The week after "Baby I'm Yours" and the duo's third UK album, *Hurtin' 'n' Lovin'*, were released (and two days after formally incorporating MAD, Ltd.), Peter and Gordon embarked on a six-week tour of Britain, with American singer Gene Pitney headlining. The Mike Cotton Sound would be the backing band for both acts. Cotton was a trumpeter who had switched a few years earlier from "trad jazz" to rock and R&B. Another solid band of professionals, they not only released their own records and played their own gigs, but they also backed scores of American acts when they toured the UK. Gordon claimed to a reporter that Cotton's Sound was giving him and Peter "the best support ever." This came as a surprise to bandleader Mike Cotton when I spoke with him about the tour. He wished he'd known at the time: "We might have asked for a raise!" Each member of the seven-man group earned £65 a week doing two shows a day with little time off. "Not exactly marvelous money, but you could live off it.

"We were working mainly at cinemas," Cotton remembered, "because they were the only decent venues in some of these towns. And we'd have to put up with the sound system that was supplied by the theater. Some weren't bad, but some were pretty primitive." Of course, with all the screams supplied by the mostly female audience, the crappy sound was immaterial. "Yeah . . . they did a good job covering it up," Cotton laughed.

Also on the bill was sixteen-year-old Scottish singing sensation Lulu, with her band, The Luvvers. Though not familiar with US audiences until her huge 1967 hit, "To Sir With Love" and her costarring role in the film of the same name, she'd been having hits in the UK for a full year at this point—most of them loud, tough R&B shouters. And how would she rate Peter and Gordon as singers? "I would never reckon either of them as 'singers.' To me, it was all about Ray Charles, it was all about Bobby Womack; it wasn't about English public schoolboys singing like choirboys!" She lets out a huge laugh, adding, "He'll kill me, Peter, but I think he knows! But they were *so* nice to me, and I really liked them very, very much."

On November 13th, more than halfway through the tour, "Baby I'm Yours" was in the Top Twenty. That week, they arrived at Abbey Road to work with producer John Burgess, who was bringing in a good amount of material for the pair to record, working with his arrangers to turn the songs into big, brassy British pop confections. Peter and Gordon, though, were also finding strong material and during these sessions recorded solid rockers like Jackie DeShannon's "The Color Blue" (which she gave to Gordon during the Caravan of Stars) and their own "Wrong from the Start." Peter was able to give full rein to his inner jazz fan and cut "Black Brown and Gold," certainly the jazziest track in Peter and Gordon's oeuvre. Sung solo by Peter, it definitely is one of his finest vocal performances, and the arrangement by John Paul Jones recalled a swingin' late-night jazz club. Legendary UK sax player Tubby Hayes, who played with Ronnie Scott and Roland Kirk, among many others, was brought in and blew one hell of a solo. How many of Peter and Gordon's teenaged fans got their first blast of modern jazz courtesy of this track?

As the winter of 1965 neared, Paul McCartney approached Peter and mentioned a new song he'd written that he thought would be perfect for him and Gordon. Paul went into Abbey Road with the pair and, utilizing a harmonium, produced a lovely demo of the song, entitled "Woman," which Peter put in the hands of producer John Burgess. Later, as Burgess was walking the halls of Abbey Road Studios, he ran into McCartney, who asked him if he'd heard the song and what he thought. Burgess told him, "Well, I didn't really care for it." Paul was a bit taken aback—not many people, other than John Lennon and George Martin, would ever give him such negative feedback on his songs. But Burgess said not to worry—it was something he could work with.

In the meantime, Peter and Gordon flew to Nashville, Tennessee, on December 15th to record an album of country songs. Gordon, especially, was a big fan of American country music, and certainly Capitol Records, who was paying for the sessions, hoped the results might give them a crossover hit— appealing to Peter and Gordon's youthful base of fans as well as pique the interest of America's large country audience.

This was a bold move for Peter and Gordon. Though country records certainly had crossed over into the pop charts before—Marty Robbins and Johnny Cash are just two examples—the term "country rock" hadn't been coined yet. Rick Nelson's first steps in that direction were still months away, and Gram Parson's influential work with The Byrds and The Flying Burrito Brothers were a couple years off. The pair even beat Bob Dylan to Nashville, who would in a few months travel to "Music City USA" and use the same studio—Columbia's legendary Studio A—for his classic *Blonde on Blonde*.

There had been a few precedents, however: Also in 1965, Del Shannon (writer of "I Go To Pieces") recorded a strong album of Hank Williams songs. But the record that was probably a direct influence on this project was *The Everly Brothers Sing Great Country Hits*. Recorded in 1963 by the duo that was Peter and Gordon's biggest influence vocally, the album, though beautifully realized, was a commercial failure—as was Shannon's.

These new sessions were in the hands of producer Ken Nelson, who knew a thing or two about producing great country records, having done so with Merle Travis, Hank Thompson, Buck Owens, and Merle Haggard, among many others. The session musicians were members of the crack studio aces of the era known in Nashville as "The A-Team," including guitarists Harold Bradley and Ray Edenton, bassist Bob Moore, drummer Murrey "Buddy" Harman, harmonica player Charlie McCoy, and pedal steel player Buddy Emmons. Even the legendary vocal group The Jordanaires was brought in to provide backing vocals.

Bradley and his brother, Owen, had built the studio—the first on Nashville's storied "Music Row"—in the mid-fifties, adding a Quonset hut onto an old house. Hit after hit came out of this building: from Patsy Cline's "Crazy" and Marty Robbins's "El Paso" to Johnny Cash's "Ring of Fire" and, more recently, Roger Miller's "King of the Road." Peter and Gordon couldn't have asked for a better studio, better musicians, or a better producer to help them realize this project.

But, according to Harold Bradley, "We were a little bit intimidated." Yes, the musicians, most of whom had played on not only the just-named hits but on records for Peter and Gordon's idols Elvis Presley, Buddy Holly, Roy Orbison, and The Everly Brothers, upon hearing they were booked to do these sessions, were concerned. They listened to Peter and Gordon's work and, upon hearing the twelve-string pop sheen Newell and Burgess had achieved, wondered how they would be able to pull off the same pop sound. Once they understood they were being hired to do what they did best, they relaxed and got down to business.

"I really loved Ken Nelson," Harold Bradley said of the project's producer. "He was very decisive. He could make up his mind in a hurry." Peter agreed: "A very efficient producer in a way I admire." Buddy Emmons added: "He was likable and easy to work with. He hired a leader he trusted and let the leader and the boys"—meaning

Recording in Nashville with guitarist Harold Bradley.

the studio musicians—"sort it out. As with most Nashville sessions, I'm sure we all had a fair amount of input." Definitely, as they didn't even know what songs they were going to play when they walked in the door. "We never knew songs before-hand—we learned 'em on the sessions," guitarist Ray Edenton recalled. If there was a rough demo of a song, it might be played for them before the first take was tried. But in this case, doing an album of well-known country hits, the studio pros simply made up an arrangement on the spot—a "head arrangement," they'd call it—as chords and notes weren't written down, they were in their head.

And if it turned out doing a song in the key of C was too high and needed to be lowered to B, no problem. "The keys didn't make any difference to us," Edenton said. "Whatever key they wanted it in, we'd play it in."

"All music and vocals on the Peter and Gordon session were done together," Emmons remembered. "The goal was to get four songs in a three-hour session, so there wasn't the freedom or proper recording facilities to afford serious overdubbing." At this point, he continued, "the recording facilities consisted of three tracks—center, right, and left," which meant that there was a designated track for the lead vocals (the center) and two remaining tracks for instruments, which could later be easily mixed into stereo. "If I made a mistake," Emmons explained, "and they wanted to keep the vocal, whoever was on my track had to go back and overdub at the same time I did."

With just four days to record and most likely a quick day to mix, the resulting album, *Peter and Gordon Sing and Play the Hits of Nashville, Tennessee,* was a fun com-bination of contemporary country and the duo's "English choirboy" harmonies (as Lulu might say). Not surprisingly, the five tracks attempted from the Everly's 1963 LP, like "Please Help Me, I'm Falling" and "Lonely Street," seem the best fit for the pair—sad and sweet and full of despair. They didn't really have enough tough swagger to pull off the up-tempo numbers, including "I've Got a Tiger By the Tail" and "The Race Is On," but it would be hard for anyone to best Buck Owens and George Jones at their own game. Harold Bradley, though, liked the outcome, concluding: "I thought they did a good job."

Ultimately, when the album was released the following October—as with the earlier Everly and Shannon country concepts—it sank without a trace, not making either the pop or country charts. It was never released in the UK.

After finishing the sessions in Nashville, Peter and Gordon flew to New York and appeared at Murray the K's Christmas Show at the Brooklyn Fox Theatre. Peter managed to do some book buying for Indica while in town. He also got together with Betsy, and the romance between them continued to flourish.

As soon as Peter and Gordon got back to London, they went into Abbey Road Studios on December 31st and recorded the song McCartney had given them. Finished in only three takes, Burgess surrounded the pair with a lush, grandiose orchestra and an arrangement written by Bob Leaper. Leaper had been working as an arranger and conductor for years with songwriter/producer Tony Hatch on many of his sessions for Petula Clark. McCartney, upon hearing the final mix, thought it *too* grandiose—he had expected something more akin to the small string section George Martin had used for The Beatles' "Yesterday," and Gordon's dramatic delivery was perhaps too much. "Burgess," Peter said, "did it his way, and Paul was pissed and still is."

But it worked. It was emotional; it rose, it fell, it crescendoed; it pleaded while trying to be patient. It showed a maturing attitude toward the female sex—putting aside girls for someone older and wiser and love that, one hoped, would last. Yes, a bit too brassy in the end, but who cares? "Woman" was and still is a great song and a great performance.

McCartney wanted to see if the songs he wrote for other artists were becoming hits simply because his name was attached to them; so, as an experiment, he asked that a pseudonym be used on the label for the song's writer. Knowing, though, that the publishing would still read "Northern Songs" (the company co-owned by Lennon and McCartney), Peter felt that something more was needed to sell the story. So together they concocted a tale, given to the press, of an art student in Paris who somehow got the song to Paul, who then published it and put it in Peter and Gordon's hands.

When the record was released exactly one month later in the United States (not until mid-February in the UK), the songwriting credit on the label read "Bernard Webb." "I think Paul chose the name," said Peter. To make it even more confusing, some pressings in the States credited the writer as "A. Smith." "They'd obviously gotten the message about 'don't put Paul McCartney,' but didn't get the proper memo," Peter laughed.

Composer and producer Bunny Lewis stated that "Webb" was the greatest songwriting discovery since Lennon and McCartney and was suspicious that it *was* Lennon and McCartney. By the time the record made the American Top Forty, the secret was out—*Daily Express* reporter Judith Simons reported that the Northern Songs clue was too obvious and put two and two together.

Despite (or perhaps because of) the ruse, "Woman" eventually became Peter and Gordon's biggest hit in the States since "True Love Ways" one year earlier.

7

LADY GODIVA

As 1966 began, the Indica shop in Mason's Yard was taking shape. All hands chipped in—even McCartney painted, mixed plaster, and built shelves. Miles needed to store his growing inventory of books somewhere, so Peter volunteered a space in the basement at Wimpole Street opposite his mother's music room. McCartney then would rummage through the boxes, choosing a few for himself and leaving a list of what he'd taken, thereby becoming Indica's first customer.

In late January, Peter and Gordon came to the United States to promote "Woman" only days before the record's release by Capitol, taping two of Dick Clark's programs—the Saturday afternoon classic *American Bandstand* and *Where the Action Is*, broadcast midday Monday through Friday. Singer Steve Alaimo, host and music director of *Where the Action Is*, recalled how acts could appear over months on many episodes: "If we had Peter and Gordon for a day, we would shoot four or five songs on 'em. Then we would take each song and fit 'em into shows as we wanted." These appearances, including prime-time shows like *Hullabaloo* or *Shindig!* that were designed to showcase music, were always enjoyable. Other times they were booked to do American variety shows hosted by stars who were completely unknown to them.

"We did a couple of odd shows," Peter remembered, speaking of his American mid-sixties TV appearances. "For instance, we went on *The Jackie Gleason Show* and we'd never seen *The Honeymooners*, so we had no idea what the fuss was all about." In 1966 Peter and Gordon arrived at the Miami Beach Auditorium, where Gleason taped his shows. "And there was this totally drunk asshole wandering around—and everyone was in *awe* of him! He was horrible to everybody.

"Of course, later I saw *The Honeymooners* and realized he had been one of the comic geniuses of all time, and I became a gigantic fan. But, sadly, by the time we got to work with him it was . . . strange." Another strange circumstance they found themselves in was dressing in overalls, standing on a makeshift farm set at CBS's

Television City in Hollywood singing Roger Miller's "You Don't Want My Love" with their best Southern accents as part of a skit on *The Red Skelton Show*, another American entertainer with whom they were completely unfamiliar.

After two weeks in the States, the pair returned to the UK and made the rounds to promote "Woman." Pop music had exploded on British TV, and the duo appeared on *Discs A Gogo, Scene at 6:30, Thank Your Lucky Stars, A Whole Scene Going, Now!, Top of the Pops, Ready Steady Go!*, plus the radio shows *Saturday Club* and *Easy Beat*, as well as at live venues—with all these appearances accomplished within a dizzying couple of weeks. But a new tool had started to be used by the pop acts of the day with a record to plug—what was then called making a "promotional film," or to use a more modern term, a "music video."

Marrying interesting images with music had been going on for decades, from the experimental films of Oskar Fischinger to Busby Berkley musicals to Walt Disney's *Fantasia*. In the 1940s, hundreds of performers such as Cab Calloway and Louis Jordan made "Soundies" shown both in movie theaters and on Panoram visual jukeboxes, a device slightly ahead of its time. In the fifties, Scopitone in France and ColorSonic in the United States again tried to succeed with visual jukeboxes, and neither really caught on, though many clips still survive.

But in 1965, The Beatles began shooting promotional clips of their hits utilizing both film and video, making them available to television shows around the world in lieu of performing live. Their contemporaries in England were quick to catch on to the tool, including Peter and Gordon. Shot quickly in a single afternoon, the duo decided to forgo lip-syncing to "Woman" and instead sullenly hang around the London docks, eventually enter an abandoned building, smash furniture, and finally row away on the Thames into the sunset. It seems they decided to play against their image of

Peter, far left, exits one of Indica's art openings.

"nice English chaps" for a change and, on reflection, Peter admitted the video is "not very good." Rarely shown in the West, it was mainly televised in Japan, Hong Kong, Australia, and the Philippines—"where we were huge," Peter said, "unaccountably."

In February, Indica Books and Gallery officially opened at 6 Mason's Yard. McCartney designed the store's wrapping paper, and Peter's mother donated an antique wooden cash register to keep track of sales. The Ashers also suggested that MAD, Ltd. use their family's bank for Indica's accounts. Miles and Dunbar, the young pot-smoking intellectuals, upon first visiting the well-established financial institution, were quite surprised to have a frock-coated footman present the company checkbook to them on a silver platter.

Peter had, over the past two years, become close with Paul McCartney—not only was Paul dating Jane and writing songs for Peter, but the two pop stars' bedrooms took up the top floor of the Asher home on Wimpole Street. "He and I would hang out together quite a lot," Peter recalled. Living with the Ashers was intellectually stimulating for McCartney, and he was introduced to many artistic concepts through Jane, Peter, their parents, and their friends—not just music, but film, theater, and modern art. Through Miles, Paul became friendly with writer William Burroughs and became interested in his "cut-up" techniques—recording audio and, after splicing the tape into small bits, reassembling the pieces in random order. Peter, who had been toying with tape recordings since a young boy, had a reel-to-reel tape machine in his bedroom and shared with Paul some of his experiments—tape loops, speed variation, and backward recording: "He had a Brenell tape recorder and we would bounce things back and forth," Peter explained, "trying out stuff—seeing what things sounded like backwards.

Peter at home with his reel-to-reel.

"We were both experimenting, trying things," said Peter, "putting cardboard over the erase head to see what it would do." Paul loved the avant-garde nature of it all; he quickly began to incorporate these ideas into Beatles sessions, including their 1966 album, which has been near or at the top of most critics and readers polls for years as the best album in rock history, *Revolver*—due in no small part to the sonic inventiveness these very methods brought to The Beatles' masterful pop songwriting.

Before flying off for an eight-week tour of the States, Peter and Gordon went back to Abbey Road to record new material, including "To Show I Love You," which would be their next UK single. The song was written by Tony Hatch, and once again, as with "Woman," Bob Leaper did the arrangement.

Eddie King, the guitarist who had been with them since their second album, was not at the session. As another "musical navvy" in the London recording scene, he had his hands full with other sessions and never recorded or toured with Peter and Gordon again. Though certainly not well-known today, King is proud of the work he helped create: "Actually, when you listen to some of them," King said of his sixties sessions, "you think: Fuckin' hell, that's not bad! You know? It sounds all right. 'Cause it actually *breathes!*"

During their first week in the States, the duo went to Philadelphia to tape an appearance on the syndicated *Mike Douglas Show*. An affable host who had been a big-band singer in the forties, Douglas's show was seen by millions of housewives on weekday afternoons. After performing, the pair sat for an interview segment with Douglas and his cohost for that week, actress Bette Davis. While chatting, Peter let slip that he was a member of Mensa, an organization whose members are in the top two percent for intelligence. Ninety-eight percent of the population score below 131 when tested (with 100 being the mean, or average, score); Peter, though, has a genius-level IQ, rated at 162. "But," he protested, "it doesn't mean I'm terribly intelligent . . . it's just that I'm good at taking these kinds of tests!"

Peter seems to be overly modest here. His smart, successful parents certainly helped genetically; plus, a childhood acting career provided numerous stimulating environments and experiences that contribute to a child's intellectual growth. Early musical training, such as Peter's, has been found to lead to a higher-than-average IQ, and his excellent schooling at Westminster didn't hurt. "Of all the qualities about him that really impress the *shit* outta me," singer David Crosby exclaimed, "that's the one—he is an *extremely* intelligent guy. And he also has a very clear vision of who he is and what's going on around him." And in 1966, Peter was smart enough to know that his career as a pop singer was bound to end eventually. From time to time, he would discuss with Betsy returning to school, completing his degree in philosophy. "And I could very much see him as a professor in an academic life. He loved science," Betsy enthused, "and he's a good teacher—very good at explaining things."

While the pair were on tour in the States, Capitol decided to release "There's No Living Without Your Loving" as a single. In 1966, when surprising sounds and experiences were materializing daily, this track did not excite the young record-buying public. Peter and Gordon did their best promoting it, but it didn't even crack the Top

Forty. As they returned home in June, their UK single "To Show I Love You" was released, and it, too, bombed. It didn't even dent the UK charts. That same month also saw the release of their new album, simply entitled *Peter & Gordon*. One of England's music papers, *Record Mirror*, called it: "Certainly a worthwhile LP—and perhaps the best tracks are the ones they wrote themselves" (adding: "and the Jackie DeShannon songs"). But despite the inclusion of solid material, including McCartney's masterful "Woman," the record also would fail to chart.

Just as their new album was released, Peter and Gordon flew to Germany to play three dates opening for The Beatles. The world's biggest band had decided they were weary of "Beatlemania" and would phase out live performances to concentrate on recording, so, though not officially announced, this would turn out to be their final world tour. It kicked off with two performances on June 24th in Munich, with the second show filmed for German television. The broadcast showed Peter and Gordon performing two songs from their set—"Woman" and "Let It Be Me"—with Peter pensively conducting the seven backing musicians. The next day they traveled by train to Essen for two more shows and performed their final two sets in Hamburg on the 26th.

"It was just a joyride, really." That's the way Roy Young remembered the tour. Young was the keyboard player and background vocalist for Cliff Bennett and the Rebel Rousers, one of the acts that took part. Young, who had started out in the house band on British television's *Oh Boy* in the fifties, had known The Beatles since their early days in Germany, playing with them both onstage and on their first proper recordings, backing singer Tony Sheridan. Times had certainly changed from those lean leather-clad days in Hamburg bars, according to Young: "They would have their private chef dishing up steaks and shrimp." With food available to The Beatles twenty-four hours a day on the train, "we spent most of our time with them," Peter recalled—ordering up food and drinks while gambling with their manager, Brian Epstein, in the opulent dining car built for royalty.

On July 29th, Peter and Gordon were back in the studio and in one three-hour session recorded three promising tracks. The first was a song they had originally heard while appearing on Dick Clark's *Where the Action Is* television show. Sung by the show's host, Steve Alaimo, "My First Day Alone" turned out to be cowritten by Phil Sloan, now going by P.F. Sloan, the young singer and guitarist who had backed them during those Hawaiian concerts on their first American tour. Sloan was only sixteen when he composed the tune with Steve Barri. When it turned up later on one of Peter and Gordon's American albums, Sloan was thrilled: "A very, very, very sweet gift," he happily recalled.

The second was "The Town I Live In," a song written by Geoff Stephens, who would soon have a North American number-one smash writing and producing "Winchester Cathedral." "I believed in religions and the message they were preaching," Stephens told me, "but I didn't like the organized church." Stephens aired his dissatisfaction in both songs—more subtly in "Winchester Cathedral," crooning about a church that does "nothing" to stop a departing lover—and more overtly in "The Town I Live In," where "nothing ever happens" despite its twenty-seven churches. John Burgess had heard the song earlier in the year when singer Jackie Lee had first recorded it for EMI. Though it failed to chart, the producer thought the song of alienation in a stifling small town would be a perfect dramatic backdrop for Peter and Gordon's harmonies. Geoff Love added horns with a Tijuana Brass flavor to the chorus, and despite Gordon not really caring for the tune, he managed to offer a wonderful vocal performance.

With the third song, it was Peter's turn to object: "I have to confess," he later said, "when it was first suggested, I had reservations about it. When it became a huge hit, I changed my mind." Smiling, he added: "In retrospect, I find it deeply charming!"

The song in question, "Lady Godiva," was written by Mike Leander and Chas Mills. Peter and Gordon's producer, John Burgess, was now recording singer Paul Jones (who had just left the group Manfred Mann) and hired Leander to do arrangements. "We always took along a song of our own to try to pop it into the session," Mills remembered. At Jones's first session, they brought out "Lady Godiva."

"Mike gave me a tune that he'd written," said Mills, "which was basically a ballad." Mills, principally a lyricist, heard it more as a "honky-tonk sort of thing." Riding in a cab on the way to Abbey Road, he dashed off the humorous lyrics, turning Leander's ballad into a music-hall update of the British legend wherein the naked lass, originally an eleventh-century noblewoman protesting high taxes, becomes an X-rated film star. Not what you would expect from a mid-sixties pop song, but Mills followed his instincts: "That's the way the best songs come—right out of your head."

Producer Burgess "loved the song," recalled Mills, and Jones reluctantly recorded it but made clear that he didn't see his first solo single being a "comedy record." Hungry for a hit, that same day Leander and Mills wrote the song "High Time" ("over lunch in about ten minutes," Mills said as he laughed) and presented it to Burgess and Jones. They recorded it immediately and released it as Jones's first solo single, eventually climbing to number-four in the UK.

Burgess, though, was positive that "Lady Godiva" would be a hit and perfect for Peter and Gordon. Using Jones's version almost as a demo, the finished production harkened back to an earlier, more innocent sound, offsetting the slightly salacious lyrics by throwing in banjos and tubas, of all things, along with the "honky-tonk" piano Mills originally imagined for the song.

Gordon later told the *New Musical Express*: "If we both really loathe something, then we won't do it. But more often than not we have to do as we're told. When your last record doesn't happen, and your A&R man comes up to you and says, 'I've got a great song here, it's going to be a big hit for you,' you don't have any alternative but to do as he says. And, let's face it, he's usually right!"

In September, "Lady Godiva" was released in the UK with Asher and Waller's "The Morning's Calling" on the flipside. In the United States, "The Town I Live In" got that position, but only on the first pressing. Peter and Gordon, by now mindful that having a self-penned song on the back of a hit single meant the possibility of a sizeable amount of publishing royalties, requested that Capitol withdraw it and replace it with the same UK B-side, inspired by Jackie DeShannon's "write from the heart" advice to Gordon on the Caravan of Stars. The switch did nothing to interrupt the disc's rise up the charts, though, and by October "Lady Godiva" was a Top Ten smash across America, rising to number-sixteen in the British charts. It would go on to sell over one million copies.

A three-week tour of the eastern United States was arranged to capitalize on the single and Capitol's hastily compiled *Lady Godiva* LP. "There was usually a band booked by the agent," Peter said, but as to how good or appropriate they were, "no attention was paid." After only two gigs, the singers decided this latest combo simply was not going to work out. Taking matters into their own hands, Peter, Gordon, and road manager "Avo" flew into New York with mere days to find new musicians to accompany them for the next three weeks.

The band they found was called The King Bees, and as their name implies, they were one of New York City's solid R&B combos. The group formed from the friendship between guitarists Richard "Dickie" Frank and Danny Kortchmar. "We met when we were about fourteen," Frank recalled. "I bought a used guitar from him, and we started hangin' out all the time, 'cause we didn't fit in that well with a lot of the other kids in high school." In 1965, a year after graduation, the group formed, adding drummer Joel O'Brien and a talented African American named John McDuffy on Hammond organ—its interracial makeup a rarity for the time. Kortchmar, "always a go-getter," according to Frank, procured an agent who was able to get them an audition for the famous New York nightclub Arthur, named after a George Harrison *Hard Day's Night* quip. Their residency lasted almost half a year and attracted the interest of RCA Records, who released their first single, "What She Does to Me," a classic slab of R&B-infused garage rock, in late 1965.

O'Brien's father, Joseph, a successful New York disc jockey, helped them get airplay, and eventually the record made the Top Ten locally, but nationally it went nowhere and neither did their next two singles. By the fall of 1966, The King Bees had moved from the upscale NYC clubs like Arthur to mostly more downscale midtown places like Joey D's Starlighter Room and Harlow's. Kortchmar says it was at Harlow's ("a dump") where Peter and Gordon caught The King Bees' act, though Frank swears it was the more upscale club The Phone Booth, which may have been a more likely spot for the well-heeled Englishmen to have scouted for talent. But either way, the pair liked what they heard and offered them the gig.

"Naturally, we jumped at the chance to work with, like, English rock stars," Kortchmar said, "even though it wasn't the kind of music we were doing." Frank switched from guitar to bass, and after a quick day or two of rehearsals, the band took off in their two Chrysler rentals—one was a station wagon driven by Frank with O'Brien, McDuffy, and the equipment; the second, a sedan with Peter, Gordon, Avo, and Kortchmar, who "was already limousine material," Frank said, laughing.

Danny Kortchmar. *Photo by Peter Asher.*

The King Bees each got about $200 a week. "It seemed like they were glad to have us, certainly at that price." Frank chuckled. "I got nothing extra for driving the car—I didn't know to ask in those days."

As usual, the absence of real management proved problematic—something as basic as a tour itinerary was completely lacking. "Gordon," Frank recalled, "would drive at about eighty to a hundred miles an hour, which in those days in those cars was really horrible. And they wouldn't tell me where we were going. It was just that level of unprofessionalism wherein he's driving the car, we don't know where the gig is, and he's driving at a hundred miles an hour—he could have just completely lost us." And remember: There were no cell phones in those days.

Police lights eventually appeared in Frank's rearview mirror, not Gordon's. "We were going so fast that they wanted to take me to jail and make me go before the magistrate," Frank remembered. "I talked and talked, and the trooper finally let me go on my own recognizance. And I never *did* answer the ticket, which made a fool of *him*, which I'm ashamed of." Frank sighed and shrugged. "It's a little too late now to do anything about it . . ."

The tour mainly went up and down the East Coast, going as far east as Canton, Ohio. Said Kortchmar: "Occasionally we would open for them, and The King Bees would come out and do four or five tunes." Peter was impressed with Danny's guitar playing and Joel's drumming and thought "John-John" (McDuffy's nickname) "was a good bluesy player," despite having trouble remembering the parts to Peter and Gordon's songs. The set list was still peppered with Everly Brothers covers, such as "Let It Be Me" and their arrangement of "Lucille." The King Bees also attempted "Woman"—"which we did badly," Kortchmar admitted, gamely trying to re-create Bob Leaper's horn and string arrangement with electric guitar and Farfisa organ. "It was a little over our heads." Kortchmar thought Gordon was a "real good singer," but he could see frustrations were getting the better of him. "Gordon was really temperamental and drunk a lot of the time," he recalled. "I'll never forget—Gordon at one time got furious with a mic stand at one of these gigs and stormed off, leaving Peter onstage. I can't remember what he said"—he laughed—"but Peter managed with his usual aplomb to escape!"

But there was professionalism in Peter and Gordon's preparations backstage—getting ready mentally to go out in front of thousands of people, dressing for battle in tailored suits made of leather—which resisted tearing when attacked by hysterical fans. The screaming, of course, made it hard for The King Bees to hear Peter and Gordon, much less each other. And the PA systems were ridiculous, Frank said, "like what you'd expect in the church rec room."

"The management was abysmal, the tours were horrible," Kortchmar stated flatly, "but it was that way for everybody 'cause it was a new area. Booking rock acts? Nobody knew what the hell they were doing. . . . It was a shambles." Peter, though, was learning what *not* to do as a manager—knowledge he would soon put into practice.

Richard Frank, then twenty, did enjoy himself: "Certainly, for me to be part of some British act with girls screaming and all was a thrill, for sure. And it was an adventure, which I certainly was eager for, growing up in the suburbs." And what about the girls? "We loaded in, we played the show, we were gone. It was really guerrilla warfare," he recalled. "I don't recall anybody coming on to me, but I was such a kid it might have happened and I missed it altogether. I got some action in the clubs, but nothin' on that tour. I don't know if they did or not . . . Gordon must've, anyway." Road manager Avo, happily, did very well on the tours himself: "They had the young ones; I had the mothers," Avison laughed.

But the fun could turn terrifying quickly, Frank recalled: "I remember after the end of the little stint in Ohio, we were driving home without sleep. I almost went off the road. I never forgot that . . . I was almost to the George Washington Bridge when I almost went off the frickin' road! And it would have been the end of the three of us in the car." Very soon after this tour, The King Bees did reach the end of the road: Richard Frank began doing session work with, among others, Neil Diamond; John McDuffy replaced Al Kooper in The Blues Project; and Danny Kortchmar and Joel O'Brien decided to form another band, The Flying Machine, enlisting the help of another old-school chum of Danny's—a singer and guitarist named James Taylor.

Peter and Gordon returned to England and within days entered Abbey Road to record the follow-up to "Lady Godiva." John Burgess requested something similar from "Godiva" tunesmiths Leander and Mills, who responded with "Knight in Rusty Armor"—even more of a novelty tune, if possible, than the previous single. Leander's arrangement opened with woodblocks imitating a horse prancing by, and though it was cute, bouncy, and well-sung, the duo seemed to be going in the wrong direction—certainly by Gordon's standards.

This was also confirmed in the following sessions for their upcoming album. Released in the UK just before Christmas, *Somewhere...* was a collection of songs from motion pictures. The title track (from *West Side Story*) and the themes from *Exodus* and *High Noon* are good examples of what the album was filled with—big, lush, romantic fare more geared toward their fans' parents (though they also tackled Lennon and McCartney's ballad "If I Fell" from *A Hard Day's Night*). Not a "real" rock'n'roll song in sight.

"Soft, sweet shit" was the way Gordon characterized the vast majority of Peter and Gordon's recorded work. "We had this tosser of a manager," he said, referring to Richard Armitage. "He never once came over on tour with us. He never once *saw*, so that he could understand what I was talking about with regard to the direction that I felt Peter and Gordon should go. This manager said, 'No, I want you to do nice songs that people can hear the words of and can understand.'"

You can imagine Gordon's frustration; as he and Peter were being told to sing "Love Is a Many-Splendored Thing" (a decent tune, assuredly), the rest of their musical compatriots were amazing the world with their creativity. The year 1966 saw the release of the aforementioned *Revolver*, Brian Wilson's masterpiece *Pet Sounds*, Dylan's sprawling *Blonde on Blonde*, and the first albums by The Mamas and the Papas, The Mothers of Invention, Buffalo Springfield, Cream, Tim Buckley, and The Incredible String Band. The Who recorded their first mini-opera *A Quick One (While He's Away)*, The Byrds flew "Eight Miles High," and Jimi Hendrix landed in London, ready to make one and all "experienced."

"I had a girlfriend," Gordon continued, "a girl called Sharon Sheeley." Sheeley was one of the first female songwriters of the rock'n'roll era, writing Ricky Nelson's hit "Poor Little Fool" and cowriting "Something Else" for Eddie Cochran, to whom she was engaged. After Cochran's death in a car crash (in which Sheeley was a passenger), she went on to write prolifically with Jackie DeShannon, who probably introduced her to Gordon just as Sheeley's first marriage to *Shindig!* host Jimmy O'Neill ended. "She knew where my heart was onstage; you know, my heart was singing rock'n'roll. And then throwing in ballads to completely confuse everybody—that this raging rock'n'roll singer could actually *sing*. And she said, 'You don't need Peter. Peter's crap. Peter can't sing.' Peter's this, Peter's that. I said, 'Well, but we're *Peter and Gordon!*' 'Fuck Peter and Gordon!' She said, 'You're the closest thing to Eddie Cochran I've ever come across.'" High praise, indeed, and from someone who should know. Gordon began to weigh his options.

Meanwhile, after only being open about four months, two things had become apparent regarding Indica: There was not enough gallery space for the art exhibitions, and there was not enough foot traffic for the bookshop. Luckily, John Dunbar had recently met Christopher Hill, who had taken over a large, old bookstore on Southampton Row. With Hill becoming a partner in MAD, Ltd. (and thanks to a loan from McCartney), Indica Books, managed by Miles, moved and became a separate entity.

While Peter toured the States in October, Miles published the first edition of the *International Times*, or *IT*—Europe's first underground newspaper. With its offices in Indica Books' new, somewhat roomy basement, the paper reported on politics, the arts, London's latest happenings, and the drug scene. Peter participated in the premiere issue with a pop music column written anonymously, attributed only to "Millionaire." "That had to be an editorial choice," Peter said wryly. "Neither was I one, nor would I have pretended to *be* one!" His column included a Rolling Stones concert review ("Certainly the Stones generate great excitement on occasions, and perhaps this was an off night"), hip in-jokes ("The Fugs album . . . is high on *Billboard*'s charts"), and even a Peter and Gordon plug ("Peter & Gordon's new record is selling exceptionally well, despite accusations of being 'morally sick' from Provosts and MPs"). That last part was *not* a joke—the Mayor of Coventry, where the Lady Godiva legend began, banned their latest hit, calling the record "obscene."

The debut column, though, was also the final one for Peter. "I don't know why," wondered Miles. "I guess because he wasn't paid! *Nobody* was paid." Miles laughed. "It was an *underground paper!*"

On November 9th, Indica Gallery was scheduled to open an exhibition entitled *Unfinished Paintings and Objects* by the Japanese artist Yoko Ono. Two days before the opening, John Lennon, invited by John Dunbar, arrived in the evening for a private preview. Dunbar introduced John to Yoko, who handed the Beatle one of her instruction cards, which simply said "Breathe." Lennon looked at her and panted like a dog, asking: "Y'mean this?" Thus began one of the century's great love stories.

On December 12th, Peter and Gordon performed as part of a charity show at the Royal Albert Hall for the famine relief organization Oxfam International. *You're Joking!* was hosted by comedians Peter Cook and Dudley Moore and also featured the Alan Price Set (led by the excellent original keyboardist for The Animals), singer Paul Jones, and at the bottom of the bill, appearing for the first time in a concert setting, Pink Floyd. "Price was actually rather snotty about us," Floyd drummer Nick Mason recounted. "Not that we're ones to bear grudges! But I remember him playing a Hammond B3, and he sort of dropped it on its corner and went: 'That's psychedelic music.'"

"A lot of those bands didn't really like that sort of stuff," Miles said, referring to the new psychedelic style, "at all! Initially, people like Ginger Baker just thought it was nonsense. They thought it was just like noodling away and nobody really knew how to play—in the way that some people later criticized punk." It seemed not just a clash of how to approach music, but life itself. Paul Samwell-Smith, bassist for The Yardbirds, recalled: "On the one hand, you had people playing some pretty heavy blues, not caring how they dressed, drinking a lot in dark and smelly clubs, and generally enjoying a debauched lifestyle. While on the other hand, you had musicians paying great attention to clothes, lighting, fashion, style, and drugs."

Weeks before the Oxfam show, over £1,000 worth of amplifiers had been stolen from the Floyd. "It was Rick's fault," Mason said, referring to their keyboardist Rick Wright, "for not unloading the van. He was paid a bit extra to do that, and he didn't. We forgave him eventually." Miles, who knew the band and their managers quite well, appealed to Peter. "I was a big fan," Peter affirmed, having seen the band at a few of their early "Spontaneous Underground" shows at the Marquee Club on

Wardour Street. He was happy to lend them some of Peter and Gordon's equipment until they could afford new gear (they soon did, thanks to Nick Mason's mum). They certainly wouldn't miss them for, as with other major British hitmakers of the day, Peter and Gordon were always getting free Vox amplifiers from Jennings Musical Industries: "They would just *give* us stuff," Peter remembered. It's amazing that at this critical point in Pink Floyd's early career, as the vanguard of the new underground music scene, they received crucial help from Peter, who, rightly or wrongly, was perceived by the Floyd's audience as musically unhip and inconsequential.

"We quite often used to go and connect with Peter when we needed advice," Mason admitted. This is right at the time the Floyd were being courted by EMI. "He probably advised us against signing with Bryan Morrison"—Pink Floyd's former manager—"which we did immediately. He would give us very good advice, and we would then ignore it." Mason said that he and the other members looked upon Peter, even then, as "a grown-up music business person, as well as an artist," even though his records were not really what they'd normally listen to—"much as I would have liked Pink Floyd to cover 'Lady Godiva'"—Mason sighed—"I could never persuade the others . . ."

Peter and pal Paul Samwell-Smith were such fans of the Floyd they discussed the idea of coproducing them—but unfortunately that collaboration never happened.

A few days before Christmas, Peter and Gordon were invited to appear on the very last episode of England's venerable rock showcase *Ready, Steady, Go!* They didn't

The Who performing on *Ready Steady Go*'s last episode. *Photo by Peter Asher.*

perform but taped a special "goodbye" message. Peter, though, spent the day on the set as a fan documenting the historic occasion, snapping photos of acts such as Donovan, The Who, and Mick Jagger duetting with Chris Farlowe.

Throughout 1966, Betsy and Peter conducted their relationship long distance, with Peter staying in her Manhattan apartment whenever he came to the city. She had begun working as an in-house publicist for manager Allen Klein's ABKCO company, getting The Rolling Stones on the cover of *Town & Country*—a major coup, helping the band achieve some high-society chic for the first time. She decided to ask Klein for a long vacation to visit Peter in London. He said no. So she quit, left New York, and by the end of the year arrived in London, where she moved into the Asher household for a time.

"To start with," Betsy recalled, "I kept very quiet." She laughed and said, "They ate much faster than I did and used two hands for eating, so I quickly learned to eat with both hands. Putting the knife down every time you were gonna take a bite, it would just take forever!" The discussions at dinner could get lively: "The dining room was set up as a library, and people were always jumping up and looking at reference books.

"Very brilliant" was how she described Peter's father. "He was very interesting and very animated and had a very playful attitude—sort of an impish humor about him." She remembered when a finial atop the fence outside their Wimpole Street residence disappeared (probably taken by one of the fans who would hang around to catch a

Peter outside his bedroom at 57 Wimpole Street.

glimpse of Paul or Peter). "He would be outside there on Wimpole Street, and he'd put one of those boiler suits on and he would be replacing it on the black wrought-iron fence, only it was papier-mâché"—she laughed—"painted with black lacquer. And if anybody asked him directions as they went by, he'd respond in a cockney accent: 'Over there, gov'nor!'

"And Mrs. Asher was tireless—an amazing person. She was a huge influence on me and taught me the ways of the world with her upbringing. I have a feeling she did the same for Paul McCartney. You know? It was like a finishing school!" Betsy laughed, and then concluded: "She was very enthusiastic in what all of her children were doing and very involved."

Her children were certainly doing quite a lot lately: Youngest daughter, Clare, had decided against an acting career and, following along the family's musical path, became an organ scholar at St. Hugh's College, Oxford, setting her sights on becoming a teacher. Jane continued with her successful acting career, performing Shakespeare onstage and costarring in one of the biggest British films of 1966, *Alfie,* with Michael Caine. And Peter had just released his latest single, was planning to tour the United States yet again, and was madly in love with Betsy. The two soon began looking for a flat of their own.

8

YOU'VE HAD BETTER TIMES

On February 6, 1967, before taking off for a monthlong tour of the United States, Peter and Gordon recorded their next single, "Sunday for Tea." The song was written by John Carter and Ken Lewis, who earlier had composed tunes like "Can't You Hear My Heartbeat"—a British hit for the American group Goldie and the Gingerbreads and, conversely, an American hit for the British group Herman's Hermits. John Carter was also a singer, working with Geoff Stephens on his New Vaudeville Band concept (that's John's voice you hear on the hit "Winchester Cathedral"). Carter was sure that "Sunday for Tea" was perfect for the New Vaudeville Band, but Stephens said he had enough material for the time being and passed.

The recently married Carter had just moved with his new bride to a top-floor flat on Park Street, near Marble Arch. Coincidentally, the first floor contained the offices of a brand-new company called AIR. Associated Independent Recording was a consortium of England's leading record producers: George Martin (The Beatles), Peter Sullivan (Tom Jones), Ron Richards (The Hollies), and John Burgess (Peter and Gordon). Tired of the pittance they were paid as staff producers, the four went independent in late 1965, finally able to share in the royalties their efforts generated. A wise decision as, over the next eighteen months, their productions sold close to thirty million records worldwide.

Carter simply went downstairs and left his demo with John Burgess, who decided he'd use it for Peter and Gordon. Not as much a "novelty" record as "Godiva" and "Knight" had been, "Sunday for Tea" still had an old-fashioned charm, with arranger Mike Vickers utilizing harpsichord and xylophone, its violin break harkening back to a "palm court" atmosphere. It was sweet and safe—and Gordon decided finally it was time to do something.

A few days later, the *New Musical Express* splashed this headline across the top of an inside page: "NEWS EXTRA—PETER AND GORDON ACT TO SPLIT."

"Peter and Gordon are to part company as a full-time act," it stated, going on to say that Gordon would begin to record solo as soon as they returned to the UK, though there were still upcoming recordings as a duo that they would promote. "We shall get together once in a while when we feel like it," they told *NME*. "But basically, after our present US tour we are going our separate ways."

"We never said, 'I hate you! That's it!' or any of that stuff, which a lot of duos do," Peter later said. "We just gradually drifted into doing other things."

"We only really recorded to fulfill our contract," Gordon admitted. "And Richard Armitage," he continued, speaking of the duo's manager, "convinced me that Peter and Gordon was not going to be going very much longer, but *I* was going to be a *superstar!*"

Peter, unlike Gordon, was never interested in being a solo artist. Gordon couldn't wait, releasing one single in 1967 through Capitol in the States—EMI's Columbia Records passed on a British release—but it didn't make a ripple. At the same time, Armitage made a deal for Peter and Gordon to sing the title song to an upcoming British comedy entitled *The Jokers*. The plot, about two brothers out to steal the Crown Jewels, was discussed with songwriters Leander and Mills, who did their best to encapsulate, in two sonic minutes, mad, swinging London. But unfortunately, that media construct was about to flicker out, replaced by a much more experimental mind-set. Within days of releasing the track, The Beatles' album *Sgt. Pepper's Lonely Hearts Club Band* hit the culture like a sonic boom, and *The Jokers*, both the film and the song, were quickly forgotten.

Meanwhile, Peter and Betsy finally moved into their own flat on Weymouth Street in Marylebone, not far from the Asher residence on Wimpole Street. "Not far at all," Miles agreed. "He wanted to stay nice and close to get the home cooking and get his laundry done for free!" At the same time, now that he had some money to invest, Peter bought a house in Surrey.

Named Laudate by the previous owner, Sir Peter Scott (famous conservationist and cofounder of The World Wildlife Fund), the house sat on eleven lush acres overlooking a large lake. Peter used it himself only occasionally, mostly renting the property to tenants—with varying degrees of success. One renter seemed promising, giving Peter six months in advance—"in cash," Peter recalled—only to later skip out, owing Peter money. An estate agent gave Peter the forwarding address, and he went to ask for the missing rent. "There were seven or eight guys there," Peter said. "They gave me a cup of tea and said no, they couldn't pay.

"I remember saying something like, 'Look—you paid me the first load in cash; can't you do that again?'" He was met with much laughter: "Oh, we wish we could!"

Well-known British DJ Kenny Everett moved in next. He and John Lennon spent an evening ingesting LSD at Laudate, later insisting to friends there were "men in the bushes" watching them. "Everyone thought it was the acid" causing Lennon to hallucinate, "but it wasn't," said Peter. "There really *were* men in the bushes." It was Scotland Yard spying on the house, as that last tenant who had paid in cash leased it under a false name and was, in reality, Bruce Reynolds—the mastermind of Britain's Great Train Robbery and still on the run.

Betsy and Peter at Laudate.

Betsy, now working as a freelance publicist, began to use her connections on behalf of clients Peter and Gordon, Tyrannosaurus Rex (featuring Marc Bolan), and Pink Floyd. Betsy organized the Floyd's first photo session to introduce new member David Gilmore and help publicize them back in the States. "And you can imagine, without fax or email or anything"—Betsy laughed—"it was pretty primitive at that point!"

Betsy got her own publicity in *New Musical Express*'s April 15, 1967, edition. "Betsy—in love with boss Peter Asher," read the headline, one of a series of articles the paper ran under the heading "Star Boy Friends." Reporter Dawn James described her as "tall and slim, with long fair hair, an elfin face, and a soft American accent that soothes rather than grates." Betsy speaks of not being in a hurry to get married so as to concentrate on her career, that she and Peter hardly ever argue, and that she is not jealous of groupies, as "they have nothing lasting to offer." The piece ends with Betsy saying that, according to Peter, he would leave her if Brigitte Bardot beckoned, but she rightly concludes: "I don't think it will happen."

There was a backload of unreleased Peter and Gordon tracks on EMI's shelves, and though no albums were released in the UK in 1967, Capitol Records managed to drop three that year in the States—*Lady Godiva*, *Knight in Rusty Armour*, and *In London For Tea*—and three times the duo dutifully toured America. While there, Peter was also on assignment from Miles to interview Frank Zappa for an in-depth article to be published in the *International Times*. Peter got an up-close look at Zappa's world—watching him rehearse with The Mothers of Invention and observing him recording tracks at Capitol for his first solo release, *Lumpy Gravy*—all the while taking photographs.

Peter didn't feel he was a very good interviewer, though—at one point during their chat, Zappa took over and began interviewing Peter! After all his effort, *IT*'s

Zappa recording *Lumpy Gravy*.
Photo by Peter Asher.

editors ultimately published Zappa material licensed from the American underground newspaper syndicate, and Peter's work went unused, leaving him "pissed off," Miles recalled.

Indica was a continuing business concern, and Peter would have weekly lunch meetings with Miles on Southampton Row to discuss the state of things. Though he was away touring much of the time, he helped out when his schedule permitted. "Whenever I was there, as indeed when Paul was there, we would be in the shop helping out and doing what we could and encouraging customers," Peter recalled.

But business was not good. "We didn't have a clue about business at all," Miles, who managed the bookstore, admitted. "It was a complete nightmare." Betsy also laughingly remembered incidents such as Peter "going into Indica and just writing on a piece of paper, 'Embezzled £10,' and taking a tenner out of the register." "That's my sense of humor, rather than 'borrowed,'" Peter explained. "When we had a good day, we would take the money and spend it collectively—go out to dinner or something."

Though a lover of books, running a bookstore was not the career Peter imagined for himself. Fortunately, an opportunity was about to materialize that would take advantage of Peter's musical sensibilities and knowledge of the recording process, pointing the way toward the future.

Paul Jones, the singer who got first crack at "Lady Godiva," originally met Peter when they toured the United States together in 1964, back when Jones was the front man for Manfred Mann. (This was after he turned down an offer to be lead singer for a little blues band Brian Jones and Keith Richards were forming in 1962.) He related how they got acquainted: "Fog-bound in Cleveland, I think it was, we had an enforced night off, and Peter and I spent the whole evening chatting. I seem to

Peter and Miles behind the till at Indica.

have got the impression that he wasn't committed to touring with Gordon the rest of his life." Now a solo artist, also managed by Richard Armitage, Jones was becoming quite frustrated recording under producer John Burgess, who was very dismissive of Paul's songwriting efforts. "When I was looking for a new producer, I asked Richard if he thought Peter would be interested." Armitage replied, "Ask him—he might well be." According to Jones, "Peter seemed surprised that I'd even had such an idea, but to me it seemed a very logical next move for him, and I was confident he'd be good at it."

The production process had long fascinated Peter. Miles recalled the two of them listening to Motown records together: "He would point out the bassline and the fills. . . . He could really deconstruct a song and tell you exactly how it was put together." But this was the first time someone had specifically asked him to take on the responsibility of producing their session. Taken aback, he hesitated, prompting Betsy to step up (as all good, supportive girlfriends should) and say: "Peter—you really should do this!"

"I *was* surprised—in the sense that he was making a leap of faith," Peter remembered. "He provided an opportunity based on very little evidence. Usually when you hire a producer, you can at least ask, 'What have you produced lately?' You know? And the answer was, '*Nothing!*'" But realizing what a fortuitous bit of happenstance this was, Peter immediately got to work.

First, Peter needed to find a good song that would be right for Paul as well as a possible hit. He found what he was looking for on The Bee Gees' second album, *Horizontal*, which had just been released. "And the Sun Will Shine" was one of those dramatic ballads the Brothers Gibb did so well. Mike Vickers, who had been arranging Peter and Gordon sessions as of late (and was himself a former member of

Manfred Mann), remembered Peter excitedly telling him: "I have this GREAT Bee Gees song for Paul!"

Vickers, originally a saxophone player, had started arranging and composing in his teens and came to London with the idea of finding work as an arranger. "But then Manfred Mann happened," he said, "so that took the backseat." Vickers joined The Mann-Hugg Blues Brothers (as they were then called) as a flute and sax player, later becoming their guitarist. When producer John Burgess began to work with them, he told them to, first, change their name to simply Manfred Mann (which he thought would be more memorable), and second, to record "Do Wah Diddy Diddy," which Burgess was sure would be a hit. The group didn't want to do either, Burgess recalled. They feared keyboardist Mann would get all the attention if they only used his name, and as for the song, it certainly wasn't a *blues* number! Burgess insisted—and was right on both counts. The record went on to top the charts in both the US and the UK.

Vickers stayed with the group for only another year and then began his arranging career in earnest. He scored films and began arranging sessions for artists, including the Peter and Gordon track "London at Night" (an early Cat Stevens composition and one of the highlights of their US *In London For Tea* album). Another session of note occurred in 1967, when George Martin, overwhelmed with preparing for The Beatles' appearance in the *Our World* TV satellite broadcast while also dealing with his extremely ill father, asked Vickers to handle arranging "All You Need Is Love," which The Beatles would perform live within days on the worldwide telecast. Martin eventually couldn't let the arrangement go without *some* input, and the score ended up retaining about half of Vickers's work. (That's Vickers you see conducting the orchestra during The Beatles' live performance of the song, released as a single only days later.)

After he and Vickers discussed ideas for the string arrangement, Peter then began to select the musicians to use on the session. His choice for bass player was his good friend Paul Samwell-Smith, a member of The Yardbirds, one of London's leading blues-based rock bands. "I went to Peter's house one evening, and we listened to the Bee Gees track and spent some time chewing it over," Samwell-Smith recounted. "We came up with a bass riff that seemed to fit." Hiring Eric Clapton, The Yardbirds' original lead guitarist, was initially considered, but Peter took the opportunity of asking Samwell-Smith if he could get the group's current lead guitarist, Jeff Beck, to play the session. McCartney got wind of what was happening and wanted to join in. As a bass player had already been procured, he offered to play drums.

Vickers, who played piano on the track with the assembled supergroup, said of McCartney: "Playing with him, as a drummer, he's just amazing! His time is so *fantastic.* I've hardly ever played with anybody who's as solid . . . a complete, natural, instinctive musician."

Vickers could see Peter enjoying himself at the session: "It just appealed to him—working in the studios and with the musicians," he said. "I don't think he was nervous at all. I think he was very confident."

Once the basic tracks were laid down, it was time for the overdubs. Peter had a specific sound in mind for the choir, remembering how the Asher family would sing together while he was growing up in postwar Britain. He wanted to infuse the chorus with that same warm sense of resolve (and, as a thrifty producer, save on all the union fees hiring a professional choir would entail). So Dr. Asher and sister Clare walked into Abbey Road Studios and gathered around the mic with Peter, combining their voices once again—only this time adding them to a recording that included some of the top rock musicians in the world. Clare, putting her Oxford music studies to use, actually starts off the track playing the stately organ intro.

"And the Sun Will Shine" was released in March 1968 and was reviewed glowingly by England's *Melody Maker*, which stated: "It's Jones' best effort in months and cries out for hit status." As the first record released with the credit "Producer: Peter Asher" on the label, Peter proudly sent a copy to his American friend Danny Kortchmar: "I listened to it and I went, 'Holy shit! You produced? Oh, *man!* He's a producer! Listen to this! He made a record!' I couldn't believe it! 'Cause nobody I knew had ever created anything like that before. I was over the moon! To me, 'producer' was several steps above President of the United States in terms of somebody with authority and ability," Kortchmar enthused.

Paul Jones, also impressed, asked Peter to helm the session for his next single. Of historical note, "When I Was Six Years Old" could quite possibly be the first instance of a pop record to use what we now term "sampling." Jazz fan Peter looped a section of a live recording of "A Night in Tunisia" by Charlie Parker and Dizzy Gillespie and used it both in the middle of the track and during the closing fade. When I reminded Peter of this, he exclaimed, "God, that was sampling before sampling, wasn't it?" But as he thought, he admitted, "It might have been Paul as well, to be fair, because he's a

Peter's first official production credit.

jazz fan, too. But I'm pretty sure, you know . . . it sounds logical it would have been my idea, 'cause that's one of my favorite be-bop classics of all time."

"We'll take joint credit on it," said Jones, who first heard Ronnie Burns's recording of the tune while touring Australia. "When we were recording it, I wanted to borrow the break at the beginning of Parker's solo," he explained, "partly because it's one of the greatest moments in the history of music and partly because, when he originally played it, I was about six years old myself. I knew nothing about tape loops," Jones admitted. "Any expertise there must have come from Peter."

Peter and Gordon owed EMI one more album and insisted on having artistic control over the project. For the first time, they produced the sessions themselves and wrote all (save two) of the album's songs. But this time, instead of writing jointly as in the past, all songs were written separately. Peter's were the more adventurous, with tracks such as "Freedom Is a Breakfast Food" (with lyrics from an e.e. cummings poem) as intriguing, not to mention as well-produced, as anything else labeled "pop" that year. And Peter continued to put his tape experiments to use—using a backward drumbeat, for example, throughout the album opener, "I Feel Like Going Out." Gordon's songs were quite solid, particularly "You've Had Better Times." That track was tackled after a few hours of drinking, and its very loose feel made it one of the most rollicking, fun tracks released that year. Gordon even misses a piano chord in the intro—"Whoops" he deadpans, with his fellow musicians' laughter left in (one of whom was The Rolling Stones' Brian Jones).

Columbia released "I Feel Like Going Out" in April 1968 as a single in the UK, and it met with universally great reviews. *Disc and Music Echo*, another of England's music trades, called it "their most progressive and best record to date." EMI touted it with full-page ads, highlighting Peter's name as writer, producer, and co-arranger (with Mike Vickers). The record-buying public, though, did not seem interested in what Peter and Gordon were up to at this point, and EMI began to rethink releasing the full-length album, which the duo called *Hot Cold & Custard*.

An intriguing title—but what does it mean? Peter explained: "When all three of us children were young, we loved (and I still do, actually) custard. And I mean that in the English sense: a hot, sugary, vanilla-flavored sauce (made from Birds Eye Custard powder and milk), which tastes amazingly good on any kind of dessert—or on its own with just a spoon. My mother was heard to lament that she made custard with such frequency and in such quantity that she wished she just had three taps at the kitchen sink, labeled 'HOT,' 'COLD,' and 'CUSTARD.' I liked the phrase and thought it would sound curiously mysterious." Mission accomplished.

In June, both Columbia in the UK and Capitol in the States decided to release Gordon's promising track, "You've Had Better Times." The US record trade publication *Billboard* called it "a sure-fire chart-topper," and the duo came over that month for a round of American television appearances to promote it, one of which was *The Mike Douglas Show*. After running through the song during a technical rehearsal, they were approached by one of Capitol's associates.

"This woman with her clipboard comes up to me," Gordon recalled snidely, "and says, 'Can you tell me what the words are in this bit?' I said, 'Yeah: *They just jump in your bed / It goes to your head*—in other words, you think you're wonderful.'" Unfortunately, this proved problematic as, obviously, anytime the words "bed" and "head" are in the same line, oral sex *must* be inferred, and word got back to "The Tower." "Capitol," Gordon fumed, "fucking banned it!" Just as the record started up the charts, it was withdrawn by Capitol, which insisted the pair rerecord their vocals and remove *any* lines about spending the night, jumping in bed, or anything remotely arousing. The pair reluctantly made the changes, but the record's momentum was derailed, and it didn't return to the charts or the airwaves. What should have been one of the summer's big hits was spoiled by corporate stupidity.

"I was just *really pissed off* that one opportunity to be something else other than Peter and Gordon—in other words, to write a double-sided hit song" (as Gordon had written both sides of the single) "was just pulled away from me by, by, basically a load of wankers." Puffing on his cigarette, Gordon continued: "Anyway, so, then my sort of rages, through people doing things that in my eyes were totally *wrong* and I was totally *right*, got worse and my temper just got worse and worse and worse and worse and worse. And I just turned into sort of"—he sighed—"an *evil* person."

Gordon's drinking certainly wasn't helping matters. Jennifer Dunbar, who met him in 1959 when they were fourteen, remembered his drinking being under control during their relationship. But when she broke it off the year of Peter and Gordon's success ("Because he wasn't 'intellectual' enough for me or something." She laughed. "How awful!"), his drinking and his moods escalated. "After we split, it seemed . . . well, he was very violent and very drunk."

"He drank with almost an angry energy," his old friend Roderick Peters recalled. "I always associated it with the pressures of becoming famous." Disappointed in love, pressured by fame, and chafing against authority—with both his management and record label—all must have been factors in his moods.

Regardless, "He was incredibly charming and smart," said Peter, who laughed knowingly when I suggested that Gordon must've been a handful to deal with, but he immediately came to his friend's defense: "He wasn't *that* bad," Peter said. "*Occasionally* he was—it was mostly when he was drunk. He *rarely* really screwed up—he wasn't the kind of person that missed gigs. No, it wasn't that much of an effort. We approached things rather differently, you know, but his input musically was always valuable, and whatever crazy things he would get up to would affect his personal life more than his professional life."

Gordon lamented the fact that even though manager Richard Armitage had faith that he could be successful on his own, "he still, nevertheless, didn't take me by the scruff of the neck and say, '*But*—you've gotta get your *fucking act together!*'"

Unfortunately for Gordon, the days of interventions and drug and alcohol rehab were at least a decade away, and Richard Armitage's attitude—indeed, the attitude of many at the time—was expressed by his son, Alex: "I could well believe he wouldn't have seen it as part of his job to pack someone off to rehab. He saw himself as a

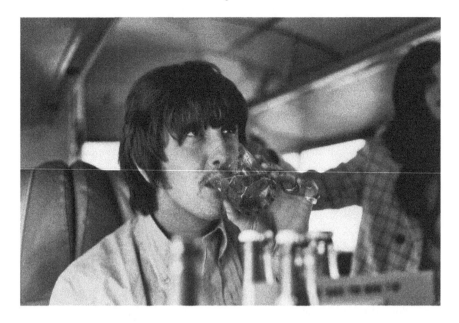

professional manager/agent. I think it would have surprised him had a client's career gone off the rails because of a personal problem like that. I think one of the great truisms of our business is: If there's a huge success, it's the client's fault—if there's a failure, it's almost certainly the agent's fault.

"But, finally, you're an adult—hopefully," Alex Armitage said. "My father once told me it was very much easier to look after intelligent people than . . ." He paused, then continued: ". . . less intelligent people. I think he might have used a different word."

Gordon, recalling the end of his career, had no problem using the correct word: "I'd love to genuinely think I regret it," he said wistfully, "but I had so much fun being an asshole."

9

CAROLINA IN MY MIND

Throughout 1968, The Beatles were formalizing plans to expand their own company, called Apple, into various divisions. Brian Epstein, who had managed The Beatles since spying them at Liverpool's Cavern Club in 1961, originally imagined a string of retail stores. After his sudden death in 1967, the group decided it made sense to expand their corporation into four areas that really interested them: films, electronics, music publishing, and records.

"An overall hospitable arts company," is how Peter defined Apple Corps. "The major labels then were *very* formal; it was *terribly* official." He recalled meeting the then-chairman of EMI, Sir Joseph Lockwood, when Peter and Gordon had their first success: "When you went in his office, you felt like you had to kind of bow—you'd be kind of terrified." Though American labels might have been less imperial—and some, like A&M, were actually started by musicians—giving artists free rein was not standard operating procedure. Times, happily, have changed: "The labels that exist now," Peter said, "where they're trying to be artist-friendly and actually listen to what the artist and the musicians have to say and take them seriously, didn't exist at all. And that's something that Paul and the rest of The Beatles wanted to create."

Though Peter and Paul were no longer sharing the top floor of the Asher Wimpole Street home—McCartney having moved into his own place on Cavendish Avenue, mere blocks from Abbey Road Studios, and Peter now living with Betsy on Weymouth Street—they continued to maintain a close relationship. "I'd be over at his house," Peter said. "He was telling me all about Apple as he was planning it, and we'd smoke a lot of dope and get these great ideas on how it was gonna be, and he had diagrams and stuff. It was great. And he said, 'Would you produce some stuff?' I said, 'Absolutely.'"

McCartney, who had played drums on Peter's first "official" session as producer, Paul Jones's "And the Sun Will Shine," had been impressed with Peter's abilities in

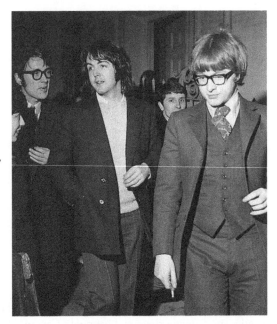

Paul and Peter outside Apple.
Trinity Mirror / Mirrorpix /
Alamy Stock Photo.

the studio. "He liked my approach, I think." Soon the talk grew from "producing some stuff" to something grander: "He said, 'Well, would you like to be head of A&R for the label?'"

A&R—which stands for Artists and Repertoire—is the division in charge of sign-ing acts and supervising the material they record, a combination of talent scout and record producer. It was, Peter recalled, "a position I gratefully accepted. Obviously, what could be better than working for a brand-new super-cool label *and* working for The Beatles?" Apple's corporate headquarters were, at this point, at 95 Wigmore Street, where Peter, after being officially granted his corporate title, was given a small room with a chair, a desk, a bookshelf, and a telephone.

Ron Kass had been brought in from Liberty Records to run the Apple label. "He was the boss. He made the deals with Capitol," Peter explained. "We figured we needed a pro to represent us in America." Ken Mansfield, who worked with both Peter and The Beatles in Los Angeles as a Capitol Records rep, was tapped to head up Apple Records in the United States. When he flew into London for his first meetings, Peter was waiting at the airport to pick him up, paying back Ken for all the times he'd greeted Peter and Gordon when they arrived in LA. Mansfield smiled, recalling this: "I thought that was really neat."

A second suite of offices was located at 94 Baker Street above the short-lived Apple Boutique—The Beatles and Co. soon tired of the retail hassles and, in a fit of pique, gave all the store's clothes away. But upstairs, executives were getting down to business. The second floor housed Apple's publishing arm and was already signing promising songwriters, including Benny Gallagher and Graham Lyle (who would both go on to write many hits). To make things easier for songwriters and musicians to get ideas down quickly, one large room was set aside as a studio of sorts. Hired to watch over the space was Neville Chesters, a former road manager with The Who, Cream, and The Jimi Hendrix Experience. "The idea was if we had people that didn't have instruments or didn't have a place to do something, that's where they could do it," Chesters explained.

On April 19th, full-page ads ran in Britain's music trades asking all aspiring singers and musicians to send Apple tapes of their best efforts. As visions of fame and fortune danced in the eyes of hopeful wannabes across Europe, hundreds of packages began pouring into Baker Street. Chesters was eventually given the job of Peter's assistant in the A&R offices and was saddled with the task of listening to the submissions, the majority of which he described as "cats playing grand piano. . . . It was pretty dire.

"There was a period where we would write to people and say, 'Thank you for sending in your tape. I'm sorry, it's not suitable.' And then," Chesters said, "we decided we'd have to do a form letter." Peter wasn't happy about it—wanting to keep Apple from becoming the typical faceless corporation—but, said Chambers, "he was the one who suggested it!" And no wonder—they were receiving almost a hundred tapes a week.

So what was it like having The Beatles as your boss? "They were inspiring bosses, they were brilliant bosses, they were exciting bosses," said Peter, "but not unanimous or coherent. I mean, they didn't present one coherent *policy*—I don't mean they were individually incoherent. Well, *sometimes*, but so were we *all* at that point in time." Peter's job was simple on the surface but, with four bosses, certainly difficult. "I was responsible for who we signed and who we didn't," he said. "I would run weekly A&R meetings at which a quorum of Beatles would attend (if they were around) and argue a lot (which they did)." Each Beatle had their own pet projects, but Peter had assurances from Paul that if he found someone he wanted to sign, he could.

Back in New York, Danny Kortchmar (who had backed Peter and Gordon in 1966 with his old band, The King Bees) could only watch helplessly as his current band, The Flying Machine, crashed and burned—due mainly to the heroin that had half of the group hooked, including longtime chum James Taylor. "As close as I was with James, even though we were childhood buddies, we had stopped being close," Kortchmar recalled, "because he was getting high and I wasn't."

Like Peter, James Taylor's father was a doctor, and in another striking similarity, his mother had also studied classical music (though as a vocalist). Music and performing seemed to be locked into the Taylors' DNA—James's maternal great-aunt was Lottie Collins, who caused a sensation in the 1890s singing and dancing to her signature song "Ta-ra-ra Boom-de-ay" in British music halls and on the American vaudeville circuit. James and his siblings grew up fairly well-off in North Carolina, spending summers in Martha's Vineyard, Massachusetts—which is where thirteen-year-old James met fifteen-year-old Danny.

Danny Kortchmar had been playing guitar for a few years, learning licks off Howlin' Wolf albums and hanging out at folk clubs. He quickly realized that young James, who had started out playing cello at school, was already a fairly decent singer and guitarist. The two soon formed a duo, "Jamie & Kootch," playing at various coffeehouses. James also got additional experience playing in his older brother Alex's rock band back in Chapel Hill.

But a few years later, at the same time Danny was in New York having some luck with The King Bees, James had a serious bout of depression—so serious he left school and voluntarily committed himself, spending nine months at McLean Hospital outside Boston (the inspiration for his song "Knockin' Round The Zoo" on his first album). Not long after being released, James called Danny in New York. The two reconnected and decided to form a band, which ultimately became The Flying Machine. The group also included another former King Bee, drummer Joel O'Brien. Unfortunately, Joel had his own demons and was using heroin to escape them. Eventually, James did the same, and with both now addicted, the group folded under the weight.

James Taylor picked up the story: "I spent some time at home, basically recuperating, down in North Carolina. And then, not knowing where to go or what to do next, I just sort of thought I'd go to Europe and see the world a little bit—travel around on my own and just make my way as best I could. I took a guitar with me and assumed I'd try to work in some clubs or busk in the street." Danny gave him Peter's address and phone number with a parting tip: "This should be your first stop, 'cause he can help you."

Staying at a friend's flat in London, James met a group of people who responded to his talent: "They were people in the arts in a general way—in commercial arts and some in show business a little bit. And they liked my stuff." They encouraged him to record a demo, which included early songs like "Something in the Way She Moves." James then remembered what his old friend "Kootch" had suggested, leading to a historical bit of "happenstance" and a magical moment in Peter's life.

James Taylor.
Photo by Henry Diltz.

Kortchmar laughed as he recalled Taylor, unannounced, simply walked up to Peter's door: "He didn't even call—he just showed up!" Betsy remembered she had her hair in curlers when she answered the knock, ushering in this lanky American with his reel-to-reel tape in hand. "I'm Kootch's friend," Taylor said and explained he'd recorded some original songs, handing his tape to Peter. Unsure what to expect, Peter politely spooled the tape onto his Ferrograph deck and pressed "PLAY."

Betsy recalled that before the end of the first song, she and Peter turned toward each other "with our mouths open."

First, there was James's distinctive style of guitar playing—he approached the instrument like a pianist, with his years of classical cello studies adding a solid yet melodic bass to the folksy finger picking. Second, his voice—it was soothing, yet fragile, with impeccable phrasing (along with quite clear pronunciation—odd for the time). And finally, the songs themselves—besides being well constructed, they had a sensitivity and wisdom for one so young. It was an irresistible package, and Peter recognized it immediately.

"I loved the tape," Peter recalled, "and I said, 'It just so happens, I've just become head of A&R for this label. I'd like to sign you.' So it was peculiar for him—because within two weeks of arriving in London as a penniless folkie junkie, he was hanging out with The Beatles." Peter brought James to Apple's offices, where both Paul and George were treated to an informal audition. They were impressed, and James became Apple Records' first signing. (Incidentally, George, taken by James's "Something in the Way She Moves," "borrowed," as Peter put it, the same six words to begin his biggest Beatles-era hit, "Something," written about six months later.)

Peter booked the rehearsal studio every afternoon for Taylor and the band that had been assembled to back him. Peter was focused on bringing the best out of James, wanting to make sure that the songs were well-rehearsed and tight before recording commenced. He also had specific ideas when it came to how the songs would be arranged. "I'd worked with Geoff Love, I'd worked with Bob Leaper," Peter said. "I knew all about arrangers and *didn't want to use one!*"

Peter decided to call up his old friend Richard Hewson, whom he had jammed with during his jazz phase in the early sixties. Hewson ("a brilliant musician," said Peter) had only one professional job under his belt—assisting Herbie Hancock with the score for the Antonioni film *Blow-Up*—and Peter's phone call brought him his second. "'Now,'" Hewson recalled Peter asking, "'you've studied orchestration, haven't you, Richard?' I said, 'Yes, I have. But I don't know anything about pop music.'" Hewson laughed, recalling his disastrous attempt years earlier to write a pop song with Peter. "I still didn't!"

But that's what Peter wanted: "I consciously hired someone with no pop experience in order to make the arrangements different," Peter explained, trying his best to make the album stand out. "I thought the songs were so great, I just didn't want them to get lost in the sort of 'folk' world," Peter said. "I wanted to say, 'Look, this is really special stuff.' So I tried to give each song a very different kind of arrangement, different instrumentation." "Something in the Way She Moves" was left stark—just

James's voice and guitar. Others, like "Sunshine Sunshine," ended up with harp and string quartet accompaniment.

On the evening of May 4th, Paul McCartney received a phone call from his friend Lesley Hornby, also known as Twiggy—the fashion world's first true supermodel. She was watching *Opportunity Knocks*, ITV's popular talent contest, and was floored by a young eighteen-year-old Welsh singer named Mary Hopkin. "You have to turn your TV on," she told McCartney. "This girl is amazing!" Paul, in turn, phoned Peter who, unfortunately, tuned in too late to catch her performance. But having won that week's competition, Hopkin would be brought back the following episode. "We had to wait till next week, 'cause there was no 'rewind the TiVo,'" Peter said, recalling that technologically simpler time, "and nobody had a tape." Paul and Peter watched her second appearance together, with Peter agreeing "she was wonderful.

"The genius of Paul is, as he signed her, he already knew the song he was going to produce," Peter recalled admiringly. McCartney had heard "Those Were the Days" months earlier at the Blue Angel nightclub performed by Gene and Francesca Raskin, the tune based on a 1920s Russian ballad by Boris Fomin. Captivated by the melancholy melody and Raskin's sentimental lyrics, Paul knew upon hearing Hopkin's pure soprano voice that they would fit perfectly. Now needing someone to score an arrangement, Paul went to Apple's head of A&R for help. Peter, impressed with the job Richard Hewson was doing for James's album, suggested him to Paul.

Hewson went to McCartney's house, and after listening to a demo of Hopkin singing the song accompanied with only an acoustic guitar, the two discussed ideas. "I thought it would be great to have a banjo," Hewson said, with Paul wanting a sound akin to a zither. Hewson instead suggested using an instrument called a cimbalom—sort of a Hungarian hammered dulcimer.

"Then it became my mission to find the guy to play it," Peter recalled. "Which we did. He was the king of London cimbalom players"—he laughed—"which I imagine was a fairly limited circle!" Hewson proudly proclaimed it "the one and only time it's been used on a pop record!"

The resulting single, Apple's first commercial release after The Beatles' "Hey Jude," was a worldwide smash, and her album, *Post Card*, was a big seller. Though Paul was the record's producer, Peter was basically "executive producer." Peter agreed: "Oh, definitely. In the modern parlance, that would have been what I was," he stated. "I was helping Paul execute his ideas. But it was his record."

Peter also was the executive producer for the recording of McCartney's song "Thingumybob," written as the theme for a new British television comedy. It was originally tried with a small ensemble in London, but Paul's dad suggested he go with The Black Dyke Mills Band—the winner of several national championships. Peter arranged to use Victoria Hall in Saltaire, Yorkshire, for the session, overseeing the remote recording while McCartney, radiating charm and encouragement, sat with the musicians. What other record label would release a brass band march as one of their initial batch of singles? "Exactly," Peter said as he laughed.

Apple Records, though, did not take all of Peter's attention—he also was continuing to produce tracks for Paul Jones (seven of which would be included the following year on Jones's album *Come Into My Music Box*). One song Peter suggested was Robbie Robertson's "The Weight." He had first heard The Band's debut album, *Music from Big Pink*, in Los Angeles while promoting "You've Had Better Times" with Gordon in June.

Peter remembered hanging out at the LA home of Alan Pariser ("He had the best drugs," Peter noted). A hip man about town, Pariser had come up with the idea for The Monterey International Pop Festival and, as heir to a paper fortune, helped finance it. On this particular day, an advance copy of *Music from Big Pink* began to waft from the speakers—its sound mixing with the marijuana smoke that hung in the air. Also in attendance and hearing the album for the first time was Eric Clapton, who was changed completely upon experiencing The Band's alchemic amalgam of American roots music. "He was overwhelmed," Peter said, recalling Clapton's reaction. "He thought it was the best album he'd ever heard." Clapton would soon disband his virtuosic group Cream and head off in a similar rootsy direction with the help of the Southern husband and wife duo Delaney and Bonnie, who, not coincidentally, were managed by Pariser.

As if both record producing and his Apple gig weren't enough, Peter was approached by producer/director Tony Palmer to join with him in putting together a new arts program for BBC Television. The show, called *How It Is*, "was quite revolutionary," Palmer said. "It was designed primarily to make the arts understandable to young people." Peter was tapped to be cohost along with, among others, author and playwright Amanda Huth and Richard Neville, publisher of the soon-to-be infamous underground magazine *OZ*. "We commissioned poems," Palmer continued, "and we were the first people on television to show an extract from *Hair*. But at the same time, we had quite distinguished literary reviewers talking about the then-unknown extent of Stalin's great terror. So it was a complete cross-section.

"Peter was hired because I thought that he would be an ideal conduit for the arts," Palmer confessed. "The fact that it got off the ground at *all* was very much due to his enthusiasm. Because he saw the point—which, of course, was very much a part of the thinking of that time—he saw the point of not dividing the 'high arts' from the 'low arts,' as it were." Peter's contacts in the show business world in general, and the rock world in particular, were a great help in attracting guests—Yoko Ono agreed to come on the debut episode (airing July 19, 1968), and he recommended the jazz/folk band Pentangle for the second show.

But a problem soon arose, said Palmer: "We did have Auto-Cue and Teleprompters, but they were really very clumsy and unsophisticated. And for one reason or another, he didn't seem to quite cope. And he always looked rather stiff on the screen." Artist, journalist, and political activist Caroline Coon, also asked to host, had the same difficulty. She, along with other counterculture leaders, "were thrown into presenting this program with no TV training," Coon noted, "as if presenting wasn't a skill! I lasted all of ten minutes in the presenting audition . . ."

"It really wasn't his fault," Palmer explained. "But because it was on at super-prime time, on the main channel, I was put under enormous pressure (which I resisted for quite a long time) to ask him to leave. I was told at one point, 'Either he goes or the show goes.'

"The real problem was it was BBC-1 at six o'clock on a Friday evening!" Palmer said, laughing. "You know? I mean, that's a slot that the world and his uncle wanted! And I was having to fight my corner to defend having got it and I was determined to keep it. And if Peter had to be, you know, shunted aside in order to keep it, well, I'm afraid . . . that's show biz."

After only six episodes, "He fired me without talking to me," Peter recalled—his agent broke the news. Though this failure must have hurt personally, professionally he carried on with the business of managing Apple's A&R department, now head-quartered at 3 Savile Row—a hip record label tucked amid posh tailoring shops. Peter had a top-floor office *and* a new assistant—a young American woman named Chris O'Dell.

Compared to the rest of the Apple staff, "he carried himself in a different way. He was very proper and very respectful," O'Dell said. "He dipped his head when people would come into the room, almost like he was giving them a little bow. He had that way about him.

"He would get very angry if people were being stupid," she said, then laughed, clarifying: "He *maintained* his anger; he kept it in check." Along with the A&R de-partment, the top floor of 3 Savile Row now also housed Apple Publishing, brought over from the original Baker Street location. Label head Ron Kass had hired Ameri-can Michael O'Connor to manage the publishing division.

O'Connor was originally a drummer, playing club dates to finance his college education. He eventually stopped pursuing his doctorate in English literature, he said, "because I was making more money playing the drums than my professors were teaching—*and* I was having a better time!"

In San Francisco, O'Connor fell in with guitarist Steve Miller, and they formed a band called The Subterraneans ("Very Jack Kerouac," O'Connor said as he laughed). A chance came to tour Europe, but Miller decided to stay behind, forming a new and quite successful band. At the end of the tour, O'Connor remained in England and began booking gigs for American artists, which is where he became friendly with Ron Kass, then president of Liberty Records—now running the Apple label.

With their offices in such close proximity, O'Connor became friendly with Peter Asher. "Peter and I would just have lunch together," O'Connor said, "and listen to music." O'Connor would toss ideas around with Peter, including the possibility of Apple administering the publishing of American acts they admired. O'Connor did manage to secure for Apple, among other San Francisco acts, old friend Steve Miller's publishing for Europe and the UK, as Miller's second album had become a hit.

The sessions for James Taylor's debut album were being held at Trident Studios in Soho—one of the first studios in Britain with eight track–recording capabilities. "Trident was run by two brothers, Barry and Norman Sheffield, who were kind of cockney tough guys," Peter recalled. "Norman was the owner, and Barry was the engineer—he did the *James Taylor* album with me." Michael O'Connor was an observer at the sessions, describing Peter as "a purist about the music. He was very thorough and precise and a perfectionist about what he was doing."

Paul McCartney, also a visitor to James's sessions at Trident, was so impressed he not only used it for Mary Hopkin's album, but he also convinced the rest of The Beatles to leave their familiar confines at Abbey Road and use the studio to record their first single for release on their new label. Peter remembered visiting Trident on the evening the new track was being mixed with co-owner Barry Sheffield at the board. "They had these big old Tannoy speakers that were much louder than anything at Abbey Road, which used Altecs. I mean, Abbey Road was actually a better mixing environment 'cause you don't want hypey speakers for mixing, but for *listening*—for *fun*—they can't be beat. And so, they played it back fairly loud and . . . and . . ." He shook his head at the memory of being one of the first listeners to experience "Hey Jude." "I was just totally knocked out! 'Cause the first time you hear it and you don't know where it's *going*"—he laughed—"it's *really, really startling!*"

James's album was nearing completion. Hewson, the album's arranger, was a big fan of composer Jimmy Webb and loved the work Webb did on the Richard Harris album *A Tramp Shining*. "He does some lovely orchestrations between tracks, and I thought it'd be a great idea," Hewson said. Peter agreed, cleverly linking together James's songs using short instrumental passages. "That's where it came from," admitted Hewson, "to take material from the previous track and try and link into the next one." "It was ambitious," Peter said, "and I think the ambition was a little overweening, looking back now." Said James Taylor: "I would agree with Peter. I would like to hear that material done in a simpler way."

Unlike most labels, the policy at Apple, according to Michael O'Connor, was *not* to give artists money upon signing their recording contracts. Therefore, James—as broke now as when he first arrived in London—was staying with Peter and Betsy during the recording of his Apple album. Still an addict, he hid his drug use from Peter very well: "I didn't know at the time," Peter confessed. "I was ignorant in these matters." Even after hanging with the kings and queens of the London underground? "Oddly enough, yeah," he admitted. "I mean, everybody smoked dope—tons. Everybody smoked opium whenever they could get it. But the idea of actually sticking needles in your arms seemed kind of alien, you know? Seemed like an American thing in William Burroughs books, but not us.

"Eventually, when we were making the album, it sort of 'dawned' on me that he was spending an inordinate amount of time in the bathroom."

"By that time, James was a New York–style junkie," Danny Kortchmar said, "which meant, you know, you learn how to be very surreptitious; you learn how to be very cool about it."

"When people are really addicted, they're not really taking drugs for fun. It's not about recreation; it's not about partying. It's really self-medication—that's what makes it so serious and tenacious," Taylor confided. "It's not a social drug—it's something you do instead of having contact with people.

"It's like temporary suicide."

During James's stay, another guest dropped into Weymouth Street for a few days—a seventeen-year-old singer and songwriter from Lancashire named Stephen Murray, who performed under the name Timon (taken from Shakespeare's *Timon of Athens*). His first record, the trippy "Bitter Thoughts of Little Jane," had come out earlier in the year on Pye but had not done well. Richard Armitage at Noel Gay Artists, who represented not only the struggling singer but also longtime client Peter Asher, played his friend some of Timon's work. Intrigued, Peter played the Pye single for McCartney, who was quite impressed by the young lad. With an eye toward possibly signing Timon to Apple, Peter invited him down to stay at his flat in Marylebone and do a bit of recording. "Peter and Betsy were very kind," Tymon—which is how he spells his name today—remembered. "Peter had picked up that I was dedicated to my songwriting, and he wanted to do the best he could."

Three recordings were done at Trident, where Taylor's album was underway. Peter drafted James and his band as backing musicians, Paul McCartney joined in on piano, and Mike Vickers did the arranging, utilizing both strings and horns to flesh out the wistful "And Now She Says She's Young." With the bouncy "Something New Every Day," "Paul was playing some really nice, tight piano," Tymon remembered. He also recalled James Taylor borrowing John Lennon's white Epiphone electric for the track. He felt too much of their contribution was lost when the horns went on: "It sort of covered it up."

McCartney thought the unsuccessful Pye single could still be a hit and suggested the young man rerecord it for Apple. Tymon, though, felt that would be going backward and respectfully declined, also turning down an original song McCartney offered, thinking it was more suited to an act like Herman's Hermits. "Making a 'hit' for teenyboppers was not a big deal for me," he explained. Being a fan of singer/songwriters like Leonard Cohen, Tymon felt he needed to record his own material and that a full album would showcase it better than a single, which was all Apple was then offering. Overhearing one of the most famous musicians in the world offering suggestions and the teenaged neophyte standing his ground, Apple press officer and longtime Beatles confidante Derek Taylor "was impressed," Tymon recalled.

Apple eventually sent him a publishing contract for his songs. He never signed it, feeling that Apple's promise of an artist's haven wasn't working out for him and sensing that something internal there was amiss. The following year, Tymon rerecorded one of the Apple tracks, "And Now She Says She's Young," for the Moody Blues' Threshold label and continued to go his own idiosyncratic way. A decade later, he worked with The Clash on their classic *Sandinista!* album. Two of the tracks Peter produced at Trident were eventually released in 2010 on the CD collection *The Ir-repressible Tymon Dogg*.

Another act that came to Apple's attention was a band from Buffalo, New York, called Raven. Trying to build on their regional success, the band's manager, Marty Angelo, recorded one of their live shows and sent the tape to Apple: "I thought, 'Why not? Let's give it a shot.'" Soon, a telegram arrived from George Harrison: "He said he was quite interested," according to Angelo, "and wanted to produce the band."

Raven was thrilled, obviously, and as their reputation in New York grew, other la-bels expressed interest—even Jimi Hendrix offered to produce them—but the group decided to hold out for Harrison and his label. "All of a sudden, I get a call from Peter Asher," remembered Angelo, saying he was in New York and wanted to meet.

Angelo knew that Peter had been half of Peter and Gordon but thought that he'd only gotten his job at Apple because his sister was dating one of the owners. As the two men sat down together in a nightclub's kitchen, "I asked him: 'Peter, do you *know* anything about the music business?'" Peter politely tried to explain his back-ground and, confirming Apple's interest in Raven, said Harrison would not be avail-able to produce the album—he would. "Do you even know how to *produce* a group like this? I mean, you're a folkie," Angelo said derisively. "Have you ever produced anybody *else?*"

Having zero confidence in Peter's production abilities, Angelo ended the meet-ing, saying, "If we can't get Harrison in the studio and his name on the back of the album, we're gonna go with Columbia." Peter left, and Angelo never heard from Apple again. Raven's debut album was released by Columbia the following year, but ironically, "we wound up not liking the producer," Angelo admitted, and the band broke up not long after. As for Peter, "Who knew what he would go on to become?" If he had even an inkling of Peter's abilities, Angelo said, "we would have signed in a *second!*"

Back in London, weekly A&R meetings continued, with Peter reporting what had been accomplished with the artists Apple had signed and those they might want to add to their roster. Oh, and what about all those hundreds of tapes they solicited with their ad? As they were boiled down to an acceptable number, Peter would listen to them himself. None was signed to Apple.

Peter, having faith in James and seeing the potential in his songs, tried to interest others in recording them. "Peter rang me up one day," Paul Jones remembered, "and said he had a songwriter there who he thought had something very special. So I went over to his place and there was this tall guy with lank hair and holes in his sweater singing songs from what, to me, was an alien culture."

Jones has always been, in his own words, "obsessed with black music," so these melancholy folk songs were not his cup of tea. Peter couldn't believe it as Jones passed on every song James played to him, including his newest—what would eventually be chosen as his first single.

James Taylor album cover.

Begun while taking a quick trip to Spain, feeling homesick, and finished at Peter and Betsy's apartment, "Carolina in My Mind"—wherein the songwriter withdraws to a comforting place in his memory to escape feeling pain—was yearning and troubled while still sounding bouncy and hopeful. The Beatles not only appear in Taylor's lyrics as the "*holy hosts*," but one is actually on the recording, as McCartney does his usual stellar job on bass. (Contradicting rumors, Peter insisted that George Harrison, though he stopped by during the sessions, did not participate.)

Despite Peter's excellent production—his first for an entire album—and the radio-friendly kick of the single, both *James Taylor* and "Carolina in My Mind" did not do as well as expected. But Peter's work did not go unnoticed—even surprising some of his old friends: "I was really knocked out when 'Carolina in My Mind' came out. . . . There was much more to Peter than I had actually realized," Marianne Faithfull said. "I think Peter even surprised Paul . . . I don't know if he expected Peter to be able to turn out fantastic, flawless hits like that."

Faithfull then wondered, "I don't know, really, why I never asked Peter to produce *me!*" Laughing, she observed, "It's never too late, you know?"

Apple was not only deluged with inquiries from thousands of amateurish hopefuls, but even more-professional artists tried to get the attention of the hippest label in London. David Bowie's manager, Ken Pitt, for example, sent his client's first (and commercially unsuccessful) album to Apple's offices in hopes of getting noticed. But one legendary act *did* come close to having their first work released by Apple Records.

The band Yes were fairly unknown in 1968 but beginning to get a buzz around town with their progressive rock interplay. They were also lucky enough to have Roy Flynn, manager of the Speakeasy club, in their corner. The Speakeasy was one of the main hangouts of London's music elite, and Flynn knew everyone in the British music business. Within two months of becoming their manager and buying them better equipment, Flynn got them second on the bill at Cream's Farewell Concert at the Royal Albert Hall, where they garnered better reviews than the headliners.

Peter Banks, the group's original lead guitarist, had come up with the band's name—with an added exclamation point: *Yes!* He thought it would do "until somebody comes up with something better," Banks said. "And nobody did." Singer Jon Anderson "was always pulling toward the—for want of a better word—'commercial' side of the band," Banks said. "As singers usually would do." Wanting to mix The Beatles' melodicism with heavier rock underpinnings, it made sense for Anderson to pose the question: "Why don't we get Paul McCartney to produce us?" With Apple the hot new label in town and Yes the hot new band, this seemed like a good fit.

Peter, as head of A&R, wanted to first see how they fared in a studio, and he booked a session with Yes a few days before Christmas 1968, producing a demo of their song "Dear Father." "We thought that might be a possible single," Banks recalled, adding: "Although we were the *last* kind of band to think about doing singles!" Banks was impressed with Peter—not just for his abilities behind the recording console, but because he observed him reading a newspaper; not the music trades or underground press, mind you, "a *real newspaper!*" Peter loved the band and was looking forward to working with them. Had Apple made a firm offer, "we probably would have grabbed it," according to Banks, but Yes was so hot at that point they had their pick of labels to go with. Manager Flynn was enamored with Atlantic Records' roster and, along with Led Zeppelin, Yes became one of the first in a long line of British bands to sign with that legendary label. But for their debut album, Atlantic saddled them with a producer who had never produced a band before. "That was pretty much a disaster," Banks recalled.

As was Roy Flynn's experience with the music business. "I got shafted," Flynn said of Atlantic. "They never delivered on their deal and left me high and dry." Bitter, he walked away from the industry in 1973, just as Yes, the group he had sunk all his money into, became one of the biggest-selling bands in the world. Peter shrugged and said, "Atlantic, like all labels back then, was capable of acting that way."

An even bigger band from that era was Crosby, Stills and Nash. Along with Blind Faith, they were one of the first so-called supergroups, with each member formerly with other hit-making bands: David Crosby from The Byrds, Stephen Stills from Buffalo Springfield, and Graham Nash from The Hollies. In late 1968, not long after forming this new unit, the group was in London hoping to sign with the hottest new record label in town.

"We wanted to be on Apple," Nash flatly stated. "So I called Peter and asked him if he'd come down and listen to this new sound. And he came with George Harrison."

"At that time," David Crosby recalled, "Graham and Stephen and I could sing the whole first album to you—BANG—at the drop of a hat. We could sing everything on it, one right after the other, and just slay you! We did it to lots of people"—he laughed—"and it was *very, very good.*" The trio broke out their acoustic guitars and began their audition. "It's fucking Peter Asher and George Harrison, for God's sake,"

Nash stressed. "Of *course* we tried to be the best we could." For the next half hour, the Moscow Road apartment was filled with soaring harmonies, sterling songcraft, and solid musicianship. "We sang 'em the whole first album," said Crosby. "And they turned us down.

"This is one of the only mistakes Peter ever made," Crosby concluded. But Peter begged to differ: "I remember hearing them and being *enthralled!* I thought they were amazing." Peter continued, "I was super-impressed. It's exactly what I love! I would not have turned them down." Harrison, on the other hand, friendly with both Crosby and Nash, could already feel the bad vibes beginning at Apple and the looming chaotic management problems that would, within one year, help tear The Beatles apart. Harrison intimated years later that *his* rejection of the group was a "favor." In reality, Peter stated, with all the members contractually tied to other labels, it would have been "impossible" for Apple to sign them, leaving it to manager David Geffen and Atlantic Records president Ahmet Ertegun to eventually untangle it all.

Harrison was not alone in his suspicions toward this new business venture. "Apple began to fall apart," Neville Chesters stated. "It was fairly obvious in late '68 that it was crumbling."

"Well, it was a corporation that decided to have four equal presidents, and I *dare* you to find a company that has that as its business plan," Apple executive Ken Mansfield explained. "Four equal presidents that *happen* to be rock'n'roll stars! So that was one of the problems. It made no sense, you know? The doors were open to the world, and 'we want everybody to get a chance,' so that meant every crazy in the world was there. The building was a madhouse. Nobody was really watching the store—and in a proper way. And this was the 'sex, drugs, and rock'n'roll' era, so. . . . Everybody was stoned or drunk or whatever. It was just a big party."

But an amazing one: "There was this feeling," Michael O'Connor recalled, "that this was the center of the world! Because everybody that would come into London, they would want to go by Apple and see if they could see The Beatles"—he laughed—"rather than, you know, the prime minister. It was incredible."

Despite all the chaos—automobiles leased and then disappearing, Hells Angels rubbing shoulders with Hare Krishnas on Savile Row—Apple Records "did manage to turn out some pretty decent music," Peter proudly stated. Mostly because of the worldwide success of "Hey Jude" and "Those Were the Days," Apple was the most successful new record company of 1968.

ASSOCIATED BRITISH presents
EILEEN HERLIE
CECIL PARKER and
DONALD WOLFIT in

Isn't Life Wonderful ! -u-

COLOUR BY TECHNICOLOR
PRODUCED BY WARWICK WARD · DIRECTED BY HAROLD FRENCH· SCREENPLAY BY BROCK WILLIAMS
DISTRIBUTED BY ASSOCIATED BRITISH-PATHE

with ROBERT URQUHART
ELEANOR SUMMERFIELD
DIANNE FOSTER
PETER ASHER
CECIL TROUNCER
RUSSELL WATERS

Lobby card from *Isn't Life Wonderful!* with Donald Moffit and Cecil Parker. *Courtesy of STUDIOCANAL.*

Photo : *M. C. Norbury*

Unorthodoxy at the Music Competitions: P. Asher, C. Garmany and G. Waller, who were "honourably mentioned " for their guitar playing

From Westminster School newspaper *The Elizabethan*, July 1961. *Reproduced by kind assistance of the Governing Body of Westminster School.*

Gordon & Peter

Aubyn St Claire

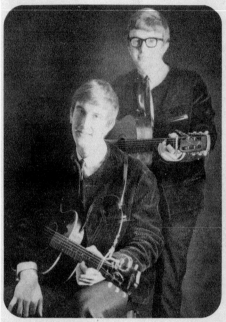

A duo whose style of blues, folk and 'country and western' songs are in the best tradition of Bob Dylan, Jimmy Reed and Peter, Paul and Mary. These two good-looking balladeers have enjoyed considerable success in cabaret where they feature a number of songs penned by themselves. Their first record is to be released shortly.

Already known to the record buying public as a hot name in the big beat music idiom, Aubyn St. Claire has an exciting delivery, a stage act that is way, way out and wild to say the least and an appeal that lies in his ability to project his personality through his interpretations of the big-sounding rhythm 'n blues numbers.

Part of a Townsend/Meaden brochure circa 1963 offering the entertainment services of "Gordon and Peter" and the mysterious performer known as "Aubyn St. Claire." *Courtesy of Philip Townsend.*

Peter and Gordon's first UK single (top) and album (bottom).

Top: Capitol Records' "Woman" release with Bernard Webb as songwriter / Bottom: The duo's final album.

An early and very informal Apple meeting. L to R: Peter, Ken Mansfield, Ringo Starr, Ron Kass, Peter Brown, George Harrison, Francie Schwartz, and Stanley Gortikov. © *Apple Corps Ltd.*

Mortimer. *Photo by Peter Asher /* © *Apple Corps Ltd.*

James and Peter. *Photo by Henry Diltz.*

Peter, left, with The Section: Russ Kunkel, Lee Sklar, Craig Doerge, and Danny Kortchmar.
Photo by Maureen McGillan-Sklar.

Peter recording the *Heart Like a Wheel* album at The Sound Factory, 1974. *Photo by Andrew Gold/ Courtesy of Andrew Gold Estate.*

Art director John Kosh holding Ronstadt's *Simple Dreams* album. © *David Jacks, 2012.*

10

ON OUR WAY HOME

"I can remember one time being in the elevator with Peter and Ken," said Michael O'Connor, referring to Peter Asher and visiting American writer Ken Kesey, "and the subject of The Beatles breaking up came up. And Ken Kesey said, 'Ahh, that could *never* happen! That would be *totally impossible!* That could *never* happen in this *world!*'" Laughing, he added: "And I remember Peter turning to him, saying, 'You are wrong. That *could* happen, and it *might* happen!'"

The Beatles were in disarray at the beginning of 1969. Along with the insane stress of trying to run a corporation, they were being filmed daily from morning till night—the cameras documenting rehearsals for a new album and, supposedly, their first official concert in years. John Lennon didn't have much material to contribute—not surprising, as he was now a heroin addict, using the drug partly as a balm against the negativity he felt the world in general (and his friends, in particular) were sending toward Yoko Ono and himself. Paul McCartney, on the other hand, was bringing in song after song—"Let It Be," "The Long and Winding Road"—and he was excited for the band to play gigs once more.

George Harrison couldn't wait for The Beatles to stop touring and was very resistant to start that up again, dreading all the accompanying hysteria. In addition, after having spent time in November recording with the cream of LA's session musicians (producing Apple singer Jackie Lomax) and being treated as their equal, he now found himself back to being relegated as "side man" to Paul and John, his songs not being given much consideration. After a little more than a week of this, Harrison announced, "I'm leaving the band now," packed up his guitar, and walked out of rehearsals.

Eventually talked into returning, Harrison made it clear that the idea of a formal concert needed to be rethought. The need, simply, was to come up with a performance idea that would not only be a fitting end to the film but so easy to accomplish that all in the group would agree to it. Two months earlier, there had been an incident involving The Jefferson Airplane performing on the roof of a midtown hotel in Manhattan. Filmmaker Jean-Luc Godard was only able to capture footage of the group doing one song before New York City police stopped the concert, kicking them off the roof and issuing a summons for disturbing the peace.

Whether a borrowed concept or a beautiful coincidence no one is sure, but after confirming the roof at 3 Savile Row could hold the minimum amount of people and equipment necessary (and getting all bandmates on board), The Beatles performed their final live gig on January 30, 1969, seen by only a lucky few—though heard by many for blocks around. Apple exec Ken Mansfield and Peter's assistant, Chris O'Dell, had the best seats for the show—huddled together with Yoko and Ringo's wife, Maureen, their backs against a chimney helping to deflect London's bitter wind. ("Chris," Peter said, smiling, "always made sure she was in the right place.") Portions of the concert were finally released sixteen months later on record, and in theaters, with the title *Let It Be* (and, in 2021, re-edited and rereleased as *The Beatles Get Back*).

Peter missed the performance, as he spent the first two months of the new year at Capitol Records' offices in Los Angeles. But doing what? "I don't quite remember," he said, puzzled, guessing that he was dealing with submissions from hopeful American musicians.

While The Beatles attempted to regroup musically, Apple continued to move forward creatively. Ron Kass, head of the Apple label, was friendly with Monte Kay, who had not only opened the famous New York club Birdland, but managed The Modern Jazz Quartet—one of the preeminent ensembles of the jazz world. Kass proposed signing the MJQ to Apple. "It was Ron's idea to show that the label was multifaceted," Peter recalled. "They thought it would bring their music to people who would, and undoubtedly did, listen to it because it was on The Beatles' label and go, 'What is this?'" Kay thought this would expand the Quartet's audience, and Kass thought it would do the same for Apple's. So, said Peter, "it was good for everybody."

A deal was made for two albums. The first, *Under the Jasmine Tree*, was already in the can when the contract was signed and was released by Apple in February 1969. For the second album, Peter recalled: "Ron asked me if I wanted to produce The Modern Jazz Quartet!" For the self-professed "jazz snob," this was a gift from heaven. "I said, 'Absolutely!'" He admitted this took a bit of nerve on his part, but "I was *such* an admirer. John Lewis is one of *the* consummate musicians," proclaimed Peter, referring to the MJQ's leader, and he absolutely idolized vibe player Milt Jackson.

The four jazz masters flew to London for the sessions, which were held at Trident Studios in March 1969. John Lewis was certainly in charge of leading the band and producing the music, but Peter acted as "supervising producer" in the control booth, trying a fresh approach to jazz recording: "I was annoyed on jazz records that the low end—you know, the kickdrum and stuff—was always practically ignored. And I always like a good 'thump,'" Peter explained. "I remember trying to record it in a more rock'n'roll style." The results were sonically different from any other jazz album of its time and, in its own subtle way—with a sound effect here and a bit of tape manipulation there—pointed the way toward future jazz-rock fusions.

Peter smiled remembering the sessions: "It was fun!" And once these four African American musical geniuses realized that this very white British pop star not only knew their music, but also, more importantly, knew what he was doing behind the console, "I got on very well with them," said Peter. Apple released the resulting album, called *Space*, at the end of the year.

Along with wanting to put out popular and commercial records, Apple also had a subversive and underground streak. To that end, a sister label—"Zapple"—was formed to release more esoteric fare. To run the label, Paul and Peter tapped their old friend from Indica, Barry Miles.

"We were just going to do spoken-word albums, but not just poetry. . . . We had the idea to get Fidel Castro and Mao Tse-tung," Miles explained, recalling the original (and, no doubt, drug-induced) brainstorming meetings: "*'They're all gonna do albums, and we're gonna save the world and let everybody communicate with each other!'* The idea being," Miles continued, "that half of the paranoia and fear was because nobody knew what the hell the real ideas behind all these things were. Everyone was scared shitless of Castro for some reason, but nobody really knew where he was coming from. So we would get Fidel to tell us and perhaps reduce the tension a bit. You know—typical idealistic sixties thing.

"I was more concerned with making poetry records. So Paul just said, 'Make a list of who you wanna record, get yourself an assistant, and go and do it.'" Miles flew to New York and California on a number of occasions to tape various writers reading their work, including Allen Ginsberg, Michael McClure, Lawrence Ferlinghetti, and the then-unknown Charles Bukowski: "He was still working at the post office," Miles said, recalling the hard-living poet. "He'd never given a public reading." Miles also taped a session with Ken Weaver of the New York band The Fugs, which he described as "humorous, stand-up comic stuff. . . . It would have *definitely* been a cult album!

"I had an office at Hollywood and Vine," Miles recalled, referring to the famous Capitol Records tower. "I was just there recording my poetry records, but I happened to be the first person from Apple to reach California. So they immediately treated me like an executive, which was *crazy* 'cause I didn't know any business stuff! They'd had advance warning—signed by The Beatles, yet—that I was to be given 'proper treatment.' So"—he laughed—"I was given this *big* office with *two secretaries*. I had *nothing* for them to do *at all!* Except show me around town . . . so they showed me around town!" When a limo pulled up to a club and management realized an "executive" from Apple had arrived, patrons were removed from good tables to make way for Miles and his secretaries. "It was strange to see the power of The Beatles," he said in wonderment.

All three Asher children were at this point excelling in their areas of interest: Peter was now an executive at the hottest new record label in the world; Jane was continuing to perform on film, on stage, and on television; Clare, leaving both acting and music behind, began training to be a teacher of geography—"the only member of the family to be educated," Peter once quipped.

Geography was a lifelong passion of Clare's: "She and Mrs. Asher once took off on a trip to Russia," Betsy remembered. "They went to Africa. . . . They were not easy trips to take. They were very adventurous and very lively, and they all were supportive of each other." The entire Asher family, according to Betsy, "threw themselves into whatever they were doing."

But Dr. Asher, the family patriarch, had changed in the five years since his dismissal from the mental observation post at Central Middlesex Hospital. He had never shaken his deep sense of disappointment at the medical establishment, and his depression caused by this perceived personal betrayal was worsening.

By late April, the sound of Dr. Asher's usual scurrying about was missing from the Wimpole Street townhouse. Thinking their father had left on another impromptu solitary sojourn, it took days before he was discovered in one of the many, many rooms that made up the Asher family residence. He was fifty-seven years old.

It was ironic that someone that brilliant, who had spent years diagnosing and helping others with mental problems, ultimately could not help himself.

Only a week after this personal tragedy, on May 3, 1969, Peter reunited with Gordon Waller at Trident Studios to record as Peter and Gordon for the first time in over a year. The song Peter chose to produce was "I Can Remember (Not Too Long Ago)," recorded originally by the American soul duo James and Bobby Purify. "I just thought it was a great pop song," Peter declared, and as the Purify version had not been a hit in the UK, he thought a certain English duo could take the song into the British charts. Just as in the past, Gordon's soulful delivery coupled with Peter's plaintive harmony came together in a memorable chorus, and Peter's production gave it a pop sheen that seemed hit-bound.

Unfortunately, pop chanteuse Billie Davis put "I Can Remember" out during the exact same week as Peter and Gordon, and the two records canceled each other out.

There was one more album Peter produced during his time at Apple—the sophomore LP by an acoustic trio from upstate New York named Mortimer. They had started life as The Teddy Boys and for a time were the house band at the New York club Arthur (just as The King Bees once were), which is where they met manager Danny Secunda. After losing a member and becoming a three-piece outfit, "we decided we wanted to try something different, so we went completely acoustic," member Tony Van Benschoten remembered. "And we decided to pick the name Mortimer because, in London, Danny had a friend who had a garment business on Mortimer Street."

Secunda was able to get the band a deal at Phillips Records, which put out their debut album in 1967. It did well—about thirty-five thousand copies were sold—but before they could record the follow-up, Allen Klein took over running the label. When a new regime comes in, acts that had been signed by the departing executives—especially bands that haven't achieved a certain level of success—get a cold reception. "He wasn't gonna give us another go," Van Benschoten recalled. "So Danny thought, 'Well, let's try England.'"

Here, a wondrous bit of "happenstance" came into play as Mortimer percussionist Guy Masson had earlier in the year attended a party at the Manhattan home of Nat Weiss—business partner and friend to Beatles manager, Brian Epstein. Masson asked Weiss to give a copy of Mortimer's Phillips album to John Lennon. Weiss promised he would and, true to his word, he did. Lennon liked it and passed it on to Michael O'Connor at Apple Publishing. So when Mortimer, after only a week or two in London, knocked on Apple's door, they were quickly granted a meeting with O'Connor.

"They invited us up, and we did sort of a live show in one of the small little offices. And we were playing away there," Van Benschoten recalled, "and George Harrison heard it and came in and said, 'Hey! Sign 'em up!'"

Peter, as head of A&R, also liked what he heard. "He worked a lot with us," said Van Benschoten. "He was a wonderful fellow. We did a whole bunch of demos down in the big basement of Apple. He just sat us down and we would play what we did. We just did tape after tape of different songs."

Peter eventually took Mortimer into Trident Studios and produced sessions for an official Apple album release. "He was trying to get the most out of us," said Van Benschoten. To that end, Richard Hewson was once again entrusted with adding strings and horns to a couple of tracks. The side-two opener, "You Don't Say You Love Me," was Peter's attempt at a brassy Brit-pop confection, but the sessions mainly highlighted the "less is more" philosophy this unplugged trio excelled at—guitar, bass, and percussion supporting harmonies not unlike those utilized by Peter and Gordon—all put beautifully into play on the record's haunting ballad, "In Memory of Her."

Peter "was always encouraging to us," Van Benschoten said, inviting the band down to his house in Surrey. He and Betsy would make lunch and then, with the autumn colors painting the trees, take them out on the small lake. "He took pictures of the three of us," Van Benschoten recalled, "and I think he was hoping it might be the album cover."

Peter then hit on a solid song to introduce the group. "He's a lover of songs," Peter's old friend Graham Nash stated. "If you start with a decent song, that's the fire that starts all that production work. You have to start with a good song, and Peter had a *great* ear for songs." Peter felt that The Beatles' unreleased "On Our Way Home" (later retitled "Two of Us") would be perfect for Mortimer and their simple acoustic approach. "Originally, they wanted The Everly Brothers to record it," Peter recalled. Phil Everly, though, regretfully said he and Don would have to pass. "It wasn't that they didn't like it," Peter emphasized; it was simply bad timing for them. So McCartney agreed to let this new Apple signing release it first, realizing this would certainly get them noticed right off the bat.

The track opens the album. Guitarist Tom Smith sang lead, changing the last words of the bridge from "out *ahead*" to "out *of here*"—perhaps simply misunderstanding McCartney's sung pronunciation. To offset the lilting, folksy feel of the track, the recording also featured a synthesizer lead. "Back then I had my Moog Series III synthesizer in my flat," Mike Vickers recalled. "So, a multitrack tape machine [probably only a four-track] was delivered there, and Peter turned up with the master tape of 'Two of Us.' I probably made something up on the spot!" This new electronic musical tool had been used recently to add color to rock album tracks, from The Monkees to The Doors; this would have been one of its first substantial appearances on a pop single—had it actually been released. Sadly, history repeated itself as, once again, another Mortimer record was stopped by . . . Allen Klein.

John Lennon, for one, was disgusted at the amount of money that was draining out of Apple. He was so upset that he began attending Apple meetings regularly, venting at those executives he felt were spending funds needlessly. Lennon had even complained to the press that, if Apple continued its profligate ways, "we'll be broke in six months." Klein, who had begun his career managing the business affairs of Bobby Darin and Sam Cooke and who eventually managed The Rolling Stones for a time, charmed his way into Lennon's confidence.

Peter, of course, knew of Klein through Betsy, who had worked for him in New York. "She told me a lot about him, and I didn't like most of it," he stated, adding: "She had a certain admiration for him—he wasn't a bad boss." But ultimately: "I didn't think he could be trusted . . . and neither did Paul."

McCartney, also realizing that something needed to be done to oversee Apple's management more strictly, wanted to bring in his new in-laws, the Eastmans—high-powered New York entertainment attorneys—but his bandmates thought that would possibly give McCartney too much power. So Harrison and Starr sided with Lennon, allowing Klein to step in and begin to manage how Apple's monies were spent.

One of Klein's first acts was to put a halt to Zapple Records. Two albums were released on that imprint the day Klein was appointed—one by John and Yoko, the other credited to George Harrison. The next scheduled release was to be the first of Miles's spoken-word recordings, *Listening to Richard Brautigan*, taped in San Francisco earlier in the year. "That one was mixed and even the preliminary designs for the sleeve were done," Miles remembered, but the record was unceremoniously terminated—as was the label. (The Brautigan album did come out a year later on EMI's Harvest imprint, garnering a glowing review in *Rolling Stone* magazine.)

Mortimer's album, also mixed and mastered, was next on the chopping block. "Anything that was recorded was put on hold," Tony Van Benschoten recalled. Mortimer continued to stick around for six months, hoping the record would eventually get put back on the release schedule—even jamming with McCartney at one point during a rehearsal at Apple. "Finally we were just told no," said Van Benschoten. "It wasn't gonna happen."

This disheartening episode brought an end to Mortimer. "We had been together for about ten years then," Van Benschoten recalled, "and I think we were just pretty well fed up with the whole business. The three of us didn't really see any future in what was going on, so we all decided to go our own ways." Though the band folded, Van Benschoten holds a fairly positive view of their time at Apple: "How lucky we were to actually get there," he said. "Yeah, it would have been nice to go further, and it would have been nice to get that album out, but we did it. And it's something we had dreamed about, you know? Not many people got a chance to play with The Beatles and also to get on Apple Records."

Forty-eight years after the record was shelved, Apple licensed the master to London's RPM Records—better late than never. On the cover of the disc, entitled *On Our Way Home*, the band sits in a rowboat on the small lake at Peter's Laudate estate. Peter's photo freezes them in time—they look hopeful, but they're not going anywhere.

It was Peter, though, who escaped. It had been just over a year since he had thrown in his lot with Apple—and the atmosphere had certainly changed. The naïveté of the lunatics running the asylum had begun to crash into the realities of what a multimillion-dollar corporation needed to survive. Klein felt he knew what was needed—to show who was boss. Projects were halted, divisions were shuttered, and people were fired—including the head of publishing, Michael O'Connor. "Allen Klein was very big in publishing and brought in all of his own people," O'Connor remembered, putting a halt to deals that were in process, including Apple administrating the songs of both Harry Nilsson and Randy Newman. It was as if Klein were cutting off his nose to spite his face.

Klein also fired Apple Records president Ron Kass, who wasted no time: "Kass went to New York and—this all happened FAST—he made a deal to become president of MGM," O'Connor recalled. "He came back and offered me the equivalent position with Robbins, Feist & Miller—which was their publishing company." Ken Mansfield, who, before running Apple Records in the States, was a Capitol Records promotions man, was asked by Kass to be vice president in charge of marketing and promotions. MGM Records was also going to need a new head of A&R, and Kass's first choice was Peter Asher. "I said, 'Great,'" Peter recalled, asking Kass: "'Will they pay for me and my belongings and cats to move to America? And wife? And everything?' And he said, 'Yes.'"

On announcing his resignation from Apple to the press, Peter said: "When I joined Apple, the idea was that it would be different from the other companies in the record business. Its policy was to help people and be generous. . . . It was a nice company to work for. Now all that's changed. There's a new concentrative policy from what I can see, and it's lost a great deal of its original feeling."

Peter and Betsy packed up their belongings and their two cats, Pudding and Sarah, and booked passage on the *QE2*, sailing from Southampton on July 12th to the city of New York. This great steamship, in operation for only one month, was one of the last of her kind. Mike Vickers and his wife saw them off for this new adventure, as they sailed to the States rather than flying due to Betsy's crippling fear—traced back to her publicity days at Klein's ABKCO organization. "Coming back from a Rolling Stones event," Betsy remembered, "we got caught in a fog bank, and I saw all these other red lights out there. Somehow I just got totally freaked by flying."

The trip lasted four and a half days. There was time to look in front of them, at what lay in store for their new life, and time to reflect on the hard times of the past year—the fracturing of both The Beatles and the dream of Apple, and the suicide of Dr. Asher. Hopefully, they were leaving all that death and chaos behind them.

"On the ship, we had the cats in the kennel," Betsy remembered, "and one of the people that we would run into in the kennel there was Sharon Tate, who was eight months' pregnant. And then we were in New York, and there was the headline about Charles Manson . . ."

11

THE ONES WHO REALLY CARE

The initial New York hotel Peter and Betsy booked would not allow cats, so they quickly made arrangements to move to an establishment that *would* give Pudding and Sarah sanctuary—The Hotel Chelsea.

An infamous residence for both the illustrious and the superfluous, this twelve-story redbrick structure on West 23rd Street was the tallest building in New York when it opened in 1884. As the city continued skyward, tenants such as Mark Twain, Lillie Langtry, Frida Khalo, and Leonard Cohen walked its grand staircase, and two classic novels, *On the Road* and *2001: A Space Odyssey*, were written within its walls. But when the Ashers arrived in June 1969, the Victorian Gothic landmark was going downhill.

Their suite was "decrepit," according to Betsy. "It was filthy and loaded with cockroaches." As she worked to turn their rooms into something more livable, Peter began his new A&R position at an American record label.

As he walked through the door of MGM's New York offices, the label was in trouble—losing millions of dollars due to poor chart success, expensive failed ad campaigns, and unrealistic sales projections. Their most successful acts at this point were British rockers Eric Burdon and The Animals, country singer Hank Williams Jr. (whose legendary father had also been on the label), and family popsters The Cowsills. Their subsidiary, Verve Records, was mainly known as a great jazz label, releasing classic albums by John Coltrane, Stan Getz, and Wes Montgomery, for example. But its roster also included Tim Hardin, The Mothers of Invention, and The Velvet Underground—all critically acclaimed or influential, but *not* big sellers. As Peter began to get his bearings at his new corporate home, he also turned his attention once again toward helping James Taylor.

Taylor had returned to his home country in the spring of 1969 toting a heroin addiction. "I was in rough shape when I came back," James admitted, "and I went into an institution for a while to try to clean up." While undergoing treatment in Stockbridge, Massachusetts, James finished a song he had begun just before leaving England. "Fire and Rain" began by addressing his grief upon learning of the suicide of a close friend. The news had been withheld from him by his old compatriots, who decided they should wait until *after* James had completed his Apple album before telling him, worried that the information might prove devastating. The second verse began as a plea for help in overcoming his addiction—an admission of needing assistance to leave his demons behind. He finished the final verse while a patient at the Stockbridge clinic, depressed over his current state and looking back over earlier disappointments, such as the demise of The Flying Machine—his band with boyhood pal Danny Kortchmar.

Taylor's innate genius manifested in his ability to take these subjects—suicide, addiction, depression—and weave them gently together with a sweet melody that masked the gloominess with a feeling that there was still something just out of reach to be hopeful about.

Part of James's hope—a large part—was the faith Peter had in him. Peter knew the handling of an emotionally sensitive artist like James would take a great deal of sensitivity itself. What manager could he trust to do the job? "We didn't know," Peter admitted. "So even though I was entirely ignorant of how to do it at the time, I said, 'Okay . . . I'm your manager.' And he said, 'Okay.' I think I knew a *lot* about how *not* to do it." No doubt—recalling bad contracts, chaotic tours, no itineraries, abysmal sound, and even missing money during his Peter and Gordon days.

Both Peter and James were making it up as they went along, which was not uncommon in that more innocent time. "Nowadays people have a lot more information about what it means to get started in a professional career in music," Taylor observed. "But at the time, it felt like living day to day with me . . . I really didn't look very far into the future."

After completing treatment, James stayed in a borrowed house in Martha's Vineyard with no telephone. If Peter needed to contact him about a gig, "he'd leave a message for me at the gas station," Taylor recalled. "I'd go there and call him back and he'd say, 'There's a job here or a college to play there,' and I'd take down the information and go.

"It was very sorta on a shoestring back in those days," Taylor admitted. "And people in the record business were really people who loved music, and it wasn't a sort of high-money, high-ticket thing to get into, or particularly glamorous. It was a left turn, still, to decide to do that.

"But in those days, things were pretty simple. You'd be a kid who pretended you could do something, and then it turned out you could."

To move beyond the "shoestring" phase and set up his management company correctly, Peter turned to Nat Weiss, the New York lawyer he'd met through Brian Epstein. Originally a divorce lawyer, Weiss had helped Epstein set up Nemperor Artists, a US management company that looked after The Beatles' interests in the States and handled new artists, such as the pop group The Cyrkle ("Red Rubber Ball").

Epstein introduced Peter to Weiss backstage at NBC Studios during the taping of *Hullaballoo*'s final episode in August 1966, which featured performances by both The Cyrkle and Peter and Gordon.

But Weiss was more to Epstein than just a business partner—he was a good friend. "Nat engineered Brian's revelatory experience that being gay wasn't the end of the world," Peter said. A closeted gay man in a sexually repressive society, Epstein had never been to a gay bar in his life. But at the beginning of their friendship, Weiss introduced Epstein to the gay club scene in Manhattan. The very idea that this part of his life actually could be fun "changed Brian's life," according to Peter. "It's one of the reasons Brian liked coming to New York so much—it was a different world."

Weiss was effusive in his praise of Peter: "He's extraordinary," Weiss simply stated. "He's consistently been one of the most perceptive and talented men in the business." Peter pronounced Weiss "brilliant. He helped me set up the management company and gave me some good advice in that regard."

Peter decided to book his client for a week of shows at The Troubadour, a small club but an important venue in Los Angeles with a good reputation for showcasing promising acts, especially in the world of folk music. James made his official solo debut there on July 7, 1969. One person who happened to catch a set that week was

Nat Weiss observes Peter playing poker. *Photo by Leland Sklar.*

a teenaged Karla Bonoff, who would later pen a handful of songs that Peter would produce for Linda Ronstadt. She was simply dumbstruck at how good Taylor was.

The week following James's Troubadour gigs, Peter booked him to appear at the Newport Folk Festival. The festival has occurred yearly since 1959 and is still one of America's premier musical events. On Saturday, the 19th of July, Taylor took part in a songwriter's workshop, which is where he met Joni Mitchell (with whom he would become romantically involved one year later). James performed a solo set before a rapt audience on the last afternoon, Sunday, the 20th. That evening, James was introduced to Joe Smith, president of Warner Brothers Records.

Smith had first taken notice of Taylor when the gatefold cover of his Apple debut took up an entire billboard high above Sunset Boulevard in West Hollywood. "It covered, like, two blocks! So I had heard about him and was interested," Smith confessed. Now, months later, Smith and others from the Warner Brothers label ran into Taylor at one of the many nighttime parties taking place in mansions all around Newport.

"The Everly Brothers were in my group," Smith recalled. The harmony duo, who had so influenced Peter and Gordon, as well as countless other acts, enthused that James's track "Carolina in My Mind" was one of their favorite songs. In fact, the brothers had recorded their own version of the song just days earlier for their next Warner Brothers single. Smith asked Taylor, "How can we get in touch with you?" James replied, "Peter Asher is my manager." At breakfast the next morning, Smith asked Peter about James's contractual obligations. Admitting that James was still signed to Apple Records, Peter noted that this could very well be a sticky problem.

James was dissatisfied—just as Peter had been—with the new atmosphere at Apple, and his initial meeting with Allen Klein was not promising: "He had one sitdown meeting with him," Peter said, "and was not impressed." Now that Peter had an overture from what was fast becoming one of the best record labels in the world, he needed to formulate a strategy to free James from his Apple contract.

To that end, Peter again received help from Nat Weiss. Having been a confidante to The Beatles for years, Weiss went to George Harrison and personally pleaded James's case. Weiss remembered George's reaction: "I'll never forget it—he said, 'I don't want to be a twit or a twat.' That was a way of George's." Weiss chuckled, defining, as Harrison saw it, the conflict twixt "twat" and "twit": "I don't want to stand in the way of an artist. On the other hand, I don't want to be a jerk and let an artist go."

"We knew we wanted to be on Warner Brothers," Peter stated, "because of the ads." Both Peter and James were very impressed at the advertisements for both Warner and Reprise artists that were cropping up in the alternative press. Stan Cornyn, head of Creative Services for both labels, was the author behind this irreverent groundbreaking salesmanship.

Beginning with Warner Brothers signing The Grateful Dead in 1967, Cornyn knew that the marketing hype usually employed in ads was simply not going to work for a music consumer mistrustful of "the establishment." Cornyn, in his early thirties, was left alone by his bosses to break any marketing rule he wanted. With his quirky sense of humor, his first ad for the Dead announced the "Pigpen Lookalike Contest," referencing the hirsute keyboardist of the group. Cornyn dictated the same simple look for each Warner/Reprise ad (inspired by Volkswagen's print ads of the day)—black letters on a white background, a catchy bold headline at the top and a small photo near the center of the page. In other words, stripped of all hype.

As people became seduced by the writing, which was playful and corporately self-effacing, they found themselves wanting to explore the music of the artist being discussed. And what artists they were: Neil Young, Joni Mitchell, Randy Newman, Van Dyke Parks, Ry Cooder—all total unknowns to most record buyers of that era. Intrigued by these ads that, while not taking themselves seriously, obviously took good music *very* seriously, many consumers took a chance and promptly fell in love with these singular singers, songwriters, and performers. Peter and James adored the ads, marveled at the roster, and felt this was the place to be.

But at the moment, Apple was still James's label, and it was Apple that picked up the tab for James's next session—an early try at "Fire and Rain." Old friend Danny Kortchmar booked the musicians, including a trio of women to contribute background vocals on the song's chorus. That was probably misguided, Peter now admitted: "I tried to R&B it up a bit too much." Both he and James were ultimately not happy with the results, and the tapes were shipped on to London, where they still sit in Apple's vaults.

What momentum James was beginning to build through solo appearances on the college circuit, though, came to a halt quite suddenly: "He was drunk, riding a motorbike through a forest," Peter recalled, "and drove into a tree." James broke both hands and both feet in the accident. "And when I visited him sometime later, he showed me the tree," Peter said, describing a huge chunk missing where James's fist and handlebar smashed into the unfortunate trunk. "You have to punch a tree pretty hard to knock a piece out of it! *Not* good for your bones.

"He was worried if his guitar playing would ever return," Peter confided. It did, of course, though his playing had subtly changed: "To be honest, I believe he had more full-on classical fluidity before," Peter stated, adding confidently: "He plays brilliantly and totally worked around it." As his manager, Peter had to cancel some important bookings, unfortunately, as Taylor rested and healed for more than a month, halting momentum. "It was a big deal."

Early one summer evening, Peter and Betsy strolled into the Chelsea lobby and were spotted by a thin young man who quickly recognized the bespectacled gentleman with the flaming red hair. "I just went up to him and said, 'Hi, I'm Chris Darrow. I'm working with Linda Ronstadt down at The Bitter End. You wanna come down and see us play?'"

Darrow, a singer and multi-instrumentalist, had first been a member of the Southern California band The Kaleidoscope—an eclectic group mixing rock, folk, and influences from around the world. Leaving after two albums, he next played fiddle in The Nitty Gritty Dirt Band for a year. Taking along the Dirt Band's Jeff Hanna, Darrow then formed The Corvettes—a solid four-piece country-rock band that caught the ear of Mike Nesmith, who produced a couple of singles for Dot Records that went nowhere.

Nesmith, besides being one of The Monkees, had written "Different Drum"—the first hit for The Stone Poneys featuring singer Linda Ronstadt. Now that Ronstadt was beginning to forge a solo career, she needed a tight band to back her, and The Corvettes fit the bill. "That band," Darrow declared, "was the band that really set her country-rock *tonality* and sort of created her country-rock sound."

Peter and Betsy, accompanied by Michael O'Connor, caught Ronstadt and The Corvettes that evening in Greenwich Village and went backstage afterward, which is where Peter met Linda for the first time. Ronstadt was still signed to Capitol Records at this point, but The Corvettes were available. Impressed by the band (which then included future Eagle Bernie Leadon), he expressed an interest in signing The Corvettes to MGM. "They were good," Peter declared. "I was just discovering all this country-rock-flavored stuff. And Chris," he added, "was *very* good."

While in New York, Linda received a call from her manager, Herb Cohen, offering her and The Corvettes a spot on the bill for an outdoor festival. Darrow remembered Linda and the band mulling it over but ultimately deciding it seemed like too much of a hassle, so Linda called Cohen back to tell him this Woodstock thing would have to go on without them.

But Betsy Asher had known singer/songwriter Arlo Guthrie for years, and he extended an invitation for the Ashers to accompany him to the festival, now moved from Woodstock to the town of Bethel, New York. "Arlo had special-ordered a black Checker cab," Betsy laughingly recalled, adding: "It had no suspension in it!" The cab picked the Ashers up at the Chelsea, where old friends Barry and Sue Miles were staying for a few weeks. Betsy left instructions for Sue to feed Pudding and Sarah while they were away but neglected to leave her key. "She eventually talked the key out of the front desk," Betsy said. Later, Sue confided to Betsy her Plan B: "I was thinking about sliding anchovies under the door!"

Despite the traffic nightmare of half a million Aquarians descending on upstate New York, the Checker cab bounced its way to the organizers' hotel, not far from Max Yasger's dairy farm, where the festival was taking place. There was such chaos getting musicians to the site that the first guitar wasn't strummed that initial day until 5 p.m., as Richie Havens was pushed to the mic and told to play *anything*.

Eventually, Peter and Betsy made their way to the side of the stage, where they decided to stay put, the hillsides now a dizzying mass of youth. "I remember looking out into the crowd," Peter said. "It was just mud and madness." From this somewhat safe vantage point, they watched the first evening's performances, including Ravi Shankar, Tim Hardin, and Melanie, with Arlo Guthrie not starting his set until almost midnight.

In the wee hours of the next morning, the exhausted group made their way back to the organizers' headquarters. Peter said, "I *do* remember walking along the corridor and stepping over somebody who was asleep." Looking down, he recognized Janis Joplin. "Like a caricature of herself," added Betsy, "with a bottle of Southern Comfort." It was as close as Peter would ever come to meeting her.

Back at MGM, Peter and his Apple cohorts dove into their jobs—getting the feel of an American record label circa 1969 and impressing coworkers with their approach. "They were just such nice, thoughtful people," Randy Nauert remembered. "Considerate and polite. *Honest*, you know?"

One of rock'n'roll's great forgotten soldiers, Nauert started out a Southern California kid who not only loved surfing but also was a natural musician. He bought himself a bass guitar and, in 1962, joined his buds in the newly formed band, The Challengers—one of the most popular of the original surf music combos. They recorded for various companies under different names, releasing dozens of albums over the next few years, including their biggest seller, *Wipe Out*, for Dot Records in 1963, masquerading as The Surfaris.

A friend at World Pacific Records turned Nauert onto the music of Ravi Shankar. Upon meeting the sitar master, he was invited to India, where, in 1966, he studied alongside George Harrison. As Nauert worked his way around the world, The Challengers disbanded. Drummer Richard Delvy (who, realizing early on the value of song copyrights, retained the publishing rights to "Wipe Out") got a job with MGM's music publishing arm, Robbins, Feist & Miller—known in the industry as "The Big Three." Upon Nauert's return to LA, Delvy offered him a position: contemporary A&R for the publishing wing.

MGM's offices were at 55th Street and 6th Avenue in Manhattan. Ron Kass, as the new head of the label, had a corner office with a framed Picasso and top-of-the-line Empire turntable and speakers. Nauert, Michael O'Connor, and Peter would use Kass's luxurious office for any major meetings they would have. Used to the swagger and hustling of industry types epitomized by Allen Klein, Nauert marveled at the different style utilized by Peter and his Apple crew: "They never really came and dominated you. They didn't really mess with what was going on; they just brought . . ." Nauert searches for the right word: "their *presence*."

Peter, as head of A&R, began meeting with various artists signed to both the MGM and Verve labels—"to find out what we were gonna do with them and who we should keep." One of these artists was Domingo Samudio, also known as Sam the Sham. They had last met sharing the bill at Atlantic City in 1965. Now Peter was in a position to cancel Sam's contract, which he didn't. "Always mellow," Samudio said of Peter, admiringly, "always cool." Peter also had a somewhat disastrous meeting with Lou Reed, the leader of New York's influential art-punk band The Velvet Underground. Peter recalled, "We tried to go to some local French restaurant, and they wouldn't let us in because we were in jeans."

Peter realized too late that he might be intimately knowledgeable on London's music scene but not quite as hip when it came to the Big Apple. "I liked him," Peter said, "but I hadn't done enough research 'cause I didn't realize quite what The Velvet

Underground were in New York as opposed to London—they were *such* a big deal. I think he may have kind of thought, 'I don't think this guy really knows who we are.' I *did!* But," he admitted, "I didn't, really.

"And I *did* go to a gig. I thought they were awful, but"—he laughed—"that's not necessarily considered relevant to the relationship."

Among the guests at The Hotel Chelsea that summer was Barry Miles. Miles was working with poet Allen Ginsberg on a recording of William Blake's *Songs of Innocence and Experience*. Still believing in the spoken-word projects Miles was doing, plus hoping to add a bit of intellectual hipness to his new company's roster, Peter arranged to have MGM/Verve release this new Miles production. The album, which featured Ginsberg performing Blake's poems with musical support from jazz greats Don Cherry and Elvin Jones, garnered high praise in both *Rolling Stone* and the *New Yorker* when released the following year.

Also, hoping to free his last record production from limbo, Peter tried to convince Apple to allow MGM to license and release the Mortimer album, but his old label turned him down.

A young singer and songwriter named Barbara Keith was another artist on Verve's roster. At Peter's initial meeting with her, Keith asked if anything could be done regarding the royalty rate she was getting. "My strongest memory is the look on his face as he read the contract I had signed without consulting anyone," Keith said. "He murmured, 'I'm going to have to get them to fix this' . . . and he promptly did." Not much had changed in the business since Peter had signed his own substandard contract with EMI back in 1963. "Peter got the points up a bit," Keith recalled admiringly.

"I started playing guitar in the fourth grade," said Keith, "inspired by my teacher—a female country musician with a Telecaster." Her father would read Sherlock Holmes stories aloud to her and, she recalled, "I drank in the cadence of words." Attending Vassar when it was still purely a women's college, she began writing songs and playing local clubs. Eventually she dropped out and headed to New York, becoming a regular at the Café Wha?—one of the city's folk music showcases. She would sometimes share the bill with a band called Kangaroo, which included guitarist John Hall (later of the hit seventies band Orleans). Keith decided to throw her lot in with them, and Kangaroo soon landed a record deal with MGM, courtesy of Tom Wilson, producer of Dylan's "Like a Rolling Stone" and Simon and Garfunkel's "The Sound of Silence."

The promising band went on the road, opening for The Who and The Doors, but the album went nowhere, and the band broke up. MGM wisely thought Keith had potential and signed her as a solo artist. Peter, as the new head of A&R, was also taken by her songs and her personality. She, in turn, was impressed with him: "I am only too glad to remember how kind [he was], and in the midst of the craziness of that era, the brotherly quality of Peter toward the 'Holly GoStupidly' girl who had no idea what she was doing." Keith explained: "He took me under his wing—to the theater, to other artists' performances." Most importantly, he decided to personally helm the sessions for her first solo album.

Peter booked A&R Studios (owned by the legendary producer/engineer Phil Ramone) for the second week of October. But as an Englishman new to the rituals of the United States, he was oblivious to the fact that this coincided with baseball's World Series. And these particular games would soon become legendary, with the perennial underdog New Yorkers finally able to celebrate their own "Miracle Mets." Bassist Joe Colegrove remembered complaining loudly, "Ah, gee, we're gonna miss the game!" Reminded of this, Peter laughed and remarked, "Even now, as a full-fledged American who understands about the World Series, I still wouldn't give a shit."

Ultimately, though, Colegrove was happy as the sessions went very fast. Peter had learned his lesson with Taylor's Apple album—not to "overproduce," but to get the right feel among the musicians and then let the tapes roll. It was almost a test run for the production style he would make his name with throughout the seventies, especially the first few Linda Ronstadt albums he oversaw. As with those records, here he had a group of musicians who understood the marriage of country and rock. Keith had hand-picked her players, and Colegrove, steel player Bill Keith, drummer N.D. Smart, and keyboardist Jeffrey Gutcheon all went on to do solid work in that genre—Smart with Gram Parsons and all four with the legendary Great Speckled Bird, led by Ian and Sylvia Tyson.

Barbara Keith was a strong, soulful vocalist whose vibrato style rivaled Buffy St. Marie. She could also write solid material; artists from Delaney and Bonnie to Barbra Streisand would later cover her songs. One standout from this Asher-produced effort was "The Ones Who Really Care," whose chorus spoke of wolves that would "*strip you bare.*" She could have easily been referring to a music industry full of wolves ready to chew up naïve artists like Keith herself. Luckily, a regime was now in place at MGM that really cared about the artist. "All of a sudden," Randy Nauert remembered, "you had thoughtful, uncorrupt, polite, nice people that had *stuff to say,* that dealt with *quality!*" Nauert shook his head at how unbelievable it all seemed. "It was like, all of a sudden, MGM's gonna be this wonderful thing, 'cause we have wonderful people with good taste that everybody respects."

But before Peter had signed a single new artist, businessman Kirk Kerkorian purchased a forty percent share of MGM Studios in October. "Everybody in the building was abuzz," Peter recalled, unsure of what it might mean. He was also slowly becoming aware that there was a strange underside to the corporate culture into which he had stepped: "People were telling me, 'Oh, by the way, you realize this whole building is completely corrupt—everyone's on the take' . . . which they were."

Label president Ron Kass would pass on to Peter the information he gradually was uncovering: "There were people taking kickbacks," Peter recalled, "and people selling records out of the trunk of their car, and you'd just hear all this amazing stuff." At MGM, padding an expense account was mere chickenfeed. Now, with the uncertainty of Kerkorian's takeover added to the mix, according to Peter, "Everyone thought: The ship's sinking, so let's steal the cutlery from the *Titanic*."

In another October surprise, music producer and entrepreneur Mike Curb recalled being asked by his good friend (and former CBS Television president) James Aubrey to meet him for dinner. Aubrey ordered wine and said, according to Curb: "I got a question for you: Would you be willing to have your company become MGM Records, and we'll merge our assets into your company?" Curb laughed at the memory. "I said, '*What?*'"

Curb was now appointed president of the new MGM Records Corp., to be based in Culver City, California, and the housecleaning quickly began. Said Curb: "There was a huge issue over printing schlock records that they would sell to Morris Levy." Levy was a tough, legendary figure in the record business, and besides playing fast and loose with royalties, Levy was making a fortune dealing in pirated and deleted records. Curb described the practice as "a whole industry-wide thing, and MGM was in the middle of it. And their legal department decided to close down MGM Records." The folks currently on staff in New York, including Peter, were handed their pink slips.

"When I first joined," Curb said, "I wasn't even allowed to talk to anyone who had been previously at MGM because of all the issues going on," though Curb admitted that "there is no indication whatsoever that Ron Kass or anybody like that was involved" in any of the illegal activities that permeated the company. Curb didn't even know that Peter, whom he had been so impressed with at that Jerry Naylor session he produced at Capitol back in 1964, had been running MGM's A&R department. "I'm embarrassed that I didn't know," he told me, adding that Peter would have been "spectacular" in the job and "good for our image."

MGM Records Corp. ended up being sold to PolyGram three years later, as corporate mergers began gobbling up most major record labels. Mike Curb went on to become not only an amazingly successful music mogul and philanthropist, but he was also lieutenant governor of California for a time.

"I actually ran into Mike Curb some years later," Peter recalled, "and said, 'Oh! It's really funny; I've never really met you properly but, you know, you fired me years ago!' And I told him the story, but he didn't quite get it—he kept saying, 'Oh, I'm really sorry! That was nothing to do with me!'" Peter, laughing, continued: "I went, 'No, it's okay! I'm not here to complain! . . . It was the right thing to do. You fired everybody—that was correct. I was already over here, that was what I wanted.'"

Peter now had both feet planted in the "Promised Land." With only James's career on his plate, Peter and Betsy packed up, left Manhattan behind, and headed out to the town that was establishing itself as the new music capital of the country, if not the world. Los Angeles.

12

SWEET BABY JAMES

The Ashers left New York with its mid-forty-degree temperatures and arrived in Los Angeles as the heat soared into the eighties. Unfortunately, the paranoia was also soaring. "There was such a strange vibe in town," Betsy remembered, and no wonder—the city was gripped by fear in the aftermath of the Tate-LaBianca murders, committed by Charles Manson and his followers earlier that summer. Consequently, it didn't seem as welcoming to Peter and Betsy as they had hoped.

One who did welcome them as they adjusted to their new surroundings was Neil Portman, a former agent at the William Morris Agency. WMA had established an informal relationship with Apple Records early on, signing James Taylor for individual representation. Portman, as Taylor's agent, helped to secure both his week at The Troubadour and his gig at Newport. Young and hip (signing not just musical acts like Creedence Clearwater Revival, but also surreal humorists The Firesign Theatre), Portman had invited Taylor to stay in one of his guestrooms as he continued to heal from his motorcycle injuries.

Portman's house was an A-frame structure up the hill from Sunset Boulevard's infamous Continental Hyatt House (or, as it became known in LA music lore, the "Riot House"), with a pool and an incredible view of the laid-back metropolis. As he had with James, Portman also opened his doors to Peter and Betsy while they got their bearings in the City of Angels.

One morning, Peter walked down to the Hyatt for a breakfast meeting with Joe Smith, president of Warner Brothers Records. Smith had recognized what a singular talent James was after hearing him perform at Newport. Over eggs, the two men finalized a deal for James Taylor to join the Warner label. There was no bidding war; the songwriter and his manager knew what they wanted. "We had the kind of company—'on the move'—that James and Peter were comfortable with," Smith recalled. "It was Mo Ostin and myself dealing with the artists personally." Ostin ran Warner's sister imprint, Reprise, and the pair, known in the business as Warner/Reprise, were the hottest, hippest labels in Los Angeles. "Not *trying* to be hip," Smith pointed out, which other labels obviously were.

Peter was upfront with Smith about the nebulous legal circumstances James was in with Apple. "We just left," Peter explained, without a torn-up contract or blessing from any of the board of directors. In case Allen Klein decided to sue, Peter wisely made sure any Warner Brothers contract would include a clause indemnifying him and James—"which they would *never* do now," Peter flatly stated, but in the cool, artist-friendly tenor of the times, it was agreed to easily. "I had visions of James and I starting to actually be successful and make money and Apple immediately taking all of it." The money Smith offered this morning was $20,000 in advance and $20,000 on delivery of a finished album. Another sip of coffee, a handshake, and it was done.

Eventually, Betsy found, for $450 per month, a two-story house for her and Peter to rent at 956 S. Longwood in the Brookside neighborhood of Los Angeles, about a mile southeast of the La Brea Tar Pits. Built in the 1920s, it was cozy—a wood-beamed ceiling in the living room, French doors that opened to a small pool out back, and above the garage, a tiny guesthouse—perfect for the new LA offices of Peter Asher Management.

The neighbors on this quiet, upper-middle-class street thought that hippies had moved in down the block—young people so poor they couldn't even afford furniture. Currency controls were in place in 1969, and most of the Ashers' money back in the UK was unavailable to them. "We didn't have much money," Betsy remembered. "We didn't have any credit rating. And so we wound up renting a TV from someplace down on Pico Boulevard"—she laughed—"and every time we turned it on, cockroaches crawled out of it."

The mostly empty living room, though, seemed perfect for Taylor to rehearse the songs that would soon make up his second album—his first for Warners. As producer, Peter needed to book studio time and find solid musicians to back James. But, being new to Los Angeles, Peter was completely unfamiliar with the players in the area and had only recorded in one LA studio before. "I came here knowing nothing," Peter admitted, "and I was asking advice of anyone whose opinion I would respect."

One of those was multi-instrumentalist Chris Darrow. Darrow first met Peter when his group The Corvettes backed Linda Ronstadt in New York, and came *this close* to being signed to MGM Records himself before Peter's abrupt exit from that label. He was a Southern California native who had played in various venues and studios around LA with multiple musicians for years.

Peter asked Darrow what he might suggest regarding both a solid studio and sympathetic players. According to Darrow, "I said, 'Well, if I were you, I'd record at Sunset Sound, and I'd use Bill Lazerus—my favorite engineer, great studio, always puts good stuff out.'" To handle the bass playing, Peter thought of Darrow's former Corvettes bandmate, John London. Though agreeing that London was a fine choice, Darrow said, "If you want to do more rock'n'roll-y kind of stuff, I would use Randy Meisner." Back when Darrow was a member of the eccentric and celebrated band

The Kaleidoscope, they occasionally shared stages with a Colorado band called The Poor, which included Meisner. "They were a *great* band," Darrow recalled, "and I always loved his bass playing."

Darrow was now backing folk singer John Stewart, formerly of The Kingston Trio, on both guitar and fiddle, and he invited Peter down to one of Stewart's rehearsals, leading to a lovely bit of musical happenstance.

"My brother was a drummer, and I grew up in a house where his band was re-hearsing," Russ Kunkel said, recalling his first time experiencing his brother's set: "He sat me on his knee behind the snare drum and showed me what to do with my hands." The drums were always set up, and the younger Kunkel got more and more interested: "As I got a bit older, I just kind of took it up myself." Many bands later, he found himself drumming behind folk singer John Stewart.

"I was the first artist he'd played with outside of his rock'n'roll bands," Stewart remembered, calling Kunkel "just a *dream* to work with." Kunkel, sensitive to the introspective nature of Stewart's songs, was a master of the quiet groove and inven-tive with the placement of his fills.

"The standard LA archetype was Hal Blaine," Peter explained, naming the legend-ary session drummer whose powerful beats launched a thousand hit records—from Phil Spector's "Wall of Sound" productions to "Up, Up and Away" and "MacArthur Park." Peter described the style as "complicated, impressive, virtuoso drum fills." Kunkel's style was more simplified, yet with tasty touches, and observing Kunkel be-hind Stewart, Peter was impressed: "Here was somebody who'd been listening more to Ringo Starr than Hal Blaine," Peter observed. "I loved the groove . . . I remember within a few songs going, 'This is my guy.'"

James in Peter's living room. *Photo by Henry Diltz.*

Peter called Kunkel the next day, and by week's end, rehearsals with James got underway in the Longwood living room—still empty, save for a stereo (of course), a few rented chairs, and a piano. "I brought my drums in there," Kunkel recalled of his first rehearsal, "and James was sitting on a chair playing guitar, and Carole was playing piano"—Carole being Carole King, unknown to the general public at this point, but a legendary songwriter revered by musicians everywhere.

For Peter, spying the songwriting credit "Goffin/King" on hit records in the early sixties, King was "purely a name—we knew nothing about her; didn't even know it was a *her*." Eventually a hit-maker himself, Peter became aware of King's own high-quality songwriting demos, which her publisher, Screen Gems, would send to prospective artists. "That's when I realized," said Peter, "what a good pianist and singer she was." James's old friend Danny Kortchmar, also taking part in the living room rehearsals, had recently befriended King while both were members of a short-lived group called The City. Danny, agreeing with Peter that her soulful feel on keyboards would be perfect behind James, arranged for King to provide her piano skills to the proceedings. According to Carole, it was immediately clear upon meeting Peter that "he believed in James and had a passion for his work.

"Peter is a very generous and cooperative person," King said, "in terms of trying to make everything work the way it should to the benefit of the *artist* and the *work*." Peter knew what needed to be done here, and it wasn't being too clever with the arrangements and accompaniment, as with the Apple sessions.

"Peter," said Kortchmar, "being the quick learner that he is, figured out for the second record, get everything out of the way and just make sure that you hear nothing but James, James, James. And he was right.

"At the time, I thought, 'Well, this is . . . not really exciting; it doesn't have any "rock" in it. Gee, I hope people get it,'" Kortchmar recalled. "But Peter, he believed in James enough to say, 'It doesn't need all this stuff; it just needs to make sure that you *get* who this guy is.' And so *that* is a major lesson, certainly, about record production, and that's the essence of Peter."

During the living room rehearsals, "there was nothing being amplified," Kunkel remembered. "We were just running through the songs, so I couldn't very well start playing loud drums." Using soft brushes instead of hard wooden sticks, Kunkel got quiet enough to hear his fellow musicians: "When you're playing with instruments that are soft, you're really forced to listen to what's going on around you. And when you listen, I think you play better"—which may sound obvious, but many musicians still overlook this simple fact. Nevertheless, much of Kunkel's sensitive brushwork became part of the final arrangement for a handful of the songs, fitting the material perfectly.

And what material . . . "Sweet Baby James," written as a lullaby for Taylor's months-old nephew, gently evokes both the lonesome cowpoke and the weary traveler, its waltz-time rhythm rocking all Aquarian children toward magical dreams. "Country Road" is also about a traveler, a bit broken but almost joyful on the journey. "Sunny Skies" is a happy, jazzy shuffle; upon hearing it, you can't help but smile, though the song is infused with solitude and doubt. All the new material, even the pretty love song "Blossom," is permeated with loneliness and sadness, yet is so sweetly melodic that the listener both aches and blissfully hums along.

And there was another go at "Fire and Rain." The first attempt a year earlier was deemed unsuccessful, but now, stripped down to bare essentials, its deep yearning was perfectly supported by the four empathetic players gathered in Peter's living room.

One participant has fond memories of those late fall days on Longwood: "I remember going over there in my little Austin-Healey Sprite," Randy Meisner recalled, and instead of lugging over his usual stage setup, "I brought a tiny Champ Fender amp—they got a kick outta that." The five-watt amp might have made his fellow musicians chuckle, but its low output was perfect for the low-key living room atmosphere.

The rehearsals would take up the afternoons. In the evening, Peter and the musicians would drive over to Sunset Sound (thanks to Chris Darrow's suggestion) and put to tape what they had spent the day perfecting. Bassist Meisner, though, did not have much experience with studio recording at this point, and his enthusiasm sometimes got the better of him: "I might have rushed the beat a little bit 'cause I was excited." He laughed. "I'd start playing a little ahead of the beat, and he [Taylor] would just look over and smile at me like, 'Come on, now!'"

Engineer Bill Lazerus worked his sonic magic, micing Taylor so intimately he sounded as if he was in the listener's own living room, the space between his lips and their ears mere inches, enhancing the confessional nature of James's performances. And, being a drummer, Lazerus made sure Peter got the most out of Kunkel's kit. On "Fire and Rain," Peter wanted the soft brushes Kunkel wielded on the toms to sound "as big as possible." Lazerus cleverly employed Neumann U47 and U67 condenser mics—placing them close, but, cautioned Peter, "positioned where they could not accidentally be hit!"

"I still get asked about those drum fills," Peter proclaimed, "more than any other detail in my entire body of work!" But how the music is played is always first—the engineering second: "The way Russ tuned and played the drums," Peter emphasized, "was at least as important—likely more so—as the way we recorded them."

Peter credits Taylor, a former cellist, with the effective idea of adding a low, cello-sounding ache to "Fire and Rain," achieved by bringing in an upright bass player. Engineer Lazerus suggested musician Bobby West for the job, and the following day, Peter clearly remembered a handsome black man strolling into the studio with the words *Bobby "Wild Wild" West* emblazoned on his instrument case. Laughing, Peter recalled thinking, "Clearly we've booked the right cat!"

Peter said West was "ridiculously cool and played great." Taking a bow to his instrument, West added a poignant bassline through the track, finally sitting on the same root note for the entire last verse—an ominous drone that underpinned Taylor's dashed hopes. West then doubled his part, "because," said Peter, "it gave it that slightly phasey, grindy effect that I thought would be cool."

Peter's old friend from Apple, Michael O'Connor, attended the sessions that day and remembered Peter coming up with that sonic touch, adding: "Peter was just very gifted, in terms of those kinds of ideas."

"Peter had great taste, and he's very smart," Kortchmar said, noting that it wasn't supposed to be a one-way street: "He'd always say, 'Well, any ideas? Anyone got any?' And he'd expect you to have 'em!

"We were well-paid as session musicians," Kortchmar continued. "So we were supposed to come to the table with some shit, not just stand around and read the newspaper. A lot of session guys—who were burned out, especially—'phoned it in.' We were supposed to come bright-eyed and bushy-tailed with a whole bunch of ideas and moves and grooves.

"You were hired, basically," Kortchmar stated, "to learn the song, and then come up with a really good part that did *not* get in James's way but *helps* the song rather than hurts it."

Decide on the best material, assemble perceptive musicians, lock down the right feel, and then cut the song live—this was the basic method Peter used for the next decade and beyond, always doing his best to serve the artist's vision.

And it's a method that, in the twenty-first century, has mostly disappeared from pop music production.

"Back then," Kortchmar recalled, "we had something called 'the ensemble.' Now, this is something that doesn't even *exist* anymore; we might as well be talking about Dixieland or ragtime—the idea of six or seven guys getting in the studio and making a pop record *with* the singer *and* a song? I mean, WHAT?" Kortchmar then proceeded to mockingly explain the modern method: "First, you get loops, and then you get drum machines, then you get programming and sequencing. Then the record company president comes down and says, 'I don't think it's a hit. Yeah, let's bring somebody else in.' Then you hire another eight programmers and fifteen different producers, and everybody's *very serious* and you take *months* on one song.

"That's the way pop music is made now—it's all done by a guy sitting behind computers, correcting and fixing every line. The culture of ensemble record making, where you get a band together and make a record, is over. But that is, basically, the essence of what Peter brought to the situation: assembling a cast."

"A producer in recording is more like a director in film or television," James Taylor mused, "or maybe a certain kind of editor in journalism. And it really is a matter of who the person is. Depending on what the artist on the other side of the glass needs, there are some who are just doing organizational stuff. There are some producers, like Arif Mardin, that are really writing charts"—meaning arranging and writing out musical notation for, say, horn and string players. "And then," according to Taylor, "if you're producing Lowell George, your main job is to sort of hold his hand and make sure he gets to the studio alive!" George, the fun-loving singer/writer/guitarist for the seventies band Little Feat, did eventually let his lifestyle get the best of him.

"So it's a very varied experience," Taylor continued, having decades now to observe how record producers approach their job. "I depended on Peter largely as a sounding board and, as the first person to hear these songs, initially he would be very encouraging—that's what's called for, in my case, 'cause I can kind of stall out on this stuff and lose faith in it."

The encouragement James got from his producer was not simply strategic, it was genuine; Peter had *tremendous* faith in the material they were cutting at Sunset Sound. And all the preproduction time in rehearsals paid off—after only two weeks of recording, the album was nearing completion. Peter and James drove up to the offices of Warner Brothers Records in Burbank and proudly played Joe Smith the songs on which they'd worked so hard.

"They played the album for me," Smith recalled, "and I said, 'Gee, that's not enough music.'" The ten recorded tracks clocked in at just over twenty-five minutes. The problem: James was fresh out of polished, finished songs. Peter remembered asking him about a few works-in-progress that sounded promising, but James pessimistically told Peter, "These fragments don't seem to be getting any bigger . . ."

This hadn't hampered The Beatles, though—as their latest album, *Abbey Road* (released only three months earlier), ended with a suite of half-completed tunes strung together expertly by the band (with producer George Martin's considerable help, of course). Perhaps unconsciously influenced by their former bosses, Peter and James took the bits and pieces and fashioned together a final five-minute flourish to close the album. And, unsure what to call it, James decided on being upfront about the reason for its existence; as this would get them the final twenty grand they were after, the track carried the title "Suite for 20G."

As the album was being prepared for release, Peter turned his attention to another Taylor—James's younger sister, Kate. Peter had first met Kate when, at the age of eighteen, she came to London in the summer of 1968 to visit James as the Apple album was in process. "I went to tea at Betsy and Peter's house in the country," Kate remembered, where, at one point, she and James wandered into the empty swimming pool to take advantage of the good acoustics, playing guitars and singing, enjoying the sunny afternoon. "I had no idea I was auditioning! It was just me being me." The

Kate Taylor with brother James.
Photo by Peter Asher.

youthful girl, exuberant and possessing a voice well beyond her years, would burst into song whenever the spirit moved her, and said: "I'm the same way now!"

Her host smiled at the soulful singing coming from the youngest Taylor. Though pleased she had seemingly impressed Peter, she thought nothing more about it as she returned to Martha's Vineyard. As 1969 ended, Kate remembered suddenly receiving a call from Peter "asking if I wanted to make a record." More than a bit surprised, she took a day or so to think it over, but eventually called him back: "I said, 'Sure—let me at it!'"

The sessions began in February 1970 over at Sunset Sound. Kate said, "I always felt secure that he knew what he was doing and was taking care of business." This time it was Kate's turn to be impressed as she observed Peter: "He would take the music in—and *think* about it—and he would know *exactly* what he wanted to hear."

Peter's "ensemble" of players was beginning to gel. Danny Kortchmar was back on guitar; Russ Kunkel was again on drums, with Carole King on piano, and, of course, James. On electric bass, though, was a new face—Lee Sklar. "Peter's abilities as a musician are good," Sklar said. "His abilities as a collector of talent are great.

"My big influence"—Sklar laughed—"was Liberace." Captivated by Liberace's lush TV show, a hit in the early fifties, young Leland threw himself into serious music study, winning awards within a few years. In high school, his music teacher needed someone to play a large upright double bass and asked Lee if he was game. "I said, 'What's that?' I really wasn't familiar with it," Sklar recalled. "And as soon as I put it in my hands and hit that first note and felt the vibration, I went, '*This* is cool!'"

Lee began playing in various bands, mostly jazz combos, but the acoustic instrument left him always struggling to be heard. Then his dad bought him an electric bass and amp and, enthused Sklar, "It opened a whole world to me."

In the late sixties, Sklar was a member of a hard-rock band called Wolfgang. The group's drummer was friendly with recording studio owner John Fischbach, who would occasionally drop by at rehearsals. Fischbach brought a curious James Taylor with him one day. Wolfgang was looking for a new lead vocalist, and James tried a few numbers with the band. "*Totally* the wrong call," Sklar said emphatically, "but we hit it off great."

James phoned Peter immediately: "I absolutely remember with clarity him calling me up," recalled Peter, "saying, 'I've found a bass player who's as good as Paul McCartney.'" As Kate's sessions continued, Sklar got the call to come and play. As Sklar's bass began to pulse around Kunkel's beats on the funky "Look at Granny Run, Run," Peter knew a good thing when he heard it.

The sessions with Kate, though, came to a halt as Peter, switching from producer to manager, gingerly began to send James out on the road—doing a tour of mainly college campuses. "He was staying in the dorms," Peter recalled, all part of an effort to keep costs low. "I just wanted him to play to as many people as possible, 'cause I'd seen the effect that it had. And gradually," Peter said with typical understatement, "things started to happen."

"I was living up in Laurel Canyon," photographer Henry Diltz remembered, "and I got a call from Peter Asher." Diltz had been a singer and musician in the early sixties with his band, The Modern Folk Quartet, who went from more-than-worthy "folk boom" practitioners to delivering "Wall of Sound" pop perfection (with Spector producing their epic track, "This Could Be the Night"). When the band folded in 1966, Diltz found that the photographs he had begun taking of his musician friends—The Monkees, The Lovin' Spoonful, Buffalo Springfield—could actually bring in money; thus, a second career began.

"Would you come down to my house," Peter asked Diltz, "and photograph this young singer? We're doing an album." Warners wanted some black-and-white publicity stills, and Diltz was perfect for the job. He arrived and almost immediately began snapping away as James, sitting on the floor of the Ashers' living room, played "Oh, Susannah"—"finger-picking," Diltz said, amazed, "like a music box!" Betsy served breakfast to those assembled, and more shots were attempted outside the house. Diltz, though, didn't like the light, so he suggested they jump in his car and try a spot in Burbank he thought might prove interesting.

"On Barham Boulevard," Diltz explained, "there was a little artistic commune—a couple of houses and little sheds—and we called it The Farm." Wandering over to a weathered shed, a few more shots were taken—mostly black and white, which was what all publicity departments wanted. "There was a big post," Diltz recalled, and James "kinda walked over and put his arm on it . . . and just WOW! In the frame, it was just *so perfect!*" Diltz quickly reached for his color camera and, mainly for himself, took a few more of the lanky singer—the shack's faded red paint complementing the blue of Taylor's shirt, his silent gaze mesmerizing.

Ed Thrasher, art director for Warner Brothers Records, saw Diltz's incidental color shots and chose one for the cover of Taylor's first album for the label, released in March of 1970 as *Sweet Baby James*—a title James resisted strongly. "He didn't want to use it," Peter recalled, as the song itself was written for his young nephew, also named James. "If we call it *Sweet Baby James*, people will think it's me," Peter remembered Taylor saying. "I said, 'No, no, we'll explain, and it's *such* a great title.'" Peter smiled. "Of course, he was right."

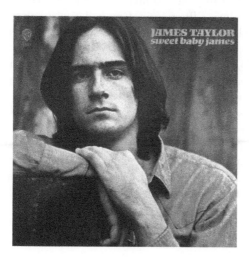

Sweet Baby James
album cover.

"It's like Madonna and 'Material Girl'—it doesn't matter whether it was intended to be a sobriquet for yourself or not, it became one. She *is* the Material Girl; he *is* Sweet Baby James," Peter said, adding with a laugh, "and they both have to lump it!"

The reviews were positive. *Rolling Stone*'s Gary Von Tersch wrote: "This is a hard album to argue with," and added: "Taylor seems to have found the ideal musical vehicle to say what he has to say." Peter, as well as the folks at Warner Brothers, hoped that the sonic palette of "sweet greens and blues" employed by Taylor would be embraced by a public just beginning to open up to introspective artists like Leonard Cohen and Joni Mitchell.

Someone who immediately got what James and Peter were creating sonically was John Stewart. This former member of The Kingston Trio had first met the pair when Chris Darrow invited them down to one of Stewart's rehearsals, which is where they poached drummer Russ Kunkel. A fan of Stewart's first solo album, *California Bloodlines*, Peter agreed to produce a follow-up record for Stewart.

James and Peter dropped by the small North Hollywood studio where Stewart was in the process of working on demos for the record. "James took out his guitar and started playing," Stewart recalled, and an immediate rapport was formed. According to Stewart, as he ran through songs for Peter, "he would say, 'I like this one better than this.' . . . It was very much a team effort—an effort of Peter and mine—to pull the best songs out of it."

Peter had every intention of using Sunset Sound once again for the sessions. But in late March, he happened to stop by John Fischbach's recording studio, known as Crystal Sound Recorders, where James was providing guitar and vocal backup on Carole King's first solo sessions. An enterprising young staff engineer heard Peter was in the building and came out to the lobby to meet him.

"I knew who he was," Richard Orshoff recalled. "I knew his background at Apple, I knew who he'd been from Peter and Gordon, and I knew his interest in music. So I went out and showed him around. And he said, 'Well, thank you very much,' and started to leave." Showing good initiative, Orshoff suggested he give the place a try, but Peter replied they were content with Sunset Sound. "I said, 'Well, I'll give you some free time.'" Peter again demurred, explaining that with the Stewart sessions about to begin, he felt he couldn't spare the few hours to give Crystal a proper audition.

"I said, 'How much time do you want?' He said, 'What do you mean?' I said, 'Tell me how much free time you want, and it's yours.'" Laughing at the audaciousness of the offer, Peter asked for two days with the ability to record as late into the evening as they wanted. Orshoff quickly checked with the owners and was given the okay, booking Peter and client John Stewart for April Fool's Day.

Crystal was "a very space age–looking studio," Peter recalled, "and very state-of-the-art." Owner Andrew Berliner was an electronic genius who built his own recording consoles from scratch. Berliner had taken a chance on Orshoff, hiring him and teaching him all he knew. "He took me from a somewhat amateur junior high school soundman to a real knowledgeable engineer," said Orshoff.

Peter was impressed enough with both Orshoff and Crystal that two days turned into over a week of sessions with Stewart. The singer, in turn, was impressed with Peter, describing him as "thorough, precise, and quiet."

"My nickname for Peter was 'Spock'—which he *loved*," Stewart recalled. "He's just very methodical. And he wanted what was best for the song."

Again, as was his habit, Peter cut many of the tracks live with Stewart and a group consisting mostly of Taylor, King, Kortchmar, Kunkel, and from Stewart's own band, bassist Bryan Garofalo. When it comes to cutting basic tracks with live players, "I love it, too," Stewart admitted. "When you've got musicians like that, it just seems to have a cohesiveness and the personality of the time it was recorded, and you can't paste that together." That being said, Peter overdubbed affective sonic touches himself on various tracks—adding an ethereal autoharp to "Great White Cathedrals," for example.

On "Clack Clack," a song recounting the trip Robert Kennedy's body made by train after his assassination, Peter put his old bass-playing talents to use on the basic track, borrowing Garofalo's Fender. "The talent just comes out of him," Garofalo marveled, "with everything he ever does." Afterward, Peter layered various passes of his voice singing an inventive harmony part on the song's chorus. The result was "one of the songs that really shined through," according to Stewart. "As important as a song can be. We worked hard on that."

"Peter and John both came from very hardcore work ethics, and there wasn't a lot of wasted time," according to Bill Mumy, who attended most of the sessions. Mumy, like Peter, had been a child actor—known for memorable *Twilight Zone* episodes and the series *Lost in Space*. Mumy first met Stewart in 1967, backstage at a Kingston Trio concert. "That was a huge thing for me, as it was The Kingston Trio that made me want to make music in the first place." Stewart would then occasionally visit the *Lost in Space* set on the Twentieth Century Fox backlot. "*He* wanted to be an actor, and *I* wanted to be a singer/songwriter," Mumy amusingly admitted. "It's always like that, isn't it?

"The sessions were fairly loose," according to Mumy. During the taping of the track "Big Joe," for example, Peter simply turned to Mumy and said, "Billy, go out

Peter playing bass during the John Stewart sessions.
Photo by Henry Diltz.

there and play cowbell." "I was kinda nervous because they placed me right next to James Taylor, who was playing acoustic lead guitar on the track." Perhaps in an effort to relax him, the older Taylor shared a joint with the sixteen-year-old Mumy during a break in the session. Ultimately, the sound that kicks off the entire album is the rock-solid beat of Mumy's cowbell.

"Peter was always a mellow guy," Mumy recalled. "He would direct things, of course, if he wanted to change an arrangement, but he let it unfold pretty naturally." "Natural" is an apt description of the feel achieved by the musicians, as Peter helped John craft a tight album that beautifully brought together strains of folk, country, and rock—all supporting Stewart's slices of life: a hobo, a trucker, a war widow, a girl on the verge of womanhood—Stewart's lyrics made each vividly real, while also sharing his own memories of childhood ("Back in Pomona") and adult longings ("Golden Rollin' Belly").

Stewart was very proud of the finished album, released with the title *Willard.* He also thoroughly enjoyed his experience in the studio with Peter: "He is a very honest guy," said Stewart. "And he never talked 'down' to you. He would say what he was feeling without thinking, 'Is that the right way to say it,' or 'Is that gonna hurt his feelings?' . . . He'd just say it! And I really appreciated that because it made things *much* easier." Stewart had to admit that, during the recording of *Willard,* "There were many times when I just drove Peter crazy." He recalled his frustration over one vocal session in particular: "I couldn't get the vocal, and I just *insisted* on getting it." If Peter feels something is simply not working, he'll usually say, "Let's leave it," or "Let's come back tomorrow," moving the session along. "Usually," Peter said smiling, "I'm pretty good at knowing when to abandon things."

Stewart wasn't having it. "I just wouldn't take no for an answer. I was *determined* to get it." Stewart sighed and admitted, "In retrospect, I shoulda come back tomorrow . . ."

Willard album cover.

At the corporate headquarters of Warner Brothers in Burbank, a decision needed to be made on James Taylor's first single for the label. "To be honest, we didn't know if *any* of them were hit singles," Peter confessed. "*None* of that record sounded like a 'hit radio single.' That wasn't the point—we'd made an *album*." Since the track "Sweet Baby James" was both a good introduction to James and also the title of the album, it was chosen—perhaps unwisely. Too country-sounding for AM pop radio and too far removed from the current countrypolitan hits on US country stations, program directors stayed away from it in droves.

But at college stations, the album was hitting a nerve. WLHA, in Madison, Wisconsin, caught on early, helping to make the album a hit in local record shops. College stations from Berkeley to Boston began to play cuts from *Sweet Baby James* over their airwaves—signals that were received avidly by the seven million Baby Boomers who, combined, made up America's student body.

More so than movies, television, or literature, it was music that propelled the youth culture in 1970—its continued importance in the lives of that specific generation cannot be overstated. Forty years before what we now regard as "social media"—Facebook, Twitter, and the like—rock music *was* social media; listening to free-form FM radio not only clued you in to where the next demonstration was gathering, messages were passed on in the music about the true state of life, of love, of society—and every young person was listening.

"It was the place where the world connected," said musician Tony Kosinec. "It was a collective soul or experience; it said that love was possible, and peace was possible—those things were very tangible.

"There was a sense of some kind of inner connection that came from the music," Kosinec stated, "and Peter and The Beatles and a couple of other key people were really the beating heart of that. So, to be able to work with him, and to have him help me shape this material, that was extraordinary."

Peter had received a call from, of all people, Murray Kaufman—better known as "Murray the K," one of America's best-known DJs. Kaufman had come across a young Canadian singer/songwriter named Tony Kosinec. Impressed with Kosinec's talent, Kaufman offered his services as manager and, using his industry connections, helped land the young performer a contract with Columbia Records.

Kosinec had an unhappy experience recording his first album, ultimately feeling the production was "overblown." When it came time to begin his second, Kosinec remembered, "Murray tried to find me somebody who could really do a good job." After various producers were considered, finally Kaufman asked, "How about Peter Asher?" To which Kosinec replied, "Oh, my God—*yes!*"

Kosinec had heard *Sweet Baby James* and was impressed with its understated, sensitive production. "This guy's gonna *know*," Kosinec recalled thinking. "It's what you put in and what you *don't* put in—the simplicity of lines. Peter was the perfect person." Kosinec's current compositions were not structured like the average folk or pop song, with predictable rhythms and choruses to sing along with—these were almost impressionistic, poetic little art songs. "I thought I was gonna have a problem with somebody willing to produce an album like that," Kosinec said, but Peter liked the creativity he heard in the demos, and he agreed to take on the project. "I couldn't believe he was gonna do it," Kosinec recalled. "That was just too much for me."

Peter met the young Canadian, and they discussed how to approach the material, which would have minimal instrumentation—Kosinec's guitar supported at times by bass, drums, piano, and flute. "One of the things we discussed," said Kosinec, "was that it was supposed to have very small sounds recorded in such a way that they sounded very big."

Before going into the studio, just as he had done with James Taylor, Peter carved out time for Kosinec and his musicians to rehearse. "He got an incredible hall for us to rehearse in," Kosinec remembered. "It was the Steinway Piano building on the second floor—opposite Carnegie Hall! It was brilliant." The 1920s landmark had large windows overlooking 57th Street in Manhattan, and Kosinec and his small ensemble set up right against the glass: "The feeling and the sense of place in the rehearsal hall was that you could reach the *whole world*—it was all there," said Kosinec. Peter created "an atmosphere and a kind of support that worked around you and inside of you," Kosinec marveled. "He sensed out what I wanted to do, and he gave me the best possible circumstance." Peter kept alert for anything in the arrangements that seemed overdone, maintaining the simple interplay between two or three instruments.

Peter also brought Russ Kunkel with him. "I just thought, rather than gamble on a New York drummer, it would be worth bringing Russ, if he was willing," explained Peter. Kosinec was quite impressed: "I gotta say, in terms of feel, sensitivity, and sound, I think Russ is the best I've *ever* played with."

The sessions were to take place at Columbia's Manhattan studios at 49 E. 52nd Street. While there, Peter ran into Bob Dylan's current producer, Bob Johnston. Dylan wanted to come in the next day with George Harrison and run through some new material. A bassist had been lined up, but Johnston needed a good drummer who could provide whatever Dylan and Harrison might need. Peter, without hesitation, suggested Kunkel.

The following day, as Peter sat in the control booth watching his friend drum behind two of the biggest recording artists in the world, he was also observing the engineer behind the console. Jim Reeves, on staff at Columbia since 1969, had recorded rock (The Chambers Brothers), pop (Bobby Vinton), and folk (Tom Rush) for the label. "Peter apparently liked what I did," Reeves said, as Peter specifically requested him to engineer the Kosinec sessions in New York.

"Wow," Reeves marveled, "what an extraordinary producer—not dictatorial at all." Likely used to more aggressive personalities sitting beside him at the console, Reeves enjoyed Peter's generous nature during the sessions. "I tend to just tell the engineer what I am looking for and rely upon his expertise to get it," Peter admitted. After a week, with almost a half-dozen tracks recorded, Reeves did his usual excellent job mixing stereo masters from the best takes. Peter, needing to get back to LA to take care of business, took the mixes and insisted Kosinec come stay at his home and finish the album in California.

With his girlfriend in tow, Kosinec moved into Peter and Betsy's Longwood Avenue home. Betsy "was really wonderful to us," Kosinec remembered. "She made sure that everything just worked. . . . A lovely person." Peter "continued this sort of 'fatherliness'—of making sure that the environment was stimulating and warm." It was, as many of Peter's friends would stop by for conversations and a dip in the pool—friends who were an inspiration to the young Canadian musician. It was all a bit much for Kosinec—even his relationship with his host: "I was in awe of Peter," he admitted. "I had to pretend that I was, like, comfortable!"

The sessions resumed at Columbia's Hollywood studios on Sunset Boulevard. Peter continued "to get everything away from that production that shouldn't be in it," according to Kosinec, while inserting small touches to enhance the work. That's Peter, for example, slapping his thighs to add a perfect unplugged percussion throughout the song "I Use Her." The track "Dinner Time" needed an exclamation point at its finale, according to Peter, so he gathered the musicians around the mic to sing "*Bahh-Dooo*," evoking a street corner doo-wop choir. "That album was really, to me, an art piece," said Kosinec. "And Peter approached it, I think, like an artist and not like a 'big-time producer.' And I'm proud of that piece of work *very* much because of its clarity and its purity, and a lot of that came from him."

"I was fascinated by him," said Kosinec. "Because he's so quiet you don't see on him what he's doing, which is usually the case with any master—you have to *be* with them and watch what they're doing. Seeing how he approached what he did taught me a great deal. It's how the music *clothed* him, how the production process works *in* him, the sort of naturalness and genius that he had in just knowing 'how much of this . . . a little of that . . . '"

Bad Girl Songs
album cover.

The finished album, entitled *Bad Girl Songs*, did well enough for Columbia to continue sending Kosinec out on tour for another year, opening for other artists on their roster, such as Blood, Sweat and Tears, but his two-album deal was not extended. Now, decades later, *Bad Girl Songs* is one of those records revered by a cult of fans who have discovered its odd, endearing tales and sparse, focused atmosphere.

When Peter delivered the final stereo mixed master of *Bad Girl Songs* to Columbia, he was a young producer responsible for a handful of records, none of which had made much of a dent in the charts or in the public consciousness. Within the next three months, that would all change dramatically.

13

FIRE AND RAIN

Back in London, Peter's old investment, Indica Books, finally went under. Paul McCartney had tried to help, chipping in £3,000 to keep the place alive, but to no avail. Part of the problem was rampant theft: "'Liberating books,' it was called," Miles said ruefully. "I *still* meet people, and they say, 'Oh, man! I stole some *great* books from your shop!' And I say, 'That's why it *closed!* If it wasn't for *you*"—he laughed—"we wouldn't have gone bankrupt!'"

In May 1970, film director Monte Hellman saw James Taylor's face on a billboard promoting *Sweet Baby James* high above the Sunset Strip. Picturing that same

Indica Bookshop on Southampton Row, before its liquidation.

handsome face on a movie screen, Hellman approached Peter and offered James a screen test for a possible costarring role in his latest independent feature. The film treatment that arrived at the office of Peter Asher Management was entitled *Two-Lane Blacktop*. As a former actor, Peter certainly saw the potential in the work, but knowing James had never tried anything of this sort before, he had his doubts about the project. James, though, found the opportunity too good to pass up and spent the months of August and September filming at various locations across the country, brooding in front of the camera and trying to write new material during the interminable downtime all actors on-set suffer through.

When it came to acting, "I didn't have any real aptitude for it," Taylor admitted, "and never had any desire to pursue it any further. But it was great traveling with those people and being part of a film."

With James preoccupied, Peter spent the first week of August in the studio with a group of musicians whom he had come to know quite well. This particular collective had become frequent guests at the Asher residence while backing Carole King on her first solo album, *Writer*. After numerous name changes, the band had settled on the moniker Jo Mama (as in the put-down street retort).

The group's driving force was singer/writer/guitarist Danny Kortchmar, or "Kootch"—a nickname bestowed by boyhood pal James Taylor. The group's bassist, Charlie Larkey, had known Kortchmar back in New York during his King Bees days, and the two had recently been in a band together called The City, which also featured Carole King. Larkey and King, now a couple, would soon become man and wife.

Jo Mama's keyboardist, Ralph Schuckett, had also played on The City's one-and-only album. Musically inclined from a young age, Schuckett learned both the piano and the cello, playing in various groups—jazz, rock, R&B, surf, you name it. "I kept getting all these offers from different bands that heard me play," Schuckett said, eventually deciding to leave college and become a professional musician, "'cause I really wanted to meet girls"—he laughed—"and get away from home!"

Designated 4F because of flat feet and asthma, Schuckett eventually joined the psychedelic band Clear Light, appearing on their only album. Just before breaking up, the band's lead guitarist was fired and replaced with Danny Kortchmar, which is where Schuckett first met him. Kortchmar "was the only one with a strong point of view" in the group, according to Schuckett. "He took over the band musically, which was kind of a good thing.

"He's like my musical big brother," Schuckett said of Kortchmar. "He really taught me a lot about arranging and about the music business." Another former member of Clear Light, drummer Michael Ney was part of the original Jo Mama lineup, as was his girlfriend, vocalist Abigail Haness—the reason there was a band at all.

"I've always been a singer," Haness proclaimed. "I had a knack for remembering song lyrics; anything I heard on the radio I could remember, and I could mimic the singer." Her proud father would show off his five-year-old daughter's talent at his restaurant and bar in Brooklyn, New York. "My father just thought it would be the greatest thing in the world if I had a career in show business." Going professional at age sixteen, she was a member of The Pussycats (a girl group in the vein of The Shangri-Las), releasing a couple of failed singles on Columbia. Then, using the name Gayle Haness, she was signed by Bert Berns to his Bang Records label, where Jeff Barry wrote and produced a few more singles (which also failed).

Moving to LA with drummer Ney, Haness appeared for six months in the Los Angeles production of *Hair* at the newly named Aquarius Theatre near Sunset and Vine. During this time, one of Haness's old friends began dating actor Peter Lawford. Lawford met Haness and became a big fan, even bringing her onto *The Tonight Show* when Lawford guest-hosted for a vacationing Johnny Carson. Lawford, along with other Tinseltown bigwigs, was an investor in the West Hollywood nightclub The Factory. When a spot for a house band opened up, Lawford got word to Haness that if she could put a band together, the gig would be hers.

The first rehearsal consisted of Haness, Ney, Kortchmar, Schuckett, Larkey, and Carole King. King decided being in the band was just not a good fit and, wisely, opted out to concentrate on her budding solo career. Now a quintet, the group played eight weeks at The Factory. During the residency, Haness fell in love with Kortchmar, which eventually led to marriage. Needless to say, Ney was out—of both the relationship and the band. Needing a drummer, Kootch knew just whom to call.

Joel O'Brien had been a drummer for both The King Bees and yet another of Kortchmar's groups, The Flying Machine. "Joel was an *extremely* talented guy," Schuckett marveled. "He was an artist, he was a photographer, he was a singer, he was a drummer, he was a hillbilly fiddle player, and he was a be-bop jazz piano player! *And* he knew more about cinema than anybody I'd ever met." O'Brien also had recorded before with Peter on Taylor's Apple sessions.

According to Haness, as everyone now in the band was already friendly with Peter, he "just seemed the logical choice" to be asked to produce Jo Mama's debut album for Atlantic Records. "I don't think we ever even *thought* about anyone else," she said. Recording live to tape, once again at Crystal Sound with Richard Orshoff at the console, the group of expert players ran through their club act, which consisted mostly of songs written by Kortchmar. Working fast, twelve tracks were recorded in four days.

Kortchmar, who became a successful producer himself (Billy Joel, Don Henley), was certainly learning a great deal observing Peter's methods in the studio: "Once you get a great team of musicians there, keep them focused on what has to happen," Kortchmar stated. "I've seen this happen a lot—where the energy just gets diffused by taking too long or with indecision. If you keep focused and keep 'em going in the right direction, you'll get focused, sharp performances."

Eventually producing projects from soundtracks to pop hits, Schuckett also first began to understand what a producer does by watching Peter: "What you're *supposed* to do is key into the artist and make everything comfortable and enjoyable and painless for *them* so that they can do what they do," he observed, "in an atmosphere where they're free to express themselves. And it takes a lot of trust and it takes a lot of selflessness to be a good record producer."

Jo Mama
album cover.

And Peter, Schuckett declared, "is a great producer."

During some of his first jobs as producer himself, Schuckett recalled, "Sometimes I would be insensitive to the artist or musicians—not in a *cruel* way, just not be present enough in the moment to notice what's really going on in the dynamic between the players, how the artist is feeling, and what they really mean even though they say something else. As I got older, I learned about all that stuff. Peter knew all that as a young man. He was very perceptive and *persistent* in a quiet, polite way."

Peter *was* persistent, as always, in making sure the artist's vision is what gets captured. The resultant album from these sessions, also named *Jo Mama*, demonstrated the band's eclecticism in material. Combining rock, jazz, funk, and Latin, the band was all over the map—with the chops to pull it off—but it certainly made them hard to pigeonhole, resulting in some difficulty gaining traction in the rock marketplace.

"That was probably the problem," Peter agreed. "People like their music to have an identity—they don't like 'Jack of all trades.'"

Within weeks of the release of *Sweet Baby James*, "Fire and Rain" first came out as a single. Not by James, though—but by the pop/soul singer R.B. Greaves. Atlantic Records' Ahmet Ertegun and arranger Arif Mardin crafted a soulful and affecting version, but it failed to chart. By mid-August of 1970, with *Sweet Baby James* continuing its slow but steady rise up *Billboard*'s album chart, a second performer released a single of "Fire and Rain." Georgie Fame, whose mastery of pop, jazz, and R&B made him a musical *wunderkind* in the UK, put out his own take of the song. Only a week later, Johnny Rivers ("Secret Agent Man," "Poor Side of Town") released yet *another* version of the song, which mainly differed from Taylor's original by adding background singers on the choruses and using a saxophone for a soulful touch. The following week, Warner Brothers, not wanting to miss out on a possible hit right under their noses, decided enough was enough and rushed Taylor's "Fire and Rain" to radio stations. The release was promoted in the trades with full-page ads proclaiming: "The original (and, we think, best) 'Fire and Rain' is now a single."

With Jo Mama's album mostly done and James still preoccupied with filming, Peter turned his attention to finishing the Kate Taylor sessions. Before going back into the studio, they spent much time together, listening to songs and discussing what material to record. Peter suggested Kate try "Handbags and Gladrags," a Mike D'Abo number that was fairly unknown at that time. He also suggested "Sweet Honesty," written by Beverly Martyn and recorded by her and then-husband John Martyn on the duo's first album together, *Stormbringer!*

In late August, Peter, Betsy, and Kate attended Elton John's American debut at The Troubadour. Elton dazzled the audience: "It was like you were watching a rocket ship take off," Kate remembered. Elton gave a preview of a handful of new tracks from his soon-to-be-released *Tumbleweed Connection*—an album now considered by many to be his best.

"He came out to my house the day after the Troubadour opening," Peter recalled, with the Ashers hosting an intimate party. Both Peter and Kate were quite taken by two of the new songs, "Ballad of a Well-Known Gun" and, especially, "Country Comfort." "I just loved that song," Kate recalled. "It made me feel like home." Kate asked Elton if he would mind if she recorded them, and according to her, "He said, 'Oh, by all means!'" In addition, Peter and Kate recently had the opportunity to hear demos of Carole King's latest works-in-progress. Rather than hold them back for herself, King graciously gave Kate the opportunity to record both "Home Again" and "Where You Lead," two brand-new songs that King would soon record. Those sessions would comprise her second solo release and one of the biggest-selling albums of the era—*Tapestry*.

"Carole's history as a songwriter is so ingrained," Peter said, "she thinks as a song-writer: 'Oh, somebody wants to record my songs.' You say: 'Yes!' It's the traditional way you think in The Brill Building"—the legendary song publishing Mecca where King got her start—"or the way Diane Warren thinks to this day"—one of pop music's present songwriting powerhouses.

While looking for a label for Kate, Peter and Nat Weiss took a meeting with the founder of Atlantic Records, Ahmet Ertegun. "We played him some Kate, and he liked it," Peter recalled, so a deal was struck. "As far as I was concerned, I was signing with Atlantic," said Peter, but when the album was released in early 1971 with the title *Sister Kate*, Peter was surprised to see it on the Cotillion label.

"That was Ahmet's pet label at the time," John Kalodner remembered. Kalodner, who went on to become one of the record industry's A&R legends, started his career at Atlantic in the seventies. "It was a wholly owned label of Atlantic," he noted, but it was up to Ertegun's whims what Cotillion would release, which included supergroup Emerson Lake and Palmer and the *Woodstock* soundtrack.

Sister Kate
album cover.

Sister Kate's final sessions took place throughout September at Crystal. For backing vocals on "Country Comfort" and "Handbags and Gladrags," Peter added both Jo Mama's Abigail Haness ("a great singer," Peter stated unequivocally) and a twenty-four-year-old Linda Ronstadt—her first appearance on a Peter Asher production.

Almost all the musicians in Peter's circle were struggling to get by—even Ronstadt. Though having scored her first Top Twenty hit with "Different Drum" three years earlier—finally achieving her second, "Long, Long Time," while participating on Kate Taylor's sessions—her career was treading water. Ronstadt's manager was Herb Cohen, who at the time also managed such characters as Tom Waits and Frank Zappa, but Cohen was quite a character in his own right.

John Boylan, a musician/songwriter/record producer of note, had run into Ronstadt at The Troubadour months earlier. She knew Boylan was responsible for assembling The Stone Canyon Band (one of the seminal country-rock outfits) for Rick Nelson and was hoping he could do something similar for her. Speaking of her then-manager Cohen, Boylan recalled Ronstadt telling him: "His idea of how to get a guitar player is to call up the union and tell them to send somebody over. I need somebody who plays my kind of music."

Before following through on his promise to assemble a band, Boylan and Ronstadt began dating and, just for fun, played some concert dates together. One that Cohen had arranged was an appearance at Capitol Records' annual convention, set to take place in Honolulu in June, right after a gig with Neil Diamond in San Jose. Boylan recalled Cohen giving him two envelopes with airplane tickets for Ronstadt and her band to get, first, from LA to San Francisco, then San Francisco to Honolulu. "Capitol's paying—first class," Cohen told Boylan.

The day after their gig in San Jose, the troupe showed up at San Francisco's airport. "I open the tickets and I look at 'em," said Boylan. "They start in Minneapolis, and then they went to Denver, and then they went to San Francisco, then Honolulu and back to LA. But the first coupons were torn out." Though a little dubious, Boylan hands the ticket agent the envelope and, within minutes, "the FBI comes from behind the screen and arrests us for receiving stolen property.

"Herbie had billed Capitol for the whole amount," said Boylan, "and bought the tickets from some guy in the lobby of the building for twenty-five cents on the dollar, claiming they were 'left over from people who hadn't shown up for some prepackaged tour,' which is why they were such a bargain.

"After that, Linda decided that Herbie had to go." Boylan recalled that Linda "asked me who I thought should manage her, and the only person I knew who was my age that I had respect for was Peter Asher." James Taylor had recently introduced Peter to Boylan, whose former band The Ginger Men used to open for James's group The Flying Machine back in 1967.

"I did want him to manage me," Ronstadt remembered, "but he was already managing Kate Taylor. And he had said yes, but then . . ." Ronstadt paused and said, "You know, Peter is really fair-minded. I think a lot of us operate with the idea that there are always a lot of reasons to do something, but if there's one good reason not to do it, *that's* the reason you should consider—not the fourteen reasons to do it. That's how I try to operate my life, anyway, and I learned that from Peter.

"So, I think the one reason not to do it was that it would not be fair to Kate, to whom he'd already made a commitment." It would certainly keep a young manager's hands full continuing to move one Taylor's career forward while trying to help a second Taylor establish herself. To then take on managing Ronstadt, Peter was sure someone would get shortchanged. Ronstadt is positive that, for Peter, turning her down "was kind of a painful thing, but he was really upfront about it, and Kate was very sweet about it."

Boylan, though, kept his promise to Ronstadt and assembled a band that would back her on tour the following year. Using drummer Don Henley (from the band Shiloh), guitarist Glenn Frey (from the duo Longbranch Pennywhistle), guitarist Bernie Leadon (who had previously backed Ronstadt in The Corvettes), and bassist Randy Meisner (from Nelson's Stone Canyon Band), the four would eventually continue as a unit and seek their fortune on their own terms . . . under the name The Eagles.

At this point, in October 1970, James's career wasn't just moving forward, it was on fire. Only ten weeks after its release as a single, "Fire and Rain" had gone all the way to number three on *Billboard*'s Top 100. In that same period, his album *Sweet Baby James* had jumped from number seventeen to number five in the album charts. Both the song and the singer had obviously struck a nerve in the country.

The sixties had been a time of turmoil for the United States: the assassination of President Kennedy; the civil rights struggles; the war in Vietnam and its accompanying protests; the killings of Robert Kennedy and Martin Luther King Jr.; riots in cities; youth rebelling against parents, against authority, against society . . . against *everything*. Youngsters had begun the decade with candy-flavored pop music (a la Peter and Gordon) and had ended it with the hard blues-rock of Led Zeppelin, the supersonic psychedelia of Jimi Hendrix, and the wild funk of Sly and the Family Stone. And The Beatles, who were heroes of this generation and reassured them all along the way with words of love, had just broken up. After a decade of endless protests, parties, and profound change, people were almost shell-shocked. They needed to slow down, look around, and reassess their place in it all.

Peter would probably use the word "happenstance" to describe how "Fire and Rain" arrived on the airwaves at just the right time. But it's clear that people responded immediately to the acoustic warmth, the sincere emotion, the quiet fragility. They could relate to Taylor's confusion and sense of loss, as well as marvel at the beauty he managed to pull from it.

On October 27, 1970, Peter and Betsy finally tied the knot at the Marylebone Register Office, going back to the London neighborhood where they had first lived together. Not even the English drizzle could dampen the spirits of the happy couple. Gordon Waller stood as the groom's best man, and Clare Asher was maid of honor. Peter wore a dazzling crushed-velvet suit along with a silk tie featuring an image of a half-eaten apple. "It seemed amusing." Peter smiled.

As the manager of a newly hot artist, Peter sent James back on the road to capitalize on this fantastic success. Backing him onstage was Danny Kortchmar, Lee Sklar, Russ Kunkel, and Carole King. With urging from both Peter and James, King would perform a short set of her own material—surprising audiences with familiar songs they didn't realize she'd helped write: "Will You Love Me Tomorrow," "Up on the Roof," "(You Make Me Feel Like A) Natural Woman." But despite years of success in the music business, performing before paying customers was not "natural" for her—in fact, King suffered terribly from stage fright. It didn't help that restless clubgoers, there to see the headliner, gave her little respect—not realizing that in one year she'd be the biggest-selling artist in the country.

Taylor was also suffering on the tour because of his ongoing drug addiction. "He had to sit in a chair 'cause he was really too fucked up to stand," Sklar recalled. Despite being handicapped by his dependency, James "never forgot a word or missed a chord! It's like the minute that body hit the stage, one door shut," said Sklar, "and another door opened. Total clarity."

During the last week of November, Taylor and his band performed for a few evenings at West Hollywood's Troubadour. Sklar was amazed at how different things were from the first time he had played the venue with Taylor just six months previously: "Literally, you could drive a truck through the place—it was so empty." And now? "The fire marshal was ready to close the place down." As Sklar looked out from the small stage, he saw the venue was packed to the rafters.

At the soundcheck one afternoon, King sat at the piano and tried out a new song. Peter and James, sitting out in the seats of the intimate club, were simply knocked out by what they heard. After she finished, Taylor strode to the stage and insisted she teach him the chords so they could perform it—that evening, together. "James remembers that he specifically asked me if he could record it," King said. "It's probable that, if he did, I said yes and then"—she laughed—"promptly forgot about it!" The song in question, "You've Got a Friend," would prove to be an important one for James, Carole, *and* Peter.

The same week James and Carole played The Troubadour, A&M Records released an album by a young British artist who performed under the name of Cat Stevens. In the 1960s, Stevens had first hit the British charts with a brassy pop sound, but lately he had adopted a more acoustic, introspective style—not too far from the stylistic vein James Taylor was mining.

Managing Stevens's career was Barry Krost, who had first met Peter when they were both child actors. In fact, during the filming of Peter's first movie, *The Planter's Wife*, Krost was on-set as Peter's stand-in. But a steady career in acting did not work out for young Barry as, he said, "I had the minimum amount of talent." His ultimate realization of this came when filming a scene for *Moulin Rouge,* directed by the legendary John Huston. Playing a young Toulouse-Lautrec, Krost overheard Huston mutter to an aide, "For Christ's sake, someone stop that child from acting!"

Krost found more success in the mid-sixties managing pop performers in London, including both Cat Stevens and Dusty Springfield. Stevens's second album for Island Records, *Tea for the Tillerman* (produced by Peter's old friend Paul Samwell-Smith) was poised to break through in the United States when released by A&M. Seeing the success Peter was now having with James, Krost felt he needed to call up his old friend for help.

"I didn't know the market," Krost admitted, "and couldn't be here." Peter and his business partner, Nat Weiss, began smoothing the way for Stevens, helping with his tour and representing him as de facto managers stateside. Within a few months, *Tea for the Tillerman* had reached the Top Ten and sold over five hundred thousand copies.

In December, Peter was off to Memphis, Tennessee, to begin work on a new album project. Tony Joe White, the swamp rocker from Oak Grove, Louisiana, who hit it big the previous year with "Polk Salad Annie," had just been signed to Warner Brothers Records. Peter was asked to produce the sessions, most likely because he was Warner's hit producer du jour. He was happy to do so: "I was a big fan," Peter said of White, who could not only write stinging rockers, but soulful ballads like "Rainy Night in Georgia."

Memphis, along with Muscle Shoals, Alabama, was beginning to attract both producers and performers from all over—intrigued by the top-notch talent pool, the funkier studios, and the atmosphere. This was the place, after all, where blues, country, and gospel had all collided one colorblind evening some twenty years earlier in Sam Phillip's storefront studio. More recently ignored as some backwater music scene, the last couple of years had brought about a change.

"Guys in Memphis, at that time, were getting used to 'outsiders' coming in," engineer Terry Manning explained. The Texas-born Manning had been working in Memphis studios for years, first learning the ropes at Stax and then becoming the first engineer hired at Ardent Studios, where some of the Tony Joe White sessions were recorded.

"You'd have guys like Arif Mardin and Jerry Wexler coming down from New York; we had Cosimo Matassa coming up from New Orleans." These "outsiders" were now producing great records around town, including *Dusty in Memphis*, the Dusty Springfield classic on which Manning assisted. And the local studio cats cutting these records were a major part of their success.

Peter had been interested in the possibility of recording in Memphis ever since he and Gordon visited the home of Stax Records while on tour. Even The Beatles had toyed with the idea of leaving their Abbey Road comfort zone and recording here. But being an "outsider," Peter needed a local liaison, and he found a solid one in Manning.

"The thing about Peter," Manning stated, "he's just such a consummate professional as far as being a musician. I mean a musician in the truest sense—not a 'player' as much as *truly* a musical person. He just really knows music and knows what he wants."

Peter knew for certain that, for the sessions to work, White needed his own players backing him. It turned out that one member of White's band had met and played with Peter before. Keyboardist Mike Utley, who would go on to record and tour with Jimmy Buffett for decades, was a member of Bill Black's Combo in 1965. When Peter and Gordon played Atlantic City's Steel Pier that summer, Black's Combo provided the accompaniment. Peter was amazed—"He didn't even remember," Utley recalled.

"Tony," Utley emphasized, "is a real opinionated person about his music." When it comes to what's being generated from the studio floor, White "pretty much calls the shots." For four days, Peter watched the musicians find their groove for each song and, sitting alongside engineer Manning at the recording console, made sure the music being created was expertly captured, keeping meticulous notes on the best takes and noting where an overdub might be needed.

"I think he was letting Tony do his thing," Manning said. "As a producer myself, I'll try not to inject myself unless I determine it's needed." Almost always wearing his large leather hat, White would come into the booth in between takes and check with Peter on the success of the last effort. The material cut consisted of swampy grooves like the album opener, "They Caught the Devil and Put Him in Jail in Eudora, Arkansas" (spoiler alert: he escapes). There are some softer tracks, as well, including a lovely take on the old folk song "Copper Kettle," with White doing a good Bob Dylan impersonation on the opening line (Dylan had released his own version of the song six months earlier).

The hit-that-shoulda-been, though, was the album closer, "Voodoo Village." Written by Lee Ann White, Tony Joe's wife, the track is a powerful rocker punctuated with urgent stabs, courtesy of The Memphis Horns. Throughout the album, the Horns add a sweet layer of soul over White's snarling Southern riffs.

Lead trumpeter Wayne Jackson—like keyboardist Utley, originally from Arkansas—had been playing since the age of eleven, when his mother bought a used trumpet from the family across the street. "I just took right to it," Jackson recalled. After years of playing in the marching bands at school, "I landed in a rock'n'roll band called The Mar-Keys," he said, "and we had the first hit record on Stax." That record—the million-selling "Last Night"—led to The Mar-Keys' horn section becoming an integral part of the Stax Records sound. Jackson and tenor saxophonist Andrew Love, after playing on almost every hit Stax released in the 1960s, formed The Memphis Horns—the best for-hire brass section the city had to offer.

Amazingly, their horn arrangements were totally improvised—nothing was written down. Jackson calls it "a gift—I could always do it." He grew up playing along to his favorite songs, thinking up horn lines, and creating a signature sound in the process. Peter was in awe of these superb Southern players, and at the overdub sessions, he happily watched The Horns work up their "head" arrangements.

"Peter, being a consummate musician and a consummate producer, really knew how to relate to any number of musicians," said Manning. That's true, but Peter might have been a little out of his element surrounded by a band of good ol' Southern boys from Louisiana, Arkansas, Texas, and Tennessee. Was he, perhaps, forced to eat barbecue and dragged to strip clubs? "Unfortunately, I think I only got barbecue out of the equation," Peter said, disappointed. "I would have gone for the whole package."

The album Peter delivered to Warners, released simply as *Tony Joe White*, was a solid snapshot of their new signing, though it didn't include a track as instantly memorable as "Polk Salad Annie" had been.

Tony Joe White album cover.

Upon his return to Los Angeles, Warners was itching to get another James Taylor track on the radio to capitalize on the massive success of "Fire and Rain," which had dropped off the charts. The *Sweet Baby James* album track "Country Road" was selected, and Peter thought it wise to go back to the master tape and remix it for AM radio broadcast. Then James suggested, after months of singing it on the road, he could do a much better job with the vocal and perhaps he should redo that part.

Peter made the decision to recut the entire song. "They'd done it live," Peter remembered, "and it was a more intense groove and would be more likely to get on the radio." On New Year's Eve, the original group of musicians assembled for a redo, with one exception: on bass now was new team member, Lee Sklar. This would be his first recording session backing Taylor.

"Lee's amazing. He's an astounding musician in general. He's one of those geniuses that can read anything and write anything," Peter said, referring to musical notation. "*And* he's an incredibly musical bass player.

"I'm often a fan of the very simplest bass parts, as well—you know, like the ones I play," Peter said, smiling. "But Lee brings a sense of melodic invention to the bass.

"James is really focused on harmonic movements and chord changes," Peter continued. "He's playing a lot of fancier chords, and Lee understood those immediately and instinctively in a way that a bass player like *me* couldn't."

Sklar claimed that the way James played guitar "forced me to create a style that justified being there! Because his *thumb* is the bass, I would have to find parts that weave around what he's already doing."

When Randy Meisner, who had played bass on the original album track, heard the single on the radio in early 1971, he was miffed—thinking they'd replaced his bass part. "But," Peter explained, "it's not as if we just took the bass off—which is one of those things that people do. What we did was say: We like the way they're doing it now because they're locked in as a *band*." A little extra percussion was layered on, and in a further attempt to make it more radio-friendly, Peter, James, and Carole put their voices together at two points in the track—adding something akin to a vocal drone—giving the song a more dramatic ending than the original.

The single did make it into the Top Forty, but barely—a bit of a disappointment. But no one would be disappointed with the performance of the next one.

14

YOU'VE GOT A FRIEND

The sessions for James's second Warners album commenced the first week of January 1971 at Crystal Sound, with the sessions for Carole King's second solo album happening simultaneously just a mile up Vine Street at A&M Studios. With all these gifted friends recording at the same time in such close proximity, there was interplay galore. Peter basically stayed with the ensemble that had served James so well this past year—Kortchmar, Sklar, Kunkel, and King, for, despite working on her own project, Carole found time to play piano on the majority of Taylor's tracks. Various members of Jo Mama were Carole's main musical support, though Taylor and drummer Russ Kunkel both pitched in when they could. With apologies to James Brown, though, the hardest-working man in show business that month was Danny Kortchmar, who managed to play on the majority of *both* projects.

Carole's producer, Lou Adler, commented on how his approach with Carole was akin to Peter's production methodology: "I've always thought we were similar in the way that we produced," he said. "I think he comes from the same school that I do, and that is the sound that you're going after isn't *your* sound—like in the case of Spector with the 'Wall of Sound.' All those records basically sounded alike. But the way that Peter and I record is—you're going after the sound of the artist.

"If you listen to four or five Peter Asher productions, you wouldn't say, 'That's a Peter Asher sound.' Which is the right way to produce," Adler said. "The song's very important, and the artist is very important. And that dictates the production; you don't go in with a particular 'sound I'm gonna get'—it's dictated by the song and the feel of the artist."

Peter emphatically concurred: "I try to come up with the best arrangement and production that will specifically suit *that* singer and *that* song."

One example from these new sessions in which the song dictated the sound palette Peter chose was the track "Riding on a Railroad." Evoking some dark, sepia-colored landscape, a stark banjo (played by John Hartford) helps to set the mood immediately as James begins to sing. A desolate fiddle is heard in the distance, placing us at some dusty crossroads. The rest of the band eventually eases in as James wearily tells of constantly moving, with those seemingly "in charge" as much of a prisoner as anyone on board. Bassist Lee Sklar weaves beautifully throughout, deftly dancing around James's guitar and vocal. Just as the minor-key lament moves toward its close, fiddler Richard Greene takes off, lifting the energy upward as we ride the train into the distance.

Though already friends with expert picker Hartford (writer of "Gentle on My Mind"), Peter only knew Greene by his reputation as the hot fiddler with the band Seatrain. But he knew they'd both be perfect for the song, and his instincts were correct, to say the least. Peter also understood that for the gentle ballad "You Can Close Your Eyes," nothing was needed—just James's voice and his melodic guitar playing were enough. Again, serving the song and the artist—or, as Lou Adler would say, the "right way" to produce.

Besides all the creativity necessary when working in a recording studio, there is also the organizational aspect of record production, which is "underrated," Peter felt. "Making sure you've got the right studio and the right engineer, and the musicians know when to be there and that you decide which songs you're cutting on which days and have the musicians you need *on* those days . . ." He took a breath finally, continuing: "That really basic, seemingly trivial stuff *is* really important because, otherwise, it all gets screwed up. You go, 'Oh, I wish we could do *that* song today, but we don't have the pedal steel. Ugghh . . .' And then it delays things—it wastes money, it wastes time, changes the mood—you know, every aspect affects every other aspect.

"So, I am quite obsessively organized," Peter admitted, "with advanced notes on how I'm going to do everything."

But there was always time to experiment and try out ideas, and "James always had good arrangement ideas," said Peter. Arrangement ideas that, at one particular point, were not *quite* welcomed. During the sessions, recalling the great feel The Memphis Horns brought to the Tony Joe White album, Peter took James and traveled back to Memphis's Ardent Studios in hopes of adding their Stax-like sound to a couple of James's tracks.

It was the middle of winter, but the activity inside of Ardent was keeping the temperature up. Large panes of glass separated the control booth from the spacious recording studio. Sitting up in the booth, engineer Terry Manning tweaked the sound coming through his console. Down on the floor, Wayne Jackson and his fellow musicians listened to the playback of James's song "Love Has Brought Me Around," working out the horn arrangement between them, as they always had.

As Peter and James watched the creative musical teamwork unfolding before them, James turned to Peter, saying, "I'm going to run out and give 'em some horn ideas." Manning, who worked with The Horns at Stax when they were part of that label's house band, raised his eyebrows, smiled, and thought: "Hmmm . . . let's see

James, Peter, and Terry Manning at Ardent Studios, Memphis, February 1971.
© 2021 Terry Manning.

how this plays out. 'Cause the only other person I knew who had ever given them parts was Otis Redding." Singing one of Redding's signature phrases, Manning explained, "'Fa-fa-fa-fa-fa-fa . . .' That's him singing a horn line."

James lankily strolled out through the heavy soundproofed door, walked into the middle of the quintet of players, and said, "Hey, guys, here's an idea: What if you played 'Da-da-da-da . . .'" James sang a strong, melodic line and looked to Wayne Jackson for a response.

Jackson looked at James, then looked up at Manning. Turning back to James, the trumpeter replied, "Well, I got an idea—how 'bout going across the street and getting us some hamburgers?"

James, unfailingly polite, immediately responded: "Yeah! Sure, I can do that. I got this—don't worry," and quickly left with Terry Manning as escort. Returning fifteen minutes later, James and Terry walked in and passed out the burgers to one and all. After a few quick bites, James tried again: "So, guys—what if you played 'Da-da-da-da . . .'"

Wayne Jackson paused for barely a second and shot back: "Well, I got a better idea—can you go get us some wine?"

Manning offered to drive, and off down the street he and James went, stopping at (of all places) Taylor's Liquor. Bringing back a few bottles, Manning pulled Jackson aside and asked, "Do you know who this is?"

"Yeah," Jackson drawled, "some guy who's bugging us!"

"No," Manning explained, "that's the artist."

"So?"

"James *Taylor?*" Manning hoped the name of the hottest new talent in the music industry would give Jackson pause.

"Who's James Taylor?"

"*That* was the beauty of Memphis," Manning said. They didn't know and didn't care; they were there to do their job and wanted to be left alone to get it done. Jackson grinned when reminded of the exchange and, ever the Southern gentleman, expressed his great respect for both James Taylor and Peter Asher, finally stating that The Memphis Horns "sounded great" on that session—which is hard to argue with.

"Two days into recording," engineer Richard Orshoff recalled, "we knew how special it was; we knew that every song was just *magic*, and that James's writing and performances were incredible." But the song and the performance that would supersede the rest was just around the corner . . .

At her session on January 6th, Carole King recorded "You've Got a Friend." James played the gentle acoustic guitar accompaniment on Carole's Lou Adler–produced session, then cut his own version of the song with Peter nine days later. Adler sweetened Carole's take with a small string section, but Peter utilized two excellent background vocalists on his production: James paired with his current girlfriend, Joni Mitchell. The two exquisitely harmonize on the choruses and helped raise King's pretty song of lasting friendship to another level of beauty.

Peter and James proudly played their take for Carole, who had forgotten all about James's plan to record it. It was a "delightful surprise," she said, and knowing a thing or two about what a hit sounds like, immediately implored them: "Yes! Please release this!"

But before the song came out as the album's first single—and even before the album itself came out—a tour had already been planned for the month of March. Jo Mama would open the show with a set based around their Asher-produced debut album, which had been released three months earlier. Carole King would then do a short set of her own (backed by various members of Jo Mama), introducing songs from her brand-new album *Tapestry*, which would conveniently hit stores as the tour began. James would be the headliner, whetting the audience's appetite for his upcoming album by sprinkling a few new songs among his more familiar fare.

One very important date on the tour was the scheduled stop on March 8th at New York's Madison Square Garden—the largest venue James had yet played. After the tour itinerary was finalized, Peter got a call from the Garden's office asking, "Would you consider moving your date?"

Peter asked, "Why?"

They explained the 8th was the date sports promoters wanted for the first Muhammad Ali/Joe Frazier fight—the most anticipated boxing match in a generation. Though not a boxing fan, Peter agreed to move James's show to the 12th on one condition: "We got four fabulous, front-row, super-deluxe, million-dollar seats."

His party found themselves surrounded by sports figures, gangsters, and captains of industry, including Warner Communications CEO Steve Ross, whose shareholders had earned a nice dividend through James Taylor's record sales.

"It was the only boxing match I've ever been to," Peter admitted. "If you start at the top, you know, why compete with that?"

While Peter was busy promoting the tour, Warner's publicity department contacted the public relations firm run by Jim Mahoney. Mahoney was old-school—his clients were Frank Sinatra, Tony Bennett, Andy Williams, and the like. When it came to someone like James Taylor, "I had no interest," Mahoney claimed. But Mahoney had Paul Wasserman working at his company. Wasserman "had the constitution," according to Mahoney, "to put up with a lot of the crap that I didn't want to"—basically, all the things that surrounded the youthful rock'n'roll lifestyle.

"He was an interesting guy," Mahoney said of Wasserman, describing him as "overweight" and "geeky." "But the press loved him," he added, and with Wasserman's connections at *Time* magazine (then the most influential news weekly in the country), he managed the coup of having James's face on the cover of *Time* the week the tour began—needless to say, promotional money well-spent.

"The New Rock: Bittersweet and Low," the cover blared, with an illustration of James staring gauntly at the reader surrounded by a swirl of Peter Max–like color. The article heralded the coming of the gentle "singer/songwriter" in popular music, with tall, dark, and brooding James as its avatar.

There certainly had been "singer/songwriters" since music began. There were lute-playing minstrels in medieval times, for example, singing tales of life and love, commenting on royalty and commonfolk alike. More recently, Bob Dylan, Hank Williams, and even Robert Johnson could, quite accurately, be called singer/songwriters. But the more direct, confessional, seemingly autobiographical approach that was utilized by James and other modern troubadours, delivered in mostly quiet, acoustic settings, *and* aimed at a massive youth market who were troubled and searching for some solace—*that* is what was "new."

As was giving fairly unknown musicians credit on album covers—a manifestation of Peter understanding just how important they were to the success of his projects. "Pop records at that time didn't have credits for musicians—jazz albums did," Russ Kunkel recalled. "Him putting our names on *unbelievably* helped our individual careers. It was like a gigantic ad campaign for us. That was Peter's idea.

"His plan was to build something that was more than just some songs and an artist," Kunkel stated. "And he really accomplished it. He really was instrumental in building that 'Southern California Sound' that J.D. Souther and Linda and The Eagles and Jackson Browne and everybody contributed to, but Peter was a *very* integral part of it."

Peter tried to make the whole experience more of a cooperative by giving the musicians points on the record—in other words, a small amount of profit participation. "It wasn't much, but it was unheard of at the time," said Kunkel. "There was a tremendous amount of loyalty, 'cause when we went on the road and did a tour, we were also promoting the product." Ronstadt later did the same with her backing musicians, but it never seemed to become a standard industry practice.

"Some do." Peter shrugged, then pointedly added: "Most people don't."

"More and more in the record industry," James Taylor observed, "record people don't like musicians and don't trust them much—sort of think of them as difficult and messy, and 'they don't understand the process they're going through.' It's not always the case, but it often is, and Peter is just the opposite."

Peter, according to Taylor, "always had a huge respect for and appreciation of musicians. Not only does he want their opinion and to bring to the arrangement what they hear, but he also pays them well. There was never any question in all the years of his managing me that keeping body and soul together for these musicians was his main priority."

"Keeping body and soul together," as Taylor put it, extended to their time on the road. And the same meticulous care, planning, and oversight that Peter practiced in the studio continued as the Taylor/King/Jo Mama tour began. "You just got the feeling that everything was taken care of," keyboardist Ralph Schuckett recalled. Each musician received a booklet with itineraries and backstage passes, phone numbers and other info, with a per diem for meals handed out weekly to each tour member.

Peter also insisted that professionals were hired for all crew positions—lights, sound, road manager—and "not some stoned-out guy who was a friend of the band," said Schuckett. Remembering how neurotic tours could be during his days with Gordon, Peter was determined to have everything go smoothly.

The tour itself was "a blast," according to vocalist Abigail Haness, with sold-out shows across the country. James was still riding a huge wave of popularity, and Carole's star was ascending. One of the high points of the show for Haness was when Taylor would return to the stage for his first encore. "Carole and I would come out"—Haness smiled—"both wearing the same-colored T-shirt." Performing matching choreography, the pair would then sing backup in their guise as Really and Truly Sincere—"The Sincere Sisters."

Each night on the road, after checking in with the sound mixer and seeing how much the evening's take was at the box office, Peter would also join the band onstage. Lending his voice in harmony and shaking a tambourine, he'd smile at how much the audience loved this music that he had believed in, helped shape in the studio, and soon would present on stages the world over.

Richard Orshoff, who engineered and mixed John Stewart's *Willard*, the debut efforts from Kate Taylor and Jo Mama, plus the new, soon-to-be-released James Taylor album, had learned much from working with Peter. "When we first started working together," Orshoff recalled, "I said, 'Tell me what you want from me.' He said, 'I want the sound to be clean, I want you to be on top of everything that's happening—if something needs changing, let me know immediately, and we'll change it—and I want you to have the tape running *all the time* . . . you never know what they're going to do.'

"I remember Peter saying to me one day," Orshoff continued, "when I asked him how he thinks about producing, he said, 'Well, I find the best artists I can possibly find who write the best material there could possibly be, I make sure they're surrounded by the finest musicians that there are, I get the best studio and the best engineer I can, and I get out of the way. And I try to make it all work together, and I say what I have to say when I need to.'

"Peter was just completely accomplished at a level of almost spiritual patience and presence with his artists that I just took as a given," Orshoff said, "since this was the first real class-A guy I was working with. And when I carried that into *my* work, it proved to have the same kind of impact."

That work began shortly after Taylor's album wrapped. Orshoff was recording Johnny Rivers performing a song by a young songwriter named Jackson Browne. Browne stopped by to play on the session and, afterward, he performed a few new songs for those assembled. Impressed, Orshoff offered to produce Browne, who was already booked to fly to London and work with producer Denny Cordell. Orshoff recalled saying, "Oh, what a shame. Well, if it doesn't work out, come on back—I'd love to produce your album."

Cordell was hoping Browne's debut would end up on his own label, Shelter Records. But halfway through the sessions, Browne's manager, David Geffen, informed Cordell that he was definitely starting a label of his own—Asylum Records—and that Browne's album would be one of his initial releases. "And Denny," according to Browne, "just didn't show up for the next session."

With the master tapes from these London sessions in legal limbo, Browne returned to LA determined to start afresh. Meeting with Orshoff, the two discussed what the album *could* be. "From the very beginning, we talked about the beauty of simplicity," Orshoff said. "Letting two or three instruments speak, rather than layering a bunch of stuff on top of it." They spent two days cutting demos and presented them to Geffen, who gave the go-ahead for Orshoff and Browne to produce the album together. Jackson Browne's first record became a classic, ultimately selling over a million copies.

"There is *no doubt*," Orshoff stated, "that you can hear Peter's influence throughout that whole album." That influence included the hiring of Russ Kunkel and Lee Sklar to back Browne, who was a neophyte in choosing musicians to work with. "Here was this world that was filled with amazing players. I didn't know how to choose any or how to pick them. I just gravitated to whatever Peter did," Browne told me. "I was only happy to have somebody whose work I really admired and whose choices seemed to be so surefooted to sort of emulate.

"I think that he was really a huge influence on everything that came to pass in those years when I made my first half-dozen records, and influenced me on every one of them, really—from either copying where he went and who he worked with or

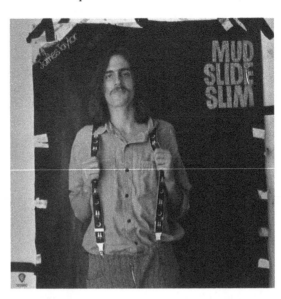

Mud Slide Slim and the Blue Horizon album cover.

taking his direct advice about what to do next or what not to do," Browne admitted. "Invaluable for me."

Peter's production influence was being felt back in Merrie England, as well. Gus Dudgeon, who produced almost all of Elton John's seventies hits, once confessed to Russ Kunkel that he and Elton would "sit down and scrutinize" the records Peter produced and "couldn't wait" to hear what Peter and James would release next.

That next release finally hit the stores in May 1971. *Mud Slide Slim and the Blue Horizon* was the title—a nickname Taylor had concocted for himself and his accompanists. By the end of July, the record sat at number two on *Billboard's* list of best-selling albums, with Carole King's *Tapestry* at the top of the chart. James's heartfelt version of "You've Got a Friend," the interpretation that had so delighted its composer, had managed to delight the record-buying public, as well. The soothing track was inescapable that summer, eventually ascending to the very top of *Billboard's* singles chart.

Though Peter had, for all intents and purposes, produced the worldwide smash "A World Without Love" seven years earlier, "You've Got a Friend" was his first number-one hit with these words emblazoned on the label:

Produced by Peter Asher

15

I BELIEVE IN YOU

The *Mud Slide Slim* sessions and summer tour were bookended by the arrival of two former Apple employees to Peter Asher Management. First, in December of 1970, came Chris O'Dell, the Oklahoma gal who had managed Peter's office while he was Apple Records' A&R director. After stints working for both George Harrison and Eric Clapton, O'Dell received an invitation from Peter to come to Los Angeles and, once again, get his office running smoothly. O'Dell dove in headfirst, moving into the Ashers' Longwood home for her first month on the job. Finding the main residence and its rear office charming, she recalled the corner location had its problems: "Every time a bus went by," said O'Dell, "the house shook."

Second, in July of 1971, came Jack Oliver. Oliver had risen through various Apple departments—from publishing to head of production. Finally, on the recommendation of Paul McCartney, he replaced the ousted Ron Kass, overseeing the label as its president during the regime of Allen Klein, who, recalled Oliver, "was a pain in the ass." When the announcement came in May 1970 that The Beatles were no more, Oliver began to wonder what his next career move might be.

After turning down an offer to run Bell Records in the UK, he remembers arriving home "legless" from a club one night to a ringing telephone—it was Peter. "And three weeks later," said Oliver, "I was in America." Working once again alongside both Peter and Chris, Jack Oliver said he felt as if this former Savile Row team had all "been transported there by some ray . . ."

Oliver had been a performer himself in the sixties as part of The Chocolate Watch Band and knew something of the concert business. But Peter threw him in the deep end immediately: "I had never produced a concert," Oliver admitted. "The first concert that I ever produced was James Taylor at the Hollywood Bowl—September 1971." Tickets started at $2.50, with the highest-priced seats at a whopping $7.50 a piece. The show went flawlessly, and Oliver continued as Peter's close associate for a number of years, eventually going off on his own, producing concerts and tours for Jackson Browne, Cat Stevens, The Eagles, and many others.

"He's very, very, very bright," Oliver said of Peter. "*Very* bright. You know, that's why I think he's not as talkative as he could be—'cause his brain is whirring a thousand miles a second"—he laughed—"computing information . . ."

As the seventies began, EMI's vaults in London were being decimated. In a shortsighted effort to save on storage space, all of Peter and Gordon's multitrack session tapes (and those of many fellow British Invasion–era compatriots) were unceremoniously thrown out, ending up in some landfill. Producer and historian Ron Furmanek discovered this when he was putting together a Peter and Gordon CD compilation in the 1990s. Obviously, Furmanek noted, when it came to The Beatles, "They saved everything." The three-track masters from Peter and Gordon's Nashville sessions survived as they remained at Capitol, never having left the United States. But practically all those original session masters that Peter recorded, work that sold millions of copies, are gone; nothing was saved other than the mono and stereo mixdowns comprising the digital tracks available today. Peter's succinct statement on the matter: "Sad."

But in 1971, Peter was looking forward, not back. *Rolling Stone* magazine's Ben Fong-Torres interviewed him on the eve of Taylor's gig at the Hollywood Bowl. "I've considered performing again," he was quoted as saying, "but I prefer Kate's voice and James's songs. So why do it? If I sent myself an audition tape, I don't think I'd take it."

After almost two years renting their house on Longwood, Peter and Betsy paid $160,000 for a home of their own: 1426 Summit Ridge Drive was a Connecticut farmhouse in the Hollywood Hills—five bedrooms, four fireplaces, lush gardens, and a heated pool. The home's original owner was bandleader Artie Shaw, whose tune "Summit Ridge Drive" became a big hit in 1940—the same year his new bride, screen goddess Lana Turner, moved into the house.

This, of course, meant that the days of squeezing the offices of Peter Asher Management into a cramped sixteen-by-twenty-foot guestroom at the Longwood residence were thankfully at an end. Peter Asher Management moved into a suite of offices on the ground floor of 8430 Santa Monica Boulevard in West Hollywood. Accompanying Peter to the new building was Gloria Boyce, who had taken over as Peter's secretary on Chris O'Dell's suggestion. "She was amazing," according to Peter. "She was very, very enthusiastic, very committed." This twenty-nine-year-old Canadian was so committed, she remained with Peter Asher Management—worrying over the details of tours, recording sessions, and various Asher minutia—for the next thirty years.

The new building was also the American office of famed French oceanographer and conservationist Jacques Cousteau and his two dashing sons, Jean-Michel and Philippe. "I remember," said Peter, "Gloria was always rather enamored of the handsome Cousteaus, who would come and go." Along with the new digs, Peter had just taken on the management of a promising band with an awful name: Country. "I'm forever abashed to say that it was me that came up with the name"—group cofounder Tom Snow laughed—"which couldn't have been worse!"

Alerted to the group's potential thanks to Betsy, Peter was happy to step in and try to help. With the band's album about to come out on Clean Records, Peter arranged a record-release gig at Los Angeles's legendary folk club The Ash Grove, and invited old friends Ringo Starr and Mick Jagger, among other musical titans, to help create an industry buzz. But Snow, one of the two main singer/songwriters in the group, soon left, due to the drugs that were beginning to envelop other bandmates. Peter, who was quick to recognize Snow's potential, turned his attention toward getting him in the studio to showcase his talents.

In early 1972, sessions began at Conway Studios, a new eight-track facility in Hollywood. As producer, Peter brought in stalwarts Danny Kortchmar, Russ Kunkel, and pedal steel guitarist Red Rhodes, who had all played on *Sweet Baby James*. Snow laughed and admitted: "It's an album of me trying to be James Taylor!" With the record's basic tracks completed, rough mixes of the songs were presented to Clean Records, who still had Snow under contract. Unfortunately, Atlantic Records, which distributed Clean, "hated the album," Snow said, and refused to release it. (These rough mixes finally saw the light of day when Slipstream Records released them with the title *Uptown Hopeful* in 2016.)

Disappointing? "Oh," Snow affirmed, "yeah!" But Peter still believed in him, encouraging his songwriting efforts, which would only improve as time went on.

On March 14, 1972, James and Peter attended the Grammy Awards in New York. The year before, the two friends sat in the audience and watched as James lost in every category for which he was nominated—Record, Song, and Album of the Year, along with Best Male Vocalist. "I was a little disillusioned by that," Peter admitted. This year was quite different, as Taylor's recording of "You've Got a Friend" won for Best Male Pop Vocal Performance, beating out Bill Withers, Neil Diamond, Gordon Lightfoot, and, yes, even Perry Como. But it was Carole King's night, taking home trophies for Album, Record, and Song of the Year, along with Best Female Pop Vocal Performance, cementing *Tapestry* as a defining work of the early seventies singer/songwriter era.

Soon after Taylor's Grammy win, sessions began for what would comprise his fourth album. A handful of tracks were cut in New York with Phil Ramone engineering, but the majority of the album was recorded at the home James was in the process of building near Martha's Vineyard. Boldly deciding to engineer the sessions himself, Peter remembered that Ramone was "very gracious with his help. He advised me about what to take . . ." Peter installed a sixteen-track recording console and accompanying tape machine on the ground floor of one of the cabins on James's property, at a time when remote recording was in its infancy. "We set it up and made it work. Amazing, when you think about it." Peter smiled. "Quite ballsy."

One photo on the album's sleeve shows Peter at the mixing board with James's road manager, Jock McLean, assisting as tape operator. Speakers hung from bungee cords and audio cables hastily draped across the room surround the pair. The room itself was rustic with butterscotch-colored wood, and the springtime sunlight from real windows was a welcome change from the usual dark, cocoonlike environs of most studios.

Upstairs, above Peter's jerry-rigged space, rugs covered the unfinished plywood floors, and more sun-drenched windows circled the room where James and his fellow musicians gathered to play. James had bought an old upright piano from Phil Ochs, and one of Steinway's main technicians, Edd Kolakowski, had been brought in from its Manhattan headquarters for a few days to make sure it was in shape.

"I was just thrilled to be a part of it," Kolakowski said and recalled the vibe Peter maintained throughout the sessions: "Nobody was wasting any time . . . it was really pro but relaxed. And self-assured."

Alongside his usual accompanists—Kortchmar, Sklar, and Kunkel—there appeared a new face: Craig Doerge on keyboards. The absence of *Peter's* face, though, due to the cabin's layout, was a bit disconcerting, as he'd "never done a session," recalled Doerge, "where you *can't see the producer!*"

Listed as one of "The 30 Greatest Rock and Roll Keyboardists" in Marsh and Stein's classic tome *The Book of Rock Lists*, Doerge (rhymes with "Fergie") began life in Cleveland, Ohio, studying classical piano at the age of six. "Everybody in the family took piano," Doerge remembered. "I stayed with it longer." Five years later, upon hearing his father's Erroll Garner and Andre Previn albums, Doerge discovered the world of jazz. "When the family would leave the house," he recalled, "I could put on these records, and I would play along with them."

Doerge's family wouldn't support him majoring in music, so he studied economics in college while practicing piano every night and playing in an R&B band on the weekends. After graduating, an old knee injury helped him escape being sent to Vietnam, and Doerge soon moved to Los Angeles, selling pianos and playing in bars while attempting to compose songs and find work as a studio musician. His persistence paid off as, by the beginning of the seventies, he managed to play on sessions produced by Frank Zappa, cowrite a Top Forty hit for Bobby Sherman, arrange tracks for Lee Hazelwood's classic cult album *Cowboy in Sweden*, and release an album as one member of the baroque-folk band Rosebud, featuring singer Judy Henske (whom Doerge soon married).

One session in 1971 proved pivotal: Barbara Keith, the same artist whose first album Peter had produced during his short tenure at MGM, was recording her next release for Warner Brothers Records. It was during those sessions that Doerge first played alongside Lee Sklar, and, suitably impressed, the bassist recommended him for a session coproduced by old friend Richard Orshoff. "That turned out well," Doerge said. Indeed, as "Rock Me on the Water," featuring Doerge's soulful piano intro, became one of the most memorable tracks on Jackson Browne's debut album.

After more sessions alongside Sklar, Kunkel, and Kortchmar—including the first David Crosby/Graham Nash album—Doerge was welcomed into the Peter Asher/ James Taylor circle, initially needing a pianist simply for rehearsals. "I was replacing Carole King," said Doerge, "which was a *huge* thing"—King now concentrating on her massively successful solo career. Rehearsing with Taylor led directly to recording the *One Man Dog* album and its odd recording setup in the cabin on Martha's Vineyard. After the musicians finished a take, Peter's disembodied voice would comment—"One more time," or "Let's move on," or, hopefully, "We've got it. Come down and have a listen."

"I think because Peter is also an artist, he had a real benefit," Doerge observed. "There were a lot of producers we had to work for who were A&R men; they're just in there waiting for the *group* to tell 'em: Is that the take or not? Because they really don't know.

"Peter always *did* know."

And Peter also knew the importance of giving musicians time to settle in, to find the "magic." The old label edict of getting two or three tracks finished in a three-hour session (as Peter and Gordon labored under) was over.

"I think most of what Peter was involved with were records that were allowed to have that magic in them," said Doerge. "The idea that you were given the freedom to make it good was a big deal."

"In many ways, he was responsible for a different kind of recording beginning to happen in LA," James Taylor claimed.

"Because he was so far ahead of things and on top of things," the singer continued, "such a bright guy, so capable, he really could ride the wave of other people's creativity *and* make a community or context where that could really happen." So, Peter let James and his band arrange the songs as they saw fit, and out of that freedom, said Taylor, "he allowed The Section to basically develop."

The Section was the name that Kortchmar, Sklar, Kunkel, and Doerge came to be known by. The recording sessions for *One Man Dog* "really cemented what we would go on to do," according to Doerge. "We were really figuring ourselves out under the inspiration of both James and Peter."

With the success they achieved contributing to the works of Taylor, Browne, and Crosby and Nash, The Section began to get calls to back other artists—many, *many* other artists. The torch was being passed from "The Wrecking Crew"—the title given to the group of musicians who dominated LA's recording studios through the sixties—to The Section, a group of players that were brought into focus by Peter.

They were "'guns for hire.' If you asked them to play on your album," said Taylor, "it's almost like you were hiring a musical director, as well."

"Really, it was Peter's innate authority that allowed that," Taylor explained. "People either have to enforce and demand authority, or else they have an innate authority that everybody just acknowledges, and they don't have to make a deal of it—and Peter was the latter.

"Peter," Taylor continued, "was a smart guy who didn't need to put anybody in their place, and he didn't need to lay down the law. He was directing things because he was the brightest guy there. And he would let the thing go wherever the creativity was coming from." And the creativity was coming from the room of musicians interacting with and bouncing ideas off each other and, in the process, "turning music into gold" (as John Stewart would later put it).

"There were never charts to anything," Sklar explained—meaning no chord changes or notes were presented to the musicians on a James Taylor recording date. "He would come in, play his guitar, and sing a song, and then we would start building it. We would sometimes come up with bridges, intros, how it was gonna end . . ." The musicians would share their melodic imaginings, and Peter kept it all heading in the right direction. "Everything was loose enough that it was all defined when we got into the studio," according to Sklar. "*Then* it could take on everybody else's personalities."

"Being allowed that freedom was really a unique set of circumstances," said Doerge. "There were no rules," Sklar marveled, "and that, to me, was the magic of it."

James's property provided its own magic—acre after acre of gorgeous woods, with various barns and cabins scattered about where the musicians were staying, along with their wives and girlfriends. Danny's wife, Jo Mama vocalist Abigale Haness, was present, as was Craig Doerge's new wife, Judy Henske. James had recently begun a relationship with Carly Simon, who was also staying on the grounds.

"Carly was living a couple of cabins away," Doerge recalled. "I can remember us walking out of our session and hearing the beginning strains of this little piano thing she's writing: '*You're such a pain . . .*'" He laughed, saying, "We heard variations of that phrase until it landed to her satisfaction." The song, of course, became Simon's monster number-one hit "You're So Vain." But Doerge recalled those hearing her efforts were somewhat dismissive: "The idea that she could be a hitmaker or write something that could sell more than JAMES? *Preposterous!*"

The team eventually decamped from Martha's Vineyard and traveled back to Los Angeles. The Section had done various sessions at Clover Recording Studios in Hollywood with engineer Robert Appere, and on their recommendation, Peter used Clover to finish up the album. A handful of new tracks were recorded there, including a beautiful rendition of the old folk song "One Morning in May," arranged as a duet between James and Linda Ronstadt.

Somewhat surprising was the inclusion of the song "Someone," written by British guitarist John McLaughlin, who was mainly known for his instrumental prowess. His current band, The Mahavishnu Orchestra, stood at the forefront of jazz/rock fusion with lengthy jams both fiery and meditative. Peter's lawyer and close advisor, Nat Weiss, was managing McLaughlin's band and played James an early demo of the song. Loving what he heard, James recorded the lyrical jazz composition during the Clover sessions. As happenstance would have it, The Mahavishnu Orchestra passed through LA at the perfect time, allowing McLaughlin to play lead guitar on the track. Engineer Appere remembered the guitarist performing masterfully, getting it in one take.

"I didn't expect to be in the song myself," McLaughlin remarked, but happily participated. This, though, was not the first time he had been in the studio with Peter; in the sixties, when McLaughlin was a "studio shark," as he put it, he got a call to come down to Abbey Road for a recording date. "The session," McLaughlin bemusedly recalled, "was for Peter and Gordon."

All of Taylor's vocals on the album were recorded at Clover, and Appere was amazed at the meticulousness of their process: "It was like working with the sons of two doctors," Appere said—astute, since that's what Peter and James were. Even though Appere insisted that James was "a one-take kinda guy"—nailing a vocal on the first pass—that was never good enough.

"James would do eight vocals," Appere remembered, "and then they would have me systematically premix those down to one track"—basically making one complete vocal pass of the song by, say, taking one line from a particular take and another line from another take (or what's referred to in the business as "comping" a vocal). But even that was not enough, as he would go through more takes, "and we would mix *those* down," said Appere. Finally, after two or even three comped vocal mixes were done, a final master composite vocal would be engineered by taking bits and pieces of the best of the previous comps, combining them together to make the final perfected vocal—quite a feat in this predigital age. It then fell to Appere to take all the recordings—from New York, Martha's Vineyard, and Los Angeles—and come up with the final mixes that comprised the finished album.

One Man Dog is an interesting mixture of songs and instrumentals. Eight of the album's eighteen tracks were also unusually short—ranging in length from around thirty seconds to less than two minutes. Peter, who described the record as "more of a hodgepodge of songs," spent a good amount of time on the record's sequencing, weaving together something akin to Taylor's Apple LP with its short, linking sections. The track that seemed the most commercial and thus chosen as the single was "Don't Let Me Be Lonely Tonight." The pretty, pleading ballad ended up a Top Twenty hit for Taylor.

One Man Dog
album cover.

But, despite another successful collaboration, Taylor felt it was time for a change. "I wanted to make an album with this group of players in New York that I had met," Taylor said—now living in that city and building a new life with Carly Simon. Though Peter would continue as James's manager, the rest of his recorded output in the seventies was without Peter's production expertise.

"I had the sense," Taylor mused, "that there might have been an element of disappointment in it for Peter, but he definitely was always, without any question, in control of his emotional life—he never got it mixed up with his work with me. He was nothing but encouraging about it."

"On a totally *personal* level," admitted Peter, "yes—the idea that he'd work with someone *other* than me . . . *Oooohh!*" Here, Peter feigned being taken aback. "But then, on a more realistic *manager* level, I *was* worried about Spinozza." Peter was referring to David Spinozza, the dazzling guitarist whom Taylor wanted as musical director and producer for his next album. "Because I think, when James is left to his own devices, or in collaboration with 'jazzy' musicians, it tends to veer in that direction—which isn't my favorite direction, and I don't think is the *public's* favorite direction.

"Even though David's an *amazing* guitar player," Peter emphasized, "a complete musical genius, I think James makes his best records when guided by someone who's *not* a musical genius—like me"—he smiled—"or Russ Titelman and Lenny Waronker—who are *very* good at making records, which is *not* quite the same thing."

Around 1973, James's sister Kate was playing a date at Passaic, New Jersey's Capitol Theatre. Linda Ronstadt came to the show and went backstage to chat with Kate, who had known for years that Peter had regretfully turned down Linda's original request to manage her. As they walked from the dressing rooms, Linda remembered Kate telling her, "You know, you really should ask Peter again, because I don't think that I'm gonna be working professionally so much."

"I had done a tour, been on the road," Kate remembered, "and I did feel that I was in the wrong place if I wasn't at home. I mean, I loved it—the work—but I missed home. And I'd come home one time, after a long stretch, and I realized I was losing my base, my home base. And I had to take the time to rebuild it.

"There were other things that I had to do in order to 'grow up,' I think . . . in order to just know more about myself. I was just a kid! And I feel like, looking back on it now, that as much, you know, 'raw excitement' that I had, I was not prepared for all aspects of it, and I needed an anchor . . . a safe harbor." Kate Taylor found that safe harbor, started a family, and didn't resume her recording career for eight years.

"Linda re-approached me after Kate sort of retired," Peter recalled, and not wanting to miss the opportunity a second time, "I said yes."

"My background, really, had been folk music," Linda Ronstadt said, adding, "and the traditional musics that I come from." From practically the beginning of her career, though, she was thought of as a rock singer. She explained: "We were all sort of put into a mold in LA when we got there."

Linda Ronstadt.
Photo by Henry Diltz

With the explosion The Beatles began in 1964, Los Angeles was a ferment of musical activity—everyone was starting bands. "There was a little club in West LA called The Balladeer," guitarist Kenny Edwards recalled, "and David Crosby and the guys in Spirit used to hang around there. It was kind of a perpetual open-mic environment." One night Arizonan musician and songwriter Bobby Kimmel came into The Balladeer and, meeting Edwards, the two hit it off. "He was very ambitious," according to Edwards, "and wanted to put something together. He said, 'I know this great girl singer in Tucson whom I've worked with in the past. We should start a band.'

"I was a traditional folkie coming into this situation," Edwards claimed, but watching friends form bands like The Byrds, "it seemed like the fun thing to do." Also wanting to experiment with combining folk and rock, the pair formed The Stone Poneys upon Ronstadt's arrival from Arizona. She was game, but for more practical reasons: "If you wanted to *eat*"—she laughed—"you had to sing rock'n'roll! And, you know, I'd listened to rock'n'roll since I was five years old. But it wasn't what I'd set out to sing. I probably would have been an opera singer," Ronstadt mused, "if left to my own devices."

Mike Curb signed them originally and produced their first single, but the group was dropped after refusing to change their name and sing surf music. A year later, Nik Venet brought them to Capitol Records, producing their three albums and the smash hit "Different Drum," which did *not* feature Kimmel and Edwards. Getting the message loud and clear from Capitol, the two soon departed, leaving Ronstadt a solo artist.

After Peter had, sorrowfully, turned down the first request to be her manager, Ronstadt asked then-boyfriend John Boylan to take on the task. "I said, 'Linda, I've never managed anyone—I'm a record producer, I'm a studio guy!'" Eventually Boylan agreed. One of the first things he did as manager was look up old friend David Geffen, who had started Asylum Records the previous year and signed many of Ronstadt's friends, including her old band, now The Eagles. Boylan told Geffen, "We'd love to get off Capitol 'cause they don't *get* her."

Capitol's problems ran deeper than a simple one of misunderstanding an artist. "The company was in a state of some flux," Bhaskar Menon, former president and CEO of Capitol Records, said diplomatically, "and it had gone through a bad financial year, and there were management issues." Al Coury was more direct on the matter: "Capitol was in the shithouse."

Coury, whom we last heard from promoting a Peter and Gordon concert on their first tour (and helping to smash Peter's head against a brick wall during their escape), was running Capitol's Promotions and Marketing Department in 1973. Coury describes Capitol Records in the early seventies as "not makin' any money, not spendin' any money. Every time you walked in to have a meeting, you had a different president! We had four presidents in one year! You know? And so she wanted to bail out of a sinking ship." Ronstadt and Menon met for lunch, and she made it unsparingly clear that, despite owing Capitol three more albums, she wanted to leave for Asylum, and that sooner would be better than later.

"Mr. Menon," Ronstadt pleaded, according to Boylan, "you don't *need* me! You've got Helen Reddy, you've got Anne Murray! *Please* let me go!"

"My general view was that it was better to seek some other path, other than that of enforcing the clause in her contract," Menon recalled. "Out of this there arose a compromise that struck me as fair and, I thought, should be acceptable to all parties." The agreement was that Capitol would let her out of the requirement of delivering the remaining albums she still owed, leaving her free to record for Geffen's label. But Capitol would be able to listen to her next three albums, "mixed and ready to be released," Menon said, and if one of those struck the Capitol brass as a potential hit, "we would have first option to exercise our right to claim that master as belonging to us and to put out the record."

Quite a savvy arrangement—Capitol would not only maintain a good relationship with Ronstadt by letting her go, but they would hopefully also reap the reward of a solid album, as the move to Asylum would most likely cause her to, as Menon put it, "blossom" as an artist.

As the sessions for Ronstadt's first Asylum album got underway, her romantic relationship with Boylan came to an end, and she began seeing fellow Asylum artist J.D. Souther. The handsome and talented Souther was born in Detroit, but grew up mainly in Amarillo, Texas. The son of a crooning father and grandson to an opera singer, Souther was intensely musical growing up, playing violin, clarinet, saxophone, and drums.

"When I was a kid," Souther recalled, "during my most formative period of music—thirteen to sixteen—I thought the best possible life imaginable was to be Miles Davis's drummer. I'd be in Paris, smokin' joints, fuckin' beautiful women, playin' behind Miles . . ." But instead of east toward France, Souther headed west to California.

He was introduced to another son of Detroit, musician Glenn Frey, at a Los Angeles coffeehouse. The pair formed a duo, christened Longbranch Pennywhistle, recorded one album, and played the Southern California clubs. Souther recalled catching one of James Taylor's first shows at The Troubadour and introducing himself afterward: "We had cut a song of his, 'Don't Talk Now,' on the *Longbranch Pennywhistle* album," he said. At the end of Taylor's set, Souther remembered he and Frey "stumbling up the stairs to the dressing room—'Wow! James! We cut your song!' And he was, like, 'Who are you?' He was polite—I mean, James is one of the most unfailingly polite people I've ever met—but"—Souther laughed—"we were *sorely* disappointed that our 'cred' wasn't such that we were taken very seriously."

It was also at The Troubadour where Souther met Linda Ronstadt. "I was lurking, as I always was in those days. I had nowhere to go but a tiny apartment and a Triumph to get there on." Watching Ronstadt walk from the bar toward the dressing rooms, he grabbed his chance: "I asked her to sit down, and I took her by the hand, and I said, 'I think you ought to cook me dinner.' And she said, 'Okay,' and gave me her phone number. And I called her, and I said, 'I'm coming over for dinner,' and she goes, 'Okay.' And I got there, and she made me a peanut butter sandwich."

As Boylan bowed out, leaving it to Souther to finish producing Linda's current sessions, his two-year management contract with her was also at an end—opening the door for Peter to finally take on Linda as his client. "I remember going to lunch with Peter and Jack Oliver," Boylan recollected, "for the official transition. Peter laughed and said, 'Well, you brought her to me two years ago—it took me two years to get her!'"

In these days of lawyers and deals and one-hundred-page contracts, it's astounding that one of the most successful musical partnerships of the seventies was cemented with only mutual love, respect, and trust. "We never signed any contracts," Ronstadt said. "Everything we did was with a handshake.

"You know, we always figured that if we wanted to work together, we'd work together. And if we didn't want to"—she laughed—"it wouldn't work very well if we didn't want to!" So, on May 18, 1973, as Peter went into the studio to produce Linda properly for the first time, helping Souther button up her first Asylum album, it seems fitting that the song they cut was Neil Young's "I Believe in You."

It was very simple: "She liked working with me," Peter said, "and I with her."

By this time, The Troubadour was one of the preeminent music spots in Los Angeles, and Doug Weston, its owner, was exercising his power—pissing off musicians and managers in the process. Artists, for example, would have to give Weston seven options for future gigs with their payday locked in at their original fee. Someone like Elton John, who made his US debut at the club, would have to play the club again years later, as one of the biggest stars in the music world, for a pittance. Elton eventually paid Weston $25,000—"just to get out of all those options," recalled producer/manager Lou Adler.

"For me, it wasn't pleasant," Adler said of the way the Troubadour management behaved, "and I imagine for the other managers/producers, it wasn't that pleasant." Spying a closed strip club on Sunset Boulevard, Adler, who had helped produce the landmark Monterey International Pop Festival in 1967, saw an opportunity "to open a state-of-the-art club with great sound," he said, adding importantly, "and treat the artists right."

Adler's original partners in the venture were LA club impresario Elmer Valentine, plus the three hottest managers in the LA music business: David Geffen, Elliot Roberts, and Peter Asher. "It wasn't a difficult sell," Adler recalled. "It was, 'Here's what we're planning to do—do you want to be a part of it?'" The Roxy opened in September 1973 and quickly eclipsed The Troubadour as Hollywood's most important nightclub.

Ronstadt and Souther became regular visitors at the Ashers'—swimming in the pool and generally hanging out. Peter and Betsy "were just nice," said Ronstadt. "They were very social. There was always a crowd of musicians in the living room, and people would be pulling out guitars and playing and singing." Laughing, she added: "And there was good food! So they were popular!"

Asylum Records released *Don't Cry Now* in October 1973 to positive reviews, and as a good manager would, Peter booked a tour for Linda to promote the record. Needing to refresh her backing musicians, Linda decided to reach out to her old friend and former Stone Poney bandmate, Kenny Edwards. Edwards's current band, The Rangers, was struggling, and Linda, having been impressed with them when they'd opened for her at a George McGovern benefit the previous year, asked if Edwards would join up with her once again. But she wanted Edwards, a guitarist, to handle the bass chores. "It was kind of an 'Earn While You Learn' program," Edwards laughed. He bought a '64 Fender Jazz Bass for $250 and began rehearsing.

She also wanted the lead guitarist from The Rangers, Andrew Gold, to come on board. The son of Hollywood composer Ernest Gold (*Exodus*; *On the Beach*) and movie-musical vocalist Marni Nixon (*The King and I*; *West Side Story*; *My Fair Lady*), Gold became proficient on many instruments, honing his singing and songwriting skills. He also learned about the recording process, working for a year at A&M's studios, second engineer on Joni Mitchell's classic album *Blue* ("Which basically meant," he admitted, "that I put away the cables"). Finally getting the chance to play good-sized venues with a well-known artist, he was "*thrilled*," Gold exclaimed, "because they were carrying my amp! I didn't have to carry my amp on stage and off! I thought this is the *height* of big-time!"

Kenny Edwards recalls those first tours backing Linda: "Everybody was just young and eager . . . what was I? Just twenty-six at the time? And Peter wasn't much older than us, but he had this natural authority . . .

"He was extremely logical and fair and honest—qualities one doesn't often find in a manager!" Laughing, Edwards went down the inventory: "He wasn't pushy, he wasn't underhanded, he wasn't sneaky and playing people off each other. He was so straightforward . . ."

"He was amazing," Ronstadt said of Peter, recalling the early days under his management. "If I didn't make money, he didn't take money." She gives a good example of Peter's managerial selflessness discussing the tour she undertook the following year, in the spring of 1974: "I wanted to buy a washing machine," Ronstadt explained, laughing. "I really wanted a washing machine badly 'cause I was having to go to the Laundromat to do my laundry, and that was a *real* drag! So, I thought, well, if I do this tour, then I could just afford a washing machine—which was about three hundred bucks at the time, I think."

She ended up getting a bad case of the flu and cancelling the last leg of the tour. "My rule is: If I can stand, I sing," she said. "But there was *no question* of me standing or anything. I was *so sick*, I had such a high fever, I was hallucinating. So we didn't finish the tour, and I think Peter didn't take part of his commission so I could afford the washing machine!"

The concerts she played from late 1973 through early 1974 helped propel *Don't Cry Now* toward a Gold Album Award—Linda's first. While she recuperated from her flu, Peter began his preproduction work on what would be Linda's next album. Within a year, she would be able to afford any home appliance she desired.

16

HEART LIKE A WHEEL

Back in late 1970, as the *Sweet Baby James* rehearsals were underway in Peter's living room, Linda Ronstadt was in New York, hitting the folk clubs and reconnecting with old friends, including singer/songwriters Jerry Jeff Walker and Paul Siebel. One evening, as the clubs closed up for the night, the troupe trekked over to the apartment of Gary White (author of Linda's first solo hit "Long, Long Time")—playing guitars and swapping songs 'til dawn.

As the sun began to rise, Linda and Jerry Jeff bid their fellow revelers adieu and hailed a cab. Continuing to discuss music and songs, Walker brought up the McGarrigles—two Canadian sisters, Anna and Kate, who had been performing throughout the '60s in the folk ensembles Le Trio Canadien and The Mountain City Four. He'd seen them recently at a folk festival and was taken by one song in particular. As their taxi rumbled through the streets, Walker sang what he could remember of it to Ronstadt: "*Some say the heart is just like a wheel . . .*"

Ronstadt recalled how dumbstruck she was upon hearing Walker's rendition of only the first verse of "Heart Like A Wheel": "I thought it was the best song I'd ever heard!"

"Their stuff sounded like latter-day Stephen Foster songs," singer Maria Muldaur said of the McGarrigle sisters, calling them "great, wonderful, sensitive, creative, talented songwriters, singers and musicians." The following year, Ronstadt was visiting Maria and her husband Geoff at their home in Woodstock, New York—long a haven for musicians and artists. As guitars were brought out and songs were shared, Maria eventually closed her eyes and began to delicately perform "Heart Like A Wheel." Linda, amazed, asked: "*You know that song, too?*" The song was sublime. She felt she simply had to record it.

When asked, Ronstadt explained what attracts her to a song: "It has to tell a story that I find to be absolutely compelling, in a way. It's not always my story exactly, but it's got a *part* of my story and maybe a part of a friend's story. And a part of something that"—she laughed—"maybe I'm afraid is gonna happen to me!

"I think the thing that will seduce me to start with," she continued, "will just be the way the chords are voiced, you know? It'll be something just in the chords that kinda rips your heart out and commands your attention. Then pretty soon there might be a lyric that starts to get you. Because lots of times there'll be a chord and a lyric that I go, 'Oh my God! That's it!' That's, you know, 'ground zero' of my emotional earthquake that I just had.

"And then some more words will come, and you go, 'Eewww! Too bad about that, but I'll get around it.' Or 'Eewww! That's a weird turn for the melody. My voice doesn't handle it too well, but I'll just jump over it and get back to the part I like.'" Obviously, with this McGarrigle tune, there wasn't anything Ronstadt needed to avoid—it was emotionally and vocally a perfect fit. She had begged Walker to ask the McGarrigles to get a tape of the song to her immediately. "They did," Ronstadt said, "and it just opened up a whole world for me."

For the next few years, Ronstadt recalled, "Every time I played it for somebody in the music business there in LA, they'd go"—and here, she snorted derisively—"'That's so *corny!* Are you crazy? *That's* not a hit!' You know? So I'd go, 'Well, it's a really great *song!*'"

With her new manager and producer, Ronstadt remembered, the outcome was quite the opposite: "When Peter heard the song, he thought it was just *beautiful* and wanted to record it right away. So, I mean, to me *that* was the difference between *him* and the other people that were sort of 'in the scene' there; that he could understand those subtler things that I thought were just really finer and had a different kind of history to them."

Peter and Linda. *Photo by Ron Galella/ Ron Galella Collection via Getty Images.*

On *Don't Cry Now*, Peter had come in at the very end of the process. Now, for the first time, Peter and Linda were starting a project together. Though it sounds like common sense, Peter admitted doing something that "not everybody did back then," he claimed, "especially to women"—and that was actually *listen* to her ideas. They began by discussing song possibilities: "A lot of song ideas come out of free-ranging conversations about favorite songs and favorite writers," Peter said. "I would present songs," Ronstadt recalled, "and Peter would go, 'Well, I like this one,' and 'That one seems a bit weak.'" "Some people," said Peter, "make the assumption that I chose all the songs, which is far from being the case. In *many* cases, she knew what songs she wanted to do." Peter's job, he felt, was to "try to get the best of her ideas incorporated and just keep things organized."

"Peter was very good, trying to help me find my voice," Ronstadt enthused, "and helping me achieve what I was trying to do." Peter also learned a few things from working with Ronstadt. "Most of what I know about country music I learned from Linda, so I owe her a debt of gratitude for that," he said, and offered an example: "I always thought The Everly Brothers were totally original until Linda started playing me The Louvin Brothers and all this other music, and I went, 'Oh! So they were copying *them!*'"

Almost all the tracks that were selected were songs of loneliness, despair, and love gone quite wrong. Along with "Heart Like a Wheel," these included Hank Williams's "I Can't Help It (If I'm Still in Love with You)"—already a feature in Linda's live shows. Growing up in Tucson, Hank's classic tearjerker was one of the tunes Linda would sing with her siblings as she learned about harmony.

During the search for material, old friend Chris Darrow had suggested "Dark End of the Street"—what he referred to as "maybe my favorite song of all time." Written by Dan Penn and Chips Moman, the soulful James Carr had searingly first recorded this tale of shameful, irresistible sin back in the mid-sixties. Another song that drew on the same subject was "Faithless Love," an aching ballad by J.D. Souther, written near the end of his relationship with Linda. Though he didn't begin writing it with her in mind, "I was conscious of the fact that she would probably do it," Souther confessed. "I just felt sure she would.

"I thought she was a remarkable ballad singer," Souther continued. "If I had an instrument like that, I would just revel in it.

"But you know? I don't—I have to work with what I got."

It should be noted that Little Feat's Lowell George was actually responsible for producing the first track completed for these sessions. "Keep Me from Blowing Away" was recorded earlier in the year, but his involvement is acknowledged only with a small "thanks" in the liner notes. When I pointed this out to Peter, he was surprised: "God, I went and screwed Lowell out of a coproduction credit! I would have happily given it to him," he said, genuinely puzzled. "I don't know why . . ."

The Asher-produced sessions began at Clover Studios, where Peter had finished up Taylor's *One Man Dog*. Bob Warford, Kenny Edwards, and Andrew Gold, then members of Ronstadt's current touring band, were hoping they'd be asked to play.

"We didn't know," Edwards recalled, "'cause we were 'just the road guys.'" "At that time," guitarist Bob Warford explained, "if you're gonna go in the studio to do an album, most of the time the producers are gonna be using studio guys."

Warford had some experience as a "studio guy," playing anonymously on albums for acts such as Kenny Rogers and The First Edition. But he had really developed a solid reputation as a guitar slinger touring behind both Roy Orbison and The Everly Brothers, along with other acts also straddling the country and rock genres. Gram Parsons had unsuccessfully offered Warford a spot in The Flying Burrito Brothers, and Ronstadt had wanted him in her band for years, finally hiring him just before Edwards and Gold came on board.

Though having not recorded with them before, Peter thought it proper to give Linda's "road guys" their chance. On June 18, 1974, they laid down the basic tracks for Lowell George's ultimate truckers ode, "Willing," followed by Paul Anka's lilting acceptance of romantic defeat, "It Doesn't Matter Anymore," which opens with Bob Warford's expert flat-picking. "Everyone was really pleased," remembered Edwards, "so we went on . . ."

Peter was particularly impressed with the breadth of Andrew Gold's musicality. "I think he really enjoyed how I could play a million instruments," Gold recounted. "For that album, it was kind of nice—as he was sort of just starting to get off the ground as a real producer—to just deal with a few people. And so, I ended up playing drums and bass and guitar, which was something I wanted to do anyway."

Edwards described Gold as "sort of this mad scientist . . . And, with Peter, they shared this love of The Beatles' musicianship." Noting that he and Peter both loved the affective touch of adding percussion to a track, as well as singing background harmonies, "we found we had a very distinct camaraderie," Gold said, "so we really got pretty close right away.

"You know, there are some people who don't find him the warmest person in the world," Gold said of Peter. "And I have always found him a complete gentleman—logical, bright, and funny as hell."

Just as Peter had built a solid team around James Taylor, he was beginning to do the same around Linda Ronstadt. At the string overdub sessions for the track "Heart Like a Wheel," another musician made his first contribution to a Peter Asher production, but it certainly would not be his last.

String player and arranger David Campbell had actually met Peter two years earlier while backing Carole King on her first solo tour following the massive success of *Tapestry*. When the tour stopped at New York's Carnegie Hall, Campbell and a colleague decided to busk in the street as the crowd waited to enter the illustrious venue, passing the hat. "We made a lot of money," Campbell recalled, but they were having too much fun and lost track of time. Finally, back in the dressing room divvying up the cash, opening night guest Peter Asher walked in and calmly said, "David—you're on," as King had started her set.

"I got out there and sat down just before I had to play my first note." Campbell laughed. "But that was my first meeting with Peter."

After the tour, Campbell began working with other artists as an arranger—notably for Jackson Browne. He had just finished recording the string arrangements for Browne's *Late for the Sky* album when Peter began Linda's sessions at Clover. Chuck Plotkin, Elektra/Asylum's head of A&R, owned the studio and, knowing Campbell's talents, advised Peter, "You have to call this guy." Campbell admitted that Plotkin "really did me a great favor there."

Campbell fashioned a delicate string quartet accompaniment for "Heart Like a Wheel," perfectly underscoring Andrew Gold's stately piano, all in support of Ronstadt's heartfelt voice. And echoing the McGarrigles' delivery, Maria Muldaur provided the lovely harmony vocal.

Peter decided to decamp over to The Sound Factory and work with owner and engineer Dave Hassinger. Hassinger, who had engineered such great tracks as The Rolling Stones' "Satisfaction," The Electric Prunes' "Too Much to Dream," and Jefferson Airplane's "White Rabbit," began the project manning the recording console next to Peter, but soon turned things over to his assistant. "Dave, being at that time about fifty-two years old and all of us being in our early thirties, kept trying to pawn them off on me because I was the 'up-and-coming guy,'" Val Garay remembered. "He wanted to go home, basically!"

Val Garay was the son of Latin entertainer Joaquin Garay, who voiced the character Panchito in Walt Disney's *Three Caballeros* and who also appeared as one of the impromptu singers on the bus in the famous scene from Frank Capra's *It Happened One Night*. Val attended Stanford's medical school, on his way to becoming a vascular surgeon. "But I met a girl who was a cocktail waitress in a bar, got in a band," Garay said with a smile, "and that was the end of my medical career!"

Garay's band, The Giant Sunflower, was signed by producer Lou Adler in 1966. Just as their single was about to hit, legal wrangling caused it to be pulled, and unfortunately, more bad breaks followed. Finally, a good break: After working alongside Dave Hassinger on a project, Garay remembers the legendary engineer saying, "You know, you have great ears. Why don't you come work for me and I'll teach you?"

Fast-forward three years: Garay began to run the board beside Peter Asher. At first perturbed that Hassinger was substituting an unknown engineer in his stead, Peter soon found he was in very good hands. "Peter and I sorta became friends," Garay stated simply. "Peter's very close to the vest and very staid in some ways, but I understood him. I liked his persona, and we really got along." A fair statement, as Val Garay would go on to engineer every Asher-produced project for the next eight years.

More fine tracks were recorded as sessions continued at The Sound Factory. Phil Everly's "When Will I Be Loved" was a standout, featuring an arrangement by Ronstadt. "I do remember telling Andrew guitar stuff to play," Ronstadt recalled, resulting in Gold's concise and startling solo. Taken at a quicker clip than The Everly Brothers' original, the combination of Linda's pleading vocal, countrified harmonies courtesy of Gold and Edwards, plus Peter's rock-solid cowbell, all equaled a track brimming with hit potential.

Peter decided to take a third try at James Taylor's "You Can Close Your Eyes," after first producing the song on *Sister Kate*, followed by James's own version on *Mud Slide Slim*. Glenn Frey and Don Henley provided guitar and drums, respectively, just as they had done back when The Eagles were Linda's road band. Afterward, Peter—for the only time during these sessions—stepped up to the mic and added a few takes of harmony to the beautiful lullaby.

"He's a good harmony singer," said Ronstadt. "I can *always* recognize his voice. He's a very accurate singer . . . and he was good at helping to sort out parts." "He sings great harmony," added James Taylor. "He has one of those voices, like Carole King or my friend David Lasley, that really fuses together a choral sound or a stack of vocals."

"You're No Good" was yet another song about a hurtful breakup, but here the singer emerges broken but unbowed. "I remember that it was Kenny Edwards's idea to do the song," Ronstadt said. "He was the one that had come up with it years ago." Edwards concurred: "I was a fan of that kind of songwriting," he said, "and I thought she would be great singing it."

This minor-key slice of American soul, written by Clint Ballard Jr., was originally recorded in 1963 by both Dee Dee Warwick and Betty Everett—with Dee Dee's version having more of an edgy rawness over Betty's slinky restraint. A year later, British band The Swinging Blue Genes had a UK Top Five hit with their cover, of which Peter was a big fan. Almost a year before recording the song, Ronstadt, due to Edwards's suggestion, had added it to her live repertoire.

"Because, you know, when you play a club," Ronstadt explained, "and we played clubs all over the country in those days, that's what we mainly did—places like The Troubadour—you had to have something really loud to begin with"—she laughed— "to shut 'em up, and you had to have something really loud to end with, so they'd be going: '*Yeeaaww!*' Because you had to get their faces out of their beer, you know? So, I remember that those songs that were *hits*—'You're No Good' and those—they were all the songs that I put in there so that I could put padding around the songs that I really loved to sing, like 'Heart Like a Wheel.'"

An early attempt, recorded on the first of July 1974, was close to what Ronstadt had been doing live the past year, but the final result—a quick-tempo R&B groove—simply didn't suit Ronstadt's vocal phrasing, and the track was shelved and left unfinished. The song was "cut about five times," engineer Val Garay said, "with five different rhythm sections." Finally, on July 5th, Peter decided to forgo another attempt to cut the track live in the studio and began to build it bit by bit.

Guitarist Eddie Black, who had also been part of Ronstadt's recent touring band, came up with the slightly ominous opening riff as arrangement ideas were being tried. Kenny Edwards on bass and Andrew Gold on drums made up the rhythm section that completed the foundation of the basic track. Gold, being the ultimate Beatles fan he was (he had even met the group at a Hollywood party during their first US tour), had Ringo's solid, unfussy drumming style down and put it to good use here.

Ronstadt delivered a live vocal that was hurt, furious, sexy, and strong—and she was not happy with it. Her vocals on the last verse especially, coming off the solo break, she felt were "screechy," according to Kenny Edwards, who strongly disagreed, calling it "one of the most amazingly exciting passages in her career. . . . It's just incisive and desperate and passionate."

Besides the work Black and Edwards did on the basic track, Gold "went in and overdubbed everything on that record—all the keyboards, all the guitars," engineer Garay said. First one pass with electric piano, then another an octave higher. A fifteen-bar hole had been left in the middle of the song, and now Gold began to work out guitar ideas to fill it.

"I think I read somewhere," Gold said regarding Peter, that "he said: 'The thing about Andrew is there's never any problem with ideas—you have to *edit* him!'" Gold laughed and confessed that "too many ideas" could be a problem for him, but Peter patiently helped Gold select the choicest riffs and discard the rest as the solo section was built.

"The solo was done in unbelievable layers," Garay said, and described the method as Gold first coming up with a part and then slowly teaching himself how to play it. Once Gold had a part down, he would double or even triple it, which took hour upon hour of work. And along with engineer Garay slightly varying the tape speed for subsequent passes, Gold would make his guitar strings sharp or flat by a mere semitone to give the parts a noticeably more jangly effect—something that John Lennon himself used to do.

With Peter and Andrew both being big fans of percussion touches, a series of handclaps were added during the song's coda. Calling Val Garay down from the recording booth to join them, the three men worked hard to synchronize their hands, clapping away on the off-beats as the track reached its conclusion.

Finally, after a couple of days of recording, "we decided to do a rough mix," said Garay. "Just a rough." This was back in the days before consoles were equipped with memory, so every mix was done by hand—or hands, more precisely: "They would work out who is gonna do what," Gold recalled. "So, I would push a fader up, and Peter would push a couple of faders up, and Val would do the rest."

"We started at seven at night," Garay remembered. The mix that was only supposed to be a "rough" was tried again and again and again, as the three men pushed themselves to perfect this track that each of them knew was special. Finally, at seven the next morning they stepped out into the sunlight. Gold remembered thinking, "Okay, we finally got it."

They played the mix for Linda when she arrived a few hours later . . . "And she *hated* it," Garay claimed. Ronstadt, along with her then-boyfriend, actor/writer/comedian Albert Brooks, thought Peter and Andrew had perhaps gone a tad overboard with the Beatle-esque guitar solo. Linda called Kenny Edwards and requested he head over with his electric guitar. "She made him play blues solos over that thing"— Garay laughed—"for, like, four hours, and we were all ready to kill ourselves."

Edwards shook his head, still in disbelief, and remembers saying to Ronstadt, "*Please* don't make me do that! This is great!" But she insisted he replace Gold's meticulously thought-out solo with something that was more traditionally bluesy— "which I was good at," Edwards said with a smile. So the solo changed from Gold's Harrison-influenced lead to a take decidedly more Clapton-sounding.

"She liked that better," Edwards recalled. But within a few hours, he remembered Ronstadt coming around to the commercial possibilities of Gold's version: "She was going, 'Y'know . . . that other one *does* sound like money . . .'"

That summer, Peter phoned his sister Clare—then getting her teaching degree at Oxford. Clare had been an organ scholar (playing the instrument on Peter's first credited production), and though she was now concentrating on childhood education, she still had musician friends in her circle.

"I'm looking for somebody in the classical field to do some arranging for me," Peter explained. "Any ideas on who might be interested?" Clare simply turned to her flat mate, Gregory Rose, and asked: "Do you want to do some rock arranging?" Surprised, Rose replied, "That sounds very cool!"

"The great thing about Peter," Rose said, "is he's always looking for a slightly new angle. I think that's why he's so successful." Peter had decided for Ronstadt's album to avoid the standard "pop" arrangements and go for someone with more classical sensibilities. Gregory Rose certainly fit that bill.

Rose—like Peter, a former choirboy—had been a friend of Clare's for years. Rose's father was the esteemed organist and composer Bernard Rose, who had studied music alongside a promising classmate named Margaret Asher. Graduating with his music degree, and after a short stint at teaching, young Gregory was in London just beginning his career as a composer and conductor.

"Peter said, 'Well, look—we'll give you two tracks, and we'll see how that goes,'" Rose remembered. He sketched in some strings over the rough mixes Peter sent, and the results were mailed back on a cassette. Peter liked what he heard and soon flew to London for the string overdub session booked at AIR Studios, with Andrew Gold in tow.

Rose recalled that Peter "gave me a lot of freedom" on the arrangements; for example, regarding the song "You Can Close Your Eyes," Rose remembered Peter telling him, "You can do what you like here." Boldly, Rose fashioned a somewhat heroic arrangement, adding a sense of strength to the fragile ballad.

For the end of "You're No Good," Peter asked Rose, "What should we do with this?" "Well, one idea might be to do a very quiet, single note that gets louder and louder and louder," Rose suggested, "and what I'll try and do is make it explode at the end." The resulting twelve-bar buildup ending in a flurry of descending notes in the song's coda was one of the unexpected, thrilling pleasures of the track. "It's so unlike what I call 'normal' rock backing," Rose said. "That's the sort of classical angle I think that Peter quite liked."

While overdubbing strings for "The Dark End of the Street," Peter asked Rose for a slight change. Lead guitarist Bob Warford had slowly bent his concluding note, and Peter felt the strings should follow suit, gently swooping upward at the very end. Andrew Gold, Rose remembered, was also heavily involved during these sessions, offering harmony ideas for various arrangements. "I very much enjoyed working with Andrew," said Rose, as impressed with Gold's musicality as Peter was.

Returning to The Sound Factory with the tapes, Peter sat with engineer Val Garay and oversaw the final mixes, adding some last-minute touches. One was having the first guitar strum of "Willing" begin before the ending harmonies of "When Will I Be Loved" had faded out; the songs were in the same key and thus dovetailed beautifully together. Now, with a mixed master of the album, Peter had to let Capitol hear it. They had passed on the previous album, *Don't Cry Now*—would they do the same with this one?

One September day in 1974, Al Coury, head of Capitol's Promotions and Marketing Department, received a call from label president Bhaskar Menon, who announced: "Peter Asher just called me. He's got a new Linda Ronstadt album finished." Coury was well known for his great ears, famously convincing Paul McCartney to release the track "Jet" as a single, resulting in one of Wings's biggest hits. Peter telephoned Coury and invited him down to the studio to hear what he and Ronstadt had created.

Her deal with Capitol stated that upon hearing the finished work, they had three weeks to make up their minds. On the phone, according to Coury, "Peter said, 'Al, do me a favor: listen to it and let me know. I can't wait three weeks to find out if you're gonna pass or not.'

"I said, 'Okay, Peter,'" Coury continued. "'I don't give a shit about what the contract says—I'm gonna listen to it, and I'll let you know if we're taking it or whether we're passing and Geffen's gonna put it out.'" Coury explained: "If Geffen took it,

Heart Like A Wheel album cover.

then we had the same deal with the next—she had to keep giving us her next album until we took one." At the end of the day, Coury headed over to The Sound Factory.

"I listened," recalled Coury. "I only listened to side one. Okay? I don't even know if I listened to the whole side. It was *Heart Like a Wheel!* It was fuckin' great! I realized, when I was listening to it, that it was the best Linda Ronstadt record I had ever heard." Laughing, Coury remembered the first words out of his mouth.

"Peter, we're takin' this album!"

17

PRISONER IN DISGUISE

Al Coury assured Peter and Linda he'd do everything in his power to make *Heart Like a Wheel* a number-one album. Once "You're No Good" was chosen as the lead single, Coury came up with a unique angle to propel the record to the top of not just one, but two charts. "In those days, you put out a 45rpm sampler of the hit," said Coury, "and you mailed it to all the radio stations—thousands of them." The promotional copy sent would have the same song on both sides of the single, to help prevent a DJ from making the mistake of playing the "wrong" side of the disc.

Coury had decided on "I Can't Help It (If I'm Still in Love with You)," a pretty country shuffle, as the B-side of the single sold in stores. At the same time that promo copies of "You're No Good" were sent to all the pop stations in the United States, promo copies of "I Can't Help It" were sent to all the country stations. A country fan would go into a store asking for one song, a pop fan would go in asking for another—and they were both the same record. Ultimately, at the end of the week, the store would report sales figures to *Billboard*, *Cashbox*, and other trade publications.

Al Coury crowed, "It worked like a charm!" When asked, "How many Linda Ronstadt records did you sell?" the store employee wouldn't say, "I sold twenty of the B-side and twenty-five of the A-side." No, according to Coury, "He'd say, 'I sold forty-five records! It's one of the biggest sellers I got!'" Peter, Coury recalled, "was flabbergasted—he had never heard of that."

Guitarist Bob Warford, who had provided memorable guitar work on much of *Heart Like a Wheel*, had decided not to participate in the upcoming tour to promote the album. He was beginning to tire of the hassles inherent in constant plane and bus travel. Though named by Led Zeppelin's Jimmy Page as one of his favorite guitarists, Warford left music and entered law school, eventually establishing himself as an expert in the field of entertainment law.

Peter, Warford said in retrospect, "is probably my favorite producer of all time, and I've played with some that I really liked and some that were really a pain. But he was particularly good at gently moving the thing where he wanted it to be.

"It was really teamwork between him and the players, instead of '*I'm* the producer—do *this!*'"

Guitarist Ed Black also chose to pass on the tour. As Peter continued to schedule Linda's upcoming spate of concerts, a replacement was obviously needed to fill the steel guitar and second lead guitar position. These two spots were eventually entrusted to one particularly talented musician named Dan Dugmore.

Guitarist Dugmore first became thrilled with the sonic possibilities of the steel guitar as a teenager, hearing Rusty Young's playing on the Buffalo Springfield track "Kind Woman." "That was the point," Dugmore recalled, "where I went, boy, I really wanna get a steel!" He approached The Flying Burrito Brothers' Sneaky Pete Kleinow between sets at The Ash Grove one evening. "I asked him if he knew where I could find one, and he said he had a couple for sale."

Purchasing a single-neck model, Dugmore began to teach himself by playing along to records, soon accompanying friends at various club dates. In 1973, he saw Linda Ronstadt open for Neil Young. "At the end of the show," Dugmore remembered, "I said, you know, I think I'm as good as those steel players up there." Now he was determined—performing on steel guitar would be his primary goal. Two days later at The Troubadour, after catching a performance by John Stewart, Dugmore made his pitch and gave his card to Stewart, who called him the following day to audition. "The next week," Dugmore recalled, "I was on the road with him."

Now, a year and a half later, Kenny Edwards attended a show headlined by his longtime friend and musical partner Wendy Waldman and, by happenstance, John Stewart was the opening act. During his set, Edwards became quite impressed hearing Dugmore play. Afterward, Edwards "introduced himself to me and said that their steel player had left and that they were auditioning guys to play steel *and* guitar." Luckily, Dugmore could do both.

At the audition, he proceeded to impress the rest of the band on such steel-heavy tunes as "I Can't Help It (If I'm Still in Love with You)." Then, switching to guitar, Andrew Gold took Dugmore through the parts for the twin leads on "You're No Good" and "When Will I Be Loved." "I was able to learn 'em really quick," according to Dugmore, "so I got the gig."

Both *Heart Like a Wheel* and "You're No Good" were released at the end of November 1974. To celebrate and kick off the tour, Ronstadt played The Troubadour, calling up her pal Emmylou Harris to harmonize during the encore. Peter filled the opening slot that evening with his former client Tom Snow, who impressed the Capitol Records folks so much they quickly offered him a contract. As Ronstadt began to perform across the country, radio stations almost immediately jumped on "You're No Good," and it began its steady rise up the charts.

"When I first heard 'You're No Good,'" producer Richard Perry remembered, "it knocked me out. Blew me away." Along with Peter, Perry was one of the top record producers of his generation, responsible for such number-one hits as Carly Simon's "You're So Vain," Nilsson's "Without You," and Ringo Starr's "Photograph," among many others. "That was not only superb record-making," Perry continued, "but he had really established his own sound.

"It was a very clean sound . . . everything was extremely well defined," Perry explained. "Everything was in its own sonic space, where they all coexisted in one beautiful whole. It was just enough 'Ooomph'—from the drums in particular—without it being overdone." Regarding Peter's work during this period, his friend and fellow hit-making producer simply stated: "They were all perfect records."

In a 2001 podcast interview with Michael Botts, Andrew Gold remembered hearing "You're No Good" on the radio for the first time: "I was driving along in my little Toyota with bashed windows and dented fenders and heard it," he recalled. "The disc jockey said, 'I've gotta find out who this guitar player is on this thing.' He shuffled some pages and went, 'It's this guy, Andrew Gold.' He mentioned my name, and I just died. I had to pull off to the side of the road."

"That's one I heard recently, and it's still pretty great," Peter said proudly. "It's quite a production. I like hearing that record—it's good. There's some I like hearing *less*," he admitted, "but that one I can still be very proud of, I think. I'll be judged by that one." He laughed, adding: "I'm *willing* to be judged by that one."

Peter knew "You're No Good" was *damn* good—good enough to get to the top of the charts—and he would bet good money on it. In early January 1975, just as the single entered the Top Forty, Peter was planning to book a Ronstadt concert the following month in Florida. "He was trying to get her price up to $25,000," Dugmore remembered. "Peter, of course, wanted to get the price up 'cause once you can show you've been paid that much, then you can ask that much."

The promoter balked, telling Peter: "I would only pay that if somebody had a number-one record." Certain he had a hit on his hands, Peter made the promoter a bet: If "You're No Good" wasn't number-one by the day of the show, she'd play for free. On the other hand, if it *was* number-one by that date, they would pay her *fifty* thousand dollars. "Double or nothing," Peter recalled. The promoter agreed. Just days before the show, *Billboard* placed the song at number-one. "He was," Val Garay recalled, "uncanny that way."

"Just never bet against Peter," Andrew Gold declared, "because Peter always wins." Due to Peter's seemingly unerring sense of how things would turn out, Gold said, "After a while, you'd go, 'Well, if *you* say so . . . '" He laughed, adding, "If Peter said it's gonna be a hit record, it's gonna be a hit record. He was hardly ever wrong."

And he wasn't wrong here. Linda's mix of cocky, girl-next-door rock and wailing country-folk heartache—paired with Peter's mix of tasteful, attentive production plus assured commercial instincts—resulted in a smashing success. The week of February 15, 1975, *Heart Like a Wheel* and "You're No Good" were not only the number-one album and single in the United States, "I Can't Help It" was in the Top Ten of *Billboard*'s Country chart. "She's about the best girl singer in the world, in my prejudiced view," Peter said at the time. Now, the rest of the country seemed to agree.

To celebrate, Peter, Linda, and Andrew Gold flew to Hawaii. It was, according to Gold, "an excuse to go to Hawaii, but also just to figure out what we were gonna do" to follow up this massive success. "We were all under great, great pressure to do something amazing—to top ourselves." With Linda's obligation to Capitol now completed, Asylum definitely wanted to replicate—as much as possible—the formula behind the hit that got away from them. "I felt a little self-conscious—I think we all did," Gold admitted, "about having to try to beat *Heart Like a Wheel.*"

The trio began brainstorming in paradise: "Every day we would get together with guitars and run over songs," said Gold. Most of the song choices Ronstadt suggested were composed by her friends, like Lowell George, J.D. Souther, and new pal Dolly Parton. She also wanted to tackle another tune from the pen of Anna McGarrigle. And, as a perfect example of how, in many cases, Linda's song choices tell a part of her own story, she wanted to cut James Taylor's fame-weary lament, "Hey Mister, That's Me Up on the Jukebox."

This Hawaiian song list consisted of some mid-tempo islands amid a sea of slow ballads. "She's always liked doing slow songs better than fast ones," said Peter. "Always." So to try to keep the record from being too ballad-heavy, Andrew Gold suggested they record an oldie that recently had been a spur-of-the-moment addition to Ronstadt's live set. One evening, after having been called back a half-dozen times for encores—and completely out of material—Gold called out to all onstage: "'Heat Wave' in D!" Though the result was completely unrehearsed, the crowd went wild.

Peter, Val, and Andrew dived into the old Martha Reeves/Motown showstopper back at The Sound Factory. "I wanted it not to speed up," Peter explained. "The Vandellas record is brilliant, but it speeds up like crazy. And it really wasn't practical to do it to a click"—referring to the electronic click track that was in standard use by then to keep musicians playing in steady time—"because the click detracts from the shuffle feel, which is what 'Heat Wave' is all about."

Gold began first by playing the drums, running through a verse and a chorus. Peter, harkening back to the audio experiments in his youth, selected Gold's most steady performance and, taping both ends of that short, edited recording together, ran it continuously through the playback head of one tape machine while the tape loop traveled around a pencil Peter held up to steady its movement. Recording that looped section onto two tracks of the multitrack master, this formed the foundation for the recording.

Later, more percussion was added, along with guitars, piano, and synthesizer—all played by Gold. Though Kenny Edwards added his bass guitar and supplied some harmonies (and Peter couldn't resist helping with the handclaps), it was Andrew Gold's track all the way—not to dismiss Ronstadt's passionate lead vocal, added at the end of the process.

Ultimately, Gold felt—perhaps because of its almost-one-man-band quality—that "Heat Wave" felt stilted. "I didn't feel our version had any soul, and it's all me on there," Gold laughed. "So I take responsibility!" Noting that it later was a Top Five single, he mused: "I guess 'A Million Elvis Fans Can't Be Wrong!'"

"But I never really liked that record much," Gold admitted. "And neither did Linda." Peter does not agree: "I think it's great," he said. "I don't think it's 'soulless' . . . it's *precise*. But I tend to like that."

By contrast, the session for Neil Young's "Love Is a Rose" was back to business as usual: Instead of spending days building a track bit by bit, all musicians played together live in the studio, with the master take captured in less than an hour. Opening the track with four plucks from his banjo, Herb Pedersen recalled Linda and the gathered musicians spending a bit of time deciding on the key that best suited her voice, but then quickly coming up with a solid arrangement.

Pedersen, who had been recording regularly with Ronstadt since her debut solo album back in 1969, recalled that Peter "wasn't a demanding person at all. He would let the musicians who he would hire do what they're supposed to do, and that's be creative and come up with something nice." Along with Gold, Edwards, and drummer Russ Kunkel, said Pedersen, "David Lindley was in there with us playing fiddle, and it was just kind of a head arrangement. And maybe Peter would, you know, quietly make a suggestion—not to come in until the first chorus or whatever, you know? It's being creative—that's part of the job."

The Neil Young song had been intended for an album, *Homegrown*, that Young decided to shelve (ultimately releasing it forty-five years later). Peter had heard the unreleased record and thought this particular track was perfect for Ronstadt, receiving Young's permission to give it a try. Ronstadt knew immediately that Peter had picked an unknown gem.

"Like all great artists, Ronstadt has a very, very good understanding of what she should be doing. It's not just being gifted with a great voice, but also knowing what to sing," said Danny Kortchmar, who played on a heart-tugging cover of Smokey Robinson's "Tracks of My Tears" during these sessions.

Besides his banjo work, Pedersen also provided expert backing vocals on a handful of the new recordings, basically co-arranging the vocals on the spot with Gold and Edwards: "You kinda pick the part that is comfortable for you to sing," Pedersen explained. "So we would just kinda quickly discuss, you know, who wants to sing baritone, who wants to sing tenor, who wants to double the lead or whatever."

Peter "was very gentle in the studio," Pedersen continued. "I could kinda tell by the look in his eye if he was approving of what we were doing. If he *wasn't* satisfied, he would mainly suggest swapping parts with somebody to see if the comfort zone was a little smoother, or whatever. But he was pretty hands-on."

Hands-on, yes, but always ready to let someone else run with a good idea, such as Pedersen's suggestion of using Brian Wilson-esque "Ooohhs" toward the end of "Hey Mister, That's Me Up on the Jukebox." According to Pedersen, the idea simply came from "growing up being a Beach Boy junkie."

"We had a rule," Ronstadt said, "that we'd always try the ideas that were thrown on the table, which were limited by the people who were there. So it wasn't that hard to try 'em all out. If the guitar player had an idea, the bass player had an idea, I had a bunch of ideas—we'd try 'em. If they didn't work, we'd go, '*Eeechh!* THAT'S a stupid idea. Next?'"

The recording sessions for the new album stretched over five months, for, with the huge success of *Heart Like a Wheel*, Ronstadt was now a major live draw, playing shows around the country. And, as usual, Peter as manager "was right there," Kenny Edwards said. "He was very much into going on the road and taking part in the thing.

"He was super hands-on when it came to making decisions about the sound and the lights," Edwards continued, "how to deal with the promoters and stuff like that. He *managed* the situation in a very literal sense.

"Because we were all on the road, all in the studio, and suddenly having a lot of success," Edwards recalled, "we became like a little family." And, once again, Peter proved how much he valued this family of musicians surrounding Ronstadt in the studio and on the road by both listing their names—acknowledging their contributions on each track—and compensating them well. "Peter *always* paid the musicians," Ronstadt stated. "I've had people working in my business that say, you know, 'Don't pay this one so much, don't pay that one so much.' I think Jackson Browne, Elvis Presley, and I were the first artists in the business to give the sidemen points. Peter just thought it was right. You treat the musicians the best—*they're* the ones that are helping you make it happen!

"They contributed a huge amount to *my* success," Ronstadt continued. "We felt they deserved to be acknowledged, and we just felt like they deserved to be *paid*. And when we traveled, we all traveled together. It wasn't ultra-first class for me and them, you know, hanging on to the wheels."

The team would grab time at The Sound Factory whenever they were off the road, pushing to have the album finished by summer's end. Peter was meticulous in keeping track of what needed to be accomplished in every stage of the recording process. "He writes every single tiny thing down, which *always* pays off in the end. He used to have a ring-binder," Ronstadt remembered, with each song written on a colored tab. He could turn easily to each song to see what needed to be done. "He'd write, '*Weird bass mistake*,'" recalled Ronstadt. "The tiniest little thing. Or if they made any change on the mixing board—he'd write it all down."

"Where did you leave off, what do you need to do tomorrow," Val Garay explained. "Copious amounts of notes. I learned that from him: You can't make a record and keep track of everything without keeping notes."

David Campbell was asked to do *all* the string arrangements this time around and, in the process, became Peter's arranger of choice for the next couple of decades. "Peter has a way of sort of mapping the whole structure of the song out on a blank piece of paper—the types of things he hears, where something should start," said Campbell. "We'll talk about what kind of instruments—how big or how small." After Campbell completes written scores for each song, "we just kind of polish it in the studio, if he wants to make any changes or additions."

"He could have been an arranger easily 'cause he had a great '*arrangemental*' mind," Val Garay claimed. "He had the ability—and that's because he has such an amazing mind—to visualize a record pretty much finished and what it needed to complete it from beginning to end."

For almost an entire year, J.D. Souther had been working on one song in particular. The first line—"*You think the love you never had might save you*"—was quickly followed by three more . . . then nothing for weeks. Later, picking it up again, he posed the question: "*Is it love or lies?*" That brought a few more lines that ended with, as far as Souther was concerned, a throwaway "*Oh my, my . . .*" and *another* stopping point. "Every time I got to where I was out of ideas," Souther recalled, "I stopped."

Though unfinished, but realizing he was on to something, Souther played what he had for friend Joni Mitchell, one of the most respected songwriters of modern times. "I'm good up to there," he told her, "but the '*my, my,*' I just threw it in there 'cause I didn't have anything to say." According to Souther, Mitchell disagreed: "It's great—I thought that was the point of getting to there. *That's* the 'sigh'!"

Happily startled, Souther replied, "Oh, *really?*" Now with Mitchell's insight, Souther stuck with the "sigh" and tried moving the song forward. Continually coming back to where he last left off, he let the emotion of the lyric dictate the chord changes and, with his jazz background, managed to deftly move into some unlikely voicings for a folk ballad, yet smoothly resolve them every time. All in all, a remarkable piece of work built slowly, step by step. "I never played the song all the way to the end," Souther said, "until it was finished."

"It's interesting to see things grow only in proportion to the amount of building materials you have on hand," noted Souther. "If it takes a year, fuck it! It takes a year. If it turns out to be a good song, you're glad. And if it doesn't, I *bet* ya, something else comes out of it!"

A good song, indeed. Peter wanted to capture this stark, delicate ballad as intimately as possible, so he directed Val Garay to set up just three mics—one for Souther's guitar and two more to capture his and Linda's vocals. With lights dimmed, the two former lovers sat just inches from each other, weaving a heartbreaking ballad into a gorgeous duet. The track was certainly one of the sessions' highlights—and ultimately used as the album's title.

Peter "is responsible for some of the best moments in the studio," Souther proclaimed. "'Prisoner in Disguise,' for many years, was the favorite thing either Linda or I had done."

Having observed his abilities on the road, Peter brought Dan Dugmore in near the end of the sessions to overdub steel guitar on five of the album's tracks, adding a sweet country sheen to her pleading heartache. On James Taylor's "Hey Mister, That's Me Up on the Jukebox," Dugmore echoed Ronstadt's closing vocalizations perfectly, adding an eerie call-and-response between her soulful voice and his desolate strings.

By May, with the sessions for Ronstadt's next album wrapping up, the second single from *Heart Like a Wheel*, a rocking cover of The Everly Brothers' "When Will I Be Loved," sat both at number-two on *Billboard*'s Pop chart *and* number-one on the Country charts. Its B-side, "It Doesn't Matter Anymore," also got enough airplay to make both charts. Capitol's Al Coury was sure this single would be a bigger hit than

"You're No Good," and it seemed "the man with the golden ears" would be proved right once again.

You might think that someone achieving this level of success would be filled with confidence in her abilities as a recording artist—but not so. With the new album completed and mixed, Ronstadt came in to hear a final playback. "Her and I and Peter listened to the whole album," Val Garay said and recalled Ronstadt's verdict: "You can't put that out."

"A couple of days later, of course, that changed," Garay remembered, but her initial reaction he has come to understand: "I don't think she ever liked anything she ever did. Anything."

"I don't," Ronstadt laughingly agreed. "That's very accurate. It's not that I don't like the songs, I just don't like the records. I don't like records anyway! I don't like anybody's records, but I *especially* don't like my own!"

She laughed and, in our 2004 conversation, tried to explain: "You know, music's just a work in progress, and it's very odd to hear something frozen. It just is. Sometimes you can do it better. Or sometimes, you know you can't! And then, maybe you could've, you know, five years ago but you can't now, and that's even worse! I just don't go there. It's hard enough to talk about it. But I *never* listen to it.

"When I say I hate everything I've ever recorded, it certainly wasn't Peter's fault—he did everything he could"—she laughed—"to try to get it right! You know? It's just that . . ." Ronstadt paused, then concluded by stating: "My own work is very unsatisfying to me."

And what was her opinion of this incredibly successful album forty years on? Ronstadt said simply, "I don't even remember what was on *Prisoner in Disguise.*"

When it came time to design the sleeve for the new album, Peter Asher Management's Jack Oliver called up John Kosh, whom he had first met back at Apple Records. In early 1969, Kosh was the art director for the British magazine *Art and Artists.* "And one evening," Kosh recalled, "I got this phone call." And here, Kosh attempts his best Liverpudlian accent: "Uh, hello, this is Mr. Lennon. Can I speak with Mr. Kosh?" The call wasn't a joke, as Kosh first assumed, and he was quickly hired by John Lennon to assist him and Yoko Ono with various conceptual art projects and designs for the rest of that year. This led to Kosh, at the grand old age of twenty-three, art directing his first album cover—a record entitled *Abbey Road.*

"EMI said, 'We need an album cover tomorrow,'" remembered Kosh, and he was quickly told to meet with photographer Iain Macmillan, who had photographed the band walking back and forth across London's Abbey Road. "Macmillan had taken all these pictures and he had them all spread out, and I said"—pointing with his index finger—"'*that* one.'" He also decided not to put the name of the band *or* the name of the album on the front cover, much to EMI's consternation. "Everyone knows who the fuckin' Beatles are," he explained to the brass at the label. "Leave it alone." Adding the names on the back cover was the compromise.

Prisoner in Disguise
album cover.

Six years later, Kosh, having moved his base of operations to Los Angeles, met with Peter to discuss ideas for the *Prisoner in Disguise* cover. It was decided to further highlight the importance of the participating musicians by including their studio portraits in the package. "You know, it'd be a great idea," Kosh added, "if we get all the songwriters to write their lyrics by hand." They did, and those disparate pages were reproduced inside the album's gatefold sleeve alongside Ethan Russell's photos of the musicians.

Once the final layout went to the printer, Peter asked Kosh what had happened to all the songwriters' original handwritten pages used in his design, and he answered with innocent bewilderment. Forty years later, Kosh smiled and said conspiratorially: "I've still got 'em!"

Prisoner in Disguise was an expensive package for Asylum—a gatefold with embossed lettering on the cover—but it achieved Gold Record status quickly upon its release that October. By mid-November, the album and its first single, "Heat Wave," were both Top Five. And, in keeping with what was becoming a Ronstadt tradition, the single's B-side, "Love Is a Rose," was another Country Top Ten hit.

J.D. Souther had been observing Peter in the studio for two years. Now good friends, he asked Peter to consider producing his next solo album. "I just saw what he had done with Linda," said Souther. "I also trusted him completely."

But things seemed to go very slowly during the first few weeks of recording. "John David's a little more plodding and methodical about stuff," Val Garay said, with Kenny Edwards describing Souther as a "perfectionist, but in an artistic way . . . looking for the elusive whatever-it-is.

"Peter really had his hands full with J.D.," Edwards continued, "who was kind of a very moody artist and had a lot of changes of heart—not as easygoing and easy to work with as Linda." Though he would later produce sessions with Souther participating, Edwards admitted that if he had been in Peter's shoes, "I couldn't handle it.

I couldn't handle *him* as an artist. I didn't have the *gravitas*, you know, to say, 'Okay, enough of this wandering—you have to pick a route and take it.'" Eventually, the very logical and organized producer of these sessions couldn't handle it either.

Peter, according to Souther, "called me and said, 'Listen—this is the *hardest* thing I've ever had to say to a friend, but I really don't think I can finish this album.' And it just caught me, and I said, 'Whataya mean?!' And he said, 'Well, I just have no idea what you're doing. You don't seem to follow any particular logic.' And I think he likened it to building a house by, like, building a stoop and then hanging a couple of bricks over here, and then coming back to a window here, and then doing a door, and then back to the porch. He said, 'I think that *you* can see the end of it, but I can't. So I can't really be the help I'd like to be to you.'

"And I said, 'Let's be honest—it's just lack of preparation on my part, isn't it? It's not coming in with the whole thing really outlined for you to work from.' And he's very kind, but he also said, 'Well, pretty much.'" Laughing, Souther continued: "So I said, 'Look, *please* don't leave me on this project, and I promise to come in more prepared and waste less time and make it easy for you to do your job. That's what I want you to do. I *totally* respect what you do. I *need* you to feel fully invested in this and fully able to do your job, and it's incomprehensible to me how I could not see that my disorganization would adversely affect your organization.' And he said, 'Okay, fine.'

"So, I came back with a better head on my shoulders about it, and we went in and made what I think is by far the best record I've made until today."

The resultant album, entitled *Black Rose*, included a photo on its back cover of Souther looking like a magician—dressed in white tie and tails, holding a black top hat, surrounded by a swirl of dark, smoky clouds. This was fitting, for the record

Black Rose
album cover.

inside contained a series of magical performances. One was Souther's re-envisioning of "Silver Blue," a song that, unlike "Prisoner in Disguise," was "written in the time it takes to sing it—complete stream of consciousness," according to Souther. Recorded first on *Prisoner in Disguise* as a duet between Ronstadt and himself, here the transcendent jazz bassist Stanley Clarke acts as Souther's musical foil. "That was live," Souther recalled. "That's just me and him and a microphone—just looking at each other."

What Souther wanted was to have the bassline be the root of the song, rather than chord changes, and he expressed to Peter his wish to have the great Return to Forever bassist on the session. "I would never have had the balls to just call Stanley Clarke," said Souther, but Peter's job, as he has said, is to listen to the artist and incorporate the best of their ideas.

Peter, Souther remembered, said, "'Call him!' I went, 'Really? Just call him?' He said, 'Sure. What's he gonna say? He's gonna say yes or no.'" Clarke said yes, and his performance was perfection.

Ronstadt made an appearance, adding an impassioned vocal counterpoint and harmony on "If You Have Crying Eyes." And Eagles Glenn Frey and Don Henley, happy recipients over the years of Souther's songwriting expertise ("Best of My Love," "New Kid in Town," and "Victim of Love," among others) added their harmonies to the album's title track. Other familiar musicians—Kortchmar, Gold, Edwards, and Kunkel, along with masterful harmonists David Crosby and Art Garfunkel—all contributed their solid playing and singing to Souther's songs. One musician managed to actually sneak his way into the sessions, but would soon become one of the most valued players in all rock'n'roll.

Robert "Waddy" Wachtel knew he wanted to play guitar at the age of five. Growing up in Queens, New York, he took a ton of music lessons, played in band after band, and, in 1968, moved to Southern California. He fell in with music producer Keith Olsen, who hired him to back the duo of Lindsey Buckingham and Stevie Nicks on their pre–Fleetwood Mac debut album. More sessions followed, and he was soon hired to play guitar behind The Everly Brothers, whose musical director at the time was Warren Zevon.

Jimmy Wachtel, older brother to young Robert, was a graphic artist designing Souther's album cover. Often dropping by the older Wachtel's home studio, Souther started to get to know this younger musical brother. "And I thought he was just the smoothest-handed guitar player I'd met," said Souther. "Even then, I thought he was just on a level with Clapton."

Waddy Wachtel recalled stopping by The Sound Factory during the *Black Rose* sessions: "I had gone by there a couple of times," Wachtel admitted. "Because that was a circle I hadn't broken into yet. I knew all the guys playing for him, but I'd go by there, and Peter would not even look at me—very, very, *very* serious about what he was doing! I thought, 'Man—this guy is *tough!* What do I gotta *do* around here . . . ?'" Eventually, Wachtel dropped by "to get something from one of the guys—Kenny or Andrew—and J.D. saw me. 'Did you bring your guitar?' Well, I *always* had my guitar in the car.

"J.D. said, 'You should play!' So, Peter kind of bit his lip and went, 'Ehhh, alright.' You know—didn't wanna hear about anyone new, and I don't blame him." Wachtel plugged in his 1960 Les Paul and listened to the band run through Souther's short, lyrically startling, and melodically beautiful "Simple Man, Simple Dream."

"As soon as I heard it," Wachtel remembered, "I felt a perfect way for me to enter into it—I just knew." Wachtel referred to the sound he produced as "phony steel guitar"—a technique he had mastered that featured, along with some intricate picking and fret work, the subtle up-and-down manipulation of the volume of his guitar via a foot pedal. Behind the studio's glass partition, Peter "took notice instantly," Wachtel said, "and, all of a sudden, started to give me a little smile."

Having impressed Peter, "Waddy" (a nickname bestowed upon the guitarist by an old bandmate) was asked back and continued to contribute tasty licks to the proceedings. Another highlight was the quasi-calypso riff played by Wachtel and Kortchmar for the eventual album opener, "Banging My Head Against the Moon," assisted in no small part by drummer Jim Keltner. "It's Keltner and Waddy's response to that song," marveled Souther. "They made it into some kind of crazy reggae thing I'm not sure I even had lined out.

"Keltner's back there like a spider, just flying—all these accents where you don't expect 'em. And a lot of that, also, is having a faultless bass player," Souther said, referring to Paul Stallworth, "so everybody else was free to dance around." Souther shook his head in admiration. "Waddy's time was faultless."

Eventually released in the spring of 1976, *Black Rose* didn't approach the sales of Peter's work with James Taylor or Linda Ronstadt but was ultimately more beautiful and sophisticated than anything he had yet produced. Bassist Kenny Edwards named the record first in a short list of his favorite Asher-produced projects. Looking back, Souther is still amazed at what Peter accomplished under sometimes trying circumstances: "He made me feel comfortable in the studio, and that's no small feat," he declared. "Anything post–Peter Asher in my career probably wouldn't have been done as well without my having known him."

More importantly, Souther concluded: "He's the kind of friend that makes you feel secure about yourself, and about your friendship, and that *some* kind of goodness—he doesn't even know he has—prevails in this world."

18

HANDY MAN

Linda Ronstadt had become one of the hottest acts in music, playing larger and larger venues as her popularity grew. Peter, now keenly aware of Waddy Wachtel's abilities on guitar, wanted to add more power to Ronstadt's touring lineup by hiring him. Currently playing behind Carole King, Peter attended one of Carole's shows to observe the guitarist in action. After the show, Peter asked Waddy to meet him for lunch the next day.

Peter made his pitch for Waddy to join Linda's upcoming tour but warned him: "I can't pay you what Carole's paying you." Nonplussed, Waddy asked, "Well, what am I doin' here, then?" "If things progress the way I believe they will," Peter promised, "everybody will benefit from it." Trusting Peter and sensing that Ronstadt had still not reached her peak in popularity, Waddy agreed to the offer.

Her touring band, now consisting of Waddy, Andrew Gold, Kenny Edwards, Dan Dugmore, and drummer Michael Botts (from the band Bread), would actually do double duty on the road; before Linda took the stage as headliner, Andrew Gold, whose first solo album had been released by Asylum at the end of 1975, would open the shows. With the same band using the same equipment throughout the evening, no interminable set change would be needed.

One day, Gold brought a newly written song with him to the tour rehearsals. "Lonely Boy" was only slightly autobiographical, and its structure—highlighting life's cyclical patterns—was reminiscent of Harry Nilsson's earlier "1941." Gold, with his gift for melodies and riffs, was also gifted in having a crack band surrounding him. They came up with a solid arrangement that gave the song real dramatic thrust.

Peter had agreed to produce the upcoming sessions for Gold's sophomore album, which thrilled his good friend no end. As he also needed to begin recording Ronstadt's next release, Peter decided to produce them at the same time. For weeks at

The Sound Factory, Peter, engineer Val Garay, and the same core group of musicians alternated between daytime sessions for one and nighttime sessions for the other.

On March 3, 1976, the first day of recording, Ronstadt and her band put to tape "Lose Again," written by Kenny Edwards's sweetheart, Karla Bonoff. Edwards remembered playing the song to Ronstadt while on the road promoting *Prisoner in Disguise*. "I said, 'Karla wrote this song, and ya gotta check this out. It would be a great song for you.' And she really liked it and went, 'Yeah! Let's learn that!' So we learned it on the road and started singing it." Realizing that Bonoff had a good musical ear, Peter decided to put her to work at his West LA office. "He used to get about three hundred tapes a month—unsolicited stuff—for Linda," Val Garay recalled. "We'd all kind of try to go through the box and listen." As with the deluge of tapes Peter had faced while at Apple, he eventually needed to delegate the responsibility of critiquing them to someone—and Kenny's songwriting girlfriend was asked if, for a nice hourly wage, she'd be up to the task.

After wading through the tapes for almost a week, "There was nothing there that I thought was decent," Bonoff concluded. Her standards might have been high, but understandably so—it would be hard to imagine those tapes contained anything as wonderful as Bonoff's own "Someone to Lay Down Beside Me." One evening after dinner, the songwriter shared this new work with her chart-topping friend. Beginning with a delicately beautiful minor-key melody, the song soon heads into an intense and desperate plea for a love that's real but resigned to the reality of never grasping it. The stark ballad stunned Ronstadt. Peter also realized the quality of the twenty-five-year-old songwriter's work, and this second Bonoff composition was promptly recorded on their second day in the studio, March 4th. A third Bonoff song, "If He's Ever Near," was cut the following week. "Peter respected me, even though I was totally unproven at the time," Bonoff said fondly, "and was always very supportive of me."

Up to this point, the majority of the recording dates Wachtel had done for other producers had utilized the method he referred to as "the pileup"—most instruments recorded separately, one after another. The guitarist was delighted with Peter's studio methodology: "These guys were doing 'em live," he explained. "Like 'That'll Be the Day'—it was live, Linda was singing live, everybody was going for it live. It was really refreshingly different." Even the background vocals, usually added later, were performed live as the Buddy Holly classic was laid to tape—also on March 4th. Only the lead guitars were overdubbed, and even then Wachtel and Gold performed their parts together—trading riffs at the break and then playing in tandem for the big finish. Playing off other musicians in the room "made for a great time," said Wachtel.

Peter urged Gold to also go for live vocals whenever possible during his own sessions, despite playing piano or guitar at the same time, and most of his takes were done in this fashion. One example was his version of "Learning the Game"—yet another tune from the pen of Buddy Holly. But where Linda's "That'll Be the Day" was an exciting slice of pure rock'n'roll bravado, Gold's "Learning the Game," a thoughtful rumination on crushed romantic hopes, was performed here as a country-folk lament, gliding by on Gold's piano, Kenny Edwards's mandolin, and Dan Dugmore's steel guitar.

Two more oldies were reimagined during Gold's sessions, both suggested by Peter. "Do Wah Diddy Diddy," the British Invasion–era smash, should have been a smash once again when Gold's take was later released as a single, but its quirky, angular rhythms were out of place at the beginning of the disco era. A more faithful treatment was given to "Stay," the old Maurice Williams doo-wop classic. And along with being in charge as producer, Peter happily lent his percussion *and* singing abilities to both tracks.

"There were *lots* of background parts" on "Stay," Gold recalled. "And he was doing it for hours, and he just adored it." The following day, Peter's wife, Betsy, told Gold, "All night long he'd been singing in his sleep! He'd been singing '*Stay!* . . . *Do-wop-she-body* . . .' He'd been *dreaming* about it"—Gold chuckled—"which I thought was so great."

When Peter sings, "he sounds very precise and pristine," according to Gold. "It was an unusually sweet side of him that he just adored singing so much. By the time he was with Linda, he wasn't that much in practice—he hadn't sung for a long time. And he really got excited about it in a way that was more . . ."—Gold searched for the right phrase—"*little boyish*."

Switching over to Ronstadt's sessions, Peter's love of percussion touches was obvious as he personally added tambourine, wood block, cowbell, and numerous shakers to various tracks, as well as handclaps alongside fellow noisemaker Gold: "He and I used to *adore* doing percussion," Gold admitted, "for days! In fact, at some point it was almost like a competition of who had the best percussion kit. Because we both got these little Anvil cases and we had our favorite tambourines—fifteen cabasas, fifteen shakers, and various cowbells—all kinds of stuff.

"And we would do handclaps for days—him and I, together. And the thing was always how close could we get it." Gold explained: "These are pretty floppy tracks, by today's standards—things went in and out of time. And we were managing to follow the eccentricities of the tracks." Gold smiled, remembering all the time and trouble to get these sonic touches right. "That was a lot of fun."

Regarding Peter, Gold laughed and confided: "I think he's sort of a frustrated artist, basically!"

"'*Frustrated musician*' would be more to the point," corrected Peter. "If it's something I can *do*—play the tambourine or sing a harmony part—I will gladly do it." And despite all his years of guitar playing, Peter insisted, "I don't play anything well enough to compete with the people I hire to play on records—*that's* for sure. So, when there *is* an acoustic guitar part or a percussion part or a vocal part that I can *do*, yes—I'm very happy to do it."

One standout track from Ronstadt's sessions was her take on the old Patsy Cline hit, "Crazy," written by Willie Nelson. The band surrounds Ronstadt's aching croon with a soft shuffle that seems to float suspended in moonlight, and Dan Dugmore's eight-bar steel guitar solo offers a slow, dizzying dance that leaves you wanting more.

"Linda was seeing a psychiatrist at the time, and she invited him to come down to the studio," Dugmore remembered. As Linda and the band were set and ready to begin a take, the good doctor came walking into the studio's recording booth just as Ronstadt began to sing the opening line, *"I'm crazy . . ."* "The whole band broke up—we had to stop." Dugmore laughed. "The timing was perfect. It couldn't have been any funnier . . ."

The recording of basic tracks stopped for a while as the tour commenced. Peter suggested to Norman Epstein, Andrew and Kenny's manager, that as he'd be accompanying his charges on the road, why not act as the tour's road manager? "Something I'd never done before in my *life*"—Epstein laughed—"but I said okay." Epstein had started his management company at the ripe old age of twenty-three, after two years under the wing of producer/manager Chuck Plotkin. With clients Gold and Edwards both recording and performing with Ronstadt, Epstein began to observe Peter almost daily, especially after moving his office to an available room at Peter Asher Management.

"I was a young kid," Epstein recalled, admitting with a smile: "I was clueless!" Epstein took full advantage of access to one of the most successful managers in the business. "He was *extremely* open and generous and kind with me about his time and letting me just hang out in his office and watch him do stuff," Epstein said. "I learned a lot. I mean, I learned some specifics about how to book a tour and things like that, but much more importantly for *me* was just how to conduct yourself and how to be a person in the world—especially in this business.

"The biggest thing I learned from Peter was to tell the truth and tell it upfront—it's *much* easier," Epstein emphasized, "for everybody! Now, that may not sound like a big deal, but in the *music business?* That's a REAL big deal—that's a weird approach to take.

"A very typical example would be: You're managing an artist, they have a band, they go out on the road, the tour ends. All the musicians come to you and go: 'When are we goin' out on the road again—you're hiring me, right?' And the general tendency in the music business would be to say"—and here Epstein affected a gruff, fast-talking style—"'Oh, man, hey, we're goin' out, you're on the team, it's gonna be great . . . !' Regardless of the truth. And Peter would say the truth. Now, sometimes the truth was, 'We're leaving again in four weeks, and you're the drummer again! Let's go!' And sometimes the truth was, 'I have no idea when we'll tour again, and if we tour again, I don't know who the band's gonna be.' Whatever it was, he'd just tell people that. And it caused *some* unpleasantness up front"—Epstein smiled—"because people wanna hear what they wanna hear, but much less unpleasantness than when you tell 'em something that *isn't* true, and then you gotta unravel it—that's *really* unpleasant!

"I didn't know anybody else in the music business who did that," Epstein recalled. "And it was great! But that was the really big lesson I got from him: You wanna make your life easy? Just tell everybody the truth all the time and tell 'em right up front and everything will go a lot better." The lessons Epstein learned from Peter served him well as he rose through the music business, eventually becoming senior vice president at Universal Music.

As Ronstadt, Gold, and their band crossed the country, David Campbell began adding strings to the handful of completed tracks. One was a composition by a relatively unknown songwriter named Warren Zevon. His self-titled debut album for Asylum was just hitting the stores, but Ronstadt had already been introduced to Zevon through his songwriting buddies Jackson Browne, Glenn Frey, and J.D. Souther, and she loved his gorgeous songcraft presenting cynical slices of life. In mid-March, she had recorded Zevon's "Hasten Down the Wind," wherein two lovers, painfully realizing it's over, agree to part.

"We had the advantage of her brilliant song sense," said Peter, quickly giving credit where it was due. "She discovered Warren Zevon, not me. I was not aware of him or his genius. She would bring me these songs and I'd go, 'Wow!'" But in an interesting first, one of the songs Linda brought Peter at this point was from the pen of a young woman from Tucson, Arizona, who had never really tried her hand at songwriting before.

Andrew Gold remembered being on the road with Ronstadt when she "came up to me and Peter and said"—and here Gold affected a shy young girl's voice—"'*I have a little song I wrote . . .*'" Startled, Peter said, "You *did*? Let's hear it!" "Well"—Ronstadt hesitated, the songwriting novice more than a bit afraid of a possibly blunt critique—"I'll play it for Andrew, but *only* Andrew. Okay?"

"And Peter was, like, just *dying*," Gold said, smiling, "'cause he was very curious, obviously.

"So, we went into a hotel room," Gold continued, "one with those two little beds. I sat on one bed, and I had my guitar, and she sang me her song, and I tried to put some chords to it." Gold did a bit more than that, helping Ronstadt write the song's bridge. Having locked down the tune's basic structure, the two songwriters rose to leave the room. "I opened the door," Gold recalled, "and it was like one of those comedy things where all these people pile in." Peter and the rest of her band, now falling over themselves, had been listening intently at the door.

Despite the high quality of "Try Me Again," Ronstadt simply didn't think composing was her strong suit and didn't aggressively pursue it. "We all have different gifts," she said. "Some of us have the gift of the ability to screw things together with material from the hardware store, and some of us have the ability to sing. I think writing's a separate gift. Occasionally something would scream out of my head, and I would be helpless to stop it, but I don't think that's what I was meant to do."

Peter encouraged her to write more, he said, "if only for the crassest of reasons: 'You should be on the B-side of these huge hit singles; you'll make a *lot* of extra money!' But we couldn't persuade her to.

"And I think part of it is," suggested Peter, "the same reason I rarely write songs: When you are surrounded by the *very best*—John David, Karla Bonoff, James, Joni—you kinda go, 'Ehhhh . . .'" He laughed, but one could certainly understand feeling insecure and intimidated by all that talent.

Andrew Gold, on the other hand, seemed destined to be a composer of memorable melodies, like his father before him. One example of Gold's delicate craftsmanship from these sessions is his song "Firefly." A complete giveaway of this particular songwriter's love of all things Beatles, the tune would not have seemed out of place on any of McCartney's albums from that period. And to top it off, Gold's solo was an obvious tip of the hat to George Harrison. Other than David Campbell's accompanying string arrangement, every note played and sung on the track was Gold's.

But "Lonely Boy" was the song Peter knew would be the album's standout track. "I love the fact that the time turns 'round at the beginning," Peter said, so the listener doesn't quite know where the downbeat of the song is until the vocal begins—a little bit of musical misdirection Peter was pleased to employ. Though an excellent take had been done near the beginning of the sessions, now that the song had been done night after night on tour—with the crowds even cheering halfway through this unknown song as Waddy's solo peaked—Peter brought everyone back to the studio in May to record the track a second time as the band's performance was now tighter. Ronstadt also happily participated, singing harmony during the second verse.

Peter's instincts were, once again, correct. When this second version of "Lonely Boy" was released in early 1977 as the lead single off Gold's sophomore release—entitled *What's Wrong with This Picture?*—it gave Gold his first and only Top Ten hit.

The sessions for Linda's album wrapped at the end of June 1976. In the shops by September, the album—named *Hasten Down the Wind* after the Warren Zevon song—was yet another showcase for Ronstadt's powerful, stylish, emotional vocals, and eventually the disc climbed all the way to number-three. The lead single, "That'll Be the Day," hit the Top Forty the week of what would have been Buddy Holly's fortieth birthday, eventually making it to number-eleven in *Billboard's* Hot 100.

The album design, again, was courtesy of John Kosh. "The one thing that happened, which was magic, is that Linda and I just got to be good friends," Kosh said.

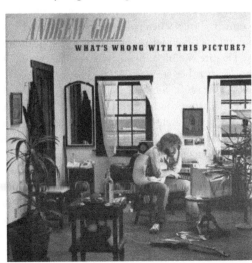

What's Wrong With This Picture? album cover.

Ronstadt fully trusted Kosh, and he became an important part of the team, continuing to work on her sleeve designs for years. Ronstadt, ever self-critical, once commented that Kosh's album covers were better than the music inside. Kosh laughed, adding: "What a load of shit!"

Famed photographer Ethan Russell took the shots used for the *Hasten Down the Wind* package. But the one Kosh liked best for the cover had, he thought, a problem—Ronstadt's right hand, coming out from her body's shadow, just looked wrong, almost claw-like. "So I photographed my wife's hand," Kosh said, "and stuck it in." Ultimately, it's doubtful anyone would have noticed the hand, as a hue and cry went up over Ronstadt's nipples showing underneath her simple cotton dress.

Some may have protested the overt sensuality of the cover, but Ronstadt, according to Kosh, "was fine with it," and he shrugged, stating the obvious fact: "She was hot!"

Peter Asher Management had outgrown its Santa Monica Boulevard offices—in size and also feel, as the neighborhood had become noisy and congested. Less than a mile west, Peter found the perfect place to set up shop. The stretch of Doheny Drive between Sunset and Santa Monica Boulevards was a fairly quiet, tree-lined residential area. The building Peter bought at 644 N. Doheny made the perfect headquarters/clubhouse combo. And, for the ultimate in convenience for our fast-rising music mogul, The Troubadour, still one of LA's premier live music venues and a hangout for many of Peter's friends and colleagues, was simply a two-minute walk away.

By the end of 1976, James Taylor's contract with Warner Brothers Records was coming to a close. The label felt it was time to release a greatest hits album and asked Peter if his client could possibly rerecord two of the tracks that had been done

Hasten Down the Wind album cover.

originally for Taylor's first and only Apple Records release: "Carolina in My Mind" and "Something in the Way She Moves."

The label had initially approached Apple and inquired about licensing the original tracks, but Apple was in such disarray at that point that, according to Val Garay, "They couldn't find the tapes."

"But if that had been the only reason," said Peter, "we would have found a way around it. Because I actually still have some backup tape copies of that record." No, the answer was more to do with insurmountable red tape: "Apple was in legal hell," according to Peter, Apple's former head of A&R. "At that point the Apple catalogue wasn't available, and Apple and Capitol were in all kinds of lawsuits, so there was no *way* that Warner Brothers could get the rights to use them."

With both James and Peter feeling that the original session was a bit overproduced anyway, and after years of performing "Carolina" in a slower and more simple arrangement, they had no hesitation cutting it in a style closer to his classic "Fire and Rain"–era sound.

Andrew Gold attended the sessions, and though credited as playing "harmonium" on the new take of "Carolina," it was actually a two-man accordion. Peter recalled that when Gold tried to play the instrument's keyboard with one hand and move the bellows at the same time with the other, "chaos ensued." He laughed. So, wielding a roll of gaffer's tape, they taped the accordion to a stool: "Peter did the bellows back and forth while I just played it like a keyboard." Gold smiled. "And it worked out great! I dare say it probably sounded more consistent than any other accordion player ever in history." He laughed, adding: "There was absolutely no breathing"—referring to the air moving in and out of the instrument.

"Well," Peter said, feigning petulance, "my affection for precision is widely derided!"

"Something in the Way She Moves" had originally been the most barebones track on the Apple debut, featuring only James's voice and guitar. Here, Peter decided to gently expand the sonic atmosphere, adding Lee Sklar's bass throughout, a dash of steel guitar courtesy of Dan Dugmore, and, on the choruses, high harmonies from Herb Pedersen. While tuning his instrument at The Sound Factory, Dugmore recalled thinking: "I can't believe this is going on *Greatest Hits*, and we haven't even cut it yet!"

With the two tracks recorded and mixed quickly, *James Taylor's Greatest Hits* was in the shops within weeks. It sold well during the post-Thanksgiving shopping season, but it didn't stop there; the album continued to sell well into the new year, and the next, and the next, eventually selling over eleven million copies and becoming the biggest-selling album of Taylor's career.

Warner Brothers, of course, wanted to hang on to Taylor, but perhaps they didn't understand that this artist, who had made them so much money, was dissatisfied with the amount he was receiving in return. "It was a standard operation, where the record company got all the best of it," Joe Smith, the former president of Warner Brothers Records, admitted. "That's what you did for the first three, five albums."

Walter Yetnikoff, then-president of Columbia Records, swooped in and offered Peter many times over what Warners currently was.

Columbia also assured both Peter and James that they had the know-how to break Taylor's albums overseas, which had so far eluded Warners. "His foreign sales were pathetic," Peter recalled. The day Taylor was supposed to sign the contract with Columbia and receive his large advance, Russ Titelman and Lenny Waronker, both senior vice-presidents at Warner Brothers and producers of Taylor's last two albums, flew to New York and did their best to convince him not to leave the label.

It almost worked. Taylor phoned Peter, who was waiting with both the contract and the check at Nat Weiss's apartment, and told him he couldn't do it. "So I went and met him at a bar," Peter remembered, leaving a fuming Walter Yetnikoff to bide his time with Weiss. "By this time, it was one in the morning, and prodigious amounts of alcohol and 'whatever' were being consumed at this time by all of us." After an hour or so, with both manager and client reviewing all sides of the situation, they made their way back to Weiss's apartment, and Taylor signed to Columbia.

"I thought Columbia would do a lot better," said Peter. Warner Brothers "had a chance to take us seriously, that we were gonna leave, and they didn't. Then they *did*"—Peter laughed—"but it was too little too late." In a retaliatory move, Warners proceeded to steal away one of Columbia's preeminent singer/songwriters, Paul Simon.

The sessions for Taylor's first Columbia album took place at The Sound Factory beginning in mid-March 1977. Having not been at the helm of Taylor's last three albums (none selling as well as his earlier releases), his new label insisted that Peter produce the sessions. He was happy to oblige, working quickly and efficiently, cutting the tracks live with minimal overdubs and finishing the album in about five weeks. Taylor brought some melodically strong material, including the jubilant "Your Smiling Face," the contemplative "Secret o' Life," and "Bartender's Blues," a sad slice of country that was sung as an homage to the great George Jones, one of country music's most iconic singers. Jones cut his own version of the song the following year (with Taylor providing harmony vocals), and his remake became a Top Ten country hit.

Taylor was obviously having fun during the sessions. Nowhere is this more apparent than in the quirky "Traffic Jam," a mostly a cappella tale of vehicular angst. The track was underpinned by Russ Kunkel's jazzy drumming, but once again, "no rules" was the rule of the day: "They kept trying drums and none of 'em were working," Lee Sklar recalled, "so they finally brought a bunch of cardboard boxes in, and *that* became the drumkit!" Taylor stacked his vocals on the choruses, which added a quasi–doo wop feel, then talked through the verses in what might be described as a proto-rap style. Of course, being a bit drunk while recording the track could be part of the reason for Taylor's surprising performance.

Due to Taylor being "a little buzzed," according to engineer Val Garay, "his voice dropped low enough to where he could sing the bass parts." Later, Garay said, "We found out that there were a couple out of tune, so we had to redo it." These were

Peter and James in the studio, 1977.
jimsheaphotography.com.

ancient days before you could autotune vocals, which is standard practice today. Therefore, Garay laughed, in order to sing low enough for the new takes, "He had to get fucked up again!" An honorable sacrifice for art.

In between takes, Danny Kortchmar began playing an old tune he'd recently been thinking about: "I got this idea of James singing 'Handy Man.'" The original 1960 hit by Jimmy Jones was produced by the legendary Otis Blackwell as a jaunty slice of pop/soul. Kortchmar imagined James doing it "as a ballad, 'cause I thought it'd be really sexy." Kootch showed James what he had in mind, and the two began playing at a slow, easy pace.

Peter, up in the booth with Val Garay, knew a good thing when he heard it. "My contribution," remembered Peter, "was *stopping* the song we were in the middle of trying to record and recording that instead. I said, *'I need to record this!'* And I just did it with James and Danny, and Russ Kunkel playing a cardboard box, and added everything else later." The trio ran through the song a few times, with Peter making sure that the guitar chords didn't get too fancy. Then the master take was quickly in the can.

"I try not to let anything go by without recording it," Peter said, adding for clarification, "anything that's gonna be *good*. And in that case, clearly, what they were doing was just a joke, for fun. But to me, it immediately sounded like a hit."

Taylor was resistant about recording the track. "Oh, don't send me to oldies heaven," Taylor pleaded. "*Please!*" Kortchmar, realizing how well his suggestion was turning out, replied, "Yeah, but *listen* to it!" Peter's attitude was similar: "The question is not whether it's an oldie or whether it's anything else," the producer patiently explained to his reticent client, "the question is: Is it great? And the answer is: yes!"

Forty-five years later, "he's still singing it," Kortchmar smiled. "Why? Not because it's some novelty, but because it's wonderful."

At that time, Taylor was wary of pandering to the commercial side of the industry. "He was very reticent about anything even approaching not just selling out," Kortchmar explained, "but appearing to want to be *popular!*" The guitarist cackles uproariously at the thought. "Now, Peter Asher *definitely* wanted to be popular! You know? And he wanted his music to be popular, and I thought that was . . ."—Kortchmar searched for the right word—". . . honest."

"It's good to do some covers," Taylor admitted, "but you know, at the time I wanted to record my own stuff." He was also wary of the mind-set of the typical label: "Whenever you handed them a cover," Taylor explained, "they immediately went for it as a single, the thing that they wanted you to promote and get behind, because that's the thing that was the safest for them; it *sounded* like a hit because it *had* been."

And it was again. When released that summer, "Handy Man" made the Top Five, Taylor's highest position in the charts since "Fire and Rain." The album, simply entitled *JT*, was also a Top Five record—his best showing since *One Man Dog* (Taylor's last Asher-produced effort)—and went on to sell over two million copies.

The album's cover was Peter's idea. He wanted the cover photo to evoke "a film star," John Kosh recalled, "a matinee idol." To help achieve that effect, Kosh took David Alexander's head shot of Taylor and retouched it considerably, which included removing a mole on the side of Taylor's face. The singer thought that was going too far: "He made me put it back again." Kosh laughed.

After finishing the mixes for *JT* with engineer Val Garay, Peter and Val had only a few weeks before they were back in the studio in mid-May to begin work on the next Linda Ronstadt album, eventually released with the title *Simple Dreams*.

JT album cover.

"I think that's the best record she made," Garay stated. "We had all evolved to a point where we really had it honed." Andrew Gold was now off concentrating on his solo career, so the music moved toward a leaner and harder rock sound with Waddy Wachtel's crunching Les Paul coming to the fore. Dan Dugmore was still playing steel guitar, and Kenny Edwards continued with bass and background vocal duties. Michael Botts was not available so, thanks to a suggestion from Ronstadt, Rick Marotta was now seated behind the kit.

Born in New York, Marotta began his artistic life as a dancer, following in his parents footsteps (so to speak). Young Rick began taking classes and entering dance contests in his neighborhood, where he kept running into fellow dancer David Spinozza. Spinozza was also a pretty good guitarist, and watching his friend on the floor, he could tell how good Marotta's rhythm and timing was. "Man, if you played drums," Spinozza once said to him, "I'd hire you for my band."

Spinozza's drummer soon went into the army, leaving his kit behind at Marotta's house. The nineteen-year-old had never played drums before but began to teach himself. "Two months later," Marotta recalled, "I had that gig."

Marotta grew to become an in-demand session player in New York, backing John Lennon, Paul Simon, and Bette Midler, to name just a few. Eventually he got the chance to back Taylor on the 1974 *Walking Man* sessions, invited by his old friend Spinozza, who produced the album.

It was during the tour promoting *Walking Man* that Marotta got to know both Linda Ronstadt (who was opening the shows) and Peter Asher. "I thought he was a little cold, sort of distant, kind of snooty," Marotta recalled. "After getting to know Peter, he couldn't be more the opposite."

Another veteran of the *Walking Man* tour was requested by Ronstadt to join her in the studio: pianist Don Grolnick.

Childhood friend Stuart Schulman remembered a key turning point for Grolnick: "His dad had just taken him to a club on Long Island to hear The Bill Evans Trio," and Schulman recalled his twelve-year-old friend "was just completely possessed by it; that's all he could think about or talk about." The pair eventually formed a band called Fire and Ice, becoming a solid Boston-area act. "It was a horn band," Schulman said, "and Don wrote a lot of the horn arrangements and a couple of tunes." Not surprisingly, with his composing and arranging talents, Grolnick also became a hot New York session player (The Manhattan Transfer, Melissa Manchester, The Brecker Brothers).

And like Peter, Grolnick was a former philosophy major. "Incredible," Peter called him. "A major intellect and a major musician. Cynical, funny, and super-smart."

After spending some time rehearsing, the sessions began on May 23rd with a song Peter had suggested: Buddy Holly's "It's So Easy." "She didn't want to do that," Peter flatly stated, but Ronstadt sang the hell out of it, using her sexy, throaty growl throughout to punctuate the lyrics. Another good suggestion came via J.D. Souther, who thought that covering the old Roy Orbison number "Blue Bayou" would fit Linda's ballad sensibilities perfectly. "I thought she was a remarkable ballad singer," Souther marveled. "Her voice was *so* beautiful." Ronstadt's performance here confirms that claim, singing with such longing the listener wants to escape to this magical place along with her, and her vocal jump to that final note—simply blissful.

Dan Dugmore once again performed an eight-bar solo with his steel guitar that is a master class in atmospheric accompaniment. "I think I've had more people comment on 'Blue Bayou' than anything else I've ever done," Dugmore admitted.

Ronstadt was at her cocky best covering The Rolling Stones' "Tumbling Dice," where Keith Richards acolyte Waddy Wachtel did his hero proud. The group had been doing the number during soundchecks on their last tour, but Ronstadt was making up half the words as she could never understand all the lyrics, due to Mick Jagger's lack of enunciation. When Ronstadt played LA, Jagger came backstage and urged her to sing more rock'n'roll. She told him, "Fine—write me out the words to 'Tumbling Dice.'" She couldn't believe it as he promptly did just that.

After singing one Warren Zevon song on her last album, here she tackled two—the postmodern Western ballad "Carmelita" and the flat-out rocker "Poor, Poor Pitiful Me." One of the sonic touches on both Zevon covers was a new electronic tool making one of its first appearances on a recording date: the Pollard Syndrum.

"Oh, those horrible Syndrums," Ronstadt sighed.

"They were brand-new," Marotta offered in his defense. "The only two guys who had 'em were me and Jeff Porcaro." Porcaro, also an in-demand session drummer, would utilize them first that year on Carly Simon's hit, "Nobody Does It Better." But with the passage of time, Marotta understood Ronstadt's distaste: "I don't disagree with Linda at all. When I hear the *'peeuuuuw'* now," Marotta said, imitating that classic descending tone, "it's nauseating to me."

Peter seemed much more at ease with the choice: "No, no, I thought they were cool," he said. "I still do."

Two weeks into the sessions, Ronstadt cut J.D. Souther's "Simple Man, Simple Dream"—a song that would eventually provide her finished album its title. Souther told me proudly that his friend Warren Zevon "thought it had the best two first lines he'd ever heard":

What if I fall in love with you, just like normal people do?
Well, maybe I'd kill you—maybe I'd be true . . .

Souther claimed to have no idea how the lines came about. When it comes to a song's first stirrings, "I can't plan when it's gonna happen," he admitted. "So I very rarely can plan how it opens." Peter's first production of the song, on Souther's *Black Rose* album, had more of a stronger pulse throughout; here, he let Don Grolnick's electric piano and Dan Dugmore's pedal steel keep the track slowly moving underneath Ronstadt's intimate performance.

The record's design again came courtesy of John Kosh. The cover photograph was taken in the ladies' room of Hollywood's venerable Pantages Theatre, a gorgeous Art Deco structure built in the late 1920s. The first session with photographer Jim Shea was done using special film stock, which gave exquisite, saturated color. But with the kerfuffle from the last cover fresh in mind, Peter's wife, Betsy, took one look at the photographer's proofs and said, "You can't use this!"

Remembering the photos, Kosh explained that Ronstadt was seated more in profile, and the problem was "what we call in the business 'SBE'—Side Breast Exposure." But by the time the reshoot was arranged, the film stock used originally had been discontinued. Various tests were then done with different stocks combined with hotter developing techniques to try to achieve a similar grainy result, which they eventually got. Kosh's design also extended to the labels used on the records, featuring the same colors and type font as the cover. Kosh pointed to the inner sleeve that held the vinyl, which featured a shot of Ronstadt's head and shoulders.

"No retouching," Kosh declared, emphasizing Ronstadt's natural beauty, and then he confided, "There's no such thing as an unretouched picture today!" The whole package was the most expensive he did for Ronstadt, but "not as expensive as *Hotel California*, for Christ's sakes," Kosh remarked, recalling the classic Eagles album he'd designed in 1976.

Simple Dreams was released in September 1977, and by October it had replaced Fleetwood Mac's mega-selling *Rumours* as the number-one album in the country, staying at the top of the charts for five weeks. Also in October, Ronstadt became the first artist since The Beatles to have two singles in the Top Five simultaneously— "Blue Bayou" and "It's So Easy."

The success Peter was achieving with Taylor and Ronstadt, both as producer and manager, was unprecedented and undeniable. Soon *Rolling Stone*, the biweekly pub-

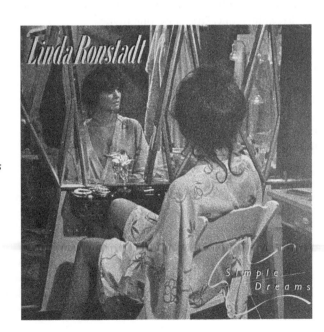

Simple Dreams album cover.

lication that had just begun to surpass its counterculture origins and stake its claim in the mainstream, came calling.

"They said, 'We're gonna do a big story about you as manager and producer, and we'd like you to come to New York and do a photo shoot with Annie Leibovitz.'" Then, according to Peter, the editors added: "And we *might* consider putting you on the cover *if* you bring James Taylor and Linda Ronstadt with you to the photo shoot."

"Generally," Peter continued, "I was the kind of manager who didn't bully his clients. I would sit down and go, 'Well, you know, we've been offered this,' and 'What do you think,' and 'Here's the pros and cons.' In that particular instance, all that went out the window! In that case, the ego was mine; I was going, 'Do I want to be on the cover of *Rolling Stone*? FUCK YES!' So, I basically bullied James and Linda into coming with me."

Peter, along with his two charges, did make the cover of *Rolling Stone*'s 255th issue, dated December 29, 1977. Along with naming Peter "Producer of the Year" in their year-end Critics' Awards, the cover story was a look back at his career, while his two famous clients sang his praises. This was followed by a two-page interview with Peter chatting with reporter Peter Herbst about his production methodology; how he prefers very clear, crisp sounds and tries to capture the intensity of early live takes before the energy starts to dissipate. He ended the interview by admitting: "I've never known what is going to happen from one year to the next," but that "things have tended to fall into place . . ."

They certainly did just two months later. On February 23, 1978, The Academy of Recording Arts and Sciences held their twentieth annual Grammy Awards presentation at Los Angeles's Shrine Auditorium. James Taylor won the Best Male Pop Vocal Performance trophy that evening for "Handy Man," and John Kosh's design for Linda Ronstadt's *Simple Dreams* won for Best Album Package. Though *JT* may have lost out on Album of the Year and "Blue Bayou" missed winning Record of the Year, the Recording Academy couldn't deny the impressive work of the man behind them both—not to mention their massive record sales. Therefore, the Grammy for Producer of the Year was deservedly presented . . . to Peter Asher.

19

HER TOWN TOO

The tour to promote *Simple Dreams* was a huge success. "We were gettin' paid pretty well," drummer Rick Marotta remembered. "Five, seven grand a week at that time was a *shitload* of money!" Marotta attributed all the successes, both the albums and the tours, to Peter: "He was an amazing delegator and leader. Peter turned into 'The Godfather' for us. The boss was Linda or James when we were onstage, but *really* Peter was in charge," Marotta declared. "Peter was the linchpin; he was the guy who held it all together.

"He handled difficult artists really well," Marotta continued. "I have to say—they were really not difficult *people*, and they were *brilliant* artists," he clarified, "it's just that emotionally and intellectually, I don't know that many people that could have done it like Peter.

"James," Marotta said, for example, "couldn't be a nicer guy, but underneath all of that, there were problems. Another *incredibly* intelligent guy, very funny, but demons like *crazy!* And Peter had a way of dealing with him that was like a friend, but more like a patriarch. Like someone that said, 'Look—you're fucking up and you have to fix it.'"

Peter, Linda Ronstadt explained, "came from a more formal background. He paid a lot of attention to manners and to protocol—which saved us! There were lots of obstacles in those days, you know? Our own silly egos and narcissism and tons of drugs, and it was just *craziness!*

"None of us needs to grow into a monster," she stated, "and a lot of people did unnecessarily because they didn't have somebody standing to the side saying, 'Do you know you're acting stupid?' Or 'Do you know you're acting unreasonable?' Or 'Do you know what you just did was outrageous, or ungrateful, or horrific manners, or inappropriate?'

"Which is not to say he kept us from doing inappropriate things—we all did all the time. Probably Peter did, too! I especially did." Ronstadt laughed.

"There's always something steady about him, you know, in the midst of quite an unsteady environment," Kenny Edwards noted. "The music business in the seventies—especially around success and all that stuff—there was a lot of drama, a lot of new money, a lot of drugs and alcohol all flyin' around. And he managed to have this equilibrium that practically nobody else I ever knew had."

But that steadiness had begun to fray when it came to Peter and Betsy's seven-year marriage. Together since 1965, they had seemed like the perfect hip and successful LA couple. Edwards remarked that Betsy was one of "the 'Royalty' of that sort of American upper-class rocker, you know? And she had this great taste; she was a great entertainer, a really great decorator, and a very smart woman." "Betsy was *very* instrumental in the early part of his career in America," according to Val Garay, "hosting the barbecues and getting the right people over. She was great.

"I just think they grew apart." Garay shrugged. "You know, the usual." Peter began living in a temporary bachelor pad near the Chateau Marmont in West Hollywood while preparing to move into a new beachfront residence in the famous and very exclusive Malibu Colony, where Ronstadt had moved after the success of *Heart Like a Wheel*. "I bought it for $800,000," Peter recalled—an insanely small amount, given the home's value today. While the divorce began its slow journey through the California courts, Peter continued to produce one great project after another.

Three years before, basking in the success of *Heart Like a Wheel*, Peter had traveled to Hawaii with Linda and her fellow musicians to select songs for the follow-up. Now, after the even bigger success of *Simple Dreams*, another trip to the islands was planned—but with a slightly different approach: "There's that thing with rock'n'roll songs," explained Peter. "The record comes out, then you go on the road, and a month later you're going, 'Shit—these are better! I wish we could redo them.'" Such was the case with Andrew Gold's "Lonely Boy"—recut after the tune was tightened on tour.

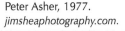

Peter Asher, 1977.
jimsheaphotography.com.

For this very reason, Linda approached Peter with the idea of playing the next album live *before* recording it. Peter, though, didn't want these "public rehearsals" to become mobbed or the press reporting on songs that might not even make the cut. Looking for somewhere to play out of the way, yet, just as important, thoroughly enjoyable, Peter found a club in Maui with a stage large enough for Linda and her band. He phoned the owner and asked, "Can we come and play there for a week?" Incredulous, the owner sputtered, "I can't afford Linda Ronstadt!" Peter, magnanimous as always, replied, "No, just pay us whatever you pay your other bands."

"He flew us all to Hawaii, and we played in this club," Dan Dugmore recalled. "These people got quite a treat to see and hear all the new songs." Some of Ronstadt's past repertoire was added into the set, but the bulk of the songs those lucky patrons heard was the material meant for Ronstadt's upcoming sessions. When recording commenced back at The Sound Factory on May 5th, "we really felt we had that energy" from playing them live, Dugmore enthused. "I think it really helped."

Much of this material, released at the end of 1978 as the album *Living in the USA*, was what you would have expected from a Ronstadt record at this point—a J.D. Souther song, a Warren Zevon number, and some tasty, well-chosen rock and R&B oldies. But within the grooves there were hints of new directions Ronstadt would soon explore more fully. One example was her performance of "When I Grow Too Old to Dream." Originally written by Oscar Hammerstein II and Sigmund Romberg in 1934, and a number-one hit the following year, this was Ronstadt's first foray into compositions that have come to be called "The Great American Songbook."

"I was born in '38," recalled Mike Mainieri, "and my mother used to sing it to me as a lullaby." As the teenaged vibraphonist began to play professionally, it was one of the songs he'd perform in his act. Mainieri amassed quite a résumé, backing jazz greats like Billie Holiday and Dizzy Gillespie, eventually forming his own band, Steps, featuring pianist Don Grolnick. "Don overheard me playing it one day," said Mainieri, "and said, 'What is *that?*'" Grolnick immediately learned the lovely, unfamiliar tune and would play it occasionally whenever the mood struck him.

Years later, playing the song to himself during a break in Ronstadt's sessions, the same thing occurred—Ronstadt asked, "What's the name of *that* tune?" "The next thing I know," Mainieri said, "I got a call from Peter." To accompany Ronstadt's take, Grolnick insisted that his old friend, Mainieri, who had taught him the tune, be a part of the track. Flying out to Los Angeles for the session, Mainieri was impressed with Ronstadt's research on the song—she had added back the original opening refrain, which Mainieri had stopped playing years ago. Equally impressive, said Mainieri, "We must have worked on it for five hours—rehearsed it all day; we tried different keys, different tempos"—all with Ronstadt singing continuously. "Man," he marveled, "what pipes!" The arrangement Mainieri and Grolnick performed on the master take manages to encompass both nostalgic front parlor simplicity and modern improvisational cool—a brave addition to a pop-rock album of that era.

Possibly more surprising to listeners was Ronstadt's take on "Alison," a ballad from the pen of Elvis Costello and a highlight from his debut album released the previous year. Peter thought the song was a potential hit and suggested it to Ronstadt, who had watched Costello perform it at his Whiskey a-Go-Go gig in November 1977. Unsure of how to approach the lyrics, the tenderest composition yet heard at this stage of Costello's career, Ronstadt hit on singing it as advice to a close friend. This change, though, meant the hurtful bite heard in the original was replaced with a pretty warning.

For many critics, during this shift away from the "corporate rock" and "California sound" that epitomized the seventies toward the punk ethos and edgy pop of the "new wave" bands then emerging, *Living in the USA* highlighted a supposed "problem" spelled out in *Rolling Stone*'s review: "Pop music is about fun and feeling," critic Ken Emerson wrote, "while Ronstadt seems to be pursuing something entirely different and perhaps antipathetic: perfection."

Peter is having none of it: "I really don't feel guilty about the perfection thing, because there are cases *now* where you hear records where the vocal is *too* perfect; where it's really been moved and tuned to death, where it doesn't sound like a real human being giving you an interpretation of the song. I was very anxious to keep that," Peter insisted, "and did my best to do so."

As an example of keeping a heartfelt performance, perfection be damned, Peter cited "Ooh Baby Baby"—the classic Smokey Robinson/Motown ballad and a highlight on *Living in the USA*. Engineer Val Garay remembered it well: "We had the background singers sing live, she sang live, the track was cut live, and I did a rough mix of it," he said, quickly adding: "Thank God!" The next day, because Ronstadt hated her performance, her vocal was erased from the multitrack master tape. "My voice was real tired from singing it all afternoon," Ronstadt explained, "and I'd gotten sorta flat." Garay, though admitting she was technically correct, exclaimed: "But so what? Who cared? It was a great *feeling!*"

Ronstadt attempted take after take of a new lead vocal. "We did, like, a million vocals," Peter said. But, despite all her efforts, "I went back to the one where the two background singers had sung live with her," Peter said, flat notes and all. Ronstadt ultimately agreed: "The whole was more important than those flat notes," she admitted, and Garay's original rough mix was the take released.

"It was soulful," Peter said simply. "I really do try to keep the magic, moving, soulful vocal."

"Moving" and "soulful" are good descriptions of Linda's rendition of Elvis Presley's "Love Me Tender"—the album's closer and a sweet tribute to the King, who had died suddenly the previous year. "We were on the road, Linda and I," Waddy Wachtel recalled, "and we got the news that Elvis died. And I just remember that she and I went out on this fire escape, and we sat there and started doing 'Love Me Tender.' And we put it in the show that night."

After Linda's version had been recorded and released, Wachtel remembered getting a call from Peter to come to his office. Once there, Peter announced: "I got a letter from the Colonel"—referring to Elvis's legendary manager, Col. Tom Parker. According to Wachtel, the letter began, "I love your version of 'Love Me Tender.'" It continued: "I have assembled a collaborative version with Elvis and Linda singing it together and, with your permission, I'd like to release it."

Peter then played the tape that accompanied the missive—a somewhat crude but effective mix fitting Presley's vocal alongside Ronstadt's, as Wachtel's guitar strummed underneath it all. As he listened, Wachtel likened the experience to being "in *The Twilight Zone*" and called it "really creepy." Ronstadt stated that she and Peter thought the idea "vulgar and silly," so the Colonel's concept was not encouraged. Ten years later, the same idea sold millions of records for Natalie Cole when she and her late father managed an electronic duet on "Unforgettable." Eventually, it was Barbra Streisand who delivered on the Colonel's idea, singing "Love Me Tender" with the ghostly Elvis on her 2015 album *Partners*.

Following up *Simple Dreams*, *Living in the USA* was highly anticipated. Asylum Records shipped two million copies to retailers, the first album to do so, and it went to number-one. The photos by Jim Shea that designer John Kosh used for the album package featured Ronstadt on roller skates, just as that pastime was becoming hip again. But "Linda couldn't skate," according to Kosh: "She was feverishly learning how"—hence the kneepads in the photos. The shot on the back cover was taken on Southern California's Venice Beach boardwalk as photographer Shea skated backward ahead of his unsteady subject.

Recalling the colorful neighborhood, Kosh noted, "It was crazy there," so a few off-duty police were hired for security. When it came time for a break, Kosh said, "The

Living in the USA album cover.

cops would come up and say, 'I guess we should sort of turn the other way while you have your *refreshments*.'" He laughed. "Yeah, this was *deep* refreshment era."

After any shoot, Kosh explained, "You'd submit a bill, and the record company would argue about the line items. 'You spent five hundred dollars on *film*? Forty dollars on *gas*?'—which was a lot, in those days. 'And how much for *food*?!'" But as they came to the line with the word *refreshments*, Kosh smiled and whispered, "They'd just skip over it!"

"*Flag* is still one of my all-time favorite records," enthused Lee Sklar. "It was absolutely a magical experience." That might have been true for the musicians, but those who could read nautical symbols might have approached the record with trepidation or concern, as the colors on the cover announced: "Man Overboard."

"There's a reason for this," John Kosh said, explaining his cover design: "James was strung out—he was overboard. This is one of the most depressing albums you ever could hear." James Taylor's second record for Columbia did seem much less positive than *JT* had been, with songs about the soul-sucking nature of the music business ("Company Man"), and a trio of tunes depicting various couples whose relationships seemed doomed ("Johnnie Comes Back," "I Will Not Lie for You," "B.S.U.R."). The album even closes with "Sleep Come Free Me"—the tale of a convict whose only escape from his endless imprisonment is found in his dreams. Though the song is beautifully composed and performed, it ends the album with the sound of a cell door slamming shut.

It wasn't all doom and gloom, though; Taylor decided to revive "Rainy Day Man," a song that offered some hope of relief from life's depressing trials. Peter had originally cut it for Taylor's Apple debut, but in 1979, "the Apple stuff was still unavail-

Flag album cover.

able," Peter recalled, "and he liked the song, so we redid it." And speaking of Apple, in a nod to his former "company men," Taylor cut a hard-driving cover of Lennon and McCartney's "Day Tripper."

"That was a jam," Lee Sklar remembered. "I just started playing the bassline, somebody jumped in, and the next thing you know, we cut it." As with "Handy Man," Peter simply knew: "It takes," said Sklar, "a real special producer who'll hear something like that happening and go, 'Let's grab it!'"

But "James has always been nervous about doing oldies, or even playing oldies," Peter confided. "I would suggest some oldie that might be a hit, and he would resist. I remember once they were doing an old Manhattans song at a soundcheck, and it was sounding killer, you know? And James saw me kind of listening at the side of the stage going, 'Hmmm . . . ,' and they stopped." Peter laughed. "He stopped! He just didn't want me to tie him into an oldie he'd have to sing onstage every night."

Despite Taylor's oldies phobia, the track that stood out as the album's likely hit, suffused with magic, was a cover of Carole King and Gerry Goffin's "Up on the Roof," a smash hit for The Drifters back in 1962. Taylor had played on King's own version, which closed her first solo album *Writer*, and the two of them had performed the song live together during their *Tapestry*-era tours.

Obviously, King's songcraft had long been an inspiration for Taylor. As with "You've Got a Friend," his take was another tip of the hat to King, and Taylor imbued the song with all the yearning and joy Goffin's words and King's melody suggested. The icing on the cake came from the string arrangement courtesy of the legendary Arif Mardin.

"We were *huge* fans of all the records he'd made," Peter declared, and who wouldn't be? The Rascals' "Groovin'," Dusty Springfield's "Son of a Preacher Man," Aretha Franklin's "Day Dreaming," and hundreds of others, all benefited from his touch. Taylor had recently worked with Mardin on Carly Simon's *Boys in the Trees* album and introduced him to Peter. "We totally hit it off. I loved him," Peter said, describing Mardin as "one of the nicest men and super-smart." Mardin's strings brought just the right touch of classical majesty to Taylor's version of what most agree is one of the greatest pop songs ever written.

Taylor also brought an exquisitely crafted song of his own to the album: "We were thinking about songs to do for *Flag*," Sklar recalled. "And he comes up and goes, 'I got this song—do you think it's worth cutting?' And he plays me 'Millworker.' And I look at him and said, 'Fuck you! I would crawl through ground glass from here to Utah to be able to come *close* to writing a song like that!'"

"Millworker," along with another track on the album, "Brother Trucker," were among three pieces Taylor had composed for a stage production based on *Working*, the best-selling oral history by journalist Studs Terkel. The interviews Terkel had gathered of working folk were woven together to fashion a musical revue, and Taylor's "Millworker" was a showstopper.

The weary tale—a single mother of three seeing no future for herself past standing at her factory loom every day until her life is over—managed to showcase the woman's dignity alongside her hopelessness. The sparse arrangement on *Flag* featured Taylor's guitar up front, with Don Grolnick's simple piano chords entering on the second verse. Finally, a cello and viola descend over the song's refrain, adding a Celtic/Appalachian coloring to the aural picture.

The viola was courtesy of Louise Schulman, a childhood friend of Grolnick's. She remembered the arrangement being worked out on the spot as Taylor and her old friend played through the song. During one run-through, Schulman recalled, Taylor took note of a particular sound Grolnick was producing. "Wow, I really like the way you're tapping your foot," he enthused, and Peter promptly instructed Val Garay to place a mic down by the floor. This subtle addition to the final mix explains why the album's liner notes for the track credit Grolnick for "Harmonium, piano & shoe."

Also in the liner notes, among all the thanks, there appeared the name "Ira." This referred to Ira Koslow, who had first arrived at Peter Asher Management five years earlier. Having lost his teaching position as an economics professor, and in desperate need of a job as a divorced parent with a young daughter, he was hired originally as Peter's driver.

"I was a chauffeur/gofer," Koslow explained. "My thing was: I'd deliver something to the studio, and I'd leave. I wasn't into staying up all night—I had a child to take care of." By now, Koslow had become more of a personal assistant to Peter, quickly learning about the business, eventually becoming the company's president.

Though Taylor's singing was superb throughout *Flag*, as was the musical accompaniment, the bleakness of most of the album's lyrics was perhaps the reason *Flag* barely scraped into the Top Ten, but it did achieve Gold Record status. And despite its beauty, "Up On the Roof" just missed making *Billboard*'s Top Twenty hits list. All a bit disappointing after the slam-dunk of *JT*, but Peter didn't have time to dwell on it—for by the time *Flag* was released, he was almost halfway through recording his next project.

"We were all, all us young teenage girls, very avid fans of every single piece of writing and film about The Beatles," Bonnie Raitt remembered. She admitted that "John was my favorite," but being keenly aware of McCartney's connection to both Jane Asher and her bespectacled older brother, Raitt also began to avidly follow Peter's career.

After Bonnie took up the guitar and began to get noticed playing the bars and the folk and blues festivals on the East Coast, she began being represented by Dick Waterman, manager of many blues artists, including Buddy Guy and Junior Wells. Waterman's lawyer was Nat Weiss, and it was Weiss who introduced Raitt to his colleague Peter. Not long afterward, "I moved back to California from the East Coast in '73 to make my third album," Raitt recalled. "In that LA singer/songwriter scene, Peter was just part of that crowd. We'd occasionally run into each other at parties and backstage at gigs."

By 1979, Raitt had a loyal following and received critical praise for her work, but her records were simply not selling all that well. Her sixth album had finally made the Top Forty, helped largely by her cover of Del Shannon's "Runaway." Warner Brothers had just renegotiated her contract—not wanting her to take an offer from rival label Columbia, as James Taylor had done. Hoping to build on her recent success, her label suggested that Peter, her friend and one of the industry's top producers, might be the perfect choice to oversee her next album.

"I have to have somebody that I respect a lot and have an affinity for. Peter was making records that were really sounding great and were getting across," Raitt explained. "And I had been making records that *weren't* necessarily getting across, and I thought it would be really good to try!"

Peter hired some of his top guns for the sessions, including Danny Kortchmar, Waddy Wachtel, and Rick Marotta. One new addition to Peter's team was bassist Bob Glaub. "I always loved music," Glaub said, and recalled he and his older brother listening to rock'n'roll radio, loving those early hits of Elvis and Little Richard. "We'd go to the record store, and we'd buy 'em together with our saved pennies."

After The Beatles hit, some of Glaub's schoolmates formed a band. Noting their lack of a bass player, "I just begged 'em—if I bought a bass, can I be in the band?" Glaub, though, admitted: "I didn't really know what a bass was, to be honest. I just knew they needed one!" After his dad bought him a bass and amp, "I started to pick bass notes off of records," and soon after these self-taught lessons, he made his garage band debut, eventually progressing to the casino lounges of Vegas and Tahoe during his college days.

Glaub soon began to jam with friends whose neighbor, in a fortuitous bit of happenstance, was Jessie Ed Davis—one of LA's top rock guitarists in the early seventies. One day, Glaub's phone rang, and it was Davis, whose regular bassist was MIA: "Bob, you gotta get your bass, come down here, and play on my record!"

"That was a big pivotal jump for me, 'cause on the session was Jim Keltner"—one of the top drummers in LA—"who immediately recommended me for a couple of little sessions around town." Within weeks, Glaub found himself alongside Davis and Keltner on a "little" John Lennon session with legendary producer Phil Spector.

A couple of years later, Glaub began working with Jackson Browne—both on *The Pretender* and Warren Zevon's debut for Asylum Records, which Browne coproduced with Waddy Wachtel. Now having fallen in with this hot group of players, Glaub was recommended to Peter for the Bonnie Raitt sessions. "Great bass player," Peter was quick to say, adding: "He reminds me of Duck Dunn"—the legendary bassist for Booker T. and the MG's, who helped guide the groove behind many of the great Stax/Volt recordings of the sixties. "It's all in the groove," according to Peter, "and Bob's an impeccable groove player."

Upon being informed that Peter was himself a bassist during England's "trad jazz" period, Glaub remarked: "That doesn't surprise me, because he's so keenly aware of every note the bassist is playing."

"In terms of musicianship," said Raitt of the players surrounding her during these sessions, "it was real '*high tide at the gene pool*.'" Being supported by this high caliber of rockers, most of them different from her usual crew, made for a fresh and enjoyable experience for Raitt.

Sessions began at The Sound Factory in late April 1979, only a month after *Flag* had wrapped. Val Garay was, again, engineering, and his assistant was George Ybarra.

But Ybarra quickly came down with hepatitis, and needing a second engineer, Garay chose twenty-one-year-old Niko Bolas, who had been working for Garay as a "runner"—as in "run and get lunch." "There was no assistant at The Sound Factory that would work with them, 'cause they were a pretty intense team," recalled Bolas. "I got the job—went from the corner of the room to 'the chair.' And made every mistake you can possibly think of!" Bolas, who went on to a lengthy career, producing artists from Neil Young to the Circle Jerks, reiterated: "*Major* mistakes . . . and Peter just cruised through all of 'em and was always a mentor.

"What he'd do is: He got a band that was so amazing, and an engineer that was amazing, and"—Bolas emphasized—"a headphone mix! *Most* important." This refers to the balance of vocals and instruments the performers heard as they played. "If you pay attention, you can see how he produces for *feel*. Peter Asher records 'feel' amazing. There's nothing about them that lines up on a grid," Bolas explained, "everything lines up with your *heart*—that's the biggest deal."

"We both decided that we wanted to make kind of a 'live' record," Raitt said. "All the songs on the record were first or second takes." For that reason alone, Peter would want musicians there he could count on. "Peter would bring you in," Waddy Wachtel explained, "because he wanted what you give"—he snaps his fingers—"spontaneously. And usually, your first throw is the thing everyone's hoping to capture.

"He was just very, very into the spontaneity of what'll happen when the red light goes on and people give it their best shot."

And their best shot was exactly what he got. The tracks burst with solid R&B energy, including Bonnie's great cover of Sam and Dave's "I Thank You," which kicks the album off with Marotta's snare daring you to hang on. Throughout, Raitt is simply a knockout as a singer. The record's final track, "(Goin') Wild for You Baby" (cowritten by Peter's former client Tom Snow), contains one of her most soulful vocals.

Between those two songs were more brilliant performances: "The Boy Can't Help It," a gender switch on the old Little Richard number, sways with a lazy strut, highlighted by Raitt's slide playing on her National Steel guitar; "Your Good Thing (Is About to End)," another great song from the pen of Isaac Hayes and David Porter, slowly seethes with resolve and regret; and Mary Wells's "Bye Bye Baby" shows no regret at all, as you can picture Raitt almost dancing away from a clueless lover. Guitarist Kortchmar suggested that old number, as well as Jackson Browne's "Sleep's Dark and Silent Gate."

"Y'know, I love Jackson's songs," Raitt confessed, and she praised Kortchmar's "interesting R&B take on it." Raitt herself contributed "Standing by the Same Old Love," a tale of two lovers who, despite their ups and downs, are still trying to make it work. "I don't write much," she said, "but I was really proud of that one."

The track that was a complete departure from the rest of the record was "The Glow," which ended up giving the album its title. During her search for material, Raitt's former bassist, Veyler Hilderbrand, had played his ex-employer some demos of his recent compositions. "She just especially liked that one," Hilderbrand remembered, and Raitt put it in the batch of songs to try.

The demo was barebones—just voice and guitar—but pianist Don Grolnick created a slow arrangement for a jazz trio that evoked Sinatra sitting in some smoky bar in the wee small hours. It's not made clear what kind of crisis the singer is struggling with—romantic? spiritual?—but the pain is palpable, the loneliness is tangible, and the need for a drink is substantial.

These sessions took place before Raitt put her own drinking and partying days behind her. "These were definitely the halcyon days of people partying," she admitted. "Rollicking days, you know? Your twenties and thirties are a *blast*," but she cautioned, "It doesn't mean people show up for the sessions completely loaded, or we would have made a bad record." Finally, she clarified that substances were consumed "mostly after the sessions." Bob Glaub said that Peter, as producer, would wait till late in the evening to have his "cocktail."

"I don't remember Bonnie partaking so much," Glaub said, "but, yeah, it was kind of the peak of that. Not everyone, but . . ." He then looked at the picture included in the album, featuring Bonnie, Peter, Val Garay, and all the key musicians. "I won't name names, but there's *very few* who didn't imbibe."

Rick Marotta readily admitted to too much mischief-making: "Yeah, yeah, I rode that train," he said. "I thought I played better when I was fucked up." Raitt was more cautious: "No, I don't ever jeopardize my gig, 'cause I don't wanna have to switch jobs!"

"Bonnie's an artist I admire immensely," Peter declared, and he wanted to do his best for her. "We had something to prove," Raitt stated. "I wanted to finally get a record that would break through and get some radio airplay, but still not compromise my integrity in terms of rootsiness—you know, rawness. And *he* wanted to prove to people that he could make a gutsy record, too.

"Ironically, a lot of people considered his style with Val Garay as being kind of 'slick' because it was so commercial at the time, but in fact, one of my most raw and *live* records was *The Glow*." She loved the collaboration with Peter: "He's *really*

The Glow
album cover.

good," she marveled. "He can hang with the rockers, but he's always been a very elegant, classy, and smart guy. I don't think he's made a stupid move since he was born.

"I was honored to work with him."

Just as Bonnie's sessions were winding down, J.D. Souther began tracking a new album at Amigo Studios with many of the same musicians—Waddy and Kootch, Marotta and Grolnick, Edwards and Dugmore. On the day vocal and percussion overdubs were being added, Peter dropped by and offered his special talents to the song that would go on to become Souther's biggest hit, "You're Only Lonely."

"The opening '*ooohs*,'" according to Souther, "are Kenny, Jorge Calderon, Waddy, and Peter. And Peter put the Beach Boys note on it—sailed in there with the absolute perfect missing note. 'Cause three-part harmony, to me," he explained, "is mostly boring—mostly because I've heard it so much, and, also, who's gonna be as good as Crosby, Stills and Nash? Eagles killed me because it was four. And, before that, The Everly Brothers killed me 'cause it was two. But mostly, we deal with three—or we were in Southern California in those days. I just wanted . . ."

Souther paused, then offered: "It's all this jazz I listened to when I was a kid. I wanted a 'thicker' thing in there. And fuckin' Peter set it down there *exactly*." By October 1979, Souther's aching ballad, a complete homage to Roy Orbison's songs of desolate beauty, was not only a Top Ten hit in *Billboard*'s Hot 100, "You're Only Lonely" would eventually remain in the top spot of its Adult Contemporary chart for five weeks.

You wouldn't necessarily call Peter "lonely" since his split from Betsy—during his move from the bungalow at the Chateau Marmont to the new beachfront house in the Malibu Colony, he'd had a fling with actress Mackenzie Phillips. That relationship was at its end by October 1979—the same month he met Wendy Worth . . . for the *second* time.

"I met Peter when I was about ten years old"—Wendy laughed—"backstage at a concert." Peter and Gordon were making one of their periodic swings through Southern California, and Wendy managed to get backstage thanks to a friend's cousin: "She was sixteen but was saying she was eighteen," Wendy recalled. "She took her cousin and me. She was meeting Gordon, and we went sort of so her mother wouldn't know, you know?" Now, years later, Wendy ran into Peter again: "It was a party in Malibu. I said: 'I met you at a Peter and Gordon concert when I was ten years old.' And he said, '*Really?!*'

"And then we started talking, and then we started going out."

Worth had grown up in the Los Angeles suburb of LaCañada Flintridge. Her father had a love of music, introducing her to Frank Sinatra and Nat King Cole. He also took little Wendy with him to movies, which began a lifelong interest in film. But an even greater interest was art: "I collected prints when I was really young, like Maxfield Parrish and things like that. I just always saved my allowance and would buy stuff." The emotional pull she felt continued as she entered her twenties: "I started saving all my money, and that's what I bought all the time," she said. "The first thing I bought was an American Impressionist painting, and then I bought Andy Warhol and Ed Ruscha and later Basquiat." Worth then added, with a laugh, "All on layaway!"

Their first date was to a Bonnie Raitt concert, celebrating the release of *The Glow*. Both Peter and Bonnie had high hopes for the album: "I thought it was a great record," she said proudly. "I don't know whether it was lack of promotion or just the climate of the day, but I was very disappointed that it didn't do better." Warner Brothers definitely put more of their promotional money behind Fleetwood Mac's *Tusk*, released within the same week. And in a bit of self-deprecation, Raitt offers another possible reason: "Looks matter."

But the real reason was, more likely, one of timing. The rock scene had received a huge boost of adrenaline lately with the arrival of a new wave of performers who took their cues from the insolent garage bands of the previous decade. The Ramones and The New York Dolls, among other bands from the Big Apple, influenced England's The Sex Pistols and The Damned—who, in turn, influenced more groups on both sides of the Atlantic. Numerous other bands, still under the thrall of the British Invasion's harmonies and hooks, were infused with this same energy, and a new flowering of power pop-ish "new wave" bands emerged alongside their more nihilistic "punk" brethren.

Though Peter, during our conversations, referred offhandedly to Ronstadt's next record as the "punk album," the singer couldn't disagree more: "It wasn't me trying to make a 'punk' record," Ronstadt declared, sighing in exasperation. "I never even set out to make a *rock'n'roll* record! I just set out to make a record of whatever songs I *liked*."

A writer whose songs she particularly liked at this point was Mark Goldenberg, a young man raised in Chicago by music-loving parents who encouraged him with piano and classical guitar lessons. When The Beatles hit, he began playing in a succession of bands and, needing material, Goldenberg decided the next logical step was to begin writing original songs. One of his groups, The Eddie Boy Band, became so popular in the Windy City that MCA Records offered them a deal. The band came out to Los Angeles to record, but despite much promise, the released album stiffed and the band folded. "I decided just to stay in LA," Goldenberg said, "and see if I could make my way as a songwriter or a musician or *something*."

As anyone in show business will tell you, having talent is all well and good, but in most cases, getting somewhere comes down to who you know. Goldenberg got a gig accompanying singer/songwriter Al Stewart for his *Year of the Cat* tour, with opening act Wendy Waldman. "Her bass player," recalled Goldenberg, "was Peter Bernstein." Waldman and Bernstein had known each other since childhood, as both their fathers were celebrated film and television composers. (The prolific Elmer Bernstein is prob-

ably best known for his theme to the film *The Magnificent Seven*, and Waldman's father, Fred Steiner, wrote the theme for the long-running television series *Perry Mason*.)

Goldenberg and Bernstein decided to form a band, which was dubbed The Cre-
tones, and Goldenberg got to work: "There was just a period there when I was writing, writing, writing," Goldenberg says. "I'd get up at eight in the morning, make a
pot of coffee, and write. I'd write every day." After songs were written, demos were
recorded. As the band tried various paths to get their material in the hands of record
labels, managers, agents, and all the usual movers and shakers in the industry, there
came a lovely bit of happenstance: "Peter Bernstein's girlfriend at the time was Linda
Ronstadt's dog-walker," Goldenberg remembered, laughing, "and she gave Linda a
cassette of our songs." Not long afterward, Goldenberg recalled getting a call from
Peter Asher Management asking, "Would it be alright for Linda to record a few of
your songs for her next project?"

Goldenberg's response? "I said, '*Yes!*'"

Thinking back on the Goldenberg tunes that caught her attention, Ronstadt recalled: "I liked that song, 'Justine.'" And with good reason, as "that might have been
the best song I'd written," Goldenberg admitted—full of hooks, dynamic starts and
stops, and lyrics about confusing, overwhelming love. That same description could
actually apply to the two other Goldenberg-penned tunes Ronstadt chose to record:
"Cost of Love" and, of course, "Mad Love," which ended up being the album's
eventual title. Ronstadt's choice of three Elvis Costello songs, with their energy and
clever wordplay, also shows the singer beginning to move out of her comfort zone
and embrace the new music that was brushing the so-called mellow mafia aside.

For Ronstadt, though, tackling Costello's work all came down to one simple fact:
"I thought he had good *songs*," she exclaimed, pointing to "Party Girl" on *Mad Love*
as an example. "They were the emerging writers of the time, and I think music was
starting to change," Ronstadt noted, adding: "Silly *me!*"

"It was a bold record," Niko Bolas, who helped engineer the sessions, observed.
"Different writers and different musicians to fortify a whole different delivery of that
voice. But it was *always* what Linda wanted. Peter makes you *decide* what you want,
and then he'll help you make the statement."

Just as Ronstadt was choosing the material for this new project, she agreed to
appear at a tribute concert for her friend Lowell George—the revered singer, songwriter, and guitarist for the band Little Feat who had died suddenly in June. The
concert at LA's Forum would be an all-star affair, featuring Little Feat as the house
band, with Ronstadt, Bonnie Raitt, Emmylou Harris, and Jackson Browne, among
other artists, performing Lowell's beloved repertoire.

The rehearsals were held at keyboardist Bill Payne's house in Woodland Hills. He
recalled: "I was listening to Linda talk to a couple of people. She says, 'I'm thinkin'
about gettin' a different band.' I just sort of ambled over to her and said, 'Ya know
what? If you're ever lookin' for a keyboard player, keep me in mind.' And she goes,
'God, Bill! I never would have thought of asking *you* 'cause you're always so busy

doin' other things.' And I said, 'Well, I'm available.' And it wasn't just because Lowell had passed away—I'd quit the band before that anyway."

"Billy's a little bit more rock'n'roll," Peter observed, and knew he'd be a better fit for these upcoming sessions. With Linda wanting to record with new musicians—and knowing that three of the tunes they'd tackle were by Mark Goldenberg—it seemed to make sense for Peter to ask the young songwriter/guitarist to also play on the project. Ronstadt even toyed with the idea of bringing in a new producing/engineering team to give the tracks more of an edge. "Peter and I talked to her," longtime engineer Val Garay recalled, "and said, 'Look, you know, we're professionals—you want it to sound that way? We can make it sound that way.' So, she decided to let us try it," he said, adding: "We purposely tried to make it sound more 'modern' and less 'classical Linda Ronstadt.'" To that end, it helped that the sessions were tracked at Garay's own newly minted studio, Record One, leaving the familiar Sound Factory atmosphere behind.

Record One, located in Sherman Oaks, an LA suburb in the San Fernando Valley, had just installed a 3M digital thirty-two-track recorder—one of only three in existence. "It was all prototype stuff," Garay said glumly. "The thing didn't really work correctly." Sometimes tracks would go into record mode on their own, erasing previous good takes. Despite the bugs, tracking digitally worked toward achieving the edgy quality Ronstadt desired, as the process lacked some of the warmth inherent in good old-fashioned tape recording. "It did," Peter attested, "have an aggressive edge to it."

Bassist Bob Glaub, also working with Ronstadt for the first time, marveled at the studio efficiency: "The tracks were recorded over five days," he said, with a couple of weeks for the odd guitar, percussion, or background vocal overdub. "I remember Linda did all her lead vocals live," Goldenberg marveled. "There were very few 'punch-ins' on that record"—referring to correcting a vocal mistake by recording a phrase over. "She just basically sang her butt off all the time!"

That statement is borne out by listening to *Mad Love*. On the title track that opens the album, Ronstadt screams the word "love" on the chorus like her life depends on it, while guitars crunch and Bill Payne's organ swirls around her. Her performance of "Party Girl" is probably the most effective of the three Costello songs attempted, with Ronstadt giving her all by the song's end—a more dramatic finish than even Costello's own version. One of the hits off the album was "How Do I Make You," an incredibly fast-paced piece of power-pop from the pen of Billy Steinberg. In fact, Ronstadt did it "too fast," according to Steinberg—so fast that the song's bridge became almost unintelligible. "A lot of the lyrics got lost in her version, but I was really happy. Who wouldn't be happy when their very first cut is a Top Ten single?"

Back in 1979, the unknown Steinberg had been struggling to get his band, Billy Thermal, noticed in the crowded Los Angeles rock scene. In yet another instance of "it's who you know" (especially if that person is Wendy Waldman), band guitarist Craig Hull was dating Waldman, one of Ronstadt's closest friends. Waldman passed the band's demo on to Ronstadt, who knew a strong song when she heard one. Steinberg's initial influence was another strong LA band: "When the song 'My Sharona' by The Knack came out, I thought it was such a great power-pop record," he said. "It really kind of inspired me to write 'How Do I Make You.'" After this first songwriting success, Steinberg would later go on to cowrite such hits as "Like a Virgin" and "True Colors."

The album also included Ronstadt's version of "I Can't Let Go" by The Hollies—possibly her way of directly making the connection from the modern power-pop of 1979 to its forbearers in the mid-sixties. "The way we played it, we weren't trying to *sound* like a band from the 1960s," Bob Glaub explained, "but we tried to emulate that energy." Though her take fails to match the manic majesty of The Hollies' version, her Top Ten cover of "Hurt So Bad" surpasses the original by Little Anthony and The Imperials. Slowed down slightly and eschewing all extraneous vocalists, horns, and strings from the 1965 hit, Ronstadt's affecting delivery alternates between hope and despair, with Danny Kortchmar's stabbing guitar slicing through the dreamy desolation.

Though not every cut worked, the album was a smash—selling over a million copies. Attempting to give the cover shot the same harsh sense of immediacy found in the grooves, John Kosh hired photojournalist Peter Howe—a war correspondent in both Northern Ireland and El Salvador. "We went to this really skuzzy part of town," Kosh remembered. "I put her in a phone booth and gave her a pile of quarters and said, 'Call Jerry Brown.'" Brown was, at that time, both the governor of the state of California and Ronstadt's boyfriend, and Howe's flash catches Ronstadt during their furtive conversation. *Mad Love*, indeed.

Mad Love
album cover.

After years of backing up other artists, Waddy Wachtel had been itching to form a rock band: "I'd look at Rick," Wachtel recalled, referring to drummer Rick Marotta, "and think, 'Jesus—why are we just doin' this for other people? We could do it for ourselves!'" He had also become friendly with fellow guitarist Dan Dugmore and, impressed with the songs Dugmore had been writing, knew he should be part of this new assemblage. For the bass slot, Waddy decided on Stanley Sheldon—the bassist he'd had the pleasure of playing beside on a recent Warren Zevon tour. Sheldon had made a name for himself with fellow musicians as the bassist on the mega-selling *Frampton Comes Alive!*

"Then," Dugmore recalled, "he asked Don Grolnick, who'd been playing with Linda and James, to play keys. And Don went back and forth about it, 'cause Don was really more of a jazzer than a rock'n'roller." Eventually, after a week with the band rehearsing in his living room, Grolnick decided this wasn't for him. According to Wachtel, "The way he put it was so great: 'Waddy, I know you—you're goin' for that 'millions of dollars' thing . . . I'm in jazz—I'm goin' for *tens* of dollars.'"

"It was such a good band," Peter declared, and he was ready to help however he could—acting as manager, working to land the group a record deal, and promising to produce their debut disc. But what would the name of this new group be? "Peter used to call us 'The Boys in the Band' all the time," Dugmore said, "so we were gonna just call ourselves 'The Boys.'"

While "The Boys" began to rehearse their material, Peter began to approach various record labels. "The most they would give us was, like, a $70,000 budget to do the album," Dugmore recalled, which Peter felt was not enough. Eventually, Bob Skoros, Mercury/Polygram's head of A&R on the West Coast, met with Peter and Waddy and "loved it," according to Wachtel. "He loved the idea, loved the band, and wanted to do it." Skoros may have envisioned "The Boys" as a hard-rock version of Toto—another group of studio musicians who had recently banded together with considerable success.

When it was time to hash out the deal, Peter brought in a high-powered attorney. "They were gonna get us a guaranteed two-album deal for $225,000 for each album," Dugmore said, remembering the paltry $70,000 previously offered by other labels. "We said, 'Man! *That* was a big difference!'" The lawyer, obviously an excellent dealmaker, mentioned that his fee for negotiating the contract would be $25,000. "And we were all kinda shocked. Then he said, 'But I worked on the people at the record company harder and got it up to $250,000 an album, so I figured I'd earned my money.' So"—Dugmore laughed—"we went, 'Okay!'"

The album was recorded digitally by Val Garay at Record One, having worked through most of the kinks that made the *Mad Love* sessions problematic. "I didn't want to do it 'studio-fied'; I wanted to do it the way we'd perform," Wachtel said, and the group set up much as they had during rehearsals in Don Grolnick's living room—in a circle, all facing each other. "We performed the songs live," remembered Wachtel, "I sang the leads live, everything went down pretty much live, and it was a gas."

"We blew through that record *fast*," drummer Rick Marotta recalled, finishing the basic tracks in two weeks. "We knew what we were doin,' we had rehearsed it, we had it all down."

The album certainly showcased the solid, crunching guitarwork at which Wachtel excelled, making his tune "Feels Right," for example, a total head-banging anthem. Another song Wachtel brought in, "Love's Coming into My Life Again," was a bouncy, hook-laden rocker whose nonstop motor was thanks to Grolnick's piano. "America the Beautiful" was not the patriotic classic from the late nineteenth century, but a new take on the subject, as solid in its sincerity as in its riffs. And to make it as grand as possible, Peter hired the USC Men's Chorus to belt out the song's refrain.

The rhythm section of Marotta and Sheldon were solid throughout, but Dan Dugmore particularly shone with his steel guitar touches on two of the slower numbers: "It Touches Everyone" and "Hey Nadine." His original composition, "All I Can," was a slow-stomping piece of country blues that would have been right at home on one of Ry Cooder's albums. It was also Dugmore's first lead vocal. "My only one." He laughed. Because Wachtel was singing lead on almost every song, Dugmore recalled, "Waddy just kept pushin' on us to sing."

"I sang pretty well, actually, considering I was shrieking my brains out," Wachtel said. "Peter was really proud of me. I didn't fix very many vocals." But having recorded the tracks live, with the band playing all together in the same room, a technical problem arose when it was time to fix those few lines: the leakage of the other instruments into Waddy's mic.

According to Dugmore, "Val Garay said, 'Well . . . we'll have to re-create the leakage.' And so, they took the drums off the riser and put these big speakers up and piped the drums back through there and ran live out from the tape machine back into our amplifiers, so it would sound like the whole band was playin' in the room again. So then, when they punched in on lines from Waddy—which was only a few of 'em—that way they had the same sound of all of us in the room."

Just as the album was being finished, the band got some bad news: The name "The Boys" was already taken—a UK punk band had been releasing records under that name since 1977, and an Australian group called simply "Boys" was having some success Down Under. So what now? "Ricky was reading that book *Shogun*," Dugmore recalled. "And in there, they talk about the Ronin—the samurai who had left their masters and gone off on their own. And they were real badass guys, 'cause they already had samurai training, but they were sorta like loner guys. So, Ricky said, 'That's what we are—top musicians leaving our masters, goin' off on our own . . .'" With no one able to come up with anything better, the title of the album would be the band's new name: *Ronin*.

Then worse news: Skoros and his team at Mercury/Polygram were out, and a new regime was in. "When we turned the project in, there were new guys," Dugmore remembered, "and they didn't care anything about us because they hadn't signed us. So they really didn't promote the record or do anything." The band hit the road,

Ronin album cover.

opening for The Rossington Collins Band. "We toured it, and we had a great tour," Wachtel said proudly. "We sounded really good, and it was strong and loud." But when they came into a new city, Dugmore recalled, "We'd go to the record stores, and there'd be no albums."

Another problem had slowly begun to dawn on the guitarist, and it was inherent with the material itself: "I come to records through the music," Waddy began. "I probably know more songs than most people you'll ever meet. But I learned 'em all phonetically." Trying to be clear, he explained: "Learning them as *sound*—that's what I mean.

"I know a *million* tunes, but I've no idea *what* I'm saying, you know? I just know *how* they go, how the lyrics go. I never stopped to realize, 'Oh, my God! This is a fascinating story here!'" The guitarist laughed, continuing: "So a lot of the tunes on there are not lyrically strong, unfortunately—they're not really sayin' too much. Unless you're sayin' somethin'," he concluded, "you don't have a record." Peter had to agree: "I don't think their songwriting matched the power of the band."

Wachtel wanted to make the next Ronin album as strong lyrically as the first was musically, so as soon as the band had rested up after the tour, he and Dan Dugmore began writing new material for the "guaranteed" second album. With the new songs rehearsed, they played them for Peter, who promptly informed the powers-that-be at Mercury that they were ready to start recording.

And the response came back: "No, thank you."

Not all that surprising, as this new team at the label didn't really care about the *last* album, practically sabotaging it. Peter once again called on his lawyer to negotiate exit terms, and he ultimately walked out of his meeting at Mercury with an $80,000 check for the band to please go away. Dugmore had to laugh: "I said, 'Waddy, we must *really suck*, man! They're payin' us $80,000 to *not* do a record!'"

Mercury might not have wanted an encore, but others are still waiting: "Not two months ago," Marotta told me recently, "Waddy called me and said, 'Rick, it's the *weirdest thing*, man! People are comin' up to me wanting to know when we're gonna release our next record!'"

After Mercury let them go, "James Taylor invited Waddy, Ricky, and myself to join his band to do the *Dad Loves His Work* album," said Dugmore. But as Taylor already had longtime bassist Lee Sklar lined up, that left Stanley Sheldon behind. "But he offered us a quarter of a point on the record, which was a huge offer," Dugmore continued, giving them a small percentage of the upcoming record's profits, not to mention the promise of a very good payday off the inevitable tour. "We had to take it—'cause it was James. But we felt really bad that all of a sudden, we were makin' good money and Stanley was makin' nothin'," Dugmore said sadly. "So that kinda broke up the band at that point . . ."

James Taylor began pulling together songs for what would become *Dad Loves His Work*, his third album for Columbia. One evening, Taylor was brainstorming ideas over at J.D. Souther's house along with Waddy Wachtel. "All of a sudden, James started spitting out this beautiful music," Wachtel recalled. The three friends spent the rest of the night working on lyrics to this delicate melody and, in the process, crafting a piece of art out of Peter and Betsy's pain:

But now he's gone and life goes on . . .
She gets the house and the garden
He gets the boys in the band . . .

The song "Her Town Too" was "written out of respect and sadness for Betsy and Peter and the whole thing going away," Val Garay explained. "And it was innocently done." But Betsy didn't find anything "innocent" in it, according to Waddy: "James wanted to play it for Betsy—Betsy was very fragile then—and she freaked out, thought it was this big 'insult.'"

"What's she gonna do about it," asked Souther, "sue us later for libel, slander, or something? About something that she couldn't prove was about her? She's nice, anyway—she would have never done that. But after a while"—Souther shook his head in frustration—"I threw up my hands and said, 'Look, we wrote a song. As far as I'm concerned, you can say it's about *my* girlfriend. I don't care. It's a song—not a historical document.'"

Waddy continued: "So James and I—J.D. didn't want to take part in this at *all*—we were summoned to come up to her house and have this meeting about it, with her and Joni Mitchell." Mitchell was a close friend of Betsy's, there for moral support. Betsy argued it was cruel for them to write this, and she seemed certain if it was released everyone would know exactly whom they were describing. Exasperated, Waddy turned to Joni: "I went, 'Joni, why don't you tell her everything's fiction'"—meaning songwriting in general, even songs inspired by real events—"'no matter whose fuckin' name is in it, or no matter who wrote what or who inspired what! It's all a bunch of bullshit, and it's all fiction! Tell her!' And she goes, 'Well, he's right. He's basically right, Betsy. Nothing's really literal around here, you know, it's just art . . .'"

When eventually released in February 1981, listeners could tell the song was about a divorce, but ironically, almost all assumed it was about Taylor's recent split from Carly Simon.

Peter didn't seem ruffled by the song at all: "I thought it was great," he said, admiring the cleverness of the concept. He also knew a hit when he heard one, and of course, his instincts were right. "Her Town Too," recorded as a duet between James Taylor and J.D. Souther, was the big hit off *Dad Loves His Work*, and it stayed in the Top Forty for ten weeks. "No one else"—Peter smiled—"has had the details of their divorce settlement revealed in the lyrics of a hit song!

"At the time, it looked like a real shitty deal"—he laughed—"'cause '*the house and the garden*' were very nice! And '*the boys in the band*' were a bunch of drunken layabouts. In retrospect, it wasn't a bad deal at all . . ."

20

WHAT'S NEW

"To make *Dad Loves His Work*, we all lived together for two, three weeks," remembered Niko Bolas, who helped engineer the sessions. "The rhythm section was there every day. You'd cut a track, you'd do the overdubs, and you would keep cutting until you got an amazing vocal. Waddy would run in and do a background part, they would go rewrite a bridge, J.D. would come down, and then all of a sudden, we'd listen to some of J.D.'s record, and that would inspire something else. It was just . . ." Bolas searched for the right word, then said: "Community. And that required budgeting and accounting and an acceptance of that process. And because it was a company, the company had reverence for the talent."

The "company" Bolas referred to here was Columbia Records, Taylor's label. Columbia had been the record division of parent company CBS since 1938, but in the late 1980s the label was acquired by the Japanese electronics giant Sony. "*Now*," Bolas continued, "it's a corporation, and corporations don't have reverence for anything except for a bottom line. So, people don't get music anymore like we did, people get 'events' that are audio—it's event-based. You have, you know, meaningless lyric that'll evoke an emotion, loud chorus, meaningless lyric, loud chorus, and then it's done. And if it can sell a cell phone at the same time, terrific.

"It's *so* marketing-based and event-based and *shareholder*-based that it has nothing to do with bringing music to light; therefore, no one's going to fund a family to create something special—it's so passé in the mind of a corporate person. Which is why none of us really have fun like we used to anymore. It's not the same," Bolas said wistfully. "It's just not the same . . ."

Which is not to imply that small, independent labels were all about musical creativity and not worried about profit: "Sometimes the little labels were *much* more worried about the bottom line because they didn't have any money," Peter pointed out. "A lot of people would say, 'Oh, indie labels are great,' and then you'd actually

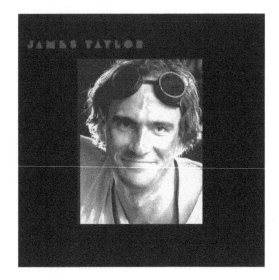

Dad Loves His Work
album cover.

go work for one and they'd be *incredibly* tough because they *had* to be—they literally
did not have the cash. So it can work both ways."

Dad Loves His Work was both another Top Ten album and another Gold Record
Award–winner for James and Peter. Besides "Her Town Too," the disc was bedecked
with beautiful performances: "Hour That the Morning Comes" was a sly slice of
modern Americana, as if Taylor was dually possessed by both Randy Newman
and Ry Cooder. Each verse was a slightly twisted take on the humanity found at a
late-night gathering, and drummer Rick Marotta, the former dancer, deftly plays
across the track—stepping, turning, dipping through Taylor's tale. "That Lonesome
Road," cowritten with Don Grolnick, was both haunting and resolute—accepting a
sad, regretful fate and soldiering on. Reminiscent of nineteenth-century ballads like
"Shenandoah," the song's seven-voiced choir (including both Jennifer Warnes and,
of course, Peter) brought the album to a stark but majestic close.

Wonderful work—but it would be four years before Taylor could complete another album. During that period, Peter would manage him and put tours together,
but mainly focus on Linda Ronstadt's career and advise her as she began to explore
various new directions—which mostly meant eschewing the "new" entirely. The first
surprising turn came immediately after the release of the ultramodern *Mad Love*,
when Ronstadt was offered the part of Mabel in Joseph Papp and The Public Theatre's revival of *The Pirates of Penzance*, scheduled to open in the summer of 1980
for a month's run in Central Park. This classic Gilbert and Sullivan musical had
originally debuted 101 years earlier and was considered by most to be a stuffy and
old-fashioned theatrical experience.

When actor Kevin Kline was first offered a role in the production, "I thought"—
here Kline shuddered and exclaimed in mock horror—"*Eeeeew, GOD!* I remember
in the Woody Allen film *Bananas*—I think one of the ways that they're torturing

people is to tie them to a chair and force them to listen to Gilbert and Sullivan!" Kline laughed, concurring with Allen's assessment. "But," he explained, "as I sat and listened to the score and read through the script and pictured it in the park . . ." Kline began to realize what a delightful romp this could actually be. "It seemed Monty Python/goofy-silly/absurdist," the actor said, "and the music was *beautiful!* I thought: 'Hey, how bad could this be for four weeks in the park?'"

"I was a huge Gilbert and Sullivan fan," Ronstadt confessed, having grown up singing Sullivan's melodies, learning them alongside her sister, Suzy, who had performed in an amateur production of *HMS Pinafore* back in Tucson. Ronstadt, who stated that Gilbert and Sullivan's work is "so solid you can't beat it with a hammer," was thrilled to take part, temporarily moving to New York. With his background in acting and experience in stagecraft, Peter happily advised Ronstadt in the etiquette of the theater: "Ralph Richardson said, 'Know your lines and don't bump into the furniture,'" Peter recalled with a laugh. "But I remember telling her: 'The most important thing is be on time, 'cause they're expecting you to be late; they're expecting a diva.'" He quickly added: "Which she's not!

"I said: 'Don't be what they're expecting. Just show up and be Linda and you'll be fine.'"

According to Kline, on the first day of rehearsals, director Wilford Leach told the cast: "I want us to pretend that this was written for us." Throwing out the historical way of staging Gilbert and Sullivan—very staid and proper—the production exploded with improvisation and fun. "Every night, it was like a party," Kline enthused. "And the audience went crazy!" The production was a smash, and it reopened on Broadway in January 1981. At Linda's request, Peter agreed to produce the Cast Album for the show, recorded in New York less than a month after finishing *Dad Loves His Work* in LA.

After all the tech rehearsals and a couple of weeks of previews, the first week of Broadway performances began. "At the end of the opening week, you do the Original Cast Album on whatever your day off is. You know, just when you're exhausted and your voice is shot"—Kline laughed—"but that's how they do it." Right before the session, Ronstadt recalled coming down with the cold that had been making its way through the cast and was (as usual) harsh about her performance: "You're doing eight shows a week, so your voice is dead. And I'm singing E-flat above high C, you know, twice in the show. You're just tired," she said. "And it was early in the run, so I hadn't really settled into the part the way I did eventually."

In the dead of winter, having only one day to record, the actors gathered at Columbia's 30th St. Studio. With its one-hundred-foot ceilings, it was known in the business as "The Church" because, when the building originally opened in 1875, that's what it was. Such classic recordings as Glen Gould's *Goldberg Variations* and Miles Davis's *Kind of Blue* had been captured there. Peter, wanting to have a trusted engineer at his side, had asked Val Garay to help him with the sessions. "There was no budget," Garay recalled being told, so he worked on the project for free as a favor to both Linda and Peter.

The Pirates of Penzance
album cover.

"We tried to do it as much as a live performance as possible," Garay explained, with Peter directing him to "Try to mic *everything*." "So," Garay continued, "aside from the microphones I used on individuals, I had a couple of PZM mics that were attached to the floor." These Pressure Zone Microphones gave Peter and Val the ability to add into the mix, when appropriate, a visceral sense of a full, live stage performance. "To my knowledge," said Garay, "I don't think anyone had ever done that before."

Because of the horrendous time constraints, "I don't think we did more than one or two takes of each song, if *that*," Kline recalled. Afterward, Garay then had to edit the best takes together: "What a *nightmare*," he said, moaning at the memory of life before computerized editing. "Each little thing in a bit—phrases, you know? *This* section of the thing and then *that* section . . ." Garay shook his head. "There must have been two hundred little pieces that I had to finally cut together."

"It took a very long time," attested Peter. "Yeah," harrumphed Garay, grousing about his "sore fingers." Happily, the resulting two-record set was a success, probably selling more than any other Gilbert and Sullivan recording in history. But Ronstadt was ready to move on and explore another musical path.

As she finished her Broadway run, which brought her a Tony nomination for Best Actress in a Musical, Ronstadt struck up a friendship with legendary music industry vet Jerry Wexler. Wexler had originally coined the phrase "rhythm and blues" and became one of the driving forces behind Atlantic Records, where he helped produce countless hits, like Ray Charles's "I've Got a Woman," Wilson Pickett's "In the Midnight Hour," and Aretha Franklin's "Respect."

One day, as Ronstadt and Wexler listened through his vast record collection, paying particular attention to singers whose heyday was the pre-rock era, she spoke of her love for these songs and her desire to become a stronger singer: "I felt that rhythm and phrasing were not my strongest gifts," she admitted, "and I wanted to get them better. And I just felt like the more I studied the stuff that came before, the better I could get.

"So, I started listening to those singers I had listened to a lot as a kid—Billie Holiday and Ella Fitzgerald and Louis Armstrong and Sarah Vaughn—and I just started pounding that stuff," she said, adding: "And a *lot* of Frank Sinatra." Ronstadt eventually came to a realization: "I started thinking, well, learning them with a band was when I would *really* learn the phrasing. And then I thought, well, I'd like to sort of tape the rehearsals"—she laughed—"so I could really listen to it . . ." Thus, the idea of an album of pop standards began to take shape.

According to Linda, Peter "didn't really know anything about American standard songs. In fact, he told me that he thought that they were just kind of Mantovani and stuff you'd hear trapped in elevators. He had paid some attention to American music and American culture, but it was Buddy Holly and that kind of stuff—which is *great* stuff! But, you know, when you compare that stuff to Rogers and Hart, and Gershwin"—she laughed—"which I grew up loving and listening to and hearing my father sing and play on the piano, it's a totally different thing. And I really always have felt that to go forward, I had to go back."

Though dubious about the project, Peter could see Linda was following her creative heart, and he helped convince her label to finance the recording. Peter also had no problem in stepping aside as Ronstadt's longtime producer and letting Wexler helm the sessions. "He knew that Wexler was interested in that kind of music. But we got into trouble in a hurry," Ronstadt confessed, "because I was used to a very custom fit, and I was used to playing a big part." The successful collaboration she'd enjoyed with Peter for the past seven years, having her song choices and arrangement ideas respected, was suddenly missed: "I didn't realize how *much* of a part I took until I tried working with a different producer who was used to sort of doing it *their* way."

For example, Wexler would "play me a mix over the phone," Ronstadt said incredulously, though she quickly added: "A *lovely* man, and very, very helpful to me in terms of holding my hand as I went into this material from a different point of view—as a professional, not just as a listener. I've great respect for him, but . . ."—she paused—"*you can't hear a mix over the phone!*" She laughed, adding: "And I'd like to *be* there helping to mix it, so it was just a basic kind of communication that we were having a hard time with."

It was more than just communication. Bill Payne remembered hearing selections from the sessions at Ronstadt's house one evening. She asked him, "What do you think?" Payne told her: "I think he's taking you for a ride." Ronstadt was puzzled: "What do you mean?" Payne said, "Look—Jerry Wexler's amazing, but this is not the way this music is supposed to sound. You got world-class players," he said, noting the caliber of the session musicians. "I'm just talking about the arrangements, Linda. The music deserves better. *You* deserve better. You're a song *stylist*."

After Wexler finished his mixes, the results were not thought releasable. Peter's assistant, Ira Koslow, heard the tapes: "It was sort of a big-band sound, not orchestra," he said. "It wasn't that it was *bad*; it's when she heard it, she said, 'That's not really what I wanna do.'" As far as Peter was concerned, Linda's standards project seemed, to his and the record company's relief, over.

Peter now undertook the extraordinary task of recording *The Pirates of Penzance* for a *second* time. With the show's success on Broadway—winning numerous Tony Awards, including Best Revival of a Musical—the money was found to turn the production into a motion picture. Peter, again, flew to New York and settled on Right Track Recording, located on West 48th Street, to handle the sessions. Val Garay, remembering the "nightmare" of the Original Cast Recording, declined an invitation to once again participate, but he sent his trusted assistant, Niko Bolas, to help. Bolas left after two weeks, once it was clear that Right Track's chief engineer, Frank Filipetti, was more than capable.

As a youngster, Filipetti began drumming in various bands, then learned guitar and began writing songs, recording demos at his home: "That was the beginning of my recording career," he said. More bands came and went, but Filipetti kept honing his songwriting skills, eventually signing a publishing deal with Screen Gems-EMI. One day, he was playing some self-recorded demos to a Capitol Records A&R man, who told Filipetti: "You know, I'm not crazy about the songs, but the demos you play always sound great. Have you ever thought about engineering?"

Eventually deciding to give it a shot, Filipetti landed a job at Right Track Recording. A year and a half later, now chief engineer, he was asked to participate in the new *Pirates* sessions because Peter requested the presence of "someone who knew the room," according to Filipetti. Within days, "Peter and I became very fast friends.

"As someone who had only been engineering for about a year, to suddenly be involved in a project of *that* scope," Filipetti said, disbelievingly, "one: It's a movie; I'd never worked on a movie. Two: It was a Broadway production, which meant recording a fairly large group all at once. Plus, it involved recording full string orchestras," he explained. "A lot of stuff I'd never done before. But Peter trusted me, and could have easily at any point said, 'I think you have good ears, but you're not ready yet.' But he was behind me a hundred percent.

"Early on, we were having all kinds of difficulties," Filipetti remembered, as he attempted to get the equipment at his studio set up for this complex session. "It was a bigger session than we had ever done before. And there are some producers who would have come in and, if we weren't ready in the first hour, would start screaming. Peter was very calm about the whole thing and realized that it wasn't the first hour of the session that was important, it was setting up properly for what was gonna happen for the next couple of weeks.

"He had a very holistic view of things," Filipetti explained. "He didn't take it frivolously, but he wanted people to not only get the work done but to have a good time. One of the things that was unusual: He definitely had a dinner hour. We broke, he took everybody out of the studio, and we all went to dinner together, as opposed to sitting in the studio, scarfing down our food, and then getting back to work. It was like a boss at a company that really takes care of the people who are working there, knowing that that's the best way to get the best out of 'em.

"I had always looked at producing from the musical side," said Filipetti. "But Peter is the one who really made me focus on the *extra*-musical side—the part of production that doesn't always get the attention that it deserves, and also the part that generally separates the men from the boys. It's not just about putting the band together, picking the studio, picking the songs. It's also the psychological parts of the session—it's *running* a session, it's *controlling* a session, it's heading problems off at the pass, and it's knowing how to deal with problems when you have them."

Kevin Kline, reprising his role as the Pirate King, had also not done a movie musical before and had his doubts about the process: "They said, 'We're gonna prerecord everything and then lip-sync.' And I said, 'Well, that's *absurd!*' 'Cause on the day that we shoot any given scene or song, how will I know what I'm doing? What the action is? And how can I match my voice when I know that I'll be swinging on ropes and falling? And since the whole characterization was very physical, I said I don't want to have all my instincts or impulses in the performance to be circumscribed by it needing to fit into something I recorded *three months* earlier! It, it . . . it has no *liveness!*"

Ed Pressman, the executive producer of the film, explained: "Well, this is how movie musicals have been made since they started *making* movie musicals." Kline, the master thespian, laughingly recalled his confident response: "Well, it's *wrong!*" But Pressman reassured him: "No, no! If something changes on the set and it doesn't match, then we can always go in and record it *afterward*, in post! So, you'll *still* have the freedom to invent whatever on the set, and if it doesn't match what you've prerecorded, *we fix it!* Later!" Ultimately, Kline admitted, matter-of-factly: "It all matched up fine."

Peter, having more time available than his first attempt with this material, was producing the tracks "completely recording studio style," he recalled, "one element at a time." Being able to spend more time on the vocals, Kline was happier with his performance: "Oh, it was a *much* better track!" Ronstadt was neither sick nor exhausted while recording her part this time; she had even received some vocal coaching since the Broadway Cast recording, strengthening the upper extension of her range, so, not surprisingly, she, too, stated that her performance was far superior on the movie's soundtrack.

But the musicians had only been paid for working on the *movie*—they would have to be paid again if a soundtrack album was released. And, unfortunately, "the film was such a flop," Peter explained, "to put that movie's soundtrack out as an album involved another thirty to forty thousand dollars in costs, which nobody seemed inclined to take. Because they figured—probably correctly—the public wouldn't really know the difference between that and the live version of the stage play."

So, the superior motion picture soundtrack was never released. And where is the tape now? "I bet it's lost," said Peter. "Everything's lost. Record companies lose stuff all the time. Every time they move, they lose everything."

Ronstadt returned to the States from shooting *The Pirates of Penzance* in England, determined to take another stab at the standards project. "Now, I'd already *failed* trying to do this," Linda admitted. "And then I went to my record company and said, 'I want even more money, 'cos I wanna do it right.' They just thought I was *crazy*. And Joe Smith"—then head of Elektra/Asylum Records—"came to my house and sat down with me in the living room and just said, 'Look, you're throwing your career away with *both hands*. *Don't do this!* Other people have made some attempts at this. It just doesn't work. People aren't interested.'"

History seemed to confirm his warnings: Ringo Starr's first solo album was *Sentimental Journey*, consisting of songs his Mum and Dad loved, featuring arrangements from folks like George Martin, Paul McCartney, and Richard Perry; it tanked. Harry Nilsson had put an album of standards out in 1973; beautifully sung, with gorgeous string arrangements by Gordon Jenkins, the album did not do well and seriously interrupted his career momentum. In 1975, Rita Coolidge tried something similar—recording an album of standards with a jazz trio—but her label, sensing a sales disaster, refused to release it.

"He was right!" Ronstadt couldn't argue with the facts. "Joe Smith was a lovely man and a good record man and had my best interests at heart. And so did Peter when he said, 'You know, I just don't think this is a great idea.' And they were completely right. But I was so in love, I was so far down the path with this material. And I could hear it in my head! So, once I could do that, I'm *doomed*. I just have to carry it out. I can't stop!"

Peter, as her manager, tried to convince Ronstadt that, having been away from the pop charts for almost two years now, perhaps an album that the public could immediately embrace would be her best career move at this point—*then* he would help her realize this dream. "He was great," Ronstadt said. "It could be real easy for somebody to fall in a trap and say, 'Well, I told you so, you idiot!' You know? 'Now you've failed, and I was right and you were wrong.' I mean, that's a wonderful feeling sometimes!" Ronstadt laughed heartily. "When you go, 'Ohhh, see? You *moron!*' And he didn't surrender to that! So I gotta give him a lot of credit." She agreed with Peter to first record a more modern-sounding album and began to search for material.

"Material," said Ronstadt, "was *always* the hardest thing! And it seemed like every album we made I was just *scraping* the bottom of the barrel. You know, every time I'd think about a song, I'd have a little notebook in my purse, and I'd write it down on this list. And a lot of songs would be carried forward from one list to the next. There were Jimmy Webb songs," she recalled, "that were on lists from 1972. We kinda couldn't figure out how to do 'em, and they just didn't quite work out right . . ."

The stars must've been perfectly aligned this time around as, on the second day of recording, Peter produced an exquisite version of Webb's 1974 composition "The Moon Is a Harsh Mistress." Webb stole the title (with permission) from Robert A. Heinlein's science-fiction take on workers' rights and crafted a love song that's at once depressing and beautiful. Bill Payne not only played piano throughout the track, he also arranged and conducted the string section. In crafting his arrangement, Payne, the former viola student, admitted: "I reserved the best parts for the viola section." In reality, the best parts are all Ronstadt; the lyrics, the melody, and the sentiment had all she looked for in a song, and her performance—soft, tough, lost, regretful—simply gives you chills.

Ronstadt's tracking dates were temporarily set aside while a tour began to roll through Japan consisting of the A-list of Peter's musical cohorts—Linda, James, and J.D. Souther, with Ronin acting as both opening and backing band. The Japanese promoters wanted to call the tour "California Live," which "everyone hated," Peter recalled, and told the promoters before they finalized the contracts: "Nobody's happy with this title because no one's really from California. I know where you're coming from with this, but I'm not from California, Linda's not from California, J.D.'s not from California, James is not from California—James doesn't even *like* California! Let's think of an alternative title." Various ones were offered to the promoter to choose from, and having seemingly solved that problem, Peter turned to a looming one with larger ramifications . . .

For six weeks, Peter had been asking James, "Will you be straight for this tour?" And James's answer was always, "Yes." "The day before we're going," drummer Rick Marotta observed, "he comes to Peter and says, 'I've got to make a confession to you: I'm not okay.' And Peter said, 'Oh.' Now, you *knew* when Peter got pissed because he would turn *beet red!* Really—you *didn't* want to be around him. He said, 'Okay.'" Then Marotta, speaking as Peter, said very calmly: "'Well, here's what we're gonna do: We'll cancel the tour, you're gonna pay all the guys in the band their salaries, you're gonna pay the promoters back, you're gonna pay my cut,' this, this, this, this, and this . . .'" Taylor, realizing the cascading chaos this monkey wrench would now cause, responded: "No, no, no—wait." It was extremely touch and go, according to Marotta, but Taylor made the plane the next morning at the *very* last minute.

"I know for a fact that was a wake-up call for James," Marotta stated. "James was up for twenty-four hours; he sat next to me on the plane, sweating and going through the DTs. But James is, physically, one of the strongest human beings I've ever, EVER met in my life, and any other mortal would probably have died." This experience, coupled with the death a few months later of John Belushi—who had become a close friend of Taylor's—moved the singer/songwriter toward a concentrated effort to get clean once and for all.

Upon arrival in Japan, the troupe was greeted by posters proclaiming: *"Peter Asher presents the California Live."* Confused, Peter questioned the promoter on the alternative titles supposedly agreed upon. "Well," they explained, *"California Live* much better." Peter shook his head and added, "The Japanese, as you probably know, smile and say 'yes' to everything, and it means *nothing.* Absolutely nothing. They do whatever they want."

Edd Kolakowski, who had first come to Peter and James's attention when he was sent by Steinway to tune a piano at James's Martha's Vineyard property, had been hired consistently by Peter Asher Management over the years—first as a piano technician on James's road crew, then adding guitar tech to his résumé, and finally

Press conference for "The California Live"—Tokyo, September 9, 1981. *Koh Hasebe/ Shinko Music/Hulton Archive/Getty Images.*

becoming stage manager on tours for both Taylor and Ronstadt—the job he handled for this two-week tour of Japanese stadiums.

"There was no 'auto tune' or 'digital backups' back then—that was all musicians playing their *asses* off," Kolakowski proudly proclaimed, and his whole team strived to make the stage a comfortable and familiar space so these performers could shine. "Every time they'd walk onstage, no matter what city we were in," said Kolakowski, "everything was right in the same place . . . make it a 'home away from home' every day."

Peter joined his friends onstage every night, singing harmony and adding touches of percussion to the proceedings. Kolakowski noted Peter's powers of observation as they stood next to each other at a soundcheck: "He'd point and say, 'What's *that* cable do? *That* wasn't there yesterday.'" He laughed, adding: "Peter's so meticulous, he didn't miss *anything!*"

Wendy Worth accompanied Peter and the gang to Japan. "I actually *was* the only one from California," she laughed. The Japanese, seeing her tanned good looks and sun-bleached hair, begged for her autograph. Observing her scribbling her name on souvenir programs thrust at her, Peter exclaimed, "*What* are you *doing?*" "I *told* them I'm nobody," Wendy laughed, but she continued signing away.

Once the tour was over, Peter wanted to book more time at Record One with Ronstadt and finish the album. Val Garay had begun engineering these new Ronstadt recordings right beside Peter, as always—a spot he had been ably filling for almost a decade. But now, the success of Garay's own career was becoming a distraction; he had finally become an award-winning producer in his own right (Kim Carnes's "Bette Davis Eyes"—a Garay production—was 1981's biggest hit), plus he was about to take over as manager for The Motels (whose new album, *All Four One*, including the hit "Only the Lonely," was also produced by Garay). He simply had too much on his plate and, not able to commit to Peter, chose to step away from the sessions. The two would not collaborate in the studio again for eight years.

Looking back on their work together, Val Garay commented: "He created that atmosphere of you wanting to do better than the best. I mean that's the way *I* was always motivated." Peter also, Garay explained, "allowed you the time and the room to get to a new place that no one had ever gone. Because when you go to those places, you know, there's no map . . . so, you know, it takes time.

"He had the most patience and least patience of anyone I've ever known," Garay continued. "He would give them all the room and all the time to get what they needed to get," he said, speaking of the musicians agreeing on the right arrangement and locking into a groove, "and once we got to getting, if they didn't get it then, *then* he would lose his patience. But not in a way that would offend anybody, in a way that would *inspire* them to 'let's get this thing right!'" Garay smiled as he reminisced on the close working relationship they shared. "I don't ever remember him raising his voice—in ten years. Not one time . . ."

Peter had an important position to fill—requiring not just an engineer, but a true collaborator in the studio. Luckily, Linda Ronstadt had a suggestion . . .

Producer, engineer, teacher, inventor—George Massenburg has been a whiz kid from the start, working in both recording studios and medical electronic labs by the age of fifteen, then majoring in electrical engineering at Johns Hopkins University in his hometown of Baltimore.

Massenburg was an early champion of the then-unknown singer Emmylou Harris: "I'd started recording Emmylou," he recalled, "back in the sixties on two-track—did demos and things." One of Harris's friends was Dr. John Starling, a physician whose side gig was performing bluegrass with his band, The Seldom Scene. Massenburg and Starling also became great friends, with Massenburg engineering sessions for both Starling's band and their acclaimed dobro player, Mike Auldrige.

When Ronstadt came down with the flu and had to cancel her tour in 1974 (the tour she did in order to afford a new washing machine), she recuperated at Starling's house near Washington, DC. "He's an EMT," Massenburg noted, "and we trust him for medical advice as well as musical advice!" The musical doctor was a good choice to keep an eye on both Ronstadt's health and well-being. Friends were constantly dropping by—including Emmylou Harris and Ricky Scaggs—and it was there that Massenburg was introduced to Ronstadt.

Informal jams formed with regularity in the Starling living room. "As soon as I got my voice back, after two weeks, I started joining in," Ronstadt recalled. Before going back to Los Angeles, inspired by the healing musical environment, she went into a nearby studio with Starling, songwriter Paul Craft, and producer Lowell George and cut "Keep Me from Blowing Away," with Massenburg engineering. Impressed with his abilities, intellect, and personality, Ronstadt stayed in touch and suggested Massenburg as a fitting replacement after Garay's departure.

"George moved to LA, and I introduced him to Peter," said Ronstadt. "I said, 'I'd really like to work with this guy. He's a really good engineer.' And that became a partnership—a musical partnership that I think I particularly benefited from. I think we *all* grew."

"*Get Closer* was the first record," Massenburg noted, "that Peter and Linda and I did. And it was a *real* paradigm shift—for Peter not working with Val.

"What I felt going into it is: Let's make a modern sound with *clear vocals*," Massenburg said. "I brought this methodology that was really germinated by Jackson Browne and Lowell George and myself, which is how to do a convincing comp vocal that sounds like a live vocal." Again, a comp vocal—short for compiled—is a method whereby a skilled engineer can expertly craft a seamless vocal track by compiling words and phrases from different vocal takes. "Linda," Massenburg explained, "wanted to do better than just to have to sing live."

"Peter," Ronstadt recalled, "discouraged me a lot from overdubbing because I'd go in there, start to do it, and we'd get bogged down on little things pretty fast, and he didn't like that. And he was right to not like getting bogged down. But George gave us a very definite method for keeping parts sorted out." The standard method would be to have the lyrics of a song in front of you, marking each line with a track number representing the take you thought seemed best—for the first line, a 2 would mean the second vocal take should be used for that lyric, for instance, while a 4 by the next line would mean the fourth vocal seemed superior for that particular phrase.

The Ronstadt/Asher/Massenburg team took it much further: "We'll listen to five different takes of a line," said Ronstadt, "and we'll write down stuff on each *word* if we hear things—it's not just that line. I have a whole little series of marks that I make," she continued, "all the way through the line, so you can take little, tiny slivers of things. So it was way more *listening* to sound and *detail* than I'd ever been able to do before."

But separate from the purely technical side of record making, Massenburg understood that communication was paramount to a successful collaboration: "What I *had to do*, somehow, was to discipline myself to organize my work so that I could collaborate—*really collaborate*, you know? And make it an artists' mix as well as my mix, an artists' record as well as my record.

"And the way I collaborated," Massenburg continued, "was to organize my work extremely well, where I could *speak* to what I wanted to try; I could speak to what I was hearing. And this has been really important, and I can't underscore it enough—that somehow you *have* to develop a language and a communication to *talk* about what you hear and where your dreams lie, and how to describe that dream-space. AND how to describe the process of *exploring* it! Because it *does* need some discipline."

Massenburg paused. "Am I getting too wacky?"

There are times, according to Ronstadt, "George will disappear down the rabbit hole. Somebody has to reach in the void down there and just grab the tips of his ears and pull him up again! Or else he'll be gone—you'll never hear from him again!

"George is *such* a genius; he has been one of the great innovators in the recording arts and sciences," Ronstadt continued. "Very few people really understand what it is he does; even those of us who've sat next to him for twenty or thirty years don't know it all the way.

"I think that George being subjected to Peter's discipline really helped him a lot," Ronstadt said. The two men certainly recognized kindred spirits: "He's one of the only people who is a technical genius," noted Peter, "*and* very musical, as well—they don't usually go together. Usually, the people who build that equipment actually don't know what it's for—and George is the exception." The equipment Peter is referring to is a line of pro-audio gear produced by George Massenburg Labs, founded in 1982, the year the two began working together. "He'd invent stuff and draw it on the back of a napkin," Peter recalled with awe.

"That was a great thing for Peter, 'cause finally he had somebody sitting next to him that was more of an intellectual match for him," Ronstadt explained. George "is quite opinionated and can be quite grumpy"—Peter smiled—"but he's one of the most brilliant people I know."

"Any engineer is kind of a neurotic, tortured creature"—Massenburg laughed—"'cause we're trying to glue together technology, which is accelerating faster, and art, which is escaping from reality with an increasing sort of velocity. I mean, there's a gap between art and technology, and we're trying to stand, like Colossus—one foot on each pillar. And Peter's very tolerant of that."

On April 13, 1982, with only a few tracks of Garay's in the can, the sessions moved to Massenburg's studio, known as The Complex, located on Corinth Avenue in West Hollywood—"a converted Bank of America check-processing facility," noted

George Massenburg and Peter. *Photo by David Goggin / Mr. Bonzai © 1997.*

Massenburg. That day, Ronstadt and her backing musicians took their first stab at recording an upbeat number from the mind of Jonathan Carroll entitled "Get Closer."

Carroll was still a young man but had already tasted success as a member of The
Starland Vocal Band, whose debut single, "Afternoon Delight," had topped the
charts six years earlier. The group traveled to Los Angeles to record their second
album, rented a house in Malibu, and befriended neighbor Linda Ronstadt, who
loved their intricate harmonies—arranged, in many cases, by Carroll. After the
group's demise, Carroll continued to arrange and record when opportunities arose,
writing songs and looking for a record deal. He signed on as a client with manager
Bill Danoff, another former Starland alum, and gave Danoff a demo of some new
original material. The first track on the cassette was "Get Closer."

Carroll remembered he was in between takes in an Alexandria, Virginia, studio,
and walked by a piano. "I went over," Carroll said, "and I played pretty much *that*
riff"—the riff that anchors what became "Get Closer." The engineer hit the TALK
BACK button in the booth and said, "That's weird. What's that?" Carroll replied,
"I dunno, it's just a riff." The engineer responded, "Well, it's a good one." Carroll
immediately recognized the riff's close kinship with The Pointer Sisters' hit cover of
Bruce Springsteen's "Fire." But where that riff rocked sensuously between two notes,
Carroll's forcefully ascended with an Elton John–ish swagger. And in a surprising
twist, the melody was not in the standard 4/4 time signature of most pop songs, but
in something closer to 7/4. Carroll claimed that, for a song with this sort of pulse,
"there's no reason to hang out for that extra note!"

The first line of the song instantly came to Carroll "as soon as I started working
on it," he said, evoking the gospel-based blues shouting of early rock'n'roll songs by
writers like Leiber and Stoller. Carroll said the lyrics came quickly, and laughingly
admitted: "It's not the most complex lyric in the world!"

"Bill went out to Los Angeles," remembered Carroll, "to do a promotional visit
for Danoff Music, and while he was out there, he got in touch with Emmylou." Emmylou Harris and Bill Danoff had both kicked around the Washington, DC, club
scene together, and Emmylou invited Bill to accompany her over to Ronstadt's place.
In between glasses of wine, Linda asked him what his former bandmate had been
doing since the group split up. Danoff pulled out the demo tape Carroll had given
him, slipped it in a tape deck, and hit PLAY.

Before the song was even finished, Ronstadt said, "Wow! Has anybody cut this?"
Assured that it was hers if she wanted it, Ronstadt quickly claimed it.

Peter and Linda were fairly certain of the song's hit potential—so much so they
cut it three different times that month, trying to get it right. On one attempt, a
drum machine was used to set the rhythm. For another go, they tried the song with a
standard 4/4 time signature, but later agreed the dropped beat was a big part of what
made the track unique. "I loved the idea of trying to make a hit with a weird time
signature," Peter said. Ronstadt's vocals were a master class in rock chick delivery,
shouting out the song's refrain with a throaty growl that made grown (and not-so-
grown) men swoon.

"That girl can *sing*, man," her old bandmate Chris Darrow declared. "She just had that nasty *EEEHHHHR!!* kinda stuff," he said, imitating her growl. "And I would . . ."—he closed his eyes and sighed—"*Ooohhh!* Every time." He shook his head at the memory. "Fuck, man."

"She underestimates her rock singing *massively*," Peter noted with more than a little incomprehension.

Despite Ronstadt's claim that material was always a problem, the songs that were attempted during these sessions were very good, indeed. A second number from Jimmy Webb, "Easy for You to Say," was a haunting, midtempo ballad, with Ronstadt's voice nailing the ache from an affair's dissolution. Joe South's "I Knew You When" had been a hit originally for Billy Joe Royal back when he and Peter traveled together on Dick Clark's Caravan of Stars. Ronstadt manages to make the song her own, transitioning from a full-throated yell on the choruses to a pained whisper to start each verse. Even Royal himself was impressed with their version.

The same day "I Knew You When" was cut, Ronstadt and her team tackled "Mr. Radio," an eerily evocative song from the pen of Roderick Taylor—also known at that time by his *nom de plume*, Roderick Falconer. Originally recorded under his given name back in 1974 for Asylum Records, Taylor recalled trying to "seek out desolation" back in the sixties.

"We'd drive up in the mountains, someplace like North Carolina or Virginia, to these old, abandoned farms," Taylor said, where he would experience "a kind of vicarious melancholy. We'd look at these ruins where people would leave all their stuff—photographs and magazines." These desolate places from another era made Taylor wonder "what the world was like before electronics came in."

He imagined a radio first arriving at one of these homesteads: "Suddenly, this new thing comes into your world," he explained, "and it contracts all the distances, and it introduces completely foreign storylines to your life." Bill Payne's synthesizer opens the track, bringing an electronic sunrise to this dusty rural scene. Dan Dugmore's pedal steel glides throughout the poetic cautionary tale of change wrought by modern magic, alongside Andrew Gold's finger-picked acoustic guitar. It was Gold who alerted Ronstadt to the song, having both played on and coproduced Taylor's original recording.

Along with "Get Closer," another delightfully fun track from the sessions was the old Ike and Tina Turner hit, "I Think It's Gonna Work Out Fine." Done as a rollicking duet with James Taylor, he and Ronstadt play off each other joyfully. Peter had always liked the song and suggested they give it a try. Unlike other "duets" recorded separately, "they worked their parts out right there on the spot," Massenburg recalled. The band, led off by drummer Rick Shlosser's call to order, lays down a groove as solid as stone, while the brilliant harmonies have you smiling from beginning to end. An added attraction is the baritone sax break courtesy of Jim Horn, a studio legend who had accompanied everyone from Frank Sinatra to Ike and Tina Turner themselves.

Get Closer was released in September 1982 and eventually sold over a million copies—not that its success gave Ronstadt pause; Jonathan Carroll recalled going over to

Get Closer
album cover.

Ronstadt's house with his family, not long after *Get Closer* came out. "She was very unabashed when we were visiting, saying: 'Naw, that's it—that's the last record I'm gonna make for kids.'"

Even before Peter recorded the final tracks for the *Get Closer* album, he was true to his word and began discussions with Ronstadt toward helping her realize her standards project, though he was feeling somewhat out of his depth. "That project was *really* a leap off a cliff for him," Ronstadt marveled. "That's, again, a thing that really separated him" from other producers. "Something that I've learned from Peter is how important it is to listen to every word the artist says," George Massenburg added. "I think Peter *always* responded to his artists. Maybe there are occasions when he did so *reluctantly*"—he smiled—"but that's okay!"

Just as Peter listened to J.D. Souther, wishing he could get Stanley Clarke to play on his album and suggesting he simply call him and ask, so he listened to Linda Ronstadt as she spoke of wanting these sessions to have the same feel as those great Sinatra albums that featured arrangements by Nelson Riddle. Peter simply called Riddle in for a meeting to see if he would be interested in arranging a track or two.

Riddle's album work had dried up at this point in his career, with him turning to television for most of his income. "He was doing *Newhart* and *Cagney & Lacey*," Terry Woodson recalled. Woodson had once been a trombone player for Riddle but was now in charge of turning Riddle's arrangements into sheet music for musicians, then archiving them all. Woodson remembered Riddle mentioning the upcoming meeting regarding some possible sessions for Ronstadt, with whom he was unfamiliar. "I don't know if she can sing them or not," Riddle mused.

California governor Jerry Brown visits the *Mad Love* sessions, 1980. Standing, L to R: Russ Kunkel, Peter Bernstein, Bill Payne, Mark Goldenberg, Dan Dugmore, Bob Glaub, Niko Bolas. Seated, L to R: Peter Asher, Linda Ronstadt, Gov. Jerry Brown, unknown roadie. *Photo by Bob Glaub.*

Peter and Wendy welcome Victoria Asher. *Photo by Paul Harris / Archive Photos / Getty Images.*

Peter meets with 10,000 Maniacs in a Jamestown, New York, bar for pre-production meeting. L to R: Peter, Robert Buck, Dennis Drew, Steven Gustafson, manager Peter Leak, and Jerome Augustyniak. *Photo by Barbara Gustafson.*

Linda Ronstadt and Aaron Neville with Steve Tyrell in his studio recording their demo for "Don't Know Much." *Courtesy of Steve Tyrell.*

Peter and Gordon performing at Gordon's wedding, August 1998. *Photo by Georgiana Steele-Waller.*

Peter at sea with friends Robin Williams and Eric Idle. *Photo by Wendy Worth Asher.*

Peter in his Sony office displaying his two Grammys for Producer of the Year and his third for producing Robin Williams's *Live 2002* album.

Peter listens intently to a "Turn, Turn, Turn" playback during the *California* sessions.
Photo by Jay Ruston.

Peter and Gordon reunite at Mike Smith benefit, August 2, 2005. © *Bobbi Lane.*

Peter and Pamela Anderson at London Fashion Week, 2009. *Doug Peters / Alamy Stock Photo.*

Seated left to right: Gabriela, Rodrigo, mixer Rafa Sardina, and Peter as mariachi—Rodrigo's birthday party, Mexico, 2012. *Photo by Rafa Sardina.*

Dave Stewart and Peter hold the sheet music for their song "Love Always Comes as a Surprise" from *Madagascar 3: Europe's Most Wanted*.

Peter with Steve Martin and Edie Brickell recording the basic tracks for *Love Has Come for You*. *Photographed by Frank Filipetti.*

Peter and Elton—"The Boys in Red." *Photo by David Furnish.*

Peter proudly displays his medal after his Investiture, February 23, 2015. *Photo by Nich Ansell/PA Images / Alamy Stock Photo.*

The meeting happened at The Complex, where George Massenburg was still recording and mixing *Get Closer*. When asked about doing a few arrangements for this upcoming project, Peter's assistant, Ira Koslow, remembered Riddle replying: "I don't do arrangements—I do albums." Ronstadt quickly showed Riddle the list of song possibilities she had compiled, and looking them over, he agreed to work up arrangements for all of them.

Massenburg recalled that, as Riddle studied the list, he said, "You wanna do 'What's New?'" He then opened up the briefcase he had brought, which contained many of the original scores he had written over the years for Sinatra, Rosemary Clooney, Nat "King" Cole, and others. "He pulls out the original chart," according to Massenburg, "crosses out Frank's name and pencils in 'Linda.' He says, 'What key?'" Massenburg smiled at the memory. "Linda's impressed!"

After locking down which key was the best fit for each song, Riddle began to fashion his arrangements, at times incorporating some of Ronstadt's suggested colorations. Finally, on June 30, 1982, after the failed Wexler sessions and much doubt and discouragement, Ronstadt stood at a microphone facing a forty-piece orchestra. "It's a big boat to steer—that many people and that kind of investment," Massenburg explained. "Peter was the guy to do it."

The first track recorded was "What's New?" with Ronstadt singing live while hearing Riddle's arrangement for the very first time. The experience was unlike anything she had ever done, and it took some getting used to. "The orchestra was following *her*," Peter observed. "Nelson kept explaining to her that she didn't have to wait for him to do *this* . . ."—and here Peter waved his arms as if conducting. "She sang! He was doing *this*"—miming more conducting—"to make sure *they* followed *her*! Which is the opposite of rock'n'roll, where she would always be following the drummer; even though they were accompanying her, the groove is the groove. And the singer has to fit in and around the groove." Now, with these songs and under these circumstances, Peter explained, "*Linda's* the 'groove.'"

"It took her a while to *get* that," Peter continued. "She could slow down as much as she wanted to—it was all her. And Nelson was there to make this brilliant arrangement accompany her properly." He added, "It's like dancing—and she's leading."

Despite his reticence regarding Ronstadt's abilities at the project's start, "Nelson was very pleased," Woodson said. "She *could* sing them." The sessions continued, off and on, over a nine-month period, mainly due to Peter's concurrent commitment—accompanying James Taylor on the road, trying to support his friend through a raw period both post-divorce and post-drugs—certainly not because Riddle would labor over his arrangements: "Nelson, in many cases, when he knew the song really well, would get up in the morning and write the chart in ten minutes," George Massenburg noted. "*Very* fast."

Ira Koslow declared that Peter and Nelson got along "fabulously." Peter described Riddle as "very funny and very cynical." He would regale them with stories of Sinatra, whom Nelson respected as a singer, according to Peter, but not so much as a person. Both men were determined to get the music to Linda's satisfaction, even if it meant forty musicians sitting around for hours while parts were rewritten. "Once we were listening to a track and just marveling at this cello and woodwind line," according to Massenburg, "just stunning idiosyncratic work. And the tape gets done, and Linda says, 'You know, I don't know about that thing in the second verse . . .' And Nelson called out: 'Okay, everybody. Pencils? Delete bars 59 through 69 . . .' And the most brilliant part was gone! Just gone. And not coming back, either!

"He had no agenda but to make it work for Linda."

Once the songs were recorded, Peter and Linda sat with Massenburg and began the mixing process. "The three of us were a good team, I thought, in terms of editing and comping," Ronstadt said. "We were really good. And we'd finish each other's sentences. We rarely disagreed." Riddle simply didn't have the patience for that sort of slow meticulousness. But at times the team was stuck, and Riddle's input was needed. Ronstadt recalled: "We'd say, you know, 'When you mix this, how . . . ?' And he would *tell* us *exactly* how he had cast the woodwinds, or exactly how he had cast the strings in any given arrangement.

"And he could give you such a literate, clear, full-color description," she continued. "He could build a little story and say, 'This is kind of hiding in the basement—it's supposed to be under there kind of moldering away, and you only get the *fumes* of it rising through the floorboards. So it should be *there*.' You know? 'And the rest of this is dancing in front of your eyes.' And you'd get it so clearly, and you'd just tweak the mix that way, and it'd be exactly right."

These songs of romance—songs he'd once dismissed as "elevator music"—just might have had a subtle effect on Peter, for right after *What's New* wrapped, songs like Side One's closer, "Someone to Watch over Me," seemed almost prophetic . . .

Peter and Wendy married on May 20, 1983, in the Chelsea District of London. James Taylor stood as Peter's best man, and Lorraine Kirke, then married to Bad Company's drummer Simon Kirke, was Wendy's maid of honor. Peter's mum and both his sisters attended, as did old friends like singer Paul Jones.

"I adore her to death," Lee Sklar said of Wendy, smiling. "There's an energy level and a kind of funny lunacy there that's hysterical. They're one of the funniest couples, because he's very restrained, very British, and very proper, and there's this maniac there that's just carrying on. I sit there and look at them and just laugh. What a couple of characters who found each other . . ."

Their reception was held at Langan's Brasserie, where Barbra Streisand crashed the party. "She'd arrived to have lunch," Peter found out, with the hostess telling her it was closed for Peter's wedding reception. "Oh! I know him," she announced, brushing past the staff. "Who's going to stop her anyway?" Peter laughed.

Along with marrying Wendy, Peter managed to acquire a new assistant from the relationship: Wendy's cousin, Cathy Kerr. "She called me one day and said, 'Peter's looking for a receptionist.' And I was just outta high school and didn't really know what I was gonna do." Kerr laughed. "I knew *nothing* about being a receptionist!" After meeting with Peter, Gloria Boyce, and Ira Koslow, she was told, "Well, this is the company. There's not a lot of upward mobility, but it's a fun job!" With all three principals often gone—at recording studios or on the road—Kerr found herself alone at the Doheny office on many occasions. She kept busy—maintaining the newspaper clippings file and, more importantly, reading: "Peter said," according to Kerr, "'If you want to learn, read. *Everything*. Contracts, my mail—whatever you want. *That's* how you're gonna learn.'" Kerr was smart enough to follow this sage advice.

In September 1983, the album *What's New* was released to an audience that would seem to be totally uninterested; the music the masses were then gorging on was such MTV fodder as The Eurythmics, The Police, and The Stray Cats—all excellent in their own right, but light-years away from Sammy Cahn and Jule Styne, the writers of "Guess I'll Hang My Tears Out to Dry." The folks at Warner/Elektra/Asylum were expecting the album to be Ronstadt's biggest flop.

But despite all the dire predictions of career catastrophe, *What's New* was a sizeable hit—peaking at number-three on the charts and selling well over two million copies. Stephen Holden, writing in the *New York Times*, called the album "the best and most serious attempt to rehabilitate an idea of pop that Beatlemania and the mass marketing of rock LPs for teenagers undid in the mid-sixties."

With the record's success, Ronstadt, Riddle, and his orchestra took their show on the road, bringing the songs and staging of another era to an audience that had never experienced such sophistication before. Ira Koslow, placed in charge of producing the tour, remembered: "We went to all of the venues where we played rock'n'roll," he said. "Pine Knob, Merriweather Post, all of these sheds. And we put up big, lush curtains, we put up velour, we put up chiffon, we put in beautiful lights. It was the first time these places had ever seen a front curtain—ever! They were blown away."

The project's success caused a revival of the songs from the first half of the twentieth century—what is now referred to as "The Great American Songbook." And in Ronstadt's wake, many rock artists—from Rod Stewart to Paul McCartney—have

What's New
album cover.

successfully released their own albums interpreting these classic songs. Peter, who had originally equated these standard American pop songs to "elevator music," had to admit that Linda succeeded in her mission to "take them out of the elevator."

Just as Ronstadt and Riddle began their tour, a daughter, Victoria Asher, joined Wendy and Peter on January 20, 1984. One of the album's highlights, the Gershwins' "I've Got a Crush on You," would open Ronstadt's upcoming shows, and its lyrics—"*The world will pardon my mush/For I have got a crush, my baby, on you*"—had taken on a whole new meaning for the couple.

21

IN MY TRIBE

James Taylor contacted Peter, saying he was finally ready to go back into the studio and deliver his follow-up to *Dad Loves His Work*. Peter's plan was to make the experience as relaxing as possible, booking a few weeks at AIR's facility on the Caribbean island of Montserrat. "Getting away from distractions," was how Peter looked at it. "And maybe James thought it would help him resolve his issues, you know, whether psychological or chemical." Opened in 1979, the studio was co-owned by Sir George Martin and Peter and Gordon's former producer, John Burgess. The buildings, nestled into the lush hills on the island paradise, had been the birthplace of many hit albums, including *Ghost in the Machine* by The Police and Paul McCartney's *Tug of War*.

For the past few years, Edd Kolakowski had begun assisting Peter at recording sessions when not needed on the road, and he accompanied Peter's team to the island. The studio, despite its good word-of-mouth, was found to be not quite "state of the art": "We spent so much time," Kolakowski complained, "waiting for them to fix things in the studio, because it turned out that any time AIR Studios in London had a piece of gear that was on its last legs or they weren't really happy with, they'd ship it to Montserrat. It was a dumping ground." The studio "wasn't working well," agreed Peter. "They'd always had problems; in fact, that Police album *Ghost in the Machine* is a reference to the eternally malfunctioning recording equipment." And if a part needed replacing, you were out of luck: "I remember *that* being a *real* issue," groused Peter. "Anything you needed a part for would be weeks of delay."

The problems were as basic as the inability to plug in your amp: "We discovered the studio was wired to English standard," Kolakowski explained, with a major difference in voltage and wall outlets, "and all of our gear was American." Equipment could have been plugged into transformers, but according to Peter, "that's yet *another* source of hum and buzz and confusion." It certainly wasn't a good working environment for Peter—or the poor engineer tasked to make it all work: Frank Filipetti.

Peter had introduced James to Filipetti during a visit to New York the previous year. This particular trio had gotten along so well, Peter asked Filipetti to engineer Taylor's upcoming sessions in Montserrat. "This was the biggest thing that had happened to me," Filipetti said. "I just felt on top of the world."

Unfortunately, Taylor decidedly did not: "James was trying to kick methadone at that point," bassist Lee Sklar recalled. "He was just a mess." Taylor's personal problems, combined with all the studio delays, meant only a couple of usable tracks were cut on the island, including a breezy cover of Buddy Holly's "Everyday." The sessions were eventually halted, and Taylor spent the rest of the year getting free of yet another chemical dependency, albeit one meant to free him from the first.

Though Taylor's session was somewhat shambolic, *What's New* and the resulting tour had been a smashing success. With Ronstadt feeling as if she had finally found her voice performing these musically complex and emotional stories, it seemed natural to record a sequel. From late August to early October of 1984, Peter produced a second album—with, of course, Nelson Riddle once again arranging and conducting such classic songs as "When I Fall in Love" and "You Took Advantage of Me." Released just in time for the Christmas buying season, *Lush Life* came conveniently packaged like a gift, courtesy of designer John Kosh. Looking like a lady's hatbox from the forties tied up with ribbon, the package won Kosh another Grammy Award for album design.

For close to a decade now, Peter Asher Management's efforts had been concentrated almost entirely toward the promotion of only two clients—James Taylor and Linda Ronstadt. And because of that laser-like focus, Peter had made both clients hugely successful and very rich—as well as, it should be noted, himself: "One day, I was sitting in his office," Rick Marotta recalled, chatting as Peter shuffled papers across his desk. Peter stopped as he glanced at one particular page and, chuckling,

Lush Life
album cover.

handed it to Marotta. "A bill from his tax accountant; it was what he had to sign the next day to pay his taxes." Marotta took a look and gasped: "I literally *fell on the floor* with my feet up in the air! It was around a half a million dollars!" Marotta had no complaints about his own compensation as a gun-for-hire; certainly no beef with Peter, who was fairer than most, always paying his musicians well, even giving them hefty bonuses at the end of tours. "I thought, FUCK, man! I'm not even making *close* to that in a year"—Marotta laughed—"and I think I'M rich!" Peter had become one of the most successful managers in the music business.

"When people ask me what the secret of being a great manager is," Peter remarked, "tragically, it's very simple and annoying: The secret is having a great client. It's pretty easy to be a great manager when you have James Taylor as a client." Peter made this confession soon after the Rock and Roll Hall of Fame asked him to give a speech at their 2014 ceremonies inducting the first two artist managers into the Hall. "And the first two were Brian Epstein, who managed The Beatles, and Andrew Oldham, who was the first manager of The Rolling Stones—which kind of proves my point. 'Great managers'—well, guess who they managed?" He smiled. "Not that astonishing."

Now, for the first time in years, Peter became the manager of two more iconic clients—Roger Waters and Joni Mitchell. The creative force within Pink Floyd during their years of massive success, Waters was about to leave his band amid much acrimony. But before the official break, his first solo album, *The Pros and Cons of Hitch Hiking*, was released, and to promote it Waters embarked on a US tour. "I'd known him off and on for ages," said Peter, who'd met the band during their early days with Syd Barrett, loaning them equipment and offering advice. Now his old friend had asked Peter to come aboard and help manage things as he toured stateside with an ensemble including Eric Clapton and Michael Kamen.

"We were all out on the road together," Peter recalled, smiling at the memory: "It was fun." But there were problems: "His relationship with the label was a bit fraught"—meaning Columbia Records, which found Waters difficult to deal with. "He *can* be a bit difficult, and his wife at the time could be very difficult and demanding." Though Peter was willing to continue his managerial relationship once the tour wrapped, Waters went his own way. Regardless, the two maintain their friendship today. "I'm a huge fan," Peter enthused.

Peter had first met Joni Mitchell when she and James Taylor played on the same afternoon at the Newport Folk Festival back in 1969. "She's one of the most brilliant women on the planet," Peter stated emphatically. "Managing her was an honor and a pleasure." After a pause, he added: "It wasn't always easy!" Asked why he never went into the studio to produce one of her albums, Peter smiled and said: "Only Joni produces Joni."

Along with these client additions, and after years on his own, Peter began to discuss the possibility of bringing another artist manager into the fold as a partner. Barry Krost was someone whom Peter had crossed paths with for years, beginning as children back in 1952, when Krost was Peter's stand-in during the filming of

The Planter's Wife. Later, during Peter and Gordon's heyday, Krost was managing hit British artists like Dusty Springfield, so they would see each other at parties and television tapings. In 1971, Peter helped another of Krost's clients, Cat Stevens—offering advice and tour support as the young troubadour began to break though in the States. As the decade progressed, Krost became more involved in the worlds of film and theater. Eventually, he began to imagine creative ways to combine his love of theater, film, and television with the musical artists he managed and admired. What if he and Peter combined forces?

"The Barry alliance was based on the fact that we were gonna try and find ways for film people and music people to work together," Peter explained, "and grow in that regard." The idea seemed a natural one, coming right as MTV was showing what could happen, both culturally and financially, when you smashed music and media together. But it was still years before rock music began to invade Broadway, and only *Miami Vice* had started to experiment with hit songs as TV underscore—both ideas commonplace today.

"The industries were very closed," Krost remembered. "In those days, if you had a recording career it had been proven that, if you made films, the films didn't work, or it messed up your recording career." Prince seemed to prove that conventional wisdom wrong with *Purple Rain*, which came out just as this proposed partnership was in the talking stages, but most entertainment executives thought it an exception. "The general mood of television and film was that they were competitive" with the music industry, Krost explained. Nonetheless, Peter Asher Management became Asher/Krost Management (alternatively, Peter said as he laughed, "Elton John used to call us *Bialystock and Bloom*," with a nod to Mel Brooks's *The Producers*). Soon, old friends like Carole King and Randy Newman changed their representation to Asher/Krost.

"The people who've made the most money in show business," noted composer Randy Newman, "are the people who know how to tell the people who the public loves a million different ways how great they are. Saying, 'Not since Shakespeare has there been a writer like you!' Or: 'You're the new Marlon Brando!' And you'd be surprised—you almost can't go too far. You almost can't overpraise someone in this business. It's shocking—I've seen it."

Peter, Newman said, "doesn't have that in him, really. But what he *does* have . . ." Newman paused and related a story: "I was once in a room with him, and there was a bunch of record company people—executive types. You know—money people. And they were playing something. And I noticed that he was the only person, outside of myself, who was tapping their foot.

"He *loves* the music," Newman declared. "In fact, where music is concerned, it's the main thing to know about him—his genuine enthusiasm." Engineer Frank Filipetti agreed and added another observation as to why clients and colleagues respect him: "Peter's generosity and fairness is remarkable." He was commenting on the fact that, when James Taylor was finally up to the task of finishing the sessions begun in Montserrat the previous year, Peter had no problem in sharing the production credit with Taylor and Filipetti. The singer and engineer decided to continue tracking at Filipetti's New York studio, mostly without Peter—due to scheduling conflicts. "There was certainly no major falling-out," Peter insisted. "I think it may have been partly conflicts, partly James kind of going, 'Let me try this on my own for a bit.'" But despite his lack of physical presence, "Peter was *always* involved in the production; even when he wasn't there, we'd be sending him things, and he'd make his comments," according to Filipetti. And when Peter ended up sharing the credit, "he just felt that was the fair thing to do, and he did it!

"Most of the people I've worked with—if you're hired on as the engineer, but you end up doing a lot of production," Filipetti claimed, "you *still* get an engineer's credit. Not only James, but Peter, as well, were both incredibly generous in giving me production credit for the work that I did.

"There are very few people I've worked with in this industry with that kind of fairness. And who are secure enough in what they do that they don't need to take credit." Though Peter was the one hired to produce this James Taylor disc, his producer's credit was kept only on the two Montserrat tracks that ended up on the record, released in 1985 with the title *That's Why I'm Here*. The liner notes accompanying the album offer this simple praise: "Fond thanks to Peter Asher, cool and thoughtful throughout."

In July 1985, just before the release of Taylor's album, Peter again went back into the studio with Ronstadt and Nelson Riddle to produce the third and final project in their trilogy of American pop standards. Unfortunately, Riddle had become quite ill—at times needing to lie down during breaks in recording. The track "'Round Midnight" was from one of Riddle's very last sessions. "Nelson's best direction to the orchestra," George Massenburg related, came just before the tape rolled on that particular tune: "For this terribly sad song, his direction was 'Play this as *coldly* as possible'—meaning play this with no emotion whatsoever." The track, which closes the album, begins with Riddle's count-off for the orchestra. Terry Woodson, who had worked with Riddle for over thirty years, said wistfully: "I thought it was really nice that Peter left Nelson's voice on there."

Nelson Riddle passed away on October 6, 1985. On the 18th of November, Ronstadt, the musicians, and the production team reconvened at The Complex to complete the project without their musical leader. Weeks earlier, "Peter called me," according to Woodson, "and asked was there any music that Nelson hadn't finished. There was one: 'I Love You for Sentimental Reasons.'" Woodson stepped up and filled in for Riddle, finishing the orchestration his old friend had sketched out, then conducting the final recording sessions.

This last album from the Ronstadt/Asher/Riddle collaboration, entitled *For Sentimental Reasons*, was released in September 1986, just as Peter was in the studio producing the hit that wasn't supposed to be . . .

Steve Tyrell had been in the music business for years, getting his foot in the door at New York's legendary Brill Building—befriending, in the process, hit songwriters

Barry Mann and Cynthia Weil. Later, as head of A&R for Scepter Records, Tyrell suggested old friend B.J. Thomas as vocalist for Burt Bacharach and Hal David's song "Raindrops Keep Fallin' on My Head," written for the movie *Butch Cassidy and the Sundance Kid*. The record was a number-one smash, with the tune eventually winning the Academy Award for Best Original Song. After moving out to Hollywood, Tyrell began managing Barry Mann and focused on trying to get his client work in the film industry.

"Barry and Cynthia," Tyrell said, "got a job working on *An American Tail* as songwriters with James Horner"—the composer of the film's score. Tyrell laid out the reasons why the two veteran songwriters were excited by this opportunity: "They'd get paid a lot of money, work for Steven Spielberg"—the film's executive producer—"and *didn't have to write a hit*. They just had to do the job and move the story along." This animated film's plot, under the supervision of Don Bluth, presented the travails of immigrants coming to the United States from Russia in the late 1800s to find freedom, all told from the perspective of a heartwarming family of cartoon mice.

One day, as Mann worked at the piano, he began to play the melody for what would be the opening lines to the song that, once finished, would be entitled "Somewhere Out There." Overhearing those first eight measures from the next room, Tyrell walked in and asked, "What the hell is that?" Mann answered, "Well, that's a little tune we're writing for the mice to sing to the moon. They're lost." Tyrell remembered replying, "Well, that's a fuckin' hit!" Mann protested: "We don't *have* to write a hit!" "I think"—Tyrell laughed—"you wrote one anyway!" As his music supervisor instincts kicked in, Tyrell said, "That song should be reprised at the end of the movie . . ." adding the kicker: "with pop singers to sing it!"

James Horner's contribution was the alternating notes that made up the song's bridge ("DA-da-DA-da-DA-da," Peter sang, parenthetically adding: "That's 'Somewhere Over the Rainbow,' but whatever—it works"). Horner, though, seemed bothered with Tyrell's interference, not wanting to sully "his" film with this pop music nonsense. But it wasn't just Horner—"No one could hear it," Tyrell said of the potential hit he heard in his head. No wonder: The only existing version—the one familiar to the animators and studio executives—was a simple piano track accompanied by a temporary vocal. But Burt Berman, head of music for Universal, had a hunch and gave Tyrell money to cut a demo to show the tune's possibilities. Berman liked what he heard, played it for Spielberg, who also liked it, "and," Tyrell said, "we were on."

Since the movie featured the song performed by a brother and sister, Tyrell first pitched it to Michael and Janet Jackson. But having done the *Captain EO* film for Disney the previous year, Walter Yetnikoff—president of Columbia Records, the parent company of Michael's label—didn't want their number-one artist involved so soon with yet another "cartoon" project and nixed his involvement. "We were disappointed," said Tyrell, "'cause *that* would have been a home run." Next, Irving Azoff—then head of MCA Records, who would be releasing the movie's soundtrack—suggested they use his label's band The Jets, another popular sibling act with a handful of Top Ten hits under their belt.

Tyrell went into the studio with The Jets and cut the song. "As soon as the session was over," he recalled, "we got a call from Irving Azoff saying, 'Linda Ronstadt wants to do the record.'" Ronstadt, then dating Steven Spielberg's friend George Lucas, had been asked personally by Spielberg if she would listen to Tyrell's original demo and consider providing her voice to the project. Always a sucker for a good ballad, Ronstadt loved the longing in Cynthia Weil's lyrics, understanding how the song, sung in the film by two lost siblings, could also be interpreted as two lovers searching for one another. Once she said yes, the finished version by The Jets, to the band's chagrin, was unceremoniously shelved.

Peter, as Ronstadt's longtime producer, was now brought onboard. But rather than flex his ego and take over, Peter asked Tyrell ("whom I like a *lot*," he added) to assist him in producing the track. Peter mentioned that Ronstadt was leaning toward using Panamanian performer—and Elektra/Asylum label mate—Rubén Blades as her duet partner, which flummoxed Tyrell. "I can't imagine it being a hit with that combination," Tyrell thought. "But," he reasoned, "Linda can take things to another level," so he was willing to try to make the idea work.

As the session at United Western commenced, Ronstadt sang her half while Tyrell—an accomplished singer himself—sang the male half of the duet as a placeholder for Blades, who would be adding his vocal later. Hearing Tyrell's interpretation with his bluesier delivery, Ronstadt began to have second thoughts, eventually telling both Tyrell and Asher, "I don't think Rubén's gonna be right for this." "*Thank you, God!*" a relieved Tyrell said to himself. Ronstadt asked his opinion on who might be best to bring onboard, and Tyrell immediately suggested his old friend James Ingram. Years earlier, when he was a struggling vocalist, Ingram had been hired by Tyrell to sing on Barry Mann's demos. Now, signed to Quincy Jones's label, Ingram was beginning to enjoy a successful career of his own.

Ingram was sent the rough mix of the song, loved it, and within days his vocal was recorded and mixed with Ronstadt's. Then the brakes were applied once again, as Quincy called, according to Peter, "and said, 'We don't think so.'" Quincy's label, Qwest Records, a joint venture with Warners, felt it important to establish Ingram as a hit vocalist on his own. After duetting with Patti Austin, Michael McDonald, Kenny Rogers, and Kim Carnes on hits, as well as taking part in the all-star "We Are the World" charity single, they thought the track was "nice" but one duet too many.

A deadline was looming—Peter needed to deliver the finished track to Universal in order to get it into the movie. He again reached out to his friends at Elektra/Asylum and brought in vocalist Peabo Bryson, an excellent R&B singer who specialized in romantic ballads. All agreed this was a great opportunity, and Bryson, whom Tyrell called a "great gentleman," was rushed into the studio to try to complete the track before time ran out. In the meantime, Mo Ostin, head of the Warner Brothers record division and one of the most respected men in the business, contacted Quincy

Jones and politely asked: "What the hell is wrong? C'mon—don't you *want* James on a smash hit?"

"In the middle of Peabo's session," Tyrell recalled, "in the middle of him *singing*, they call us up and say, 'You can have James.' It's really fucked." Tyrell shook his head, sympathizing with Bryson. "This poor guy . . ." Peter is caught in the middle—having been told to go back and change the vocal and now wondering if he should continue.

On the phone with Ostin, with Bryson still standing at the studio mic, Peter remembered saying: "Well, *I'm* not telling him! That is really above and beyond. I'm just gonna finish this, and *you* guys have to sort that out. With all respect, I don't know *what's* going on anymore!" Hanging up and telling Tyrell the latest twist in the saga, Peter announced: "We're going to finish both versions, *then* we'll decide!" The following day, Linda's old friend Don Henley dropped by just as George Massenburg was tweaking the final mixes. Peter played both versions for him, and, after listening, Henley observed politely: "I think Mr. Ingram did a good job." The next day, Peter played both versions for Ronstadt and Tyrell, asking them to vote. "I've always felt the same way," replied Tyrell frankly. "James did it great, and I think it's a can't-miss hit by him." Peter then looked to Linda, who paused and said: "I think I agree with Steve." That was all Peter needed to hear, and the winning master mix was immediately delivered to Spielberg's production team.

"Peabo delivered a *perfectly* good vocal," Massenburg was quick to point out. "I know his heart was broken . . ."

After not even trying to write a hit, after all the maddening stops and starts throughout various recordings, Ronstadt and Ingram's version of "Somewhere Out There" was released as a single in November 1986, and by the following March, it peaked at number-two on *Billboard*'s chart. Ultimately, at the thirtieth annual Grammy Awards ceremony, it was named Song of the Year.

As 1987 began, Elektra's senior vice president and head of A&R Howard Thompson approached Peter about the possibility of producing the next album by 10,000 Maniacs—a young band who had recorded one LP for Elektra, selling only a meager 180,000 copies, but with great promise. Peter agreed, as the band, especially their lead singer, Natalie Merchant, intrigued him: "I loved her voice," he said.

"We were really excited about it," band keyboardist Dennis Drew recalled, stating the obvious: "Peter was a hit-makin' guy!" Drew also recalled what Peter warned the band from the beginning: "We had to play on time and in tune, or he'd find someone who could—that's exactly what he said!" The band understood. "It was no more fun and games," Drew noted. "It was serious work." Peter asked to hear their best compositions.

When it came to songwriting, 10,000 Maniacs proved different from other bands—always crafting their melodies first. Drew explained their methodology for coming up with material: "We never had a monitor when we practiced," he said, referring to the typical amplification system for a vocalist, so Merchant never sang along. "She didn't wanna struggle singing over us at rehearsals. She sat in a corner and wrote lyrics and notes." Once the band had polished a new melody, Drew said, "we would tape 'em on a Fostex"—an early four-track cassette portastudio. "Then she'd take 'em home and sing over 'em"—recording her finished lyrics on the remaining open track.

The group came out to Los Angeles, and Peter asked Edd Kolakowski to meet them at Massenburg's studio. "Help them with their gear," Peter instructed, "'cause I hear they're pretty rustic." Kolakowski laughed, recalling guitarist Robert Buck's homemade effects rack featuring navy surplus gear: "And if you didn't set it up right, you'd electrocute yourself!" Once the equipment was safely operational, the band spent three days simply running through the new material with Peter, laying the songs down demo-style to two-track tape. With five members in the band, "there were always a lot of different ideas on where to take songs," Drew noted, and they soon realized Peter "was a good arbiter of ideas." A comfortable "authority figure," he helped steer the band to open one song with a brief intro, for example, or double the chorus on another. In other cases, he knew when the song felt right; after listening to the band perform "What's the Matter Here?"—an observation on child abuse—Peter simply said, "That's great," and moved on.

"Be willing to experiment," was Peter's credo for the sessions, according to Drew: "He was only gonna do the project if we were willing to try new technology and experiment in new ways of recording. He wanted to have fun with this and explore." Recording with engineer George Massenburg at his studio, The Complex, Peter could take advantage of the full panoply of up-to-date equipment offered by Massenburg Labs, which mostly would have been out of place if utilized on the Nelson Riddle sessions, say, or a James Taylor recording. With these tools, he would be able to deliver to the label an album with an aural sheen similar to other recent alternative rock albums.

According to Drew, as recording commenced, Peter "really worked on Natalie," who had some pitch issues at the start. He and Massenburg would record six or seven takes of vocals, followed by the comping method they had perfected with Ronstadt, editing right down to the syllable. The band, Peter commented, "had timing issues" as well, which he was loath to tolerate.

Bassist Steven Gustafson offered an example: "Our drummer, Jerry, plays on the front edge of the beat, propelling the song forward. This would lend the songs to accelerating at times—something we were used to and even liked on some songs." As they labored to record the track "Campfire Song," Peter was gently pushing drummer Jerry Augustyniak to remain steady throughout.

"Jerry would start," Gustafson recalled, "and at about the same spot in the song, Peter would get on the talk-back, stop him, and make him start over." Take after take was tried, with Gustafson, up in the booth with the production team, observing Asher and Massenburg: "Every time that one spot in the song would come up, I could see them tensing in anticipation. When it wasn't right, they would hang their heads and mutter an expletive," with Massenburg eventually calling out: "Take thirty-seven."

"No one wanted it right more than Jerry," observed Gustafson, noting: "We got the take eventually."

"He put us through the ringer," Drew said of Peter's drive, "but made us all a lot better."

"I think we were still a bit raw when Peter signed on to work with us," agreed Gustafson (adding: "Maybe still are . . ."), "and it was a new challenge for him." Peter, as well as Massenburg, Gustafson noted, "were used to perfection and we played on emotion, damn the blemishes. Don't get me wrong: We wanted to be perfect for Peter. We all had a lot of respect for him, but sometimes it was just out of our grasp."

Jerry Augustyniak was "a good guy," Massenburg attested, "but we needed something that would steady his tempo." Most drummers would "float" to one degree or another, according to Massenburg, "with rare exception." Click tracks had been used for decades in the movie industry, helping orchestras synchronize to film clips during soundtrack recording. Beginning in the sixties, when many untrained drummers began recording, click tracks were utilized more and more in pop music, fed into the drummer's headphones to help steady the beat, "but not a lot of people knew how to *follow* them," Massenburg stated. "That was something that had to be learned." Many producers, when faced with this dilemma, would have simply brought in a session drummer to do the job—as was done, most famously, when George Martin brought in Andy White to drum behind The Beatles on their first single, after having doubts about Pete Best's steadiness during the group's first session.

Peter, though, to his credit, felt it was important *not* to bring an outsider in, but maintain the band's identity. One day, Drew recalled, a group of technicians wheeled into the studio "two *huge* racks that, together, were the size of a side-by-side refrigerator—racks of computer stuff. And this big Synclavier keyboard." The Synclavier was an early digital workstation and sampling synthesizer. "Jerry," Drew remembered, "would go in and play his drums. He would hit his snare, and they'd record it into the Synclavier." This went on for days until, finally, his entire kit was recorded one sound at a time. Augustyniak would then play the Synclavier like a piano—triggering his prerecorded drum sounds. This, for example, was how the drum track was achieved on the song "Like the Weather"—Merchant's somewhat chipper tale of depression. Once a drum take was completed, "They'd *quantize* it—make it all perfect—and then they'd go back in and make it a little *un-perfect*, so that"—Drew laughed—"it sounded more realistic! Hours and *days* of that stuff . . ." Remarked Massenburg: "It's what you do in ProTools *so* easily now, but it was *such* a pain in the ass then." Ultimately, the drum tracks ended up being about fifty percent sampled and fifty percent live—though so expertly done, it's almost impossible to tell which is which.

"It was a real departure for us," Drew said of the tech used during the production. "A lot of attention to detail—and we were never quite that detail oriented!" For their production team, it was like kids in a candy store: "Peter and George loved it—they had a great time doing that stuff." But because of all the time involved achieving the level of perfection they were looking for, "we spent a lot of time sittin' around," Drew laughed.

During some of this downtime, one member of the band had a little run-in with the authorities. It seems Miss Merchant decided to take a walk through Hollywood, but without her ID. Plus, "I think she'd smoked a joint," Peter postulated. "She was staying at the Chateau Marmont, was walking along Sunset Boulevard barefoot, and was stopped by the police, who 'claimed'—you know, they always say that they were looking for 'somebody' who'd allegedly 'escaped' from some mental institution who fit her description. It's what they always say. And they stopped and asked her a lot of questions, and she gave them kind of vague, Natalie-ish answers, upon which they looked in her bag and found this notebook full of lyrics—which they read, getting more and more convinced that she was a complete nutter. And then they said, 'What are you doing?' And she said, 'Oh, I'm here in LA recording an album with my band.' So they asked the name of the band.

"Of course, when she told them *that*"—Peter smiled—"they became a hundred percent convinced! But anyway, she finally dropped my name, which apparently one of the policemen had some reaction to—probably a James fan or something. So, they called me up at the office, and I did my best impression of a grown-up and said, you know"—and here Peter lowers his tenor voice to a baritone—"'Oh, yes, well, of course she's very eccentric—*you* know artists. But she's absolutely harmless.'" Satisfied, the patrolmen released her on her own recognizance.

"At the end of the day on Fridays," Gustafson remembered, "Peter would toss his car keys in the air and ask one of us to go get a bottle of vodka, and we would sit and sip cocktails while listening to the week's progress. Peter had a NICE car"—indeed, a Rolls Royce Silver Cloud III—"and we would almost wrestle each other for the keys to drive down a Hollywood street for a few minutes in a cool car. We were like kids: 'I want to drive Peter's car!' I took extra laps when I had the keys . . ."

Those fun Fridays came to an end as the final song was finished. The record was full of sparkling tracks, bursting with jangly guitars and imaginative lyrics. Merchant's graceful voice offered observations on environmentalism and militarism, bards and bums—a thinking man's folk-rock, hitting head and hips in equal measure. But even with all of Peter's efforts making sure the group's essence was captured in full, when they presented the album to Elektra, the response was: "Weeelll . . . yes, but we don't hear a single . . ."

Peter was a bit taken aback but understood the needs of the promotion department wanting to immediately grab the ears of radio programmers. The label staff asked if it was possible for the band to record a cover song. And, as we remember from an earlier chapter: "That's the thing that's the safest for them," James Taylor said of record labels. "It *sounds* like a hit because it *had* been."

Peter asked the band if they did any covers. "Well, we do Cat Stevens's 'Peace Train,'" came the reply. Peter exclaimed: "Incredible! Brilliant!" The band was not thrilled with the idea, and Peter agreed he thought the album was perfect. But, he explained, after all this work, rather than have the label not be behind you all the way, let's make the record company happy. "What the hell," he cajoled. "Let's try it."

In My Tribe
album cover.

The track needed to be done in a hurry, as there was a release date already on the schedule; plus: "We'd been goofin' around on some of these experiments," Drew conceded, "for weeks," so the recording budget was running low. To move things along, the band's manager, Peter Leak, asked his friend Fred Maher to participate. Drummer for the bands Material and Scritti Politti, Maher and the Maniacs' own drummer together programmed the rhythm track. Peter brought in friend and keyboard ace Don Grolnick to provide the piano part. Dennis Drew gave all the credit for manufacturing the track to Peter, who modestly offered: "I thought it was quite a good version."

In June 1987, it became the lead single off the album, entitled *In My Tribe*. The band toured behind the record, opening for R.E.M. and appearing on *Saturday Night Live* and other important shows of the day. But it wasn't "Peace Train" that broke the album, but "Like the Weather." Released as a single in May 1988, with its lilting melody and quirky rhythm (thanks to all that Synclavier programming), it brought new fans into the fold, helping to push *In My Tribe*'s sales past double platinum.

Peter's old friend, Joe Boyd, was happy—both for the band and for Peter. A legendary producer—helming sessions for Pink Floyd, Fairport Convention, Maria Muldaur, and the McGarrigles—he had produced 10,000 Maniacs' first album for Elektra, the one that had sold only 180,000 copies. "I prefer mine, of course," he confessed. "But his sold millions and mine flopped."

Linda Ronstadt, continuing with her credo "to go forward, go back," had spent her time since the Riddle sessions immersing herself in the Mexican music of her childhood. Her father, Gilbert, of both German and Mexican heritage, was blessed with a lovely singing voice of his own. Performing professionally for a while, he eventually set that dream aside to run the family business. Along with introducing his children to the sounds of Sinatra and other pop singers of the day, he would soothe them at night with Spanish lullabies. Luisa, one of Gilbert's sisters, also sang and performed, specializing in traditional Spanish songs—*rancheras* and *corridos*. She eventually published her favorites in a collection she entitled *Canciones di Mi Padre*, or "Songs of My Father."

Linda Ronstadt had long ago proven herself a consummate crooner of country music, wowed Broadway audiences with her operatic range, and successfully tackled the complexities of interpreting the likes of Gershwin and Porter—all genres she first encountered while a youngster in Tucson. This last piece of her early musical education—these Spanish songs with their passion, their poetry, these "songs of her father"—were now swirling in her head, and she was determined to finally learn them properly.

In 1986, Ronstadt began to try out this new passion in public, appearing at a handful of mariachi festivals around the Southwest. Though her efforts were warmly received, it was the same old story at her record label, as Ira Koslow recalled: "Linda says, 'I wanna make a Spanish language record.' And the record company says, 'No, no, no! You're gonna kill your career! *You're gonna kill your career!*'

"Peter backed her up," Koslow said admiringly. "Peter said, 'You know, Linda, you may kill your career, but if you wanna do it . . .' Peter forced them." *Forced* may be too strong a word, but Peter certainly explained, in his polite way, that his client's musical instincts had been proven right in the past—millions and millions of dollars' worth of right—and they should leave her to follow them again.

Ronstadt insisted Rubén Fuentes take part—a legend in the Mexican music industry who knew this material inside and out. "My parents," Maestro Fuentes explained through a translator, "started me at the age of four" with music education, and he never stopped: "Elementary, high school . . . I just kept studying music." Eventually, at the age of eighteen, Fuentes joined the folkloric group Mariachi Vargas de Tecalitlan, which began an amazing musical career—composing songs that have become standards and producing a string of records that are classics of the ranchero style.

A fistful of those Fuentes-produced discs were for singer Lola Beltran, whom Ronstadt practically worshiped, and he remembered Ronstadt flying down to Mexico City to meet and discuss the project. Unlike Nelson Riddle, "I was familiar with her rock'n'roll," Fuentes explained, but like Riddle, "I thought: '*Can she do it?*'

"From the *first* moment I heard her," Fuentes claimed, "I *knew* she could!"

They both excitedly began to discuss song possibilities for the project. Maestro Fuentes agreed to both arrange and conduct the songs Ronstadt would perform, acting as producer—but only for the orchestral half of the sessions. To make sure she wasn't setting herself up for another Wexler-like situation, Ronstadt asked Peter to coproduce the record—to concentrate on recording her vocals and supervising the mix. He agreed.

Regarding Peter's willingness to, once more, participate in producing a musical genre with which he was completely unfamiliar, "*Wooohh*," Ronstadt exclaimed, "he just followed me off a cliff with that one, too!" Peter felt less anxious knowing George Massenburg would be manning the controls, having promised he'd again be

at Peter's side for this adventure, but that soon proved doubtful: "I had overprom-
ised," Massenburg sheepishly confessed, then producing sessions for Toto, among
other projects. "I was saying yes to everything.

"Peter came to me," Massenburg remembered, "and said, 'How can you *possibly*
say you can do this?' I said, 'Well, I really wanna do it.' He said, 'That's not the same
as saying you *will* do it. That wish has turned out to be a lie . . . you are *lying!*'"
Massenburg was a bit surprised by Peter's blunt critique but admitted: "He was absolutely right!" Peter, having been left in the lurch once before by Val Garay bowing
out of the *Get Closer* sessions, wanted an ironclad commitment, which his friend
had to admit was not possible, so Shawn Murphy was tapped to run the board. Fast
becoming legendary in Hollywood for his work recording John Williams's scores for
Steven Spielberg's films, Murphy was wholeheartedly endorsed by Massenburg as a
"brilliant" replacement.

Edd Kolakowski remembered Peter telling him at the beginning of the project:
"You know, I've been listening to a lot of mariachi stuff; *none* of 'em are in tune!
That's why I want *you* there—let's make an *in-tune mariachi record!*" Kolakowski,
up for the challenge, found a tuning accomplice in guitarist Gilberto Puente—"the
master of the mariachi guitar," Kolakowski stated. "Everyone looked up to him as
kind of a God."

Introducing himself to Puente on the first day of recording, Kolakowski told him
of Peter's tuning goals, and added: "I've talked to the other players, and they all tell
me that if *anybody's* gonna be in tune, it's you!" Puente's eyes lit up, and he asked,
"Really? They said that?" Nodding affirmatively, he showed Puente a stroboscopic
tuner—a device Kolakowski had employed for years in his capacity as a keyboard and
guitar technician. Its accuracy in detecting the slightest variations of an instrument's
pitch was unsurpassed.

All his life, Puente had been tuning his guitar by ear. After Kolakowski demonstrated how quickly and accurately that could now be accomplished, Puente became
a staunch ally in making sure every instrument—from the *vihuelas* to the *guitar-
rons*—were solidly in tune.

Their last adventure together in the studio, jumping into the lush complexities
of decades-old songcraft, proved somewhat difficult, as Peter and Linda were both
obviously not in their usual comfort zones. Ronstadt remarked that, as these new
sessions with Fuentes stretched through the summer of 1987, the process "was more
extreme" than the last, "'cause we were dealing with all these people who were running the music who didn't speak English, and there was a lot of translating going
back and forth." Ira Koslow's wife, Gail, a teacher fluent in Spanish, was brought in
to help bridge that language divide, but she soon realized that translating in *real time*
is a skill: "I was getting totally confused," she confessed. "I think at one point I was
speaking Spanish to Peter."

Dismissed after only three days, Gail recalled Peter pointing to Fuentes and saying: "We've discovered we have two things in common: We both love music, and
we both love vodka." The two producers would communicate just fine without her,

thank you, as all musicians can speak the language of rhythm and melody. Listening to his arrangements, Peter and Linda requested a few tweaks, Fuentes recalled—a "slower" pace for one song, "more violins" for a particular passage, that sort of thing. The musical performances Fuentes produced were focused toward achieving the artist's vision. Ronstadt wanted to keep things *very* traditional, and "once I knew," Fuentes commented, "that was what I did."

After the instrumental tracks were finished, the vocal sessions began. Ronstadt poured her heart and soul into these thirteen interpretations, from the desperate aloneness she conveys in the album opener "Por Un Amour" ("For a Love") to the fiery exclamations of "Los Laureles" ("The Laurels"), where she forcefully warns of the chaos of romance. The album's *tour de force* is Ronstadt's vocal gymnastics on "La Cigarra" ("The Cicada"), jumping octaves and holding notes for an inhumanly long duration.

That last song was one that Fuentes had produced originally for Lola Beltran in the fifties—a favorite recording of Ronstadt's. "Not *my* favorite," Fuentes admitted, laughing. He lauded Ronstadt's take, though, specifically complimenting her efforts in enunciation.

The resulting album, also called (with a nod to her aunt) *Canciones de mi Padre,* was a smash—surprising Ronstadt almost as much as the brass at Elektra/Asylum. The album, which would win a Grammy for Best Mexican American Performance, sold multimillions and eventually became the best-selling foreign language recording in US history.

Fuentes wasn't surprised: "I knew it was a hit." He called the album a "true jewel" and pointed with joy to several sonic touches: "For the first time," Fuentes declared, thanks to Kolakowski's and Puente's efforts, "a guitarron tuned!" He also praised the delicacy and precision of Shawn Murphy's mix: "The violins and trumpets placed

Canciones de mi Padre album cover.

at the right volume," he marveled, "without disturbing the voice." And what of Linda's voice? "I don't think that voice has ever been treated with so much taste," said Fuentes.

Ronstadt was excited to take *Canciones* on the road and began to plan an elaborate stage show, hoping to surpass the tour she had done with Riddle and his orchestra. Ira Koslow, who produced both touring shows, thinks what they attempted has yet to be appreciated: "With *Canciones*," he said, "this was a Broadway show! We had two trains, two moons, a boat, fog, six dancers, and thirteen mariachi." "AND doves"—Cathy Kerr laughed—"we had a dove wrangler. He would let them go from the soundboard, and one would land on her finger!" Trying to put on what was, essentially, a Broadway production in venues across America was no small feat, but Ronstadt had a vision, and Peter did his best to anticipate problems, keep things focused, and see to it that it was achieved.

And, just as in their early days, Peter waived his fees when fortunes turned. "At the beginning of the Mexican enterprise," Ronstadt remembered, "one of the major corporate sponsors that had promised—*promised* us—to be involved, backed out after we'd already started building our sets and stuff. It was really unprofessional and irresponsible and wrong of them. I mean, really shocking," she said, still irritated. "And we got left holding the bag. And he didn't take any commission for that until it started to recoup and it started to make money. He was always really good that way."

In 1987, a young duo called The Williams Brothers were recording their first album for Warner Brothers and needed a manager. Singer/songwriters Andrew and David, along with others at their label, thought Peter would more than fit the bill, so "we pursued him," Andrew remembered. "As we were recording our record, we were feeding them tracks. And, eventually, he said 'yes.'" Peter certainly saw some of the spirit of Peter and Gordon in the pair, not to mention The Everly Brothers: "The harmonies, the two guitars—I think he encouraged that approach," Andrew said. "He could relate."

"I didn't know who they were," Cathy Kerr, Peter's receptionist, recalled. Peter explained they were the nephews of recording and television star Andy Williams, had been performing together for over fifteen years, and were now signed to Warners. Peter handed Kerr their new album and said, "Listen to it. Let me know what you think."

"I went home that night like I had a homework assignment"—Kerr smiled—"took notes, and came back in going: 'I really like *this* song, and I like *this* song, and . . .' Really enthusiastic." Peter told her: "I'm going to give them to you—they'll be your clients. You're going to do their day-to-day stuff."

"I was honored and thrilled that he trusted me with that," Peter, Gloria, and Ira were there to help, but "I learned a lot," Kerr explained, "dealing directly with the record company and agents and doing everything I could for them—and asking a *lot* of questions along the way. When they had shows here *in town*," Kerr emphasized, as she was still the firm's receptionist and couldn't travel with the band, "I would be there for the soundcheck to make sure everything went right, and to collect the money." It was soon proven that Peter's trust was well founded, with Kerr becoming more and more confident in her abilities as time went on.

The year 1987 was also big for the singer known simply as Cher, due to her newly established acting career exploding with hits like *The Witches of Eastwick* and *Moonstruck* (for which she won the Academy Award for Best Actress). Along with her newfound film success came a new recording contract with Geffen Records. Most might assume this was due to Cher's continuing friendship with David Geffen (back in the seventies, they were involved in a two-year relationship), but the thanks go to A&R guru John Kalodner.

Like many American teenagers, after listening to The Beatles, "I really wanted to be involved in music," Kalodner said. "I wasn't a musician, so I had to figure out something else." After a stint as a critic for his local paper, Kalodner was hired as a talent scout for Atlantic Records in the seventies and jumped over to the newly formed Geffen Records label in the eighties.

After all her hits with former husband, Sonny Bono, and a good number on her own, Cher had not had a decent showing in the US charts in almost a decade. "Nobody wanted me," Cher recalled. Kalodner was sure he could turn her music fortunes around, though his team at Geffen were dubious—even, according to Cher, Geffen himself. But once she was under contract, "I immediately asked him to work with her," Kalodner said, referring to Peter. "I was so much in awe of him."

Peter then began a ritual that he repeated for each Geffen album in her three-album deal: He would go to Cher's house and sit with her, working out what key best suited her voice for each song she was to record. Kalodner had put the word out that he was looking for hard-rock material, and the songs that he chose ended up being, for the most part, produced by their respective composers—Jon Bon Jovi and Ritchie Sambora, Michael Bolton, and Desmond Child. The song "Dangerous Times," though, was up for grabs, and Peter decided to supervise that track himself—a metal cleanse, of sorts, something as far from mariachis as was aurally possible. The session was also notable for being the first of many Peter Asher productions to be both recorded and mixed by Frank Wolf.

Wolf had studied classical piano as a youngster, majoring in music at UCLA while playing in a band. The group booked studio time to record some demos, and as Wolf got his first look at the world of producers and engineers, he remembered thinking: "That's for me"—quickly switching majors to electrical engineering and acoustics. One class included a tour of the Village Recorder in West LA, where he impressed the studio head and chief of maintenance. "They invited me to come anytime," Wolf said, quickly adding: "I really took advantage of that!"

Once out of college, the Village hired Wolf, who practically lived there—troubleshooting technical problems. They allowed employees to use any open studio time for their own projects, and Wolf did just that—both recording and mixing his best friend's band, Maxus. Band member Robbie Buchanan, on his way to becoming a major studio musician of note, quickly recommended Wolf as engineer on other projects, and Wolf was soon working on sessions at George Massenburg's studio, The Complex. Massenburg heard some of Wolf's mixes and, suitably impressed, began using Wolf's mixing expertise for a couple of his own projects, including a handful of tracks on 10,000 Maniacs' *In My Tribe*.

Peter was also impressed and became Wolf's manager—a first for Peter to represent someone on the technical side of the business. But, again, no contract was drawn up. "And this is one of the things that I always respected so much about him," Wolf said. "He never insists on contracts or paper; if you make an agreement, you make an agreement. And if sometime later you decide that that's not working for you anymore, then you dissolve the agreement. And I just always thought that, in a world of people who are litigious and indecent and will do anything they can to promote themselves, Peter always, *always* was of the highest integrity.

"Working side by side with him for so many years," Wolf continued, "I'd, you know, hear him take phone calls, and some artist would say, 'Oh, I found this song that I just *love!*' And he would listen to it, and, literally, he would say, 'You know, I just don't hear it. I don't think it's a good song.' He'd hang up, and we'd talk about it for a minute. And he would say something like, 'I just find that I stay out of trouble by just telling the truth. And it may not be what they wanna hear, but I try to always tell the truth, because then nobody can say, '*Oh, but you said you loved it . . . !*'

"And it sounds more like a philosophy class than working with a producer," Wolf said, smiling as he continued to praise the former King's College philosophy major. "But it's really rung true for me for a lot of years."

Unlike his work with Ronstadt, who would mostly sing live as the musicians played, Peter would cut the music beds first and send those to Cher. "She's always done her homework," Peter pointed out. "She comes in, and she knows the song, and she sings it great—loud and Cher-ish and terrific." She might know the *words*, but that's different, Cher said, from knowing the *song*.

"I *do* try to be prepared, but I learn the song usually while I'm there," she said, clarifying: "I learn the *feeling* while I'm doing it.

"It's kind of like acting," she continued. "We would talk about it, you know? It's interesting how someone can suggest without telling you. They can give you word ideas. Like, a great director shouldn't *tell* you how to act at *all*—they should sit and talk with you and give you ideas that you don't realize are ideas. And that's how he would be," she said of Peter. "We would just talk, and then I would have a deeper understanding when I went to do it."

Another important team member during Cher's tenure at Geffen was Kalodner's assistant, Debra Shallman, who worked hard to keep the project organized. Observing Peter in action during the vocal tracking, "he was just amazing," Shallman marveled. "Just watching his rapport with the artist—being able to correct things in a way that was encouraging," she noted, "to get the best out of her."

There was usually more going on than just recording an album: "In the next room," Peter recalled, "there's the guy who's designing the perfume bottle to get approval, there's a costume fitting for a movie, there's the guy doing the fitness video to talk to her—I mean, all this shit she has going on! It's incredible! And she had it all really under control, you know?"

Kalodner would also be there—not up in the booth with Peter and Frank Wolf, but sitting feet away from Cher, without headphones, blissfully listening to her raw vocals. According to Wolf, Kalodner was "absolutely smitten" by Cher. He quickly clarified that he didn't mean that in a romantic way (though, really, who could blame him?), but totally in awe of *her*—her voice and mystique.

Peter recalled a typical back-and-forth with Cher, once a good vocal take was achieved: "I'd say, 'I think we've got the vocal. Do you want to hear it?' And she'd say, 'No, if you think it's fine. Is there anything you want me to sing?' I'd say, 'Yeah. There's two lines I need.' She'd say, 'Okay, just mark the two lines and I'll sing 'em.' She's all matter-of-fact." Shallman, though, was quick to emphasize that out of all the producers on the record, Peter "was the only one she was like that with. Honestly—she *totally* trusted Peter."

"I totally did. I love him," Cher said. "He understands how each artist needs to be treated. It's like, when I worked with Robert Altman," she added, mentioning the legendary filmmaker who directed her in *Come Back to the Five & Dime, Jimmy Dean, Jimmy Dean* along with Sandy Dennis, Karen Black, and Kathy Bates. "He had all these women, and he knew how to *treat each one*, and that's a special gift. And Peter," she concluded, "had that gift."

When it came time for the final mixes, she had a request: "At that point, she wanted the drums to be more heavy metal. She was hanging out with the heavy metal boys and liked those big, thundering drums," Peter recalled. "So, I would try to goose up the drums for her, and she'd be happy. So she always has very good, useful, and strong opinions, but she doesn't play that active a role in the making of the tracks." Peter smiled, adding: "God help you if you get it wrong, 'cause she'll make you do it again! But I love Cher, I love her sense of humor, I love her approach to life."

"Of the people that I've worked with, Peter," Cher confided, "is one of my favorites. He's also," she emphasized, "a favorite *person* because of his unbelievable humanity."

Despite all the doubters, Kalodner's instincts proved to be spot-on, as Cher's first release on Geffen, simply entitled *Cher*, went platinum and yielded a Top Ten single.

Don Bluth's follow-up to his animated hit *An American Tail* was *The Land Before Time*. Working once again with Steven Spielberg's Amblin Entertainment, the film depicted a group of young dinosaurs learning to set aside their prejudices and work together in order to survive. With the success of "Somewhere Out There" from the last film, no one had to be talked into the advantages of having a similar song attached to this new project. Composer James Horner, "really upset that HE didn't get to write the big tune" from the previous film, according to George Massenburg, "talked Spielberg into letting him write the song." Working closely with Barry Mann and lyricist Will Jennings, the trio crafted a ballad of resilience called "If We Hold on Together," which Ronstadt, once again, was asked to sing.

"Linda turned it down," Massenburg explained, "and Steven went to a number of other singers," with Anita Baker eventually coming onboard. David Foster, who'd had recent hits working with Chicago and Kenny Rogers, was asked to produce the song, but Baker's attempt was not deemed successful.

"Steven finally came back to Linda and *begged* her to do it, and she said, 'Okay, but *only* if . . .'" and proceeded to list a number of stipulations. "David did none of them," Massenburg quietly stated, and Ronstadt again demurred. Peter was then asked to step into the producer's role, and after bringing his A-Team of Russ Kunkel, Lee Sklar, and Waddy Wachtel to lay down the basic tracks, it was then time to record the lead vocal. Ultimately, this would be handled by none other than the legendary Diana Ross.

Peter confessed he had "heard all the scary stories and was full of trepidation." The former lead singer for The Supremes had garnered a reputation as a diva with a capital D. Peter had heard she could only be called "Miss Ross," and that he and engineer Frank Wolf should, under no circumstances, ever solo her vocal track—thereby letting her efforts stand naked without the instrumental accompaniment. "I'd known her socially forever, back from The Supremes days; we'd been on *Hullabaloo* together," Peter fondly recalled, "but I'd never worked with her, and I was quite nervous."

Peter remembered, after she'd laid down her vocals, he and Frank Wolf began to comp a vocal, using the best parts of various takes. Miss Ross left to let them do their work, returning after a while. "She came back in the studio and sat behind us, listening for about a half hour. We were fiddling about," Peter said, "and I felt her kind of stand up, and I went, 'Oh, shit,' you know. 'She's gonna say something. Here it is—here's the Diana Ross we've all heard about.' And she said: 'You know, you guys have been at this a long time. Can I get you some coffee or something?'

"And I went, 'Oh . . . okay.'" Peter laughed, remembering the relief. "So my experience with her has been nothing but positive. She's been amiable, friendly, helpful, and totally great."

When released as a single in January 1989, "If We Hold on Together" made the US Top Forty and barely missed the UK Top Ten. When released a year later in Japan (in conjunction with the film opening in the Far East), it shot to number-one, eventually selling a million copies. "The movie was a hit, the record was a hit, and then they made it a theme for a soap opera," Peter recalled. "It was the biggest-selling single in the history of Japan, or something crazy. I remember Diana and I talking about it—'What did we do here? We're gods in Japan!'"

In November 1988, just as *The Land Before Time* had its premiere, Peter began his next project with 10,000 Maniacs. The last album was, by now, a certified hit, and the band decided to flex their muscles. "One thing we wanted to do," bassist Steve Gustafson said, "was get Peter out of his element"—meaning Los Angeles—"and all its distractions." Consequently, the new album was recorded closer to the group's home turf in an old church out in the woods near Woodstock, New York.

"I definitely remember the cold"—engineer Frank Filipetti laughed, recalling the drafty old church in late autumn. Peter had recently recommended his friend to the manager of the band Foreigner, resulting in Filipetti engineering his first number-one record, "I Want to Know What Love Is." "He gave me my first experience in so many aspects of the business," Filipetti said of Peter. And *Blind Man's Zoo*, as this new 10,000 Maniacs album was eventually called, was no exception. "It was my first experience with digital," the engineer stated. Strictly an analog guy up to this point, Filipetti was not a big fan of digital multitracking, as the resultant recordings at this early stage could sound brittle if care was not taken. Peter was sold on the new technology, though, and Filipetti got a handle on all the 1s and 0s pretty quickly.

Singer Natalie Merchant, being the focal point of the band, was becoming a star in her own right, and this was beginning to cause some friction within the group. Disagreements between her and the rest of 10,000 Maniacs seemed to crop up with more frequency during the sessions. "There was a lot of arguing going on," Peter was quick to admit. "Natalie had some very definite opinions about what she wanted," according to Filipetti. "Another aspect to being a great producer is not being dogmatic. Obviously, I'm sure if he felt she was doing something destructive or wrong, he would say so." But Peter, Filipetti recalled, never once said: "No, do it *this* way." He was more apt to say: "I don't always have the best solution, and I'm confident enough in my abilities that I don't mind trying it your way."

Despite any tension amid the ranks, in comparison to *In My Tribe*, "*Blind Man's Zoo* was a lot more relaxed," keyboardist Dennis Drew maintained. This feeling was no doubt due to the more familiar, rustic surroundings—not to mention the complete absence of any interminable programming or sampling. And, as proof of the camaraderie that this casual atmosphere engendered, Drew exclaimed: "Peter would actually go out drinking with us!"

The songs laid down at Dreamland Recording Studios, as the deconsecrated church was now called, were again full of Merchant's stunning lyrics. They might

Blind Man's Zoo
album cover.

not be as teasingly vague as last time, but her choice of subject matter—religious radicalism, environmental disaster, wealth and poverty, wars and their aftermath, plus, of course, love and *its* aftermath—was all again wrapped in catchy melodies that continued the band's commercial climb. The song "Trouble Me" seemed inescapable on the FM dial through the summer of 1989, and the album itself, once again, went platinum.

Blind Man's Zoo, though, ended their collaboration. "I enjoyed working with them very much," Peter offered, and the band was honored to have him in their corner, if only for two albums: "He was our George Martin for a while," Steve Gustafson marveled. "How cool is that?"

Amazingly, during the sessions for *Blind Man's Zoo*, Peter would return to LA and turn his attention toward producing two other projects. The first was for Australian singer Peter Blakeley, who was attempting to break through to a wider audience. Blakeley had moved to Sydney in his teens, working his way through the Aussie music scene for a decade, "joining bands," Blakeley said, "and being kicked out of bands." He eventually signed to an indie label, but after a couple of promising singles, dealings with this label became, according to Blakeley, "a nightmare." With his recent demos in hand, he and his manager flew to Los Angeles to search for better prospects.

While shopping the demos around, getting interest from a handful of labels (eventually signing with Capitol Records), Peter heard them. Knocked out by Blakeley's soulful voice, he expressed an interest in producing some of the tracks. Blakeley was similarly knocked out by Peter: "He's the most unflappable character I've ever met. Nothing puts him in a state of confusion," Blakeley said admiringly. "Always wonderfully balanced!" Peter surrounded Blakeley in the studio with the cream of LA musicians—even Linda Ronstadt dropped by and sang harmony on the track "You Never Heard It from Me." "I was such a huge fan of Linda's as a youngster," Blakeley said, "so that was absolutely incredible." Though the resultant album, *Harry's Café de Wheels*, didn't break Blakeley in the States, it sold close to a million copies back in Australia. "I loved this record," Peter mused. "He's *so* good . . ."

So good that Peter used Blakeley as a backup singer on his *other* concurrent LA project: Cher's second Geffen release, *Heart of Stone*. Peter produced a trio of songs for the album, including the title track and the album closer, "After All." That ballad was cowritten by Tom Snow, whom Peter had first managed in the early seventies. Lately, Snow had become a songwriter of note: The Pointer Sisters' hit "He's So Shy," cowritten with Cynthia Weil, and "Let's Hear It for the Boy," used in the film *Footloose* and written in tandem with Dean Pitchford, were just two of many hits already on his résumé.

"After All" was composed by Snow and lyricist Pitchford specifically to be used in the romantic comedy *Chances Are*, and the movie's creative team decided they wanted the tune recorded as a heart-tugging duet. John Kalodner had convinced Cher to provide the song's feminine voice, but the director of the film "just didn't want me," Cher recalled, "and had to be talked into it." Even after agreeing, he later contacted Peter to try to replace Cher with Linda Ronstadt.

Peter Cetera—former lead singer for the massively popular rock band Chicago—eventually signed on to supply the male half of the equation. "Peter had to record them separately," Kalodner sighed, "in separate studios, on separate days." No one would ever realize this, of course, as the two voices intertwine so seamlessly. Kalodner was not surprised Peter would make it work: "That's how great a producer he is." The track was released as a single in February 1989 and made *Billboard*'s Top Ten. Cher's album *Heart of Stone*, released four months later, sold over three million copies in the United States alone and millions more overseas.

In March 1989, finished with his previous commitments, Peter immediately began the sessions for Linda Ronstadt's next album—her first collection of modern pop songs since *Get Closer* in 1982. She had told songwriter Jonathan Carroll that she was through making "records for kids," and, staying true to her word, she chose to record primarily gorgeous songs of grown-up longing and heartbreak. She had long ago threatened to put out an entire album of songs by Jimmy Webb (her favorite songwriter), and choosing four of his compositions for the sessions got her close to her goal. Old friend Karla Bonoff provided three solid and beautiful tunes. Peter was obviously a fan of Paul Carrack's seven-year-old album *Suburban Voodoo*, as he suggested Ronstadt cover two numbers off that LP, providing some upbeat spice.

But the heaviest dose of spice came from singer Aaron Neville—a man gifted with an angelic, soulful singing style. "One of the greatest voices of all time," according to Peter, though, he noted, inside an incongruous package: "Such an incredibly charming, thoughtful, intelligent, sweet man who *looks* like he's going to *kill you*." Neville had first come to the attention of the record-buying public in 1966 with his smash hit "Tell It Like It Is." Since 1977, he and three siblings had been performing as The Neville Brothers, becoming one of New Orleans's most acclaimed bands. Aaron had first met Linda in 1984, while she was touring with Nelson Riddle. "After her show, she came to see The Neville Brothers," Aaron recalled. "We were playing at Pete Fountain's club. Somebody told me she was in the audience, so I dedicated a song to her and called her up on stage to sing." This was something Ronstadt rarely did, but the chance to sing alongside the great Aaron Neville made her throw caution to the wind. "Later, she told the press that was the highlight of her tour," Neville recounted. "Felt like Cinderella at the ball!

"We got to talking backstage about maybe trying to get together and doing some recording," Neville recalled and, before long, Linda was sending him tapes of possible songs. It had taken a few years to get everyone's schedules aligned, but the time had finally arrived. "I was very excited to meet him," Peter confessed. Neville was similarly impressed with Peter and called him "a cool guy"—quite a compliment coming from one of the coolest guys in the business.

"He's a professional," Neville explained. "He knew what he wanted and knew how to say what he wanted and *get* what he wanted." Constantly, according to Neville, Peter was "coming up with ideas for the music and the harmonies." "We tried a lot of different songs," Peter remembered, with four duets making the final album. But the one that really stood out was a ballad entitled "Don't Know Much."

As with "After All," the last duet Peter produced, this was yet another song with a major contribution from Tom Snow. Its origins went back to the late seventies, when fellow songwriter Barry Mann came over to Snow's house one day and said: "Let's write a song!"

Sitting at the piano, Mann asked Snow, "D'ya have anything?" Snow recalled saying, "Yeah, well, I have this little jerky-sounding motif," and proceeded to play the chord progression that would eventually open the song and end each chorus. Mann, according to Snow, "went, 'Ooohh! I love that! I love that!' Then"—Snow smiled—"he went into his intense, talented genius mode and said, 'I wanna try something!'" The two of them went back and forth at the piano, eventually writing the melody that made up the verses and the song's hook, while Mann alone wrote the music for the bridge. Mann's wife, Cynthia Weil, made what Snow felt was the most important contribution: "For me, the song is so good, number one, because of Cynthia's lyrics. I think the lyric is better than the music." He laughed.

Mann recorded the song himself on his 1980 self-titled album, and both Bill Medley and Bette Midler covered it in the intervening years. Ronstadt had reached out to Steve Tyrell for song ideas for her upcoming sessions with Neville, and Tyrell pitched "Don't Know Much"—pushing the work of his client, Barry Mann, like a good manager should. Ronstadt remembered how much she liked Midler's version and said she definitely wanted to try it. Tyrell suggested that Ronstadt and Neville come to his studio on Sunset Boulevard and record a demo of it—that way he could use their rough duet to elicit more possibilities from songwriters and music publishers.

At this point, the song nearly got away from them: Film director Taylor Hackford heard the demo and felt it was perfect for his upcoming movie, *Everybody's All-American*. After being told the demo was just that—a demo—and unavailable, Hackford made plans to recut the track using Ann Wilson of the band Heart as vocalist. Fortunately, Barry Mann and Cynthia Weil took a chance and stood their ground, refusing to license the song, thereby making sure it stayed securely in Linda, Aaron, and Peter's hands.

Almost a year later, the album sessions finally got underway. As with "Somewhere Out There," Peter again agreed to share the production duties for "Don't Know Much" with Tyrell, who had already taken the pair through one recording of it, besides suggesting it in the first place. As the basic tracks were being cut, Linda and Aaron sang right along with the musicians—"face to face," Tyrell attested, unlike Cher and Cetera. "That's how they got that vibrato so tight." Neville, known for his improvised vocal flights, was going a bit overboard with them, according to Tyrell: "They were all over the place"—he laughed—"and I remember him doing one of those incredible licks and Peter looking over at me, saying, 'Who's gonna tell him?' I said, 'I'll tell him . . .'" Neville managed to pull back, saving one magnificent effort for the song's closing seconds.

The record was being recorded at George Lucas's Skywalker Ranch in northern California's Marin County. The recording studio was built specifically to record the grand scores that accompany modern movie blockbusters, and the large room's ambience would make this batch of songs as sonically powerful as possible. "That idea of big orchestral rock, and doing it *live*, was made possible by having a big room to work in," Massenburg attested. "There's nothing like the sound coming off a soundstage with sixty or eighty musicians. If the arrangement is there, if the song is there"—he shook his head—"it's thrilling. It's *transporting*." Among the final vocal and instrumental overdubs recorded at Skywalker, there was one memorable session for the Jimmy Webb–penned "Adios." A special guest drove up from Los Angeles to add classic Beach Boys–style background vocals to the ballad: Brian Wilson himself. Peter described the experience as "fascinating."

"Brian walks in," Massenburg said, "and starts talking to Peter about touring Hawaii with Peter and Gordon in the sixties: 'Hey, Peter, remember that time Jan'"—of Jan and Dean—"'put shaving cream in your socks?' He could remember that pretty clearly, but he couldn't remember where the washroom was. He kept asking," Massenburg said, shaking his head. "No short-term memory."

After requesting a specific number of tracks to begin stacking vocal parts, Wilson walked to the studio's microphone. "And he's doing the intro; he did a track. And Peter looked at Linda . . ."—and here Massenburg, with eyes widened and eyebrows raised, evoked Peter's directness: "We're fucked." Wilson's pitch seemed, at best, problematic. "And he did a second track in a *different voice* . . . and a third track . . ."

"He'd put down five vocal tracks of unison stuff," Ronstadt said in awe, "and the five tracks wouldn't all be *in tune*, even!" Wilson would repeat this for each note in the harmony, ending up with, say, twenty tracks of vocals. When he was finished and it was time to mix, Wilson would balance the tracks *just so*, and those few slightly off-pitch would, to Ronstadt's astonishment, "make a chorusing effect that would just broaden the whole pitch center and make everything sound like *cream!*"

The gorgeous arrangement of harmonies was totally improvised on the spot, but occasionally Wilson would have to stop and think for a minute. He'd go to the piano and play some old rock'n'roll number with no relation to the task at hand, suddenly stop, and having somehow worked out his harmonic problem, pick up recording where he'd left off. "His musical performance was extraordinary," Peter stated, noting: "He's crazy, but brilliant."

The album was released in October of 1989 with the title *Cry Like a Rainstorm—Howl Like the Wind*. Its title track, written by Ronstadt's old friend Eric Kaz, lived up to its name, as David Campbell's string arrangement swirled and The Oakland Interfaith Gospel Choir roared behind Ronstadt, whose voice was strong, bluesy, and totally in control. Another of the album's highlights was Ronstadt's rendition of "I Keep It Hid." Written by Jimmy Webb back in 1967, and featuring Webb on piano, the verses have a Burt Bacharach–ian feel with a slow waltz shuffle that, on the chorus, suddenly switches to a straightforward beat while Ronstadt wails and whispers of

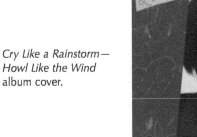

*Cry Like a Rainstorm—
Howl Like the Wind*
album cover.

the torch she still carries. It's a great performance—as is "When Something Is Wrong with My Baby," a song Neville suggested. He and Ronstadt are simply dynamite, their duet underpinned by big, soulful brass courtesy of The Tower of Power Horns.

Years later, in her memoir *Simple Dreams*, Ronstadt called this album with Peter's production efforts "our best collaboration." The record-buying public seemed to agree, as the album sold three million copies in the United States alone, staying on the *Billboard* charts for a year. "Don't Know Much" was a number-one smash, and a second duet, "All My Life," was also a hit. Not surprisingly, this reignited Aaron Neville's solo career. "It not only opened doors; as a matter of fact," Neville quipped, "it kicked doors down!"

Neville thought "Don't Know Much" was special from the beginning and felt certain upon hearing the final playback: "When we finished it, I remember telling Linda, 'Meet you at the Grammys.'" He was right; on February 21, 1990, the song earned the pair a Grammy Award for Best Pop Vocal Performance—Duo. That same evening, all of Peter's good work—for 10,000 Maniacs, Diana Ross, Cher, and, especially, Linda Ronstadt and Aaron Neville—did not go unnoticed by the Recording Academy. Lou Reed walked to center stage, opened an envelope, and announced that the Grammy Award for Producer of the Year would go, yet again, to Peter Asher.

22

MYSTERIOUS WAYS

It would be two years before Peter produced another album in its entirety. Record labels, in many cases, were beginning to hedge their bets—three or four or more producers working on different tracks for the same release, all in hopes of capturing that elusive "hit," was becoming the norm, and over the next few years, that's mostly the way Peter worked. He certainly kept busy: Asher/Krost was continuing to take on new clients, and Peter would offer his expertise—providing career management, of course, but also lending a hand when those clients were in the studio.

Or sometimes Peter would simply help out old friends—such was the case with star Sarah Brightman, who had shot to fame in the stage musical *The Phantom of the Opera*. "I'd met her already because I knew Andrew," Peter said, referring to composer Andrew Lloyd Webber, then Brightman's husband. Peter and Andrew were classmates together at Westminster and kept in touch over the years as Peter conquered the pop charts and Andrew did the same on Broadway. Brightman, a classically trained soprano, was attempting a modern pop album, to be called *As I Came of Age*, with production by Val Garay, Peter's former right-hand man in the studio.

The latest Webber musical to open on London's West End was *Aspects of Love*, which included the number "Love Changes Everything." "We decided that could be a hit," said Peter, who then worked up an arrangement of the song and coproduced the track with Garay. "It didn't succeed," he wistfully admitted, but he had nothing but praise for Brightman: "She was great—very nice, very together, very professional." Not always the case with every singer.

Over at Geffen Records, John Kalodner was working as music supervisor on the film *Days of Thunder*, starring Tom Cruise. Along with other Geffen artists, Kalodner was keen to add Maria McKee to the soundtrack. After one album under her own name, the former lead singer of LA's roots-rock outfit Lone Justice was struggling to establish herself as a solo performer in the States. Kalodner thought the song "Show

Me Heaven" could be the breakout hit from the movie and called on Peter to produce the track for McKee.

"There's very few people I would ever say were difficult. *Amazing* singer," Peter
quickly added, "but I found her difficult." He thought it possible that, rather than
being able to use a more familiar production team, perhaps McKee perceived Peter
as being foisted upon her by Kalodner. "I'm usually able to recover from that," Peter
mused, "but I don't think I did." Getting down to business, Peter programmed an
African-esque rhythm bed for the song, but despite his efforts, "she was not happy
with what I wanted to do," Peter admitted, "and didn't seem to have a clear picture
of what *she* wanted to do. We ended up communicating through third parties . . ."

One of these "third parties" was Robbie Buchanan, a pianist/composer/arranger
who had first worked with Peter on the Sarah Brightman session. A professional
musician since the ripe old age of twelve, Buchanan was an exquisite player on whom
artists and producers could count—for his broad knowledge of music, his clever
ideas, and his improvisational skills. He also worked fast: Peter "booked me for a
day," Buchanan recalled, to musically mediate with McKee.

Buchanan built an atmospheric bed of synths over Peter's undulating rhythm.
Once the mood is established, McKee begins—quietly describing, in her lower register, a cautious desire. As the chorus hits, she belts out the demand of the song's title
with her voice breaking here, sighing there. The track rises, falls and rises again, with
Peter later adding such sonic touches as baritone guitar and mandolin.

It was a solid effort. But when "Show Me Heaven" was released as a single in the
States, it was met with indifference. In the UK, by contrast, it was a smash—staying
at number-one for a month. McKee, though, refused to sing it in her live shows for
years. "Eventually, when you act like that"—Kalodner shrugged—"people start not
doing favors for you and not paying attention to you." After delivering two more
albums, both critically acclaimed, Geffen did not renew her contract.

Kalodner soon asked Peter to produce a couple of tracks for another film, *Mer-
maids*, starring Cher and Winona Ryder. "When John asks me to do something"—
Peter smiled—"I do it." The film takes place in the early sixties, and Kalodner, as
music supervisor, chose a selection of hits from that era to accompany the story. He
also picked a couple for Cher to rerecord for the movie, including a remake of "The
Shoop Shoop Song (It's in His Kiss)." Kalodner admitted choosing it "because it was
an old favorite from when I was growing up."

Originally a number-one R&B hit in 1964 for Betty Everett (whose previous
single was "You're No Good"), it was also a favorite of Linda Ronstadt's—she and
Peter almost recorded a version ten years earlier. Now let loose on the song, Peter
arranged and produced a solid track, adding a nineties rock sheen to its inherent
girl-group vibe. Cher, as usual, recorded her vocals last. "She'd sing for two hours,"
Kalodner remembered, "and that would be it—the song would be great. She's just
uniquely talented."

Neither the movie nor "The Shoop Shoop Song" were big hits in the States.
"*Nothing* here," Peter frowned. But overseas, it was a different story: "It was a huge

hit in England," Peter proudly proclaimed, staying at number-one for five weeks and a smash all across Europe and Australia. Cher still proudly sings it onstage, calling the record "one of my favorites."

"Show Me Heaven" and "The Shoop Shoop Song," both chart-toppers, were notable for another reason: It was the beginning of a long-lasting working relationship with engineer Nathaniel Kunkel—someone Peter had known since his birth in 1970. The son of drummer Russ Kunkel, whom Peter had put in charge of supplying the rhythmic backbone for hundreds of his sessions over the years, and singer Leah Kunkel, sister to Mama Cass Elliot and blessed with a comparable voice, Nathaniel had grown up surrounded by music makers of the highest caliber, and it showed: "Nathaniel's a very good drummer," his father proudly boasted. "He also plays piano, guitar, and he's a very good singer!"

Nathaniel not only grew up around Peter but was a fan of his work: "I remember listening to *In My Tribe* in school," he enthused, "and thinking '*Oh my God!*' It was so *bitchin'*!" Already intrigued by the recording process, fourteen-year-old Nathaniel began accompanying his father to various sessions engineered by George Massenburg. After being kicked out of school "for smoking pot on a ski trip," according to Massenburg, he convinced his mother he should skip college and get a job in a recording studio.

Young Kunkel managed to land the plum position of assistant engineer with Massenburg—"The only person that George ever took on," Father Russ is quick to point out. "George," Nathaniel insisted, "really gave me the ability to *learn*." Massenburg smiled at this, adding: "I call him my godson." Working alongside both Massenburg and Frank Wolf for years, Kunkel's assistant engineer credit appeared more and more frequently on Peter Asher productions as the young man learned the ropes.

As the new decade began, Asher/Krost Management was continuing to look for ways to intertwine music with other artistic endeavors. Barry Krost was able to convince Joni Mitchell to allow a creative team to put together a theatrical evening highlighting her poetic and richly musical compositions. Searching for the right creative team, Krost approached his friend, stage director David Schweizer, who immediately signed on. Schweizer asked writer Henry Edwards, a friend and former pop music critic for the *New York Times*, to help come up with a working script.

The show featured five performers on a journey, creatively presenting two dozen of Mitchell's works—"totally without dialogue," Schweizer said, "so the arrangements of the songs made a kind of emotional sense." The lyrics sung in the first act were full of life's possibilities, while the second act "was a little more sophisticated and jaded," Schweizer said, calling the staging "kind of poetic abstraction."

Presented at The Los Angeles Theatre Center at the end of 1990, *The Joni Mitchell Project* was certainly not a new concept—back in the sixties, *Jacques Brel Is Alive and Well and Living in Paris* was a similar theatrical experience—but the *Mitchell Project* predated by five years *Smokey Joe's Café*, a show so massively successful it brought forth the torrent of "jukebox musicals" that continues today on legitimate stages everywhere. Unfortunately, "I think we were just a *fraction* too early," Barry Krost admitted. Despite good reviews, *The Joni Mitchell Project* closed after only three months and has not been revived.

Asher/Krost Management was formed to be a haven where artists from music, film, television, and theater could combine disciplines. But after a little over five years into the partnership, the two old friends decided to go their separate ways. "Did we actually find the great cross-alliance of films and television and music?" Peter asked, adding parenthetically, "which has happened a bit more, of course, now that television makes such continual use of pop songs." He finally answered, "No, it didn't accomplish everything we intended." "The timing wasn't right," Krost stated, and shrugged. "We tried . . . or maybe it was *us*, you know?" Barry Krost went on to success as a movie producer with the Tina Turner biopic, *What's Love Got to Do with It*. He still speaks highly of his former partner, talking in terms every media mogul can understand: "If I think of the music business, there are two people whom I trust implicitly with my checkbook: Jerry Moss"—the cofounder of A&M Records—"and Peter Asher."

Four years after Peter Asher Management welcomed The Williams Brothers as clients, their sophomore effort for Warners got underway. Producer David Kershenbaum had mostly overseen these new sessions, but after basically finishing the record, the brothers were still coming up with material, and they played their new demo of "People Are People" for Peter. He was intrigued by the song and suggested an approach: "He liked the idea of taking something acoustic but making it a little bit more modern," Andrew Williams recalled, so, as with "Show Me Heaven," Peter started out by programming a rhythm for the song. "At that time, it wasn't quite as easy or as universal as it is now," Williams explained regarding the seemingly ancient programming technology Peter was then utilizing, but when he finished, "he knew every bar and beat of that song. The precision with which he thinks is the precision with which he produces."

"People Are People" posits that, underneath our superficial differences, we're all the same—something we, unfortunately, need to be reminded of on a regular basis. The last track recorded, it became the first cut on the new album, simply entitled *The Williams Brothers*. Adult Contemporary radio began playing a few of the album's tracks, but the boys didn't want to undertake the usual club tour. Cathy Kerr suggested to Peter that, with all the coffeehouses cropping up everywhere, perhaps the brothers could tour these newly hip establishments with nothing but their acoustic guitars—just as Peter and Gordon had back when they would play bars for beer and sandwiches. Peter thought it was a great idea, and it *was* eerily similar at first: "There was no money in it," Kerr laughed. "They played for coffee." But soon, due to Kerr's dogged promotion skills, "everywhere," she marveled, "it was sold out and they started getting paid. It was really successful." Eventually, record labels began calling her, asking: "Can we get your databases on the coffeehouses?"

The Williams Brothers stayed with Peter Asher Management for almost eight years, until the two young men dissolved their partnership. "It just sorta ran its course,"

Andrew said. "It felt more important for us to be brothers than battling collaborators." David soon exited the music industry, but Andrew continued behind the scenes. "Peter was definitely an influence," admitted Andrew, who went on to produce the critically acclaimed album *Fight Songs* for the band Old 97's, among many other projects. He and Peter still stay in touch: "He's been a great ear and very supportive."

While the brothers were playing the coffeehouses of LA, Peter was scheduled to record a track for the movie *The Butcher's Wife*, starring a clairvoyant Demi Moore, but there was a last-minute snag: "I was in LA," British singer Julia Fordham recalled, "and I got a phone call from the record company saying that Linda Ronstadt was supposed to sing a song for this film, but something had come up and she couldn't do it. Could I do it, like, *tomorrow?*"

Fordham had released only two albums at this point but was garnering both critical raves and a fervent following for her smoky voice and her poetic tales of relationships. Comparisons were being made to the work of Joni Mitchell, which Fordham didn't mind: "She is my number-one favorite iconic singer in the universe," Fordham unabashedly admitted. Soon, Peter phoned her, asking, "Do you want to do it?" Fordham was totally taken by his charm, sense of humor, and straightforwardness. "He made a little joke: 'Well, don't think you're, like, the second choice, but basically you are!'" To ensure she wouldn't refuse, Peter offered to assemble her dream band: "Is there anyone you've ever wanted to work with?" Fordham had already met bassist Larry Klein, hoping one day to record with him. She asked if that might be possible, and Peter immediately said, "Yes!" Fordham then asked for drummer Vinnie Colaiuta, and Peter responded, "I think we can do that. In fact, that's rather easy!"

A messenger soon arrived at Fordham's door with a demo of "(Love Moves In) Mysterious Ways." The songwriting team of Tom Snow and Dean Pitchford, who were also responsible for the Peter Cetera/Cher duet "After All," composed the piece. "It was unusual for me to do a song that I didn't write," Fordham explained, as each track on her two albums came from her own pen. Luckily, the ballad was "very good," Fordham thought, with interesting chord changes throughout.

She then "trotted off" to Peter Asher Management to chat and work out what key would best suit her. "I was ushered into his office," Fordham recalled, "and he was talking on the phone, sounding quite brilliant." While taking care of an important long-distance business issue, he smiled and gestured for her to have a seat. "And then Joni Mitchell walks in"—Fordham laughed—"and I'm trying to get my jaw to come back up to my lips." Mitchell wanted Peter to stop everything and give her feedback on a video project she was working on. Peter immediately switched gears over to artist manager: "I was impressed how he went from a pretty serious phone call," she observed, "to effortlessly taking her artistic tizzy onboard."

After tactfully explaining to Mitchell that he would watch the footage later because, without her presence, he could better formulate an unbiased opinion, Mitchell left in a cloud of smoke: "She was smoking like a chimney," Fordham noted, adding, "Even smoking looks good on Joni." Then Peter announced: "Alright, moving on!"

"A heartbeat later," Fordham continued, "he's got his producer's hat on. So he had three invisible hat changes in the time I was there!

"I told him that one of my concerns was I had to make it *mine*," Fordham said, and Peter, always interested in an artist's input, asked, "How do you think we might do that?" She came up with the answer at the recording session the following day: "More percussion," she suggested—"ethnic-sounding," more specifically— "something similar to what I'd done before to tie it in to my pack of songs." Fordham asked about adding an *udu* to the track—a large clay vessel, or pot, originating from Nigeria and played by hand. "I like that idea." Peter smiled. "I like that idea a lot!"

The udu, played by master percussionist Michael Fisher, is the first sound we hear in the finished mix, as Peter and engineer Frank Wolf slowly add each successive instrument—electronic beats, synthesizer, piano, bass—around Fordham's understated vocal. As she sings of unraveling love's mystery, the musicians and background singers weave their spell—much as Demi Moore's character does onscreen. The verses seem to float—almost like a mirage—and the choruses shimmer as love appears, like magic, out of nowhere.

It also appeared on Fordham's album out of nowhere. *Swept*, her third LP, had just been released when she recorded "(Love Moves In) Mysterious Ways," but after the track climbed into the UK Top 20, Virgin had the song inserted on all future copies. "I've had such success with it," Fordham admitted, and though she and Peter both were happy with the results, they parted ways on the merits of the movie for which it was done: "It was such a lovely film," she gushed, whereas Peter opined: "Terrible movie."

Fordham was especially pleased to work with Peter: "I think he's truly a fascinating individual," the singer stated. "He has a pretty high mischief factor"—she laughed— "and I do, too! But there's something about him that's *peculiar* in that English way; he's the 'charming eccentric,' but there's nothing flippant about him 'cause he has a real *weight* to him, he really does.

"The man delivers!"

After *Cry Like a Rainstorm—Howl Like the Wind*, Linda Ronstadt recorded a second album of Spanish language songs in 1991, *Mas Canciones*—this time, though, without Peter's involvement. But Peter did produce two numbers that year with his "favorite girl singer" for the motion picture *The Mambo Kings*, starring Armand Assante and Antonio Banderas as two Cuban brothers struggling to keep their musical dreams alive in 1950s New York. One of the film's music consultants was native New Yorker Ray Santos, who arranged the songs "Quiereme Mucho" and "Perfidia" for Ronstadt—both cut at Skywalker Sound. "That's where I met Peter Asher," Santos said, calling him "a very knowledgeable producer."

"He was making suggestions all the time: 'Why don't we do this and that' . . ." Santos was then unfamiliar with Peter's extensive music background and was surprised: "They were very musically valid suggestions, so naturally I went along with them!" Ronstadt sang impressively, holding the ending note of "Quiereme Mucho," for example, over a dozen seconds. "I commented to Peter, 'Wow! That's right on the money!' That note"—he laughed—"can't be truer than *that!*"

Ronstadt was thrilled and inspired with the sessions, suggesting to Santos that she'd like to attempt an entire album of Latin Jazz compositions. "She approached me at the end of the session," Santos remembered, "saying, 'I'll be in touch with you!'" These first results of Peter and Linda's collaboration with Santos were later released on *The Mambo Kings—Original Motion Picture Soundtrack*, with Ronstadt fitting right alongside such Latin music legends as Tito Puente and Celia Cruz. The movie might have left most audiences cold, but the soundtrack compilation was most assuredly hot.

Peter spent the rest of the year producing a smattering of tracks for various albums—four of which were new efforts from iconic artists who had come to prominence back when Peter and Gordon were first touring the States. He began with four tracks for Cher's third album for Geffen, *Love Hurts*. Released in June 1991, the album was yet another smash in the UK, hitting number-one and selling over three million copies. "I like that album a lot," Cher commented. One of Peter's efforts, "Could've Been You," made it into the UK's Top Forty when released as a single eight months later. A kiss-off to a lover who's skedaddled, the fun track was tough with a determined vocal from Cher and a wailing lead guitar break from Toto's Steve Lukather, yet still pop-rock sweet with a layer of background vocal support from Andrew Gold, Kenny Edwards, and Peter himself—just like in the old Ronstadt days.

Peter had programmed a rhythm track for each of his four songs, layering the other instruments on top. Then, wanting to experiment a bit, Peter and engineer George Massenburg brought drummer extraordinaire Jeff Pocaro into Skywalker Sound's big room, overdubbing live drums onto the tracks while his kit was surrounded by baffles known as Quadratic Residue Diffusers. "It blasts this incredibly diffuse sound into a room and makes it bigger," Massenburg explained about the panels his labs build. "George loves blinding people with science—he really does." Peter smiled. "But the drums *do* sound great."

This method, it turned out, worked best for the snare, toms, and kickdrum, but all the cymbals had to be recorded separately *without* the Diffusers on a second pass! A difficult job for any drummer, Massenburg agreed, but added: "Jeffery is probably the only kind of musician who can make that sound like it was one pass.

"And Peter had the *vision* to say, 'Let's go for it'—even though there was a considerable risk in it not really feeling right—AND the *imagination*"—he laughed—"of how to get out of it if it failed!

"Peter's very smart," Massenburg concluded. "He has as scientific an approach as could possibly be brought to music—without losing the art."

Two months after *Love Hurts* hit the shops, Columbia Records released *Lovescape*, singer/songwriter Neil Diamond's nineteenth studio album, with Peter's production gracing two tracks. "Brilliant guy," Peter said of his friend. "Still underrated in this country as a songwriter and an icon. He gets rediscovered every now and then—when 'Girl (You'll Be a Woman Soon)' is in *Pulp Fiction*, or they use 'I'm a Believer' in *Shrek*, or when UB40 does 'Red Red Wine.' There's always people who'll go: '*That's* a Neil Diamond song? Wow—I didn't think I liked Neil Diamond!'" Peter shook his head. "So many of those great classic rock'n'roll songs were all his . . .

"So, he's got this remarkable thing of being a figure of fun almost, in some re-spects—as if he were sort of Englebert Humperdinck or someone. But actually, he's got this deep rock'n'roll credibility; to the point where Bono and all kinds of people idolize him as one of the great American writers and icons of rock'n'roll, which he is. And he is also one of *the* nicest guys—my wife and I are both immensely fond of him. And, you know, I was actually thinking of calling him," Peter said, reaching over to make a note. "Having Neil Diamond to dinner is a wholly positive and fun experience!"

Despite Diamond's "rock'n'roll credibility," *Lovescape* is decidedly in the soft-rock category, with only a few songs liable to cause a toe to tap. One of Peter's two efforts, for example, is the emotional Bernstein/Sondheim duet from *West Side Story*, "One Hand, One Heart." Though it veers toward the overly dramatic near the song's end, Diamond put his former acting chops to use, genuinely and gracefully delivering the sentiment of two becoming one. Even if the listener's opinion of Diamond is decid-edly Humperdinck-ish, one can't help but be moved.

Next, due to the success of their collaboration on "If We Hold on Together," Pe-ter was asked to produce tracks for Diana Ross's upcoming album—her second for Motown since returning to the label that made her a star. Ultimately, Peter produced half of the record, released near the end of 1991 as *The Force Behind the Power*. He dipped back into the Paul Carrack catalog for "Battlefield," producing a track that mirrors Miss Ross's early days; once the chorus hits, a stomping beat with vocal ac-cents from Kate Markowitz and Valerie Carter seems to bring The Supremes twenty-five years into the future—plus featuring Peter on tambourine, an instrument some-what forgotten in its importance to the "Motown Sound." Peter participated further on "When You Tell Me That You Love Me," strengthening Markowitz and Carter's harmonies by adding his own, plus programmed the drumbeats that are the founda-tion for "One Shining Moment." Those last two tracks were both UK Top Ten hits, helping to push the album past one million in sales.

Miss Ross certainly did her job—caressing each love song with sweetness and longing, all in her inimitable style—but the label didn't always do theirs. "We cut the tracks," engineer Frank Wolf recalled, "and as Peter always did, we would make rough mixes." This was back in the day when everyone had a cassette player nearby, so these roughs would go on a cassette, accompanied by a note explaining, for exam-ple, that next week the guitar and keyboard overdubs would be added. The tape and note were sent to the office of Jheryl Busby, president and CEO of Motown Records. Each week, with every major addition to the tracks, another rough mix with writ-ten explanations would be made and sent on. "Finally, Diana had requested that we get a male singer to sing mockup vocals so she could study the melodies but not be influenced by a female singer," Wolf said, "so we got a high-pitched male singer who sang pretty much just the melody as it was written. And then we turned *those* in."

Now, with four or five sets of cassettes passed on to the powers-that-be, Peter, Frank Wolf, and arranger David Campbell were preparing to fly to London and record the orchestral overdubs. Sitting with Wolf, going through notes for the trip, Peter got a phone call from Cathy Kerr back at the office: "Jheryl just called and said: 'Cancel your trip—call him at his office.'" Peter tried, but was told by Busby's assistant, "He's not available." "That was it," Wolf shrugged. "He had to cancel the trip."

They later found out that Busby, according to Wolf, "had finally picked up a cassette, and he'd listened to *the very first one*—which just had skeletal tracks on it—and concluded, 'You guys are not ready to do orchestra.'" Brett Swain, who at the time was an assistant engineer at The Complex, where some of the Ross sessions were recorded, remembered Frank Wolf showing him the letter that Peter fired off to Busby the day after the cancellation: "*The* most *eloquent* letter of 'What-the-fuck-are-you-doing' that I've ever seen in my life," Swain laughed. "I mean, it really kind of dressed him down, but it was a *beautiful* letter—you didn't know you just got chewed out!"

"Peter can really write these *horrible* letters," his wife, Wendy, enthused, "but they're polite! They're awful, but they're *so good*." She eagerly takes advantage of her husband's singular talent: "Sometimes, when I'm really angry at someone, I'll have him write the letter. And he can be really rude in an English way that's *so* mean, and it's *so* great. And he'll go, 'Maybe I shouldn't go that far,' and I'll go, 'No, no, no—that's *exactly* what I want!'"

The scoring session was rescheduled, and the mix-up ultimately only cost them a day, but the damage was done. Regarding Motown, "Peter," according to Wolf, "never worked with them again."

On September 9, 1991, Peter was at Conway Studios in Hollywood, and for the first time since Mortimer's "On Our Way Home," he was producing a brand-new song written by his old housemate, Paul McCartney. To make it even more of a British Invasion reunion, the artist performing the song was Ringo Starr.

By the end of the 1980s, "Ringo was in a really bad place, career-wise," Peter's friend Ken Mansfield stated. "He had gone through the drug thing and cleaned up, but his career was really in the toilet." Mansfield, the US manager for Apple Records (that's him in the white coat sitting near Yoko during The Beatles' rooftop concert) was excited to see that Ringo had recently gone back on the road with his initial All Starr Band concept and felt that a solid album was the next step in rejuvenating his old friend's musical reputation.

Mansfield contacted Ringo, saying: "I have this idea for an album. What are you doin'?" Ringo replied, "I'm totally free—I'm totally between all contracts, and I can do whatever I want to do." Mansfield had coproduced the number-one country smash "I'm Not Lisa" for Jessi Colter in 1975 and continued to have good contacts within the industry. He decided to present this rare opportunity to Private Music—"a small, classy label, so Ringo could have proper representation and people he'd relate to," Mansfield explained, "but distributed by BMG, so basically a major label." Private Music had been primarily known for its roster of "new age" artists, but Mansfield knew it was now looking to expand into the rock and pop markets.

Mansfield met with the label's owner, Peter Baumann—once a member of electronic music pioneers Tangerine Dream. Finally getting down to the crux of the negotiations, Baumann inquired, "What is Ringo asking?" Mansfield intoned: "You're talking about signing one of the three most famous musicians in history" (the other two being McCartney and Harrison, who was still very much alive at that point). "And he just looked at me," Mansfield remembered, and after a long pause, Baumann said: "This is gonna cost me." Laughing, Mansfield added: "And it did."

For this new album, his first in almost a decade, Ringo chose four producers to work with: Jeff Lynne, Phil Ramone, Don Was, and Peter Asher. According to engineer Frank Wolf, who worked alongside Peter, Ringo "was great to work with—really fun." Assistant engineer Brett Swain remarked that the sessions at Conway Studios were "absolutely incredible," calling Ringo "one of the *sweetest* guys.

"I think he still had the same hi-hat and cymbals that he had on *The Ed Sullivan Show*," Swain marveled, "and they were just the dirtiest, grungiest-looking cymbals you'd ever seen." But when it comes to drumming, it's not about having the newest and shiniest gear; it's about feel. Ringo always provides a solid foundation, but at the same time he adds a sensitivity and soulfulness to his playing. Bassist Bob Glaub, who also took part in Peter's sessions for Ringo, had a one-word description for observing a master at work: "Unreal!"

Any rock musician growing up in the sixties took the music The Beatles made and internalized it, fusing it with their DNA. And the way the group *looked* making those sounds was just as unforgettable: "You know, Ringo has that very distinctive back-and-forth hi-hat technique," Glaub explained. "It doesn't seem as much up-and-down as other drummers." While recording, Glaub was playing bass across from guitarist Waddy Wachtel as Ringo drummed away, swishing his stick in rhythm. "I was right next to Ringo, and I saw that . . . and I looked at Waddy and both of our jaws"—he laughed—"you could have scooped 'em off the ground!" He and his fellow musicians were "in heaven," he said. "I had to pinch myself: I was playin' with *Ringo!*"

Andrew Gold, also on the sessions, wasn't merely in heaven—he had achieved nirvana. Glaub described him as "probably the biggest Beatle aficionado I've ever met." Gold, Glaub claimed, could play every note and sing every harmony part from every Beatles record. At one point the musicians took a break, sitting in Conway's lush outdoor patio. Two years before comic actor Chris Farley's clueless questioning of Paul McCartney on *Saturday Night Live*, Gold just had to ask: "Hey, what was it like being in The Beatles? Was it really great?"

According to Glaub, who said he practically spit out his drink upon hearing the question, "Ringo just looked at him and said, 'Yeah—it was fuckin' amazing.' He didn't say 'you idiot,' but he gave a *look* . . ." Glaub laughed and defended his Starrstruck friend: "Andrew was just so excited in the moment. It could have easily been *me* . . ."

Gold also had the thrill of hearing Starr record a version of "Thank You for Being a Friend," Gold's Top Forty hit from 1978 and later used as the theme for the hit sitcom *The Golden Girls*. Unfortunately, it ended up not making the album, released the following year with the title *Time Takes Time*. But Gold was in good company: The McCartney number "Angel in Disguise," which Peter said he "loved" and to which Ringo added some original lyrics, didn't make the final cut, either. "You need some *real* motivation to take a new Paul McCartney song OFF a Ringo album," said Peter, still puzzled, "but *somebody* did."

With Peter's track record as a hitmaker and considering his history and friendship with McCartney—obviously someone who also enjoys making hit records—why haven't they ever worked together in the post-Apple years? "He never asked me," was Peter's simple reply.

"When we run into each other, it's always embraces and friendship and stuff," he noted, "but then we tend not to see a lot of each other—maybe because I've been too busy, maybe 'cause he's been too busy . . ." But as far as producing Paul, "No, it hasn't come up."

Peter was quick to point out: "I remain a huge fan, of course, as does the entire world. He's brilliant."

Amid his already full schedule, Peter found time to squeeze in another favor for John Kalodner. The Geffen Records *wunderkind* had signed Olivia Newton-John in hopes of reviving *her* singing career—and, just as with signing Cher, Kalodner said the idea had no real internal support from his label. Newton-John was to record four

Backstage, Peter observes Paul McCartney warming up as Lindas McCartney and Ronstadt converse. © *1976 MPL Communications / Photographer Robert Ellis. All rights reserved*

new tracks to lead off a greatest hits compilation—both a reminder of past triumphs and a reintroduction of a still vital talent. Peter took on the task of producing a version of Brenda Lee's chart-topping 1960 hit "I Want to Be Wanted," building an irresistible romantic pop confection in the process. David Campbell's string arrangement and Jay Dee Maness's pedal steel guitar swirl together to lushly support Newton-John's vocal—breathy, vulnerable, and incredibly sexy.

"She was *really* sweet," Frank Wolf recalled, "wanted to work hard, was not pretentious. Again, with Peter, virtually everyone we worked with—no pretentiousness at all! And I don't know whether it's his demeanor that disarms them or what, but he's really respectful of the artist. He's not 'kissing their ass,' but he's respectful. And the consequence is that—and I've always seen it with him—you get that respect back."

Unfortunately, Newton-John's comeback plans were soon derailed by a breast cancer diagnosis, and rather than promote the album, entitled *Back to Basics: The Essential Collection*, she wisely put her energies into fighting the disease—successfully, it should be noted.

Peter proceeded to produce or coproduce three full albums in 1992, each as musically different from the others as possible. Linda Ronstadt's work for the film *The Mambo Kings* had whetted her musical appetite, and she wanted her next album to be a feast of mambo and salsa tunes. Only a month after working with Ray Santos on those first two tracks, she and Peter met with Santos again and began choosing song possibilities for what would comprise her next release. "I brought along a whole bunch of recordings and sheet music for her to refer to," Santos said, "and we decided on the tunes we were gonna do." As Santos finished up the arrangements, musicians were booked for the sessions, to be done, once again, at Skywalker Sound.

But three days before recording was to begin, John Brenes received a call from Janet Stark, Ronstadt's personal assistant: "John, Linda's gonna cancel the session." Brenes was introduced to Ronstadt via Aaron Neville, and the two had become close friends through their mutual love of music and almost encyclopedic knowledge of songs. It seemed, Stark explained, despite all the preplanning, Ronstadt was beginning to fall out of love with many of the tunes she and Santos had agreed upon.

"'I want you to do something,'" Brenes remembered Stark saying: "'*Find some songs!*'" She had asked the right man; music had always been Brenes's passion, and for over sixteen years he'd owned The Music Coop, the coolest record shop in Petaluma, California. But more importantly, blessed with Costa Rican and Panamanian parents, he had grown up listening to Latin Jazz and Afro-Cuban music and knew what tracks might appeal most to Ronstadt for this project. Brenes still had a couple of his parents' old Toña la Negra records, and they were the first to go into the pile to play for Ronstadt. He recalled, "I listened to records for, like, seven hours!"

Armed with over twenty-five song possibilities, he called Ronstadt the next morning, saying: "I'm coming over, and I'm not leaving until we have a record." By midnight, Ronstadt had chosen seven songs from Brenes's trove and finally felt secure—the sessions, only forty-eight hours away, were back on track. George Massenburg stated emphatically: "John saved that record."

Having Ray Santos onboard was also immensely important. Inspired to pick up a saxophone in 1945 after hearing Coleman Hawkins's rendition of "Body and Soul," Santos eventually graduated from Juilliard and dove into the Latin Jazz scene—composing and arranging for such masters of the genre as Machito, Tito Puente, and Tito Rodríguez. He arrived at Skywalker with dynamic charts but, with the many last-minute song additions, he really had to scramble.

"Ray Santos! He was *great*," Massenburg exclaimed. "He was the kind of guy who could follow her with these new songs and just whip off an arrangement on the spot!" Peter would also contribute arrangement ideas: "'Leave her alone with the rhythm section for the first eight bars and *then* bring the saxophones in'—things like that," Santos noted. "These were suggestions by Peter that worked out very well."

Ronstadt's vocals were uniformly excellent, and the musicians supporting her were exquisitely passionate, experts at improvising around Santos's charts. Pianist Joe Rotondi, for example, kicks off the album with a beautifully lyrical display and provided outstanding solos throughout the sessions. Percussionist Armando Peraza, in his sixties, was simply a firecracker—with a long career playing alongside greats like George Shearing and, more recently, Carlos Santana. "Peraza," Massenburg noted, "taught us how to calibrate a song, and it's basically this: If, during a playback, you have a conga line going around the control room, you've pretty much got it!"

Though Peter had worked with George Massenburg for years, this was the first time they shared production credit for an album. Peter, Massenburg said, "couldn't commit all his time to doing it, and I couldn't commit all of my energy to doing it, so it was a great compromise." From start to finish, Ronstadt worked hard to do the material justice and, in the process, reached a new performance plateau: "Linda has said," Massenburg noted, "that it wasn't until that record that she learned how to *phrase* in time."

Frenesi album cover.

"That record" was called *Frenesí*—or "Frenzy"—and was the last of Ronstadt's trilogy of Spanish-language releases. It certainly sold well in Puerto Rico and other Latin American markets, eventually earning a Grammy for Best Tropical Latin Album the following year.

Peter's inability to devote all his attention to the Ronstadt sessions was because he was simultaneously diving into a project that would continue through most of 1992—producing Neil Diamond's first collection of Christmas songs. Diamond himself contributed the original "You Make It Feel Like Christmas," hoping it might become a new seasonal standard, but mostly the song selection was what you'd expect—a mix of traditional tunes ("O Holy Night," "Hark! The Herald Angels Sing") and more modern fare ("The Christmas Song," "White Christmas").

Though Robbie Buchanan played keyboards for the majority of the sessions, Diamond's musical director, Alan Lindgren, performed the piano intro to "White Christmas." After hearing Diamond's take on Irving Berlin's classic tune, Lindgren suggested adding back the song's original preamble, wherein Berlin describes a beautiful Christmas Eve day in Beverly Hills under the palm trees, before he shares his dream of a perfect "White Christmas"—the verses that today are such a part of the holiday season. "I remember," Lindgren said, "I had to convince Neil that *that* was actually a part of the song."

At one point during the sessions, Diamond sensed something was wrong: It was during a playback of "Silent Night," Peter recalled, "and Neil, at that time, was still smoking a lot of dope—he doesn't anymore—but he went . . ." Here, Peter mimed taking a toke and, pretending to be Diamond, asked, "'Ya know, isn't there something *weird* about this?' And I went, 'What do you mean, Neil?' He said, 'An atheist producing a Jew singing a Christmas song?' And I went, 'Yeah, it's weird.' And he said, 'I thought so!'" Peter then pretended to take another toke and laughed, concluding: "I love Neil."

When it comes to weird, though, it would be hard to beat the arrangement of "God Rest Ye Merry, Gentlemen" featuring Diamond backed solely by a barbershop quartet. It sounds bizarre but works beautifully; though you've probably heard this song a hundred times, the intricate harmonies of the 139th Street Quartet force you to hear it afresh.

The Christmas Album, as it was straightforwardly called, was wrapped by August and under trees by year's end. Year after year a strong yuletide seller, almost two million copies have been purchased since its release.

The LA band Mary's Danish signed with Peter Asher Management for representation. Both fans of the local band X, fronted by John Doe and Exene Cervenka, singers Gretchen Seager and Julie Ritter had been inspired to form their own group, aiming for the same powerful expression of ideas behind a similar interplay of two voices. Experiencing some early success with their song "Don't Crash the Car Tonight," Mary's Danish decided to sign with Morgan Creek Records—a new independent label formed by parent company Morgan Creek Productions, producers of various successful films.

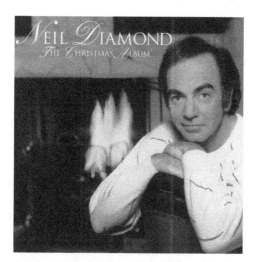

The Christmas Album cover.

The band was friendly with Niko Bolas and suggested he produce their upcoming sessions. Bolas, who had last worked with Peter ten years earlier as assistant engineer on Ronstadt's *Get Closer* and Taylor's *Dad Loves His Work*, had become a damn fine producer himself—recently helming the R.E.M./Warren Zevon collaboration *Hindu Love Gods* and Neil Young's *This Note's for You*. As Peter met with Bolas to discuss the project, they decided it would be fun to do it together. "They were very good," Peter said of the band, and after producing one album of Latin Jazz and still tweaking Diamond's holiday tunes, Peter confessed: "I wanted to make a tough rock'n'roll record."

Mary's Danish certainly had eclectic tastes, and the songs they brought in were wide-ranging: "Some were country-twang, others were hard punk, others were poppy," vocalist Seager said. "It was really nice to have a guy like that who understood how to make it all cohesive." As with 10,000 Maniacs, Peter enjoyed the challenge and offered ideas on song structure. Seager gave examples of his suggestions: "'Let's try a different approach to the song . . . maybe add a piece here . . . I think you need to rewrite the chorus . . .'" She described him as "very influential—helping if melodies weren't quite clicking."

Rather than record in Los Angeles, Peter called up George Lucas and asked if Skywalker Sound had ten days of studio time available. "Not bad knowing people in high places," Seager smiled, recalling how gorgeous the Marin County compound was: "I just remember the guest cottages we all stayed in. I was, like, 'Okaaay! I could get used to this!' It was fantastic."

As recording got underway, the band rocked hard—Louis Gutierrez and David King had developed a crunching twin-guitar attack, and along with the rhythm section, took such songs as "Leave It Alone" into a punkish/metal zone. But, instead of the usual snarling male vocal on top, Seager and Ritter's dual feminine perspectives on love and hate were a refreshing change, doling out poetry and protest in equal measure.

Also surprising was the sonic clarity of it all—every instrument and voice was clearly heard, never fighting one another. "Two things do that: one, the way you record it and mix it, and the other—the arrangement," Bolas offered, then claimed: "There's no such thing as a good mix without a good arranger, and any mixer who tells you otherwise is lying. That's it. The mix happens on *this* side of the window," he said, sitting in the middle of one of Capitol Records' spacious and legendary recording studios. "Everything that happens in *there*," he said, pointing toward the control room, "is fruitcake bullshit to justify charging a lot of money." He laughed.

"And Peter," Bolas continued, "would spend the right amount of time makin' sure that it was fast enough or slow enough, that it was the right key, and that this guitar player knew what that guitar player was playing so they never fought each other. And those are the things that I cherish as lessons."

If Peter thought the band was firing flawlessly, there was no need for his input. But he'd offer suggestions when the band seemed stuck. "Because he came from a different kind of musical background, the ideas he'd throw out in the recording studio were not ones that we would have naturally come up with," Seager explained. "Sometimes they worked and sometimes they didn't, but I appreciated the direction he was always trying to push, and I loved working with him in those terms.

"It was kind of like working with another artist," Seager said. "The guy knows music inside and out."

The plan was to finish the basic tracks, then come back to The Complex for any overdubs. But just as the sessions at Skywalker were wrapping up, riots broke out in Los Angeles when four white police officers were acquitted in their trial for beating black motorist Rodney King. The team didn't want to return to a city in chaos, but their recording budget was running quite low, and Skywalker was at the costlier end of the studio spectrum. Therefore, said Bolas, "We all decided to cut some of our pay, stay there, and finish it." One problem, though: Peter, having brought only enough to wear for the time originally booked, realized that he was out of clean clothing. Never one to ignore an excuse to buy new clothes, Peter invited the band to accompany him into San Francisco for a shopping adventure. Before they left, Seager remembered asking Peter, "Why are we going into town to go shopping? There's a laundry in *my* cottage—there's gotta be a washer and dryer in *yours* . . ." He answered: "I don't know how to work a washer and dryer."

"I said, 'Whatdya mean, "I don't know how"?' He said, 'I don't.' I said, 'You've *never* done your own laundry?'" Peter proudly answered: "Never!"

"I said, 'Well, I can *show* you! C'mon, Peter, I can show you how to turn on a *washing machine!*' He said, 'No, that's okay.' So"—Seager smiled—"we went into town, and he bought ten more outfits."

"That's Peter," according to his wife, Wendy. "One hundred percent."

The album was released under the title *American Standard* and with the credit: "Produced by Peter Asher/Recorded, Mixed and Co-Produced by Niko Bolas." That coproduction credit is due to Peter being "generous," as far as Bolas is concerned, "because all of the musical decisions always get run by Peter." He added: "Whatever

American Standard album cover.

level of comfort or inspiration I brought," due to his friendship with the band, "Peter acknowledged it and gave me the credit."

After receiving praise in *Rolling Stone* and other press ("Great songs," proclaimed the *Chicago Tribune.* "The troupe's best record yet."), the band hit the road to promote the album. But signing with a new independent label has drawbacks, and such was the case with Morgan Creek—or, as Gretchen Seager referred to them, "More Than Cheap." As Mary's Danish made their way across the country, they couldn't find *American Standard* at record stores, their food and hotel per diems were slashed drastically, and promotion from the label seemed nonexistent. Things got so dire they had to borrow money from Peter to finish the tour.

Eventually, Seager said, "Morgan Creek was gonna fold as a record company and was trying to sell Mary's Danish on the open market"—in order to recoup their investment. "And I forget what they were asking, but it was an absolutely ridiculous sum of money for a small indie band. So we were in a holding pattern, and Peter did his best to try to negotiate our release." As he met with the label's chief operating officer (whom Peter described as "horrible"), it was obvious there was no sympathy for the situation the band was in and certainly no interest in letting them go. "So basically," Seager recounted, "the only way we could get out of our contract with Morgan Creek was to break up as a band." It would not be the last time a promising group, full of potential, was sabotaged by an uncaring label—as you shall see.

23

DON'T SAY GOODBYE

"I didn't have a lot of time with him."

Singer/songwriter Laura Satterfield was speaking of her relationship with her biological father. "Never did get enough," she said. "But I had seen him recently around that time." That time was 1992, and with her writing partner, Ira Walker, Satterfield began to craft a song about disappointment and forgiveness—of a parent, yes, but ultimately of oneself. Its evocative melody came mostly from Walker, and the pair worked on the lyrics together—"written from the heart," Satterfield said. With both songwriters raised in families of varying ethnicities, the sentiment that completed the chorus was a lesson they understood early: "*Love is the only color.*"

While the song was in process, Dick Rudolph, a friend of Satterfield's, invited her and Walker to view a rough cut of a new film he was working on, hoping they might be inspired to come up with an original song for the project. The movie concerned a young African American woman, conceived through artificial insemination, discovering her biological father is white. Though the familial bonds that begin to form during the film were at times played for laughs, yearning for a parental connection and questioning one's racial identity were serious ideas the songwriters already had in play. As they watched, Satterfield recalled, "We just kept elbowing each other in the side, like, '*Oh my gosh! Oh my God! This is incredible!*' Because we could just keep doing what we were doing, and it was gonna work!" After the screening, Rudolph introduced the songwriters to Richard Benjamin, the film's director. Walker immediately said to Benjamin: "We have a song for this movie!"

Their work had echoes of Native American chanting, African American gospel, and blues, with the mixture succeeding due in large part to Walker's gifts as a musical shaman who can deftly weave these spiritual strains together. Satterfield, though, acknowledged her own role in the song's evocative mixture: "Makes perfect sense, really, if you think about how I was raised and brought up in all of those influences,"

Satterfield explained, "because of my mother, and her being married to Booker"—referring to singer Priscilla Coolidge and stepfather, Booker T. Jones, one of the architects of the Stax Records sound—"them being in an interracial marriage and us being from the South. My grandfather is full-blood Cherokee, yes, but a southern Baptist preacher!"

Once finished, "I Know I Don't Walk on Water" was recorded as a demo, with Satterfield handling the vocal, and sent on to Rudolph. It was quickly approved for the film, which was to be released as *Made in America*, and Peter was approached to produce the track. "I *loved* the song," he stated, and met with Rudolph to work out the details. As her demo played, "they were trying to figure out," according to Satterfield, "what 'name artist' could they get to do this song. And it was Peter—in all of his wonderful preciousness—who said, 'Well, I really like *that* girl's voice!'"

Satterfield had been around music her whole life, as her mother and stepfather recorded albums together and her aunt, Rita Coolidge, enjoyed a high-profile career of her own, but this would be Laura's first major recording experience. "It was all I'd ever dreamed of since I was little," Satterfield confessed. With Peter giving her this chance, "I just felt so honored."

Peter also impressed Ira Walker, who had been writing, recording, and performing for years: "I have been around so many top-notch executives," he said, "but Peter Asher is A-Number One. He calls me and says, 'I want you to come to the session,'" telling Walker there's a ticket waiting for him at the airport. "'Come and hang out with us.' *Who DOES that, man?*" Walker asked incredulously. "They don't make 'em any nicer."

The film's soundtrack album was to be released by Elektra Records, whose executives suggested Ephraim Lewis participate in the recording. Lewis's debut album for Elektra was garnering much praise, mostly for his exquisite soulful singing, and it was decided that "I Know I Don't Walk on Water" would now be a duet. "We met," Satterfield recalled, "and ten minutes later, we were in the vocal booth doing the song together.

"When he opened his mouth, I was standing there *staring* at him, you know? With my mouth hanging open, just listening to this *incredible* voice of this dear, dear soul." She was so taken by the artistry she was witnessing she'd sometimes miss her cue to begin singing and didn't feel "worthy" to share the same room with Lewis. But Peter's faith was well placed, as Satterfield rose to the occasion and delivered a quietly passionate performance alongside Lewis's heart-wrenching delivery.

Unfortunately, it turned out to be Lewis's last recording; he died a few months later, falling from a balcony in his apartment building after being Tased by the police for causing a disturbance. It's still unknown what led to his behavior that evening—we'll probably never know—but the loss of this young man, so full of promise and undeniable talent, was tragic, and the events of that evening now add a completely different coloring to the song's opening line: "*Why? Why do angels fall?*"

Turning from angels to devils, Peter began working in the studio with Randy Newman at the beginning of 1993, laying down basic tracks on songs that would form the basis of *Faust*—the composer's first attempt at a stage musical. The original 1809 drama by the German writer Goethe—concerning selling one's soul to the devil—was turned into a farcical look at humanity, with Newman's cynical and comedic song-stylings leavened with beautiful ballads and arrangements that are among the best work of his career.

"It may have been the best thing I ever did," Newman concurred. Catching the busy film composer on the phone, interrupting his efforts toward the completion of yet another scoring project, his fingers would occasionally strike the piano keys in front of him, adding brief musical punctuations to his words. Peter, he commented, "was enthusiastic about the project, and I thought he was a great guy for it."

Peter certainly agreed with Newman's assessment of the quality of the finished work: "I think it's brilliant!" But as to calling *Faust* his "best," he demurred: "Randy's one of those people who actually get better and better all the time. I couldn't even *pick* a favorite Randy track or album because they're all so good. He's amazing."

Newman had first recorded demos of the songs at his piano beginning in 1991, singing all the parts—including both God *and* devil in a schizophrenic *pas de deux*. (Rhino Records released these early work tapes in 2003.) Songs were dropped and others added by the time Peter and engineer Frank Wolf began to record basic tracks in February 1993, and Newman was certainly happy to have Peter in his corner.

"He's one of the best record producers we've had," Newman said of Peter. "He's really adept in the studio, and he has what I *don't* have, which is an interest in the heart of rock'n'roll, and of pop records—the rhythm, the tracks. You know? The bass, drums, guitars," Newman explained. "And he knows it *very* well. I'm *less* interested in it—which is why my career has not been like Taylor's and Ronstadt's." He laughed. "Ahh, *one* reason! But he's very fastidious and careful about those basics. Because when you have a problem in a basic track—I've learned at my cost—it stays with you. *For life!*

"But at this point in my life, I wanna have a good time while I'm doing it. And I don't play as meticulously as he would like, you know? He made me nervous. I'm not a session musician," Newman complained, merely half-joking. Session drummer extraordinaire Jim Keltner, who accompanied Newman on such early tracks as "Last Night I Had a Dream" and "You Can Leave Your Hat On," and also played on some of the *Faust* sessions, refers to those tempos as "Newman Time," to which the composer readily agreed: "It's not Pacific Standard, you know?" As an example, he began to pound away on his keyboard. "It's not 'regular' musician time. So"—he laughed—"I had more re-dos to do than anyone else did."

Frank Wolf admitted that, during the sessions, Peter got a bit frustrated at times: "He likes it to be 'just so,' you know? Well-ordered—that's just who he is." But Newman praised Peter's work ethic: "He's a very hard worker. A lot of times you work on a project, and you think you're the only person that's working hard. But in *his* case, that isn't true—you *know* he's working as hard as you are. If not harder . . ." Newman paused and reconsidered: "Well, you can't work harder than a *film composer . . .*"

This was their first studio project together, though Peter Asher Management had represented Newman for over five years. During that time, Cathy Kerr had gone from Peter's assistant/receptionist to manager-in-training. Most of the time, "I was kind of the one who was in the office," Kerr recalled. "So everyone called me for whatever they needed, and Randy just ended up calling *me* all the time. And Peter just said: 'He's yours. He calls you; he feels comfortable with you.'" Peter ceded management duties of a major artist (and future Oscar winner) over to his former receptionist graciously and, it turned out, presciently; Newman's comfort level with Kerr remained steady, and she continued to manage his career for over three decades.

After the rhythm tracks were completed, Newman began to concentrate on the complex orchestral scores that would build upon the work already recorded. During this period, Peter turned his attention toward two other projects. First for Neil Diamond, who wanted to record a tribute to those fellow songwriters who once toiled away within the hallowed edifice known as The Brill Building. Located at 1619 Broadway in New York City, great songwriting teams—Jerry Leiber and Mike Stoller, Doc Pomus and Mort Shuman, Burt Bacharach and Hal David, Ellie Greenwich and Jeff Barry—wrote hundreds of classic pop songs for music publishers whose offices were tucked inside the eleven-story structure. Though not literally in The Brill Building itself, songwriters Gerry Goffin and Carole King, Barry Mann and Cynthia Weil, and Neil Sedaka and Howard Greenfield worked in another building across the street, so are often thought of as part of "The Brill Building era"—that period from the mid-fifties to the mid-sixties, when "The Great American Songbook" morphed from Irving Berlin's "Let's Face the Music and Dance" to Pomus and Shuman's "Save the Last Dance for Me."

Diamond began his career during this golden age and wanted to salute those composers who both inspired and encouraged the novice songwriter. "Neil and I," Peter explained, "went through a whole list of songs," eventually settling on sixteen for the project. Before cutting the basic tracks, Peter arranged a dozen of the songs along with help from Diamond's band, which included keyboardist and musical director Alan Lindgren. Who deserves credit for what, Lindgren admitted, can be a bit nebulous: "We would all just work it out," he said. "If the band has a way they've kinda been doing it, you listen to it and make changes"—with Peter adding his creative ideas. "It's kinda a collaborative effort." Those arrangements were then performed by the crack session musicians Peter hired.

Lindgren, though, personally contributed a wonderful arrangement for one song whose lyrics may have originated in The Brill Building, but whose melody was created four thousand miles away. In 1961, Italian songwriters Carlo Donida and Giulio Rapetti wrote "Uno Dei Tanti," which, two years later, became "I (Who Have Nothing)" with English lyrics courtesy of Jerry Leiber and Mike Stoller. "I love that song," Lindgren proclaimed. "I just kinda put everything I had into it." The strings are given bluesy, descending flourishes to highlight the melodramatic agony of a devastated lover. The active strings are almost a *homage* to Lindgren's "hero"—arranger Paul Buckmaster, who's best known for his seventies work for Elton John.

Along with producing the album and helping to arrange many of the tracks, Peter added percussion touches throughout—even performing the signature descending

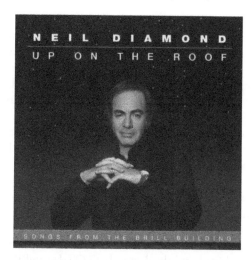

Up on the Roof
album cover.

marimba riff throughout the classic "Spanish Harlem." He laughed when reminded of this: "Really? It must've been a simple part!" That track is another of the album's highlights, with a lovely liquid fretless bass courtesy of Larry Klein. Peter had first produced a version of Greenwich and Barry's "Do Wah Diddy Diddy" for Andrew Gold back in 1976; it manages to rock even harder here by having Mary's Danish (in their last recorded appearance) accompany Diamond, giving the album some real crunch. A particular highlight for Peter during the sessions was working with another musical superstar and cultural icon: Dolly Parton. She sang a duet with Diamond on what is arguably the ultimate Brill Building composition: "You've Lost That Lovin' Feelin'," written by Barry Mann, Cynthia Weil, and Phil Spector.

"I knew her, of course, from the 'Trio' stuff," Peter said, referring to the highly successful collaboration between Parton, Emmylou Harris, and Linda Ronstadt. Those classic 1986 sessions had been produced by George Massenburg, not Peter, "but I was there a lot," he noted, and a friendship was formed. The idea for the duet came out of a conversation Peter and Neil had about adding a woman's voice and viewpoint to the song. "We're both big Dolly fans," said Peter, and he simply called her manager to see if she was interested. She was.

Dolly recorded her part at Diamond's own studio, Arch Angel Recording. "Oh, she was great," Peter said. "She was incredibly efficient and sang beautifully." The Diamond/Parton duet kicks off *Up on the Roof: Songs from the Brill Building*, released in October of 1993. The collection was the most well-received release from Diamond in years and eventually earned him another RIAA Gold Record Award.

As work on *Faust* continued in fits and starts, Peter became involved with another project in 1993—this one courtesy of old friend John Kalodner. Geffen Records had managed to sign a young band whose demo tape had created a huge buzz at music labels all over town. They called themselves The Semantics.

The group was originally formed in Nashville in early 1991, when musician Ben Folds tried to convince his old college buddy Millard Powers to move to town. "He told me, 'Man, there's this guy, Bill Owsley—he's a great guitar player,'" Powers said, remembering Folds's fateful phone call. "'If you two got together, I *guarantee* you'd have a record deal in six months!' I'm like, 'Really?'" Powers took Folds's advice, traveled to Music City USA, and roomed with musician Jody Spence. Every evening for the next three weeks, Powers, Owsley, and Spence took over the studio run by Sony Tree Publishing, where Spence was signed as a songwriter. Sony, according to Powers, would "use it during the day to do publishing demos, which was their bread and butter, and, at night, they just gave us the keys." He still can't believe their good fortune: "It was an amazing opportunity, because it was a full-blown studio that was ours from, like, ten p.m. until six a.m. We worked that thing as hard as we could.

"Either Owsley or myself would come in with the basic music or hook, and then we would all three sit together and just bounce ideas off each other lyrically, collaborating on melody ideas," said Powers, "and then record it." Less than a month later, when Sony Music Publishing heard the demos, both Owsley and Powers were also signed as writers.

Now, with seven well-recorded original songs in hand, the boys headed to Los Angeles and, over the next three months, played them for anyone who would listen. One who realized the band's potential early on was Don Donahue at Reunion Records, a Christian label with a distribution deal with Geffen. Donahue "got a hold of the tape, loved it, and sort of championed it," said Powers, and because of their business dealings, "they had Kalodner's ear."

"Brilliant musicians" was how John Kalodner described his initial reaction upon hearing The Semantics' demos, and he made his way to Nashville to see how good the boys were live. His assistant, Debra Shallman, was also knocked out, immediately hearing such influences as The Beatles and Todd Rundgren in the group's clever, melodic pop. "There was a *lot* of label interest in this band," she recalled, but it was Geffen who won them over. Kalodner, though, didn't offer the band a recording contract outright, wanting to hear more material. "He wanted us to continue to write," Bill Owsley recalled, "and signed us to a development deal."

"Owsley and myself were more of the 'song idea' guys," Powers explained. Jody Spence "was a really good creative force in the studio when we were trying to write, but"—Powers sighed—"he just kinda lost interest" and left the band, adding that he also felt Owsley had pushed Spence out because "Jody wasn't dropping everything" to cater to Owsley's obsessive drive. Powers and Owsley soldiered on, now bringing in old friend Ben Folds to help out. A great all-around musician (as were they all), Folds sat behind the drums, providing a solid backbeat as more demos were recorded.

Powers, Owsley, and Folds traveled out to Hollywood to meet with Kalodner and Shallman, playing them the new material. All were hoping Folds would be the new member of The Semantics, but he was feeling this wasn't the right path to be on. "Ben said, 'You know, I really wanna do my own thing,'" Owsley recalled, and though that may have left the group drummerless, it was the right call for Folds—

about a year later he formed his own band, Ben Folds Five, which, Owsley said with a laugh, "worked out well for him."

Kalodner, though impressed with the new demos, hesitated to offer a recording contract—"They can't market a *duo*," Owsley complained, explaining the reasoning, "they can only market a *band*." Bemoaning their lack of a drummer to fellow musician Henry Gross (who had a Top Ten hit with "Shannon" back in 1976), Owsley recalled Gross's pie-in-the-sky advice: "If you were smart, you'd get Ringo Starr's son to play in your band." Ringo's oldest son, Zak Starkey, had been playing drums professionally for over a decade and had inherited a good deal of his dad's solid abilities.

"Yeah, like, fat chance," Owsley replied. "I wouldn't know the first thing about how to get in *touch* with him, much less him like our music!" When Kalodner phoned the next day asking if they'd somehow found a drummer, Owsley replied no, but laughingly related Gross's impossible suggestion. There was a pause. Then Kalodner stated: "I know Zak real well."

A tape of The Semantics' songs was delivered immediately to Starkey, who phoned Kalodner: "I *love* this stuff," he exclaimed. "Now what?" Kalodner sent Starkey a ticket to ride, and off he flew to Nashville. "We hit it off *famously* with Zak," Owsley said. "He's just a great guy." With more demos in hand cut at Sony Tree, this new trio headed to Kalodner's office in Hollywood—now a *band* and ready for their shot at a major-label album. Kalodner arranged for them to meet with a handful of possible producers, including Jack Joseph Puig (who had worked with The Black Crowes, John Mayer, and U2), Dave Jerden (Jane's Addiction, Social Distortion, Alice in Chains), and the keyboard player for Springsteen's E-Street Band, Roy Bittan (Chicago, Bonnie Tyler, Celine Dion). Finally, the group stopped by Peter's office on Doheny Drive at Kalodner's insistence. "I couldn't even *believe* that someone of Peter's stature would even mingle with the hoi polloi," Owsley said incredulously.

"The first thing he said," according to Owsley, "was, 'Well, by listening to your tape, it's obvious that you guys know what you're doing in the studio.' He goes, 'You don't really need me.' We didn't say anything. He goes, 'But I think that Geffen's not gonna give you guys the record budget 'cause you're twenty-two years old. I can be a facilitator for you, *and* I can be part of your team. And I'll sit there every day and say *sharp, flat,* or *Hey, we need a U47 microphone.* I know whom to call to get whatever you need gear-wise and book studios and that whole part—my staff can help. But you guys can make the record you wanna make! 'Cause I can tell that you really want to be involved in the production of your record.'"

"Hired! That's what I say." Owsley laughed. "I was just like, *pffft!* Meeting over! Meeting adjourned!" Millard Powers agreed: "Other producers, for them it was just another job. Peter was exactly the opposite. He told us, 'Honestly, I just want to be involved with this record.'"

Powers was bowled over by Peter's enthusiasm for their music: "He didn't need the job! As a matter of fact, he took a *pay cut* to work on this record." Peter, impressed with their demos, advised them to stick to those arrangements: "It's all there—we just have to render it the right way." Kalodner advised them to "make sure it sounds like a rock band," according to Powers. "He was pushing for louder guitars—a little more aggression." In just the past two years, the band Nirvana, signed to Geffen's DGC label (now scheduled to release The Semantics' debut album), had become the hottest group in the country, and the post-punk thrash of leader Kurt Cobain's guitar was a sonic touchstone. Though The Semantics would never be mistaken for that Seattle trio, Kalodner—being the good record man he was—knew the market and wanted to make sure *some* of that crunch was present.

Peter phoned Frank Wolf, but not to have him engineer the project: "Here's the kind of guy that he is," said Wolf. "He says, 'I'm just calling you preemptively to let you know that the guys want to work with somebody who's younger and has less experience, so that it doesn't sound too tailored. So I'm gonna have Nate do this project.'" "Nate" was Nathaniel Kunkel, who had worked alongside both Wolf and George Massenburg as assistant engineer for the past three years. Peter felt this might be the perfect opportunity to give the young man his shot at engineering a project top to bottom. "I was disappointed," Wolf admitted, "but you can't do anything but respect somebody who calls you and tells you that; you don't find out through the second engineer at the studio calling, saying, 'Hey, I know you work with Peter—what's the setup?' 'Uhh, what are you talking about?' I've had that happen, and it's icky."

Tracking began in July 1993 at The Music Grinder on Hollywood Boulevard, not far from Griffith Park. "It was awesome," Owsley enthused. "It had the really huge open ceilings—just really tall and made for a very ambient sound. Peter loved it as well, and so that's where we kind of 'held up' for the next four weeks tracking the record"—with Frank Wolf engineering. Owsley and Powers had decided a more experienced engineer *was* needed after all. "And Frank was also a veteran mixer," Owsley noted, "which would save us money from having to hire an independent mixer; we had a man who could track the record *and* overdub the record *and* mix the record. So it was great."

"Unbelievable project," Wolf said fondly, recalling how he, Peter, and the band dove into the process of capturing the quirky alternative pop songs from the minds of these creative Southerners. The basic tracks were, according to Wolf, "plain, balls-out trio." The crunch of guitars were "loud and rude" (what Kalodner wanted, Wolf noted), and there was no question that Zak turned out to be a great drummer.

"A real *collaborative* project," Wolf added, where Peter's experience and musicality could be put in play. Owsley remembered Peter suggesting one idea: "'Follow me here. I know it's tough, but . . . do it.' And we followed him, and we were totally happy!" Peter turned with a smile and explained, "That's what I do."

And, of course, Peter added percussion throughout: "He was integral on 'Coming Up Roses,'" Owsley remembered, noting one of the album's standout tracks. While Zak drummed through the song's chorus, "Peter stood over the top of Zak, and he had these two enormous shakers that were *huge*, like two Coke cans per hand that were filled with sand. And he was doin' that *shiii-shiii-shiii-shiii* motion, you know, back and forth with Zak," Owsley continued, "and Millard and I were just standing there watching him do it, going, 'Listen to how *locked* Peter is with Zak!' I mean it was just *uncanny* how great he was at time—amazing *rhythmical* time."

The record this team ended up presenting to Geffen was nothing short of a power-pop masterpiece, containing both sides of that shiny coin: guitars and drums powerfully slicing through the catchy pop melodies, and harmonies layered throughout the album's compositions. Memorable hooks and catchy melodies abound, oftentimes four or five within the same song. Powers's "Sticks and Stones" (about an unsatisfying relationship) and "Average American" (about a hopefully satisfying one) were comparable to Rundgren at his catchiest, while Owsley's "Coming Up Roses" and "Don't Say Goodbye" were akin to top-drawer McCartney—strong ballads that made you sing along by song's end and a chorus that stuck in your head for days. "It was so well-played and so well-produced," Kalodner recalled.

After the final mix was done, "Peter and John Kalodner played our record for the entire Geffen Records staff," Owsley recalled, and much head-scratching ensued: "Alternative promotion said they thought it was too pop to be called 'alternative,' and they wanted to push it over to the pop side of Geffen and let pop promotion handle it, and pop promotion said it was too alternative for them. So, we kind of fell into the middle, and they didn't know what to do with our record." This was the height of the "grunge" era, and Geffen's radio promo team knew how to sell that, not this. The label had spent over two hundred grand on the project but decided to write it off. Peter had to break the news: "The record company has let you go from the label," were the words Owsley heard over the phone.

"One phone call—our whole lives gone. All of our work and everything." When I spoke to Owsley over a dozen years after that fateful call, he remembered it vividly: "I fell against the corner of the wall and just slid down. You know what I mean? I handed the phone to Millard because I was crying so hard I couldn't even talk. I was just coming apart." Powers kept pressing Peter for a possible solution, Owsley recalled: "He was just kinda pacing back and forth, you know, with that look of concern in his eyes, going, 'Well, can we do *this*? I mean, if we did *this*, could we do *THIS*?' I don't know what Peter was saying on the other end, but it was basically, 'No, no, no, no, no.'"

"You sign a band," Debra Shallman explained, and though the label had spent almost a quarter million dollars on recording and mixing, "the *big* investment is the marketing. And if they're not a hundred percent behind it, they're cutting their losses." Having championed the band throughout the entire process, she was devastated by the rejection and knew that her boss, John Kalodner, as well as Peter, were disappointed, but really felt for the band: "In some ways, I think it's harder on a band to get signed and then not get a shot at all than *never* getting signed."

The Semantics disintegrated soon after. The album master sat on a shelf but was eventually released in Japan a couple of years later (thanks to Aki Shimomiya at Alfa International) and developed a following among those who like their pop with an edgy quirkiness and smart studio craft. The record was given the title *POWERBILL*,

POWERBILL album cover.

crafted from the names Millard POWERs and BILL Owsley. "It did *really well* over there!" Owsley laughed and added: "It's just funny how that worked out . . ."

The band went their separate ways: Zak Starkey has had a stellar career pounding the drums for such bands as Oasis and The Who, among many other acts. Millard Powers has played bass for Counting Crows since 2005. Bill Owsley won a Grammy for his first solo album, and for years he toured and played guitar for country music superstars. But various career and personal problems took their toll, and he ended his life in 2010. He had tragically forgotten what he told me just a few years earlier when we spoke about the untimely end of The Semantics:

"What if I'd taken my own life right there after Peter Asher made that phone call? Then I never would have sung with Mutt Lange and Shania Twain or ridden in Lear Jets with Amy Grant and Vince Gill.

"Life is just hills and valleys," Owsley said. "You just never know what God's got 'round the corner for you . . ."

24

LEAVING ON A JET PLANE

One month before 1993 came to a close, Linda Ronstadt released her album *Winter Light*. Peter had been involved at the start of the sessions, producing the songs "Heartbeats Accelerating" (composed by Anna McGarrigle, writer of "Heart Like a Wheel") and the Brian Wilson/Tony Asher *Pet Sounds* classic "Don't Talk (Put Your Head on My Shoulder)." But before things progressed very far, Peter left the project.

"We were recording up at Skywalker and got into a bit of an argument about songs," Peter remembered—"in a very civilized way," he was quick to add. "That's when I started to think that maybe I should let Linda do this on her own." Together, Ronstadt and George Massenburg finished the album (with help from Steve Tyrell). *Winter Light* ultimately might not have been a commercial success, but it definitely showed that she had learned much from Peter, as the production was nothing short of exquisite.

This was her first attempt at producing herself. She would go on to coproduce three more of her own records and help produce projects for David Lindley, Aaron Neville, and Jimmy Webb, among other friends. But much like her self-deprecating remarks regarding her skills as a singer, she downplayed her abilities as a producer even more: "I've produced records on occasion, but I don't think that that's sorta what I do," she admitted to me when we spoke in 2004, just as she was about to embark on her final recording sessions. "I don't consider myself a producer. I'm really a mom more than anything—I sit around and make peanut butter and jelly sandwiches."

Throughout 1994, Peter continued to work on Randy Newman's *Faust*—specifically helping to cast the singers who would need to inhabit the story's main characters. Newman would no doubt make a fine devil, but who should play the title role of Faust? Or the innocent Margaret and her more worldly friend, Martha? And, perhaps most importantly, who had the right voice to make real the majesty of the Lord God himself? How should that part even be played?

"Randy told me at the time of the session," James Taylor, who accepted the role, recalled: "'Think of this as being a Reagan kind of a Lord—not too bright, but having a real high opinion of himself and perhaps more confidence than he's justified in having. He thinks everything's just grand—as if Van Johnson's playing the Lord. Or Arnold Palmer.' I don't mean to disparage these three great men," Taylor quickly added, "but that was his suggestion, and it was good direction."

Peter reached out to artists he had known for years; Linda Ronstadt, Bonnie Raitt, Don Henley, and Elton John were asked, and all wanted to take part. "Everybody said yes because it was Randy," Peter explained. "It's Randy's name that works magic." Vocals were recorded whenever the singers' schedules permitted. No rush, as Newman still needed to pay the bills—writing the music to two separate films during the time he was also composing new songs and sketching orchestrations for *Faust*.

Peter also had another project going that summer: As Neil Diamond's *The Christmas Album* had sold a million copies two years earlier, it was decided to come up with a second volume of seasonal favorites. And, as with the first collection, there were some sonic surprises, including a fun Reggae arrangement for "Rudolph, the Red-Nosed Reindeer." Merely two months after its release, it had already sold over half a million copies.

Near the end of the year, Peter flew to London to oversee a recording of "Love Can Build a Bridge" (originally released by The Judds in 1990). This version would be an all-star performance with vocals handled by Chrissie Hynde (from The Pretenders), Neneh Cherry (whose song "Buffalo Stance" had made a splash five years earlier), and Peter's friend Cher—all done in support of Britain's biyearly Comic Relief/Red Nose Day charity efforts. "Some songs just speak to you," Cher said, who knew the song was special.

Comic Relief cofounder Richard Curtis (writer of *Four Weddings and a Funeral*, *Notting Hill*, and writer/director of *Love Actually*) approached Peter to participate

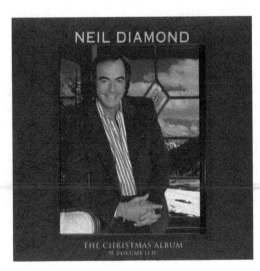

The Christmas Album Volume II album cover.

based on Cher's suggestion. "I never had met the two girls,"—meaning Hynde and Cherry—"so I think that I would've *especially* felt good," Cher explained, with Peter at the helm. The extra dash of electric spice in the final mix was a fortunate bit of happenstance: "I dragged Eric Clapton in at the very last minute," Peter said, "because I'd run into him at lunch in London.

"I said, 'This will be interesting. Would you play a guitar solo on it?' And Eric said, 'Yeah. Let Roger know what's going on.'" Roger Forrester was Eric's manager at that time, who was not happy.

"Roger yelled at me: 'You should've come to me first!'" Peter recalled replying: "You would've said 'no'—you say 'no' to everything! I probably would, too, in your shoes." Forrester asked, "Well, how do we know where the money's going?" Peter shot back: "It's *Comic Relief!*"

"Finally, Roger called me back and said, 'Okay—he'll be there.'" But he made Peter promise to not ask Clapton to do *anything else* but record the solo. The next day, he told his three principal singers who was coming by to play. "Chrissie freaks out—turns out she's never met Eric. She's a guitar player, and Eric is God; plus, he's a chick magnet." With the video scheduled to be shot the following day, Peter made sure the girls knew of the promise he'd made to Eric's manager: He WOULD NOT be asking him to take part. Understood, they said.

Clapton arrived and proceeded to lay down eight passes for the solo: "All different," recalled Peter, "all great." He asked Clapton would he "mind if I pick and choose" different parts and comp them together? Clapton agreed, but before he could exit the studio, the ladies surrounded him—sweetly beseeching the guitarist to be in the video shoot the next day. "Of course he was butter in their hands"—Peter smiled. Clapton agreed to take part.

"By the time he showed up for the video," said Peter, "I'd put a solo together from three or four takes, which of course he'd never heard." As Clapton tried to follow his pieced-together solo, the camera swirled around the "Guitar God," helping to hide the fact that, Peter admitted, "he doesn't know what he's doing." With all the star power present, the record predictably was a number-one smash in the UK.

Randy Newman's Faust should have also been a smash upon release in 1995. The songs certainly were among Newman's best work—moving from farcical religious rave-ups ("How Great Our Lord") to achingly beautiful ballads ("Feels Like Home")—and the performances on the recording were all excellent, with Taylor particularly good as a vigorously cheerful deity.

"I think it's a brilliant record," Peter enthused. But as to its lack of sales: "It's remarkable. The people who love him think he's a genius—one of the best living songwriters in America, and I happen to be one of those people. But Randy's records *don't* sell, necessarily.

"Nobody else could make a record with Elton and James and Don Henley and Bonnie Raitt and Linda Ronstadt on it and *not* sell a million copies of it." He laughed. "You know? It's something about Randy!"

Randy Newman's Faust
album cover.

Peter was still enjoying the recording process as much as he ever had, but the challenge was beginning to disappear from the management side of things. "We were making a lot of money; we were still doing well," according to Ira Koslow, Peter's right-hand man at Peter Asher Management. "But I think he saw down the line, 'Well, wait a minute . . .' James wound up having a family," Koslow explained, "and Linda adopted some kids—both wanted to tour less. Carole King was going into the theater, Joni didn't want to tour anymore—everybody was having their own little things."

Peter agreed: "There was suddenly less challenge. You know, putting together a James Taylor summer tour every two years isn't brain surgery."

So, when Tommy Motolla, then head of Sony's music division in the United States, asked Peter if he'd be interested in becoming part of the corporate team, he was very intrigued: "I said yes just to explore it. Something I'd never done was be at a record company." That's not counting Apple and MGM, of course, but both those adventures were over before they really began.

Peter pondered the ability to make change from the inside. "Sony gave him a chance," Koslow said. "We always made fun of the record companies and said, 'Look at those guys! Why don't they do something smart?' So, here was his chance to be on *that* side AND do something smart."

He asked old friends for their advice: "I discussed it with James at some length," Peter confessed, "what he thought I should do. He wrote me a letter saying that he thought I should do it . . ."

George Massenburg remarked that something else probably helped with the decision to become senior vice president at Sony Music, one of the world's most successful music companies: "Well, it was an *awful* lot of money, wasn't it?"

In February 1995, Peter became an ambassador-at-large of sorts for Sony, traveling the world giving speeches, brokering deals, and smoothing ruffled feathers of international artists and division heads alike—putting his fabled honesty and fairness into play.

And Sony took advantage of having a great hitmaker on staff, as Peter began to participate in a variety of Sony recordings, including producing two new tracks for Billy Joel's *Greatest Hits Volume III*. A wonderful cover of the 1963 Goffin/King soul classic "Hey Girl" featured a passionate vocal by Joel and a gorgeous arrangement of strings and background singers by David Campbell, with the choir cleverly echoing Joel's desperate final pleas. But the second track was less successful.

"To Make You Feel My Love," written by Bob Dylan, "is a really good song," Peter stated, and this recording would be its first release. "I was trying to make it completely un-Dylan"—with, again, a Campbell orchestration—"and suddenly there was this thing about, 'Well, it's a *Bob Dylan* song; we have to respect that.'" Donny Ienner, the chairman of the label, became personally involved and, in an effort to "Dylanize," a harmonica was added, along with an odd, rolling rhythm that appears around forty seconds into the track and distracts throughout.

"Donny Ienner convinced himself that the song was a huge hit." When it wasn't, Peter confided, Ienner "thought that was my fault and was furious."

"I'm not gonna say they hated each other," one music-biz veteran (who spoke on condition of anonymity) stated. "Ienner hated Peter. Donny's as dumb as a two-by-four, and Peter's smart. Donny's only political and Peter's musically intelligent and literary. Donny's a very powerful man, and so a lot of the projects that Peter did for Sony were suppressed by Donny, who wouldn't raise a finger to help."

"I'm a great admirer of Don's," Peter said diplomatically. "But it's a relationship that had its ups and downs, yeah."

Now spending so much time in New York, "it seemed silly to rent," Peter explained, so he and Wendy were on the lookout for vacancies in Manhattan. At a social gathering, they overheard half a phone conversation concerning someone who was vacating their longtime residence. "It was Shirlee Fonda," Peter said—the widow of actor Henry Fonda—on the end of the line; turned out her soon-to-go-on-the-market apartment was only three blocks from Sony's headquarters. "We bought it almost sight-unseen," Peter admitted. Eventually, he also helped an old friend buy in to the same building: actress Joan Collins. She had been married to Apple Records president Ron Kass and was now a much-reviled character on television's *Dynasty*. Peter was more than happy to compose a testimonial to the building's board on her behalf, saying in essence: "She's not really a bitch; she just plays one on TV."

In 1995, twenty-year-old Chantal Kreviazuk, a classically trained pianist turned singer/songwriter, was signed to Sony Canada by Mike Roth. Among her compositions, "he felt that a song called 'Surrounded,'" Kreviazuk recalled, "was worthy of international attention." Roth sent a demo of the song to Peter, who loved it and expressed interest in producing it. But not thinking Peter would want to helm a whole album, Kreviazuk suggested bringing in producer Matt Wallace, whose work with such bands as Faith No More and The Replacements had impressed her. It soon became clear that Peter had more passion for the project than initially thought, and with Wallace already on board, it was decided that they would produce Kreviazuk's debut together.

"They're very, very different people," Kreviazuk observed. "But they love comradery and they love the process of making records, and so they both brought their own brand of talent and insight and perspective to the record-making process. I think it worked quite well"—she laughed—"as a lot of people still love my first record out of all my albums.

"I'd never made a record before . . . and there was a level of pressure that I don't think a lot of twenty-one-year-olds have," she explained. Fellow Canadian Alanis Morissette's record *Jagged Little Pill* had just gone through the roof, so Sony's expectations were enormous. "I was really overwhelmed, and there were times when I just didn't know how to explain what I wanted." Understandable, as she had performed solo for most of her life; this album would mark her first time supported by a band.

At LA's Conway Recording Studios, the musicians were told to take a break. "Peter took me into another room, and I was crying," Kreviazuk recalled. "He was able, for a minute, to stop everything and make me realize that the most important thing was my stability and how I *felt*. And that made me feel really good at a time when I felt I had to just '*be strong*,'" she said, "and not reveal what it was really doing to me.

"You know, he tends to be a really strong person," she noted, with a nod toward Peter's traditional British "stiff upper lip." "But when it mattered," she continued, "Peter revealed his sensitivity and his compassion and his heart, and I was really glad he did . . ."

Matt Wallace assembled the top-notch players to accompany Kreviazuk. "Their instincts were terrific," he noted, describing them as "ego-less," devising innovative parts to support Kreviazuk's lyrics and piano and make the songs fly. Wallace worked to sonically add a youthful crunch when needed, whereas Peter was responsible for giving some songs a more open ambience, including the track "Don't Be Good"—featuring a swooping, harmonic bass courtesy of Davey Faragher.

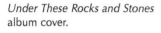
Under These Rocks and Stones album cover.

Both producers strived to instill confidence in the novice artist, and "she rose to the occasion," Wallace said. The resulting album, *Under These Rocks and Stones*, went double platinum in Canada, beginning for Kreviazuk a long, successful career. Peter later produced Kreviazuk's remake of John Denver's "Leaving on a Jet Plane," used in Sony's soundtrack album for the blockbuster film *Armageddon*, and that same year produced her cover of The Beatles' "In My Life"—used as the theme for the NBC series *Providence*.

Regarding Peter, Kreviazuk enthused: "He's one of the most informed people that you'll ever be around in your life. There's really nothing he doesn't know about. . . . It can be very intimidating, but it also feels like a privilege to be around him."

Peter himself was spending a lot of time on jet planes, helping international Sony acts when necessary. The New Zealand artist Bic Runga was a promising new signing, based on her initial EP release, but the Sony brass felt that the work on her debut album was "taking too long," Runga admitted. Peter "came out to our little practice room in New Zealand and sat on the floor and said, 'This song's good, this song's not so good.'"

Runga, who was producing herself, confided: "I'd never worked with a producer before, and to have someone in the room who knew what he was talking about was kind of a relief! And it gave me the sense that I could finish the record myself," which was the point of his presence—again, giving a young artist confidence and advice. Peter also couldn't resist adding some "airy" (as Runga described it) vocal accompaniment to one track, then using his clout to have Sony give the finished album, *Drive*, an American release. Though it didn't break through in the States, *Drive* debuted at number-one in the New Zealand charts and was named Album of the Year at the 32nd New Zealand Music Awards.

He worked his magic with another female artist from Down Under, Australia's Tina Arena. Her third album, *Don't Ask*, was a smash in her home country, and the Sony brass made it a priority to break her internationally.

David Massey, then head of A&R for Epic Records, brought Peter into his office. "I've got this idea for a song for Tina. It was a huge hit in the UK," he said, and proceeded to play Maria McKee's "Show Me Heaven"—not realizing that the man in front of him had *produced the track*.

Peter smiled, nodded, and said, "I can do that."

Which he promptly did, producing a stirring showcase for Arena's powerhouse vocals. "She's great," Peter enthused—and many agreed, as her version achieved hit status in many countries that were unaware of her talent.

Peter had stepped aside from Peter Asher Management soon after starting at Sony, taking his name off the shingle, and retitling the company PAM. Though still an owner/consultant, Peter's longtime employees Ira Koslow, Gloria Boyce, and Cathy Kerr were now running things. "I wondered how it would do without me," Peter said, "and the answer was not very well." Even initial client James Taylor eventually changed management, and as other artists slowly exited, the company finally shut its doors.

December album cover.

Peter was asked to work with many established artists on the Sony roster: Dan Fogelberg, Heart, REO Speedwagon—producing new tracks for their upcoming compilations. He developed a solid rapport with Kenny Loggins—producing the track "For the First Time" (used in the film *One Fine Day*), then two years later collaborating with Loggins on his Christmas-themed album *December*.

"Peter and I worked hard on making that record," Loggins told me. The album opens and closes with the sound of cold, desolate wind, and for the fifty-three minutes in between, Loggins's warm tenor moves through both traditional tunes and a few self-penned efforts that maintain the reflective mood, smoothly overlapping the selections, playing as a snowbound song cycle. "One of the things that I wanted to try to capture was the bittersweet melancholy of the season," said Loggins. "That still-life picture of the tree with no leaves in the snow—it has that quality of sparseness to it." The tracks move between the misty nostalgia of a Yuletide of yore and the colder reality of a season of discontent.

"The holidays are emotionally taxing," Loggins observed, "or can be. They're not all the final scene of *It's a Wonderful Life*." But the album surrounds those emotional poles with romantic warmth—a string trio here, an oboe there, a children's choir—and creative touches, such as coupling a sixteenth-century carol with, not recorders, but a *shakuhachi*—an ancient Japanese wind instrument. "It's like a recorder on acid," quipped Loggins.

After working with Peter on "For the First Time," he knew whom to call to help realize this project. "He's probably the best producer—on a number of levels—that I've ever worked with. Certainly politically, 'cause he's the most 'no bullshit' guy," Loggins stated. "When he likes something, he lets you know clearly that he likes it and *why* he likes it, and when he doesn't like something, he'll just say: 'It's not working.'"

"I found him really quick and smart," Loggins continued, "and an interesting balance of being able to *feel* what's right—not just map it out on one side of the brain, but to have *both* sides of the brain working at the same time; that's what makes him extraordinary. He's not just analytical, he's also a musician—so he gets his sense of what's happening in two different ways: As a producer he's looking at time and money, but as an artist he's looking at 'well, what's happening here that's gonna make this interesting?'"

Loggins was not only happy to work with Peter again, but also the engineer Nathaniel Kunkel. Since 1990 Kunkel had been an assistant engineer alongside George Massenburg or Frank Wolf, but five years later he had come into his own; *December* was the first time he engineered an album from start to finish for Peter. And at the time of this writing, twenty-five years later and after over a dozen album projects together, one of the most respected engineers in the business gives credit where it's due: "Peter," Kunkel stated, "really gave me the ability to have a career.

"The things that I learned from Peter in the time I've worked for him have been the *most* beneficial in building my career of all the other mentors I've had," said Kunkel. "The skill set I got from Peter was the type of ethics and the type of character and the type of follow-through . . ." He paused a moment: "And the type of *focus* that you need to really be able to survive in the entertainment industry.

"We're makin' music, you know? We're *not* sending rockets into space. And being able to keep that all in perspective . . . I really learned from Peter."

It may not be "rocket science," but you wouldn't know it by the amazing amount of detail Peter and Nathaniel keep track of during sessions: "He's *meticulous* about documentation," Kunkel emphasized. "When you leave the studio at night, you should be able to DIE in your sleep and have people come in in the morning and finish the record without having to ask anybody a question. *That's* how well things should be documented. And Peter definitely counts on that type of professionalism."

When recording at the top studios in Los Angeles, New York, or London, that type of professionalism would be expected, but Peter wasn't quite sure *what* to expect when his limo arrived at the small studio where his next project would be recorded. The Dixie Chicks, then country music superstars, had been approached to cover the old Supremes hit "You Can't Hurry Love" for the upcoming Julia Roberts vehicle *Runaway Bride*. Their label, Sony, would be releasing the soundtrack album, and the group's manager, Simon Renshaw, was debating whom to work with. "Peter was with the label," Renshaw realized, "and I just said to the girls, 'Why don't we meet with Peter Asher? He was James Taylor's producer.' They *loved* James Taylor."

With Peter enthusiastically approved, "we needed to do something quickly," Renshaw recalled, but at that time the Chicks were on tour. Peter cut the music track, which propels along as solidly as Motown's original (with Peter's tambourine work, again, a key element), in LA. He then flew with engineer George Massenburg to the Midwest, or as Peter called it, "The middle of nowhere."

The Chicks were asleep in their tour bus, and Peter woke them up, as there was no time to waste. "I had them for one morning," Peter recalled, so the closest studio "which was adequately equipped to do vocals" was booked. Within a couple of hours, The Chicks had nailed it. *Runaway Bride* went on to gross over three hundred million dollars, with the soundtrack album a Top Five hit.

Conversely, Miss Georgiana Steele did *not* run away, becoming Gordon Waller's bride on August 15, 1998. The champagne had been flowing at the wedding reception for hours by the time best man Peter was cajoled onstage by Gordon—reuniting their act for the first time in decades. Having not sung these songs in years, Peter was a bit forgetful with some words, but no one cared—the two old mates laughed and smiled their way through a set of their old hits, bringing the delighted crowd to their feet.

As the new century dawned, "My contract with Sony was drawing to a close," Peter recalled. "It was clear to me that the whole record business was entering a somewhat different phase." Quite an understatement.

With the advent of peer-to-peer networks such as Napster and the ease of trading music files, along with the advent of Apple's iPod and iTunes Music Store, there was a return to the primacy of the "single" track—similar to Peter's early days in the business. Consumers began to turn their backs on purchasing overpriced albums, and accordingly, record label profits began to tumble. Peter could see all the layoffs coming: "I don't think they wanted," he admitted, "to keep me on and pay me what they were paying me . . ."

Before his move from senior vice president to consultant became official, a couple of album productions concluded Peter's tenure at Sony. For old friend Neil Diamond, Peter was called in to assist Diamond's musical director, Alan Lindgren. After months of helping Neil with arrangement ideas for his latest batch of tunes, Diamond had asked Lindgren to produce his upcoming sessions. "I was an untested quantity producing," Lindgren admitted, and Peter stepped in to help. "Peter knew how the process went and how to deal with 'the suits'"—Lindgren chuckled—"and I really appreciated him being there!"

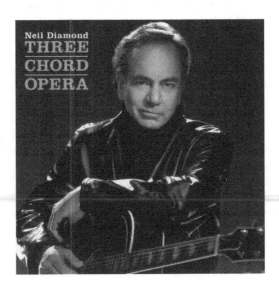

Three Chord Opera album cover.

The record, released as *Three Chord Opera*, contains the memorable, lovely waltz "Turn Down the Lights" (featuring Lindgren on organ and Peter playing autoharp). The two producers utilized some surprising sonic choices—like combining a string quartet with steel drums—and Diamond gave them free rein to embellish his work musically. "He does what the producer says," Lindgren observed. "He's more concerned with how the vocal fits with the track, how he *sits* in the whole thing." He concluded that Diamond is "not so much a musician as he is a songwriter."

Peter had no problem comparing Diamond to another legendary songwriter—Bob Dylan: "They absolutely are in the *exact* same role in life: I wrote these songs, people like 'em, I go out and sing 'em. They have different *approaches*—Neil is a very serious crowd pleaser, and Dylan is very seriously a crowd *confuser*—but the essence of what they do, their *job*, is *exactly* the same."

Next came one of the highlights of Peter's work for Sony. Canadian artist Amanda Marshall was about to embark on her next album when Sony A&R man Mike Roth gave her a tape of work by songwriter and producer Billy Mann. Listening, she became intrigued with the possibilities for this third album, noting: "I really wanted to step outside of what I'd done with the previous two." Soon after, Peter arrived in Toronto for meetings and ended up at dinner with various label execs and also, luckily, Marshall. "We just really hit it off," she said, telling Peter about what she hoped to achieve writing with Mann. Peter had been impressed with Billy when they met earlier that year and, excited at the possibilities, told Marshall: "If this works out, I'd really like to be a part of it."

Before flying to Canada to begin writing sessions, "Peter had advised me on what he thought I should think about musically," Mann recalled, and he reached out to a DJ and hip-hop artist from The Legion known as Molecules. "I have this wacky idea," Mann told him, "of doing acoustic and rock guitar stuff—pop songs—but over beats!" That idea doesn't seem at all strange now, but at the time, "people weren't putting acoustic guitars and woodwinds and strings with hip-hop beats," recalled Mann. "It just wasn't happening."

With a collection of tasty beats from Molecules now in hand, Mann cleared his schedule and flew to Canada. "I was really eager because"—Mann laughed—"I just wanted to impress Peter, really!" On their first day together, Mann and Marshall wrote the song "Everybody's Got a Story," recorded the demo, and sent it to Peter, who loved it. "Maybe," Peter suggested to the two of them, "this is something we could do together." Mann recalled his response: "Hell, *yeah!*"

When Peter arrived in Toronto, he dove into the project in a way he hadn't in decades: actively involved in writing the songs. "It became obvious he had a lot more to offer," according to Marshall, after Mann told him to grab his guitar. "We were in the studio, and he came in and we sat around and just laughed and wrote," Mann recalled. "I mean, he jumped right in!"

"It was great to sit around with a guitar like in the old days and cowrite with people," Peter confessed. "Amanda, Billy, and I got on very well doing that, and I think had some good ideas." "His comfort level as a songwriter," Mann recalled, "was as fluid and easy as his comfort level as a producer."

The tales the trio married to Molecules's beats ranged from walking in on your lover's same-sex tryst (the noirish "Brand New Beau") to waking up tattooed and pierced next to a stranger (the funny, frantic "Sunday Morning After") to the pain someone of mixed race feels from the casual racism of clueless friends (the powerfully pointed "Double Agent"). There was also the perfect pop chorus within "Red Magic Marker," where the singer tries one last time to make her intentions clear to someone missing every signal.

In sharing production duties, Mann maintains Peter became a mentor to him: "He had a way, in the songwriting *and* the producing, of making me make smart choices. Like, 'Well, we could do this here *or* we could do this here . . .'" According to George Massenburg, who engineered the sessions: "I think Peter wants to hear things to compare: 'Okay, well, here's A, here's B' . . . I mean, it's logical and maybe even a little scientific, except you're responding to your *feelings*—what feels better? A or B?" Peter's ability to steer the artist or collaborator toward the smartest choice is one of his greatest assets.

"It's like a third ear," Mann laughed. "How do you describe that cosmic extrasensory ability that he has? I'm not sure how to do it, except to say that he's an amazing, amazing guy."

"It's tremendously inspirational to hang out with him, because he has endless, boundless amounts of enthusiasm," Marshall said. "The guy is among the most driven people that I have ever met in my life, and usually 'driven' does not necessarily make for a pleasant personality." She laughed. "And he is *so* much the exception to that rule."

Though the record began as a modern slice of "folk" music—conversational lyrics over acoustic guitar with a street-edged sensibility, "it was Peter," said Marshall, "who

Everybody's Got a Story album cover.

brought all the various musical elements together that needed to be there to bump it up to the next level." David Campbell once again was called upon to arrange strings and woodwinds, enhancing songs that began as acoustic guitar and hip-hop rhythm beds by adding a gypsy violin here, a clarinet duet there.

Finally, there's Marshall's stupendous vocals. "Amanda's one of the best singers in the world," Peter enthused. "She's astounding—I mean, just astounding! She rattled off all those vocals and all the harmony parts *instantly*." He shook his head. "She sang them *perfectly* every time." Marshall was quick, though, to credit Mann: "Billy was amazing. He's really a gifted vocal arranger." The album is full of vocal asides and exclamations, layered harmonies, and strong, soulful storytelling, ending with "Inside the Tornado"—a vocal *tour de force* with no musical accompaniment.

Everybody's Got a Story, released in 2001, achieved Platinum-level sales in Canada, spawning hit singles and winning a handful of Juno Awards (that country's equivalent to the Grammys), including Pop Album of the Year. With all the fun he must have had making it, Peter had no hesitation listing it as one of his favorite productions in a long career.

25

RUN TO ME

Merck Mercuriadis heard that Peter would be stepping down from his position at Sony at the beginning of 2002 and was quick to set up a meeting. Mercuriadis had been in the music business since a teenager, and after stints in both marketing and then A&R for Virgin Records, he joined Sanctuary Music—rising to the position of chief executive officer of Sanctuary Group North America.

"Our success is based on creating an environment for our artists," Mercuriadis told me in 2005, "one that is sensitive to who they are, that can give them the confidence to be able to do their best work. And when I heard that Peter was looking to transition himself out of Sony, I was on him like a shot because he's a perfect proponent of our model." Brought in as president of Sanctuary Management, then one of the largest music management companies in the world, Peter explained they could provide "not only international representation, but representation in every aspect of the business." Along with divisions for agents and merchandising, not to mention a record label, Sanctuary would have their fingers in almost every part of a client's pie—and representing such iconic artists as Beyoncé, Guns N' Roses, and Morrissey, those slices would definitely prove profitable.

Alongside his management duties, Peter continued to accept production work that piqued his interest. Early in 2002, Peter Gelb, the head of Sony Classical Records, signed a young Nova Scotian singer named Aselin Debison. With high hopes for a pop crossover hit, Gelb and his team quickly saw that Peter would be perfect to lead the young girl through a major-label project. "I was only twelve," Debison explained. "I kind of put my faith in the hands of others, and they did a fantastic job bringing in Peter and George"—meaning Massenburg, who not only engineered the sessions, but coproduced with Peter.

Though "only twelve," she *did* have a choice in what she was singing: "A lot of different songs were pitched," she explained, "and I gave my thoughts!" Some that made the cut were "Driftwood" by the band Travis and Mike Oldfield's "Moonlight Shadow" (which ended up a Top Twenty hit in Japan). "Peter has a vast catalog of songs he just *likes*," Massenburg stated. "He remembers great songs, and he's right there with a suggestion." Another suggestion was "Sweet Is the Melody," an achingly charming tune by Iris DeMent—an Arkansas-born singer/songwriter who was a client at Peter Asher Management in the nineties.

Debison hails from the Cape Breton coast, and the sessions featured much of the traditional Celtic feel that permeates that area's sound, with pipes and fiddles incorporated throughout. Many of the songs have an enchanting, innocent quality to them, but "Once in Every Life" (written by Billy Mann with his friend Leslie Satcher) gave some adults pause: "We went back and forth over whether I should do it or not," Debison recalled. "They said, 'Well, it kind of sounds like a romantic relationship.' But I said, 'It doesn't necessarily have to be that way . . . it could be your parents or your best friend. It doesn't matter—everybody loves *somebody*,'" she protested. "So I kind of won the battle on *that* one.

"Peter was fabulous; he was *so* kind and *so* funny, *very* down-to-earth," Debison remembered, "and because I was a kid, he *approached* me as a kid." If she needed a break or there was a technical issue, he'd say: "Go out in the driveway and play basketball for twenty minutes while we work on this." She also recalled Peter's kindness after he flew off to catch a Robin Williams concert, as Peter was in charge of recording Robin's upcoming comedy tour for a CD release. "I was a big fan," Debison confided, with *Mrs. Doubtfire* one of her favorite films. "When he came back, he said, 'I have a present for you.'" From behind his back, Peter revealed a tour poster signed and personalized to Debison by Williams himself.

Sweet is the Melody was a lovely album, but not a big commercial success. "I don't think it met anybody's expectations," George Massenburg stated. "And you know, that's the other thing Peter sort of taught me: The less emotionally involved you get in a project, the easier it is to let go of it. You know? That Zen thing, where, at the

Sweet is the Melody album cover.

end of it, you know you've done the very best that you can do. You just let go. . . . It does what it does."

Peter was brought in on the Robin Williams project, "because," Williams stated, "we were looking for the best," but another reason was that Robin had become, in Peter's words, "one of my best friends." They first met in London years earlier at a party for mutual friend Eric Idle, "and then Wendy and my wife, Marsha, became great friends," Williams recounted, solidifying the relationship. Interestingly, one of the award-winning actor's most celebrated roles was portraying Dr. Oliver Sacks in the film *Awakenings*; it turned out Sacks had been a student of Dr. Richard Asher, Peter's father.

The idea was to record all thirty-eight shows in good quality, then edit together "performances from different cities," Williams explained. "Local stuff, but yet still making it play for the whole country." Peter needed someone he could trust to handle all the live recording. "Peter called me," Nathaniel Kunkel recalled, "and he said, 'Do you wanna go on the road and record Robin Williams's tour?' . . . *Are you kidding me?*" He laughed, insisting: "That wasn't even like a gig—that was like a gift!"

The trek became the highest-grossing comedy tour in history. Ultimately, Peter and Nathaniel shared a suite of rooms at the Clift Hotel in San Francisco and began to mix the material together. "Peter had wonderful ways of transitioning stuff," Williams noted, "he and Nathaniel picking the best cuts." Peter and Robin had talked from the start about incorporating music somehow, and one bit seemed especially promising, though it came from a near-tragedy: "My father-in-law had died," Williams explained, "and they revived him, and he said, 'Why'd you do that?'" Laughing, he continued: "He realized at that point the Grim Reaper wasn't a really bad guy, going"—changing to a gruff, heavy voice—"*'I've come to take you!'* It's more like"— calm and friendly now—"'Hi! Hi, how are you?'" He explained that as you age and more and more friends start to die, "it becomes a weird race where you're the last man standing," he said wistfully. "It *truly* is a game of *Survivor*."

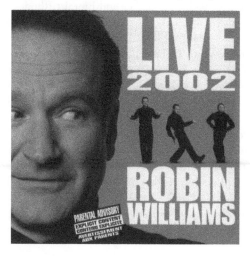

Live 2002 album cover.

Williams's comedic recounting of the Ages of Man he dubbed "The Grim Rapper." Peter thought it would be perfect to pair it with the old Apple Records hit "Those Were the Days" by Mary Hopkin, which he'd had a hand in producing. "Peter tried to license the track," Kunkel said, "and they wouldn't let him do it, so he went and recut the track," re-creating Richard Hewson's original arrangement with a few hip-hop touches on top. Eventually, Hopkin herself was enticed back into the studio to rerecord her vocal for the song's chorus. "And you *cannot tell the difference, dude!*" Kunkel shook his head. "Peter's so good."

The CD, entitled *Live 2002*, ended up winning the Grammy Award for Best Comedy Album the following year. As Peter grinned from the audience, Williams stood on the Radio City Music Hall stage and thanked members of his "posse," finally including Peter: "We call him 'DJ Mensa.' God bless you, Peter; he's English, he knows more than we do . . ."

"The Grammy I owe to him," Williams told me plainly. "He's an extraordinary man, you know. In this time when people drop the word 'Renaissance,' I think an 'Enlightenment' Man. Just skip the Renaissance and go to the Enlightenment, given his field of knowledge." The comedian added: "A sartorial genius, too; a man who can dress in colors where a pimp would go '*Noooo*,' and yet pull it off."

For his next project, Peter would again revisit music from his past. Manager Winston Simone and Columbia A&R man Mitchell Cohen had an idea for the group Wilson Phillips—as children of California pop royalty (The Beach Boys and The Mamas and The Papas), why not an album of songs by California-based bands?

Peter, though no longer a VP, was still consulting for the label and was immediately a top contender for the producer's chair. "We met with him because we were fans of his previous work," singer Carnie Wilson said, "but we had no idea what to expect." They gathered at Peter's house and began brainstorming song possibilities. "We just liked his ideas," she confessed, "and he was very open about letting us be very, very hands-on with the vocals." The label presented the group with *their* list of song suggestions, including deep cuts by Arthur Lee and Emmitt Rhodes, which Wilson described as too obscure: "We were, like, 'We've never heard these songs in our lives.'"

For the next six weeks, "I would go into a rehearsal studio with them and try stuff out," explained Peter, with "everyone bouncing song ideas." The tunes eventually chosen for the project "not only lyrically had to be right," Wilson said, but "had to have the opportunity for us to have our blend." Ultimately, she admitted, "We cheated a little bit" with the dictate of the songwriter or original artists being *from* California—simply a strong West Coast relationship was sufficient.

"He worked *very* fast," Wilson recalled. "He said, 'We're gonna track all ten songs in a week'" meaning record the basic music beds—"and I said, '*What th' fuck are you talkin' about?*'" She laughed. "I couldn't believe it. And those musicians kicked butt!"

It seemed fitting to try a song from each respective parental unit, and "Monday Monday" was selected to represent the Phillips side. Peter, Carnie said, "had more of a rock vision" for the song, using stinging electric guitars to open the track, propelling the song forward alongside the Sklar/Kunkel rhythm section. "When I heard the track, I just said, 'My God!' It really gave us this great canvas to paint on." Wilson was initially expecting to harmonize on every line, but Peter advised them to resist and insert harmonies sparingly, making the vocals (which here also included Mama Cass's daughter Owen Elliot) sound "really great," according to Wilson.

Jay Ruston, the engineer at The Park Studios, where many of the vocals were recorded, observed Peter's creativity with vocal arrangements up-close: "They could be stuck," he said, "and he'll sing them a new melody: 'Here, try this,' or 'Try this harmony here.'" At other times, Ruston said, "He would basically let them do their thing, which to me is as brilliant as telling them what to do." He laughed. "Because he recognizes when what they're doing is the right thing."

David Rolfe had been chosen by Peter to both take over production when he was away on business and come up with arrangement ideas. Rolfe decided to slow down Fleetwood Mac's "Go Your Own Way" and turn it into a moody ballad, cutting a demo merely "to pitch Peter on the downtempo concept," he explained. Peter liked it so much, he simply used the demo as the basis to begin building the master track, supplementing Rolfe's ringing guitar arpeggios with Russ Kunkel's cajon percussion and Larry Klein's fretless bass. Guitarist Dean Parks "really made the track happen," according to Rolfe, by adding a staccato acoustic guitar part over Rolfe's playing.

The final icing came with David Campbell's lush orchestration, and the vocal "blend" Wilson mentioned earlier—their voices in unison here, harmonizing there, tumbling together with overlapping lyrics during the long fade. All in all, a simply gorgeous take on California-native Lindsey Buckingham's ode to his breakup with Stevie Nicks.

For "You're No Good," Rolfe programmed the track's loping rhythm bed and added a dirty fuzz bass to give it "attitude," he said, bringing the tune sharply up-to-date. Once again, this was from his arrangement demo: "I didn't intend for any of that to end up on the record," he claimed, but they're the first sounds you hear on the album—just as the same song opened *Heart Like a Wheel* thirty years earlier. Peter had fun revisiting one of his biggest hits, mischievously deciding to sample his original production and place it at the end. "We had to change the tempo and the pitch and do all kinds of stuff to make it fit," explained Peter.

He politely sent a copy off to Linda Ronstadt and said: "Let me know what you think, because I'm not even gonna ask the record company for permission if you don't want it to be there." She had no problem: "I was very flattered," she told me later, adding: "I thought he did a great job." The next time he was with the girls in the studio, Peter got Linda on the phone and passed it around. "Wendy was too nervous—wouldn't talk to her," Peter recalled. "But Carnie and Chynna both spoke to her and thanked her profoundly, and Linda told the girls how great they sounded."

"The whole thing was a very different experience for us, because we're used to doing original material," said Wilson. "This was like a challenge." The biggest challenge turned out to be their take on "Turn! Turn! Turn!"—Pete Seeger's musical adaptation of the book of Ecclesiastes and a number-one hit for The Byrds. Wilson called Peter's first attempt "a frickin' nightmare.

"The arrangement of it," she said derisively. "The rhythm was all wrong. All three of us did not see the same vision that he did." And, once again, Peter listened to his artists: "A lot of producers walk in with that 'My way or the highway' attitude," Jay Ruston noted. "Not all of them, but a great bunch of them. But Peter—he can be firm when he needs to, but he really listens to everyone's ideas."

One day, Carnie Wilson recalled Peter saying: "I think I've got it now." Pushing PLAY on his drum machine, out came a brand-new rhythm he had programmed for the song. "He's a pioneer with technology," Jay Ruston enthused. "He'll sit there and create beats almost like a hip-hop producer!"

As the three singers listened, they knew: "That was it," Wilson said, and they started over. "Those girls don't accept anything but perfection," Ruston declared.

Finally, Carnie and Wendy's dad, Brian, took the girls through his early Beach Boys classic "In My Room"—not only playing piano, but taking the lead vocal on the song's bridge. "He didn't want to sing—he was very scared," Carnie recalled. "He was, like, ready to leave before he even got there!" They worked fast, and in thirty minutes the "Beach Girls" had the track that would conclude their album entitled *California*.

Though "Go Your Own Way" made inroads on Adult Contemporary radio, the album didn't do well. "I'm pretty let down with the sales," Wilson said four months after its release. "I don't know if that's Sony's lack of promotion, or the change in the business . . . I think it would have helped to do a tour," she mused, but with Wendy's pregnancy, that was simply not in the cards.

But as to Peter: "We'd *love* to work with him again," Carnie exclaimed. "I just love being able to trust someone like that."

California album cover.

"I always sensed that when you talked to him," actor Kevin Kline said of Peter, "he really had this wealth of knowledge and always this *taste*. . . . He appreciated a breadth of music and musical styles and knew musical history."

After revisiting the music of the sixties and seventies with Wilson Phillips, Peter dove into the compositions of the twenties, thirties, and forties with his next two projects. First, film director/producer Irwin Winkler had tried for years to get a film about songwriters George and Ira Gershwin off the ground but gave up due to rights issues. Someone suggested he take a look at their contemporary, Cole Porter, and after realizing what a singular personal life he led—a gay man married for years to a beautiful woman—Winkler worked with writer Jay Cocks to develop a script that used Porter's sophisticated, witty, and romantic songs to illustrate his story.

Along with film producer Rob Cowan, Winkler began approaching artists to per-form Porter's tunes in selected scenes. Composer and arranger Stephen Endelman, brought in to handle the film's music, recalled that once current superstar Alanis Moris-sette was on board, other artists began to say yes, including Elvis Costello, Sheryl Crow, and Robbie Williams. Not long after, MGM/UA struck a deal with Sony to release a soundtrack album, and they, of course, turned to Peter to executive-produce the release.

"He was coming in to make sure that what we were doing for the film," Endel-man said, "would also work on record," with Peter lending his producing expertise during recording: "Working with all those cool artists," said Peter, "was fun." Endel-man oversaw the film's 5.1 mix, then joined Peter in Nashville, where the record was mixed with George Massenburg.

The film *De-Lovely* was a period piece, so the performances were all in the style of that glamorous era between the World Wars. Even so, some purists were not amused; even Kevin Kline—who stared as Cole Porter—drew the line at Sheryl Crow's rendi-tion of "Begin the Beguine."

"I was always against that," Kline confessed. Winkler "wanted the tone of the song to have the same color as the action," he noted, so to connect it to the sad narrative of the scene, it was changed from a major key to a minor one. "As the living embodi-ment of Cole Porter," Kline protested, only half in jest, "I had to say: 'I didn't write it that way!'"

Peter was much more sanguine about it: "Don't worry too much about art. Trying it in a weird way doesn't do any harm at all," he observed. "My feeling is, you know, if the song's good enough, it can survive anything."

The film was only moderately successful, but there was a positive outcome: "A *whole generation*," Kline declared, "was introduced to Cole Porter's music, and be-cause those popular singers of the day were putting the songs over, they *listened* and started to appreciate his genius." Indeed, the following year saw a noticeable surge in the sale of Cole Porter song compilations.

A handful of Porter's songs also made it into Peter's *next* project: Sony Classical's Peter Gelb had signed jazz singer Jane Monheit, whose four independent releases had proven quite successful. Having been a fan of the great MGM musicals, she wanted her upcoming record to comprise classic songs from those iconic films. Gelb, a long-

time friend of Peter's, asked if he'd be interested in producing it: "I said, 'Absolutely,'"
but because of previous commitments, "I wasn't sure if I could."

"So they called me," Al Schmitt recalled, "and asked if I would engineer *and*
produce the record." Schmitt, who'd won more Grammy Awards than any other
engineer or mixer—recording everyone from Elvis and Sinatra to Dylan and Mc-
Cartney—agreed to do both for Monheit, "though I don't really like to do that," he
said, preferring one or the other: "Too many hats to wear."

Eventually, after Peter was able to clear his schedule, these two industry legends
who respected each other immensely decided to produce the project together. Peter
described the experience as "terrific."

"We worked together as a team," Schmitt explained. "I'd throw an idea out that
maybe wasn't *quite* right, and he'd say: 'That's a good idea! But if we did *this* . . .'"
And besides all the creative back-and-forth, each could take over if necessary; if Peter
was tending to Sanctuary business, for example, and recording needed to continue,
he could leave it all in Schmitt's capable hands.

"I remember the vibe in the studio being really great, really mellow," Monheit
said. "The three of us saw eye-to-eye *completely* on what we wanted to happen musically, which is"—she laughed—"a really nice situation to be in!"

Peter brought "more of a pop sensibility than other producers I'd worked with,"
she added, but jazz was still the main focus. Surrounded by excellent players, Monheit cut her vocals live—scatting and skipping through "Honeysuckle Rose" and
"Taking a Chance on Love," sighing and swooping through "In the Still of the
Night" and "Embraceable You." One highlight was the unjustly forgotten "Too Late
Now," the Lerner and Lane torch song from *Royal Wedding*. Monheit nails the melancholy ache from a failed affair with romantic precision, perfectly accompanied by
the jazz quartet led by pianist/arranger Michael Kanan.

"He's got an amazing ear," Monheit observed, as Peter detected the smallest aural
imperfection: "The way I end notes sometimes—a little sound in my throat," she

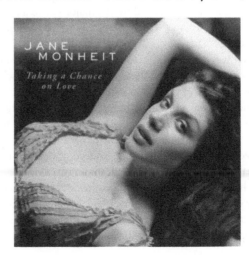

Taking a Chance on Love
album cover.

said as example. "One of those little, tiny things that I didn't even notice was there." Peter, Schmitt said, "would get on her all the time about it," advising her to drop it. "'You don't need that to be there,'" she recalled Peter saying, with Monheit not the least bit offended, but happy for his advice: "Why do you bring a great producer into the studio if not for his ideas?" she asked.

Taking a Chance on Love shot to number-one on *Billboard*'s Jazz chart upon its release. Peter certainly brought out Monheit's best. "He knows how to handle vocalists, obviously," Schmitt said of his old friend, and Monheit was ready for another album, stating: "There's a whole lot more to be learned from Peter . . ."

"When you're someone who has the experience Peter has," Sanctuary's Merck Mercuriadis explained, "you also bring him in to work with projects that require his expertise." The British singer Morrissey, signed to Sanctuary Records, was planning to record a live album at the close of 2004. "Morrissey admired Peter as much as I did," said Mercuriadis, so he was tapped to produce the project, released the following year as *Live at Earls Court*.

"All the vocals are completely live," Peter stated, but there were a few musical fixes: "If there was a mistake, for example, you'd fix it with something from somewhere else," as other shows from the tour were also recorded. Therefore, Peter and mixer Nathaniel Kunkel could take a guitar solo from a different date and fly it in to cover a bum note. "I ran everything by him," Peter said of Morrissey. "A couple of times I sat in his car with him, playing stuff and getting approval.

"He's charming and intelligent and . . ." Peter paused, then said: "Occasionally unpredictable. And, of course, *immensely* talented. He's brilliant.

"I mean, he is a bit weird, but that's part of the mystique, you know?"

Peter developed a close relationship with another mercurial artist during this time: Courtney Love. "We first met," he recalled, "because Merck and I went down to France at the time when Sanctuary was actually interested in signing her album."

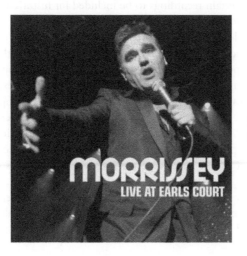

Live at Earls Court album cover.

Though Love ended up releasing the record through Virgin, "she and I got on well," said Peter, and he began managing her through Sanctuary.

Peter's assistant at the time, Brandilyn Rolfe, admitted having Love as a client wasn't all smooth sailing: "She was *exhausting!*" Love seems the polar opposite of the reserved and erudite Asher, so why take her on? "Peter," Rolfe revealed, "likes a challenge." "That's true, I do," Peter agreed, "and I like Courtney—she's smart and interesting and fun to talk to," but then added that, back then, she was "out of her mind."

"There were times," Peter recalled, "I was obliged to kind of issue actual ultimatums, you know? Like: 'You have to clean up or we're going away.' But before we actually walked, she would sort of veer off back into 'the Path of Goodness.'" He smiled. He did his best to stick beside her, accompanying her to court appearances, supporting both her musical endeavors and stints in rehab, and representing the estate of Love's late husband, Kurt Cobain. In that regard, one project Peter helped bring to fruition was the Nirvana box set *With the Lights Out.*

Jack Endino, who produced and engineered most of Nirvana's early sessions, told me research for the proposed compilation, including locating and gathering tapes, began in 1998, with the project "'on,' then 'off,' then 'on' again," explaining: "The apparent hang-up always seemed to be Courtney suing Universal, or suing Nirvana LLC, or getting sued herself, or conflicting with an ex-manager, or some such nonsense.

"Asher's main contribution to getting the damn box set process moving again," Endino claimed, "was to provide a solid organization and responsible management structure to oversee Courtney's business affairs, which I had the impression was, uh, rather haphazard for some years before."

The surviving members of Nirvana were managed by John Silva; Michael Meisel, working for Silva, had been on the project from the beginning. "I was not a Nirvana expert—he is," Peter stated. "So, going through tapes myself? No. Sitting and listening and choosing what should go on and what shouldn't based on how it *sounded,* yes." Meisel would push for certain recordings to be included for historical reasons, and, said Peter, "we collaborated very effectively."

It was a case study in diplomacy and patience—both needed because of the ill will between the parties. "They were never allowed to communicate directly," Peter cautioned. "I never actually spoke to Dave Grohl, and he never spoke to Courtney—*that* would have got complicated." Though differing points of view were expressed, "The other guys in the band were very cooperative; Courtney was very cooperative.

"In this context, I think the ambassadorial system worked very well," Peter offered with typical understatement. *With the Lights Out* sold over a million copies in the United States alone, with Stephen Thomas Erlewine writing on allmusic.com: ". . . nobody who gets this box set should be disappointed, since it is as good as it could possibly be."

During both the Morrissey and Nirvana projects, Peter was not only attending to business at Sanctuary but concurrently producing a solo album for Raul Malo, singer and songwriter for acclaimed country outfit The Mavericks. Peter, out of curiosity, asked Malo, signed to both Sanctuary Records and Sanctuary Management, "what I was gonna do for the next project," the singer recalled, now that The Mavericks had basically dissolved.

"I had always been 'The Guy,' you know? I had written all the songs, arranged everything, produced everything, and I'd never just been 'The Singer,'" Malo said, pausing—". . . which is pretty ironic, thinkin' about it . . . the one thing I love doin' the most is singing. And when Peter and I spoke of this record, I told him that that's exactly what I wanted to do."

The two of them began to brainstorm song choices: "I had my guitar," Malo said, "and I just started playing songs that I knew." Peter, perhaps thinking back to his first production effort, asked if he knew any Bee Gees songs, and Malo started singing "Run to Me," a Top Twenty hit from 1972. "He loved the way it sounded," Malo recalled. "He was, like, 'Oh, yeah! We gotta record that!'" Peter, ever the Everly Brothers fan, suggested their 1960 hit "So Sad," while Malo chose to try J.D. Souther's "You're Only Lonely"—all songs of romantic longing and perfect for Malo's magnificent multi-octave voice.

Once songs were chosen, "we mapped out arrangements and tempos and instrumentation," Malo said, "so when we got to the studio we knew on *this* song was gonna be percussion, this song was gonna have upright bass, this other one was gonna be electric bass," he said, adding: "I'm used to just, 'Alright, everybody bring everything, we'll smoke a joint, and we'll figure it out.'" He laughed. "Everything was thought out and planned meticulously before we went in. And it was great, 'cause we saved time."

Once in the studio, "I was *really* surprised by this, and the musicians were really surprised by this," Malo noted: "He produces by un-producing." As the musicians began to play, Malo observed that Peter "listens to each song, each piece of music very intensely, and everything has a purpose—every lick, every movement, every musical note has a purpose."

"I like clarity—I usually don't like clutter," Peter offered.

"Instead of letting people just fill holes as they normally would, sometimes he'll leave a hole, and *then*, when an instrument plays," Malo said, "they really stand out." He laughed. "That's where, I think, part of his genius lies. . . . He really allows a song to breathe."

One example of this occurs on "Run to Me." The recording begins with a bed of guitar/piano/bass/drums augmented with steel guitar and strings, but after the opening verses and initial chorus, suddenly everything but the strings drop away, leaving you to focus on Malo's pleading voice for a full verse before bringing back those supporting instruments one after another. "That was Peter's idea," string arranger David Campbell admitted—a simple but dramatic touch.

Including Ron Sexsmith's "Secret Heart" and Randy Newman's "Feels Like Home," Malo's *You're Only Lonely* occupies that rarified air that includes Sinatra's 1950s romantic concept albums, though the instrumentation is more contemporary, taking slight detours with a gospel touch here and a Latin touch there.

You're Only Lonely
album cover.

There's not a note out of place on the entire album, so even though there's "a lot of stuff on there, it doesn't *seem* like it," Malo emphasized, concluding: "The record is a joy to listen to because of that." Campbell agreed: "It's one of those kinds of albums that there aren't enough of now." *You're Only Lonely* is a marvelously produced pop album of impeccably chosen songs with gorgeous arrangements and meticulous engineering supporting a stunning voice.

Or, for Peter, business as usual.

26

TIME

Paul Shaffer recalled seeing Peter and Gordon perform in 1967 at a hockey arena in his hometown of Thunder Bay in northwestern Ontario, Canada. "They played on a Friday night," he said, adding: "Every Saturday night, I played with my band" at that same venue. Shaffer remembers walking into the arena's dressing room to get ready the day after Peter and Gordon's appearance and finding a surprise: "In one of the lockers was a stack of *Lady Godiva* albums, pre-autographed, that they just didn't have time to give out, I guess." Somewhere in his record collection, one of those autographed albums still sits.

"I used to perform Peter and Gordon songs in my band," Shaffer admitted, and, covering the hits of the day, their set list would also include numbers by The Dave Clark Five—a massively popular British Invasion act. Their lead singer, Mike Smith, was one of the greatest vocalists of that era. "He was really a soul singer," Shaffer pointed out, though often saddled with somewhat slight pop material. Smith cut a striking figure in the group, standing at his Vox Continental organ, and Shaffer decided he would stand at his keyboards, too—and continues to play while standing to this day.

For years, of course, Shaffer led the house band on David Letterman's various talk shows. Once, when filling in for Letterman as host, he had Smith take over his own spot—leading the band through various DC5 hits to the audience's delight. "He was fantastic," Shaffer enthused, and because of his influence on a certain young Canadian musician, "it was a kick to meet him and work with him."

On September 13, 2003, while climbing a fence at his Spanish villa, Smith fell on his head, crushing his spinal cord and leaving him paralyzed from the waist down. "I felt terrible," Shaffer recalled, and he spoke with Little Steven Van Zant about possibly putting a benefit concert together with artists like Bruce Springsteen (who, Shaffer noted, "was very much influenced by The Dave Clark Five, too"). "But the planets weren't aligned right"—he sighed—"and it just didn't happen."

Now, finally able to afford his own Vox Continental organ, the instrument occupied pride-of-place in Shaffer's home music room. "Every day I would look at it and say, 'Jeez, I should really be doing something for Mike Smith.'" Deciding to try something on a smaller scale, he phoned Smith's agent, Margo Lewis, for help in procuring acts for a show. It turned out The Zombies, another major British Invasion act, were touring the States and had an open date on August 2, 2005. They agreed to participate, as did The Fab Faux (a band including Shaffer's *Late Show* bassist Will Lee)—known for their note-perfect renditions of Beatles records. With those two acts, Shaffer was able to book B.B. King's Blues Club in New York's Times Square for the benefit.

"And then my wife said: 'If you could get Peter and Gordon together, *that* would be really something!'"

Shaffer started to dismiss the idea, thinking that Peter would simply be too busy to try to revive his decades-old act, "but she said: 'You'll never know unless you try.'"

Peter admitted: "I didn't know about Mike Smith's accident" until Shaffer called him about the proposed benefit show. "He said, 'What would it take to get Peter and Gordon back together?' And I realized," Peter continued, "it would be very hard to say 'no,' because it was such a good cause AND I knew he would put together a spectacular band!"

Gordon recalled, when contacted by Peter, "He said, 'I fear we should do this one.' '*I fear*'—like 'Oh, shit.' And I said, 'Well, okay.' And he said, 'I think we should rehearse.' And I said, 'Well, I think *you* should, yeah!'" Gordon had continued to perform his hits, playing an oldies show here and a Beatles convention there, but Peter definitely felt the need to prepare.

He began by singing along with his old records, relearning the songs. "I went to a vocal coach three times a week to get my high notes back in shape," Peter said, confessing that he had to drop the keys to a couple of songs by a full step. "I assume it's age . . . or lack of practice, which comes to the same thing." Eventually confident in his vocal abilities and lyric memorization, Peter began rehearsing with his old schoolmate, blending their voices together once again.

Shaffer asked each act on the bill to perform a Dave Clark Five number and decided "Because" was right for Peter and Gordon. The pair agreed that it was something they *would* have recorded in 1964, if given the song as a demo, and re-voiced it to fit their style. The Top Ten hit also had a personal significance to the Shaffers, as Paul's wife considered it "their song."

Amazingly, in only a matter of weeks, Peter and Gordon would finally perform an advertised concert together for the first time in thirty-seven years.

New York City, August 1, 2005: It's nine o'clock at night, 95 degrees outside, and the humidity is damn near one hundred percent. On West 25th Street, as the door to SIR Studios opens, cool air thankfully welcomes you in. At the end of a long, red hallway lined with posters signed by rock elite, a familiar (albeit muffled) sound is

Peter rehearsing for reunion show, New York City, August 1, 2005. ©*Bobbi Lane*

coming from behind a black, closed door—the hit sixties arrangement of Del Shannon's "I Go To Pieces."

Inside, Paul Shaffer, who arrived earlier from a taping of *The Late Show with David Letterman*, is putting his horn section through their paces: "From bar thirty, just the horns. Two, three, four . . ." Satisfied after a few listens, he moves to the string section, then the band alone, and finally everyone together. From behind his keyboards, Shaffer directs the group with his whole body—slouching down on the verse, hands out as if holding a small object, exhorting the musicians to clamp down on the volume; then rising up for the chorus, arms up and shaking, coaxing from those assembled the sound of a grand sixties pop orchestra.

Peter then strides into the rehearsal room and immediately smiles at what he's hearing. Following behind him is his old friend from Steely Dan, Donald Fagen—now personally managed by Peter through Sanctuary Management. Fagen stops, seemingly transfixed by the music, while Peter walks over and huddles with Gordon, who's been watching from the sidelines. As Shaffer and the orchestra reach the song's ending, Peter thrusts his fist in the air along with the final four notes, grinning broadly. He was sure Shaffer would put together a "spectacular band," and hearing them now for the first time, he's convinced of it.

The next evening, August 2nd, the two shows have completely sold out. As lines of excited ticketholders stretch down 42nd Street, the doors part, and the expectant crowd fills the curtained room. After short opening sets by Billy J. Kramer and Denny Laine, Paul Shaffer finally introduces "*Peter and Gordon!*" to a cheering crowd and motions for his musicians to get ready.

Just offstage and hearing the band begin, "I phoned up 'this gentleman,'" Gordon said, referring to his performing persona, "and I thought, 'Here we go!'" He leaned forward to Peter, standing in front of him, and said: "Go on—get up there and get 'em, boy!"

Peter described his state as "excited and apprehensive" ("I wanted to *not* forget stuff," he confessed: "That's the biggest fear"), but he walked onstage with seeming nonchalance, grinning broadly at the crowd's standing ovation. Opening with "I Go To Pieces," the duo's voices were surprisingly tight as they sang the first verse in unison, but as Peter's high harmony came to the fore on the second verse, his partner broke out in a smile. It felt "exactly the same," Gordon marveled.

They continued the set with "Lady Godiva," "True Love Ways," and, at Paul Shaffer's request, "Because." Peter then paused, saying he could understand the audience's puzzlement over their different look these days, but he had a solution; reaching into his pocket, he pulled out the same horn-rimmed specs he'd worn on *The Ed Sullivan Show* forty years prior. The crowd cheered wildly as he put them on: "The illusion is restored," he said smiling and, with Gordon, launched into "A World Without Love."

Shaffer's British Invasion pop orchestra were, as expected, exact in their re-creations of the hit arrangements—but with their set closer, "Woman," Shaffer decided to follow the horns' mid-song exclamations with a touch of harmonium, in a nod to McCartney's original demo. As the song reached its zenith, the pair exited the stage to yet another standing ovation. Among the cheering throng were Peter's wife, Wendy, and twenty-one-year-old daughter, Victoria. Wendy had witnessed Peter and Gordon in their heyday, but Victoria was experiencing her dad's legendary act for the first time. "I was crying through most of it," she confessed sweetly.

"The whole thing," Shaffer told me proudly, "was just a smashing success."

"And *did* you forget stuff?" I asked Peter afterward.

He smiled. "Not so's you'd notice!"

Back at Sanctuary Music, things were less successful. Millions had been spent on their Urban music division run by Beyoncé's father, Mathew Knowles, without much return, and there was an accounting scandal enveloping the home offices in London. Their stock took a dive, and layoffs began, though Peter was optimistic: "The 'official party line' from London is everything will be fine; we just need to restructure certain things, and we'll reorganize it," he said near the end of 2005. "I'll take that as 'gospel' until, you know, paychecks bounce or the door's locked!"

Earlier in 2005, Simon Renshaw had quit the high-powered management organization The Firm and began his own company, Strategic Artist Management, taking

The Dixie Chicks and Miranda Lambert, among other artists, with him. In 2006, Renshaw spoke with Peter: "I said, 'What are you up to?' And he said, 'Ohh, this whole Sanctuary thing is going sideways! Who knows *what's* gonna happen over there.'" Renshaw quipped, "Well, hopefully you're not one of the guys that's gonna go to *jail*, Peter!"

"Ohh, no, no, no, no!" Renshaw laughed, recalling Peter's semi-legal protestations: "I've had *nothing* to do with any of the *alleged* improprieties, or malfeasance, that people are *alleging* may possibly have been *alleged* to occur!" Peter then mentioned that Renshaw's old company The Firm had made overtures for him to come aboard.

"I said, 'You can't go to The Firm! You're *Peter Asher!* That's not the right move for you." When Peter began to moan about the difficulty in building his management company again, basically from scratch, Renshaw stopped him: "If you just want a shingle to work under and don't want to go out and build your own, just come over and do it with me," he told him. "There's an office, there's a phone—do whatever you need to do.

"That was it. It was really that simple." Thus Peter began a partnership with Renshaw's company, continuing his creative passions without pause: "I've never *not* been on the lookout for interesting new management clients or interesting new production projects," Peter told me during this transitional period. "That continues to be the case."

For his next "interesting new production," Peter was chosen by singers Sasha Lazard and Shawna Stone to helm the sessions for their album *Siren*. Both classically trained sopranos aiming for broad crossover appeal, for weeks they would meet almost daily with Peter and listen to songs that each would propose—from James Taylor's "You Can Close Your Eyes" (Peter, of course) to Donizetti's "Una Furtiva Lagrima" (Shawna) and Radiohead's "Fade Out" (Sasha).

Once the tunes were chosen, the three began to arrange how they should be sung. Peter "was part of a duo," Shawna Stone noted, "and it was so neat the way he approached a vocal blend. A lot of times you work with a producer who's a brilliant producer but isn't also a brilliant musician. Peter is an *extremely* talented singer and guitarist, and he knew what we were going through . . .

"He's brilliant at having singers sound organic," she went on, "hearing your voice in its purist form. Being a duo, the *challenge* is to get both voices to sound that way and *blend.*" Stone chuckled. "It's definitely tricky! And he's also incredibly precise in intonation and rhythms. He just did not allow for errors.

"And his energy! Sasha and I would be *dying* at the end of some of these rehearsals, and especially after some of the recording sessions, and he had hours left in him!" She laughed. "He would get there before us and leave after us. It was pretty impressive . . ."

Thirty-three years after arranging strings on Ronstadt's *Heart Like a Wheel*, Peter called up Gregory Rose once again—by now a respected classical conductor and composer. Having read recently that Professor Rose had presented a classical composition prize to a young musician named Naomi Pinnock, Peter called up Rose and

Siren album cover.

stated: "I like her name!" Laughing, Rose recalled Peter asking: "Is she any good?" Assured that she was *very* good, Peter casually asked Rose to bring her on board, and the two of them split arrangement duties for the record.

Peter insisted that the tracks that were the most operatic be recorded live—vocals and orchestra together—to capture the tension and feel of a live performance. Vocals on more modern compositions were overdubbed later, but even the "modern" compositions were classically tweaked—such as the madrigal feel on "You Can Close Your Eyes" achieved by using The Medici Quartet augmented with Jacob Heringman's exquisite abilities on lute.

Peter then actually became a wordsmith for Johann Sebastian Bach—adding lyrics to the master's well-known "Air on the G String." Johann "was a pleasure to work with," said Peter, noting: "Didn't say much." The track opens with the sound of a clock slowly ticking and a bed of strings fading up like daylight, the ticking then joined by a bass duet, setting the song's pace as the familiar instrumental is updated into a luscious vocal arabesque entitled "Time," questioning if love is finally at hand and whether its real meaning is even knowable. "And we had a hit in Japan," Peter observed, as the track ended up in a popular television commercial.

The finished album was a mix of classical and pop, moving between ancient and modern, from Bach to Sting, and probably was not enough of one genre or the other to completely satisfy either camp, resulting in poor sales. Shawna certainly felt all the hard work, though, was worth it: "I feel so blessed that I'm the musician I am now, coming out of that experience, because of Peter. He stretched my voice beyond what I thought I was capable of, and he achieved a precision that I'm very proud of."

After its release, Gregory Rose ran into Radiohead at an awards show. "I've just done an arrangement of one of your songs," he told band member Jonny Greenwood and sent him a copy of Sasha and Shawna's take on "Fade Out." And what did Radiohead think? "He wrote back and said, 'Yeah, we didn't like it.'" Rose, laughing heartily, adds: "I love it when people are really honest, you know?"

While busy handling management concerns and starting production on another Diana Ross project, Peter was contacted by film veteran Bob Balaban. A well-known actor (*Close Encounters of the Third Kind*) and Oscar nominee (coproducer of *Gosford Park*), Balaban was in the midst of directing *Bernard and Doris*—a film based on the life of billionairess Doris Duke. He'd been Peter's friend for a number of years, knew of his acting background and love for the craft, "and I knew he was interested," Balaban said, in a good role.

The first scene in the film was a short, tense interplay between Duke (Susan Sarandon) and her hapless butler. "If you have a small part," Balaban noted, "sometimes it's harder to cast that with somebody who's currently an actor, because they don't seem real enough. And I knew Peter was skillful enough, and enough of a human being, that he could probably come and act and not even *look* like an actor—he'd look like a real person, which is the best compliment you can give somebody."

Peter was also friends with Sarandon, so the three worked easily together during the single day of shooting. During one take, Peter forgot his line, and Sarandon, improvising, continued haranguing him. "And he was wonderfully flustered," Balaban said of Peter, who went with it. "Anybody less talented would have just said, 'Can I do that again?' and ruined it." Balaban knew the take was golden and used it in the film, which went on to receive multiple Emmy and Golden Globe nominations for directing, writing, and acting.

Peter's excellent manservant portrayal might have been criminally overlooked come award season, but his place in movie history had already been dubiously achieved with the recent success of the three Austin Powers films. Actor and comedian Mike Myers had conceived of the character as a tribute to his late father, a Liverpool native, who had turned his son on to British pop culture. The character was obviously an oversized spoof on the James Bond film persona, but Powers's actual *look* came from elsewhere: Peter Asher.

Peter said that Myers confessed to him that the mop-top hair, horn-rimmed glasses, and bad teeth were inspired by his own youthful appearance. Peter took the homage in stride but felt that, on the "shagadelic" scale, he could never compete with Powers.

Graham Nash thought otherwise, recalling the time he first met Peter in 1964: "At a little lunchtime show in a club in the middle of London," Nash said. "And Peter Asher had with him one of the most beautiful women I've ever seen in my life!" Her name was Linda Keith, a model straight from the pages of *Vogue* magazine. Nash, quite the lady-killer himself as the years went on, was quite impressed. With his usual understatement, Peter admitted: "I did okay."

Just a month after *Bernard and Doris* held its world premiere, the legendary West Hollywood club The Troubadour celebrated its fiftieth anniversary, with three eve-

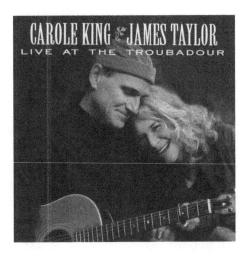

Live at the Troubadour
album cover.

nings reuniting James Taylor and Carole King onstage—almost thirty-six years to the
day when they had last played the club.

"Carole and I had not worked together since the early seventies," James Taylor
noted, other than a benefit here and there. "For years, we'd say: 'Oh, God, we ought
to find some way to do it again.'" Once he heard The Troubadour was marking fifty
years in existence, he thought the perfect opportunity had arrived.

"So I called Peter," Taylor continued. "He just got right into the project and made
it all happen—helped with the set list, arranged the rehearsals, arranged for it to be
recorded. . . . He just slid right back into the saddle." To make the evenings seem
even more like a musical dream come true, their original backing band from 1971—
Kortchmar, Kunkel, and Sklar—were right beside them.

"I couldn't even believe it," Danny Kortchmar said, thinking this group of players
would never appear together again. "I hadn't played with James in eighteen years,"
Lee Sklar confessed, explaining there'd been no falling-out—simply people going
their own way. Taking the stage, they might have looked almost forty years older,
but the special magic created between the players transported not only the audience
of gray and balding fans, but the musicians themselves, back to a time when these
songs were a balm for the soul of a generation.

Peter sat at the mixing board during the shows, with Russ Kunkel's son Nathaniel
at the controls, making sure everything sounded perfect as the three evenings were
captured for later release. Just before launching into "Something in the Way She
Moves" from his debut album on Apple, Taylor would point up to Peter at the mixing board and speak on how he'd given him his "big break."

Peter must have thought back on that sunny spring day in 1968 when a shy singer
stood outside his Weymouth Street apartment, knocking with a nervous hopefulness.
Taylor could just as well have been speaking for Peter when he told the Troubadour
crowd: "It was as if somebody opened a door, and the rest of my life was on the
other side of it . . ."

27

NOT FADE AWAY

One gorgeous afternoon, as Peter strolled along the beach near his home in Malibu, he greeted his neighbor, actress Pamela Anderson—out to enjoy the sun herself. As they chatted against the sound of the surf, Anderson confessed that she was now in need of a new personal manager. Could he help a neighbor out? Of course, Peter replied.

"She is, truly, a global celebrity brand," manager Simon Renshaw commented. "And at the same time, she's zany and quirky enough . . . like an artist! She's a pop icon, that's what she is. And I think Peter has the sensibilities that you need to be able to work with someone like that."

"I think Pamela and I trust each other quite a lot. I think it helps that, even though I haven't been managing her for very long, we've known each other a long time." This quote of Peter's is from the E! Entertainment Television 2008 series *Pam: Girl on the Loose*—an eight-part documentary chronicling a few hectic months in the celebrity's life. Peter is seen in business meetings, advising Anderson on endorsement deals and accompanying her on personal appearances.

"I ended up doing a lot of narration myself," Peter confided, "because Pamela wouldn't do it—that's why I keep showing up in the show.

"She didn't want to wear a mic all the time, she didn't want to do things over—there are concessions they expect for television that she didn't want to make."

"I'm unmanageable," the model and actress declares in one episode, but Peter described her more accurately as "a bit unreliable," adding: "I think she's cool—she's a remarkable woman." Her love for and trust in Peter is obvious for all who tune in. At one point, lounging in a bubble bath, she says her good friend Courtney Love vouched for Peter and confirmed he's very good at his job, but the well-known animal rights activist admits there *is* a problem: Cut to a shot of Peter wearing quite stylish alligator shoes. "We'll work on that," she says quietly.

After the Mike Smith benefit, Gordon floated the idea of possibly doing a tour of ten American cities. "I don't think that's gonna happen," Peter said, "but, you know, if somebody said, 'We'll give you a kasquillion dollars to do a week somewhere,' it's a yes. If someone says, 'We'll give you three months across America in a bus,' it's a no."

Though promoter Ramon Ramos's offer was not in the kasquillion-dollar range (definition: more than a billion, less than a zillion), it was enough for Peter and Gordon to agree to a couple of shows in the Philippines. Those went well, which led to the pair deciding to perform "every now and then," Peter explained, adding: "It's fun."

Something Peter never expected to be at this point in his career was an "Oldies Act," and he certainly didn't need the money, but he was surprised by the reception: "It's easy to be cynical about it," he stated, "but you see people crying in the audience and coming up afterward, you know: 'That was the tune I proposed to my wife' . . . 'Thank you for doing this again' . . . 'These songs mean so much to us' . . .

"People are genuinely moved and transported back in time."

Just as Richard Armitage, Peter and Gordon's former manager, procured a backing band for his young charges, thus Keith Putney, the re-formed duo's new manager, needed to do the same. Jeff Alan Ross remembered Putney asking him: "Can you put a band together?"

"'Well *yeah*, I wanna work with Peter Asher!'—it's, like, the first thing in my *brain*," Ross recalled, but then immediately flashed back to his one experience backing Gordon . . . or trying to: "Gordon got so drunk," Ross related, "he never actually made it to the stage." An excellent singer/pianist/guitarist/arranger, Ross had been a member in a latter-day iteration of Badfinger and for years worked as musical director for various acts. Though he'd sworn never to work with Gordon again, he took Putney's offer. "We all became really good friends with Gordon." Ross smiled. "He was a lovely guy."

There were certainly some memorable gigs: At Carnegie Hall on October 10, 2007, Peter and Gordon closed an evening highlighting the songs of Elton John and Bernie Taupin by performing a moving version of "I Want Love." Their arrangement was so well-received, Peter produced a studio recording of their rendition a month later. They performed on the Santa Monica Pier on August 21, 2008, highlighted by Joan Baez walking onstage to harmonize with them on "500 Miles," the song that had clinched their EMI audition back in 1963.

And at the Surf Ballroom in Clear Lake, Iowa, on February 2, 2009, Peter and Gordon took part in an all-star tribute to Buddy Holly on the fiftieth anniversary of his final performance. Graham Nash, also participating, had grown up idolizing Holly, just as Peter did—naming his first band, The Hollies, in his honor. "He was one of us—he wore a suit, he had glasses, and he didn't shake his ass like Elvis," Nash said of Holly. "He was an ordinary guy." Nash decided, along with Peter, to go out to the site of Holly's tragic death, occurring within hours of his last concert. "We saw the hole in the fence," Nash said, quietly adding: "It was a very emotional time, particularly for Peter and me."

So, too, for Gordon—honored to sing Holly's own "True Love Ways" on the spot where his idol likely sang it for the last time. Sadly, Gordon performed it on only three more occasions with Peter before succumbing to a cardiac arrest the following July 17th. Manager Keith Putney called Peter with the news.

"I knew he was ill," Peter said, and revealed what occurred when the paramedics arrived: "They told him he should go straight to the hospital, and he wouldn't. *He* thought he would die if he went to the hospital; *they* thought he would die if he didn't. They were really both right . . .

"Gordon was one of those people who had the warning from his doctor, 'Keep doing X, Y, and Z, and you will die,'" Peter said, quietly adding: "and he kept doing it." He was sixty-four years old.

"Gordon played such a significant role in my life that losing him is hard to comprehend—let alone to tolerate," Peter wrote in a statement.

"Without Gordon I would never have begun my career in the music business in the first place," he admitted. "I am just a harmony guy . . . Gordon was the heart and soul of our duo."

After Gordon's death, it was hard for Peter to conceive that he'd never sing their songs in public again. Despite always displaying zero interest in becoming a solo act, perhaps there was some way to fashion a show *beyond* just a sequence of songs. He decided to take a couple of lectures he'd given recently, focusing on his experiences in the 1960s and the beginnings of his career as a producer, and put together a spoken memoir with musical interludes.

The show became a multimedia production—photos, videos, and songs helping to illustrate Peter's charmingly told tales of early fame and musical discovery. Peter even found a way to sing with his old partner again, harmonizing with a clip of Gordon performing "True Love Ways." That bit of technical wizardry Jeff Lynne, Peter's friend, found "brilliant." A consummate musician and producer himself—from his own Electric Light Orchestra to producing The Beatles' mid-nineties reunion tracks—Lynne praised not only the show's technical aspects, but also the band, led by Jeff Alan Ross, which Lynne said, "sounded fantastic." First staged at the beginning of 2010, "Peter Asher—A Memoir of the '60s" entertained audiences for years. "I thought it was terrific," Lynne told me. "I went to see it twice, actually!"

The year 2010 also saw the release of Peter's latest production project: *Savages*. Its roots lay back in the year 2000, when Jeff Alan Ross found himself southeast of London in County Kent, concluding a UK tour backing guitarist John Jorgenson. "The last show," Ross related, "was in a place called Sevenoaks." Jorgenson and the band were invited out to the nearby Webb residence for an end-of-tour party, which is where Ross was introduced to the musical family. By 2003, two of the clan, sisters Charley and Hattie Webb, had released their first album, and Ross, for one, was disappointed—he had heard their voices in their raw, spectral splendor and felt the Nashville producers were trying to "turn them into something they're not."

Later, in 2007, after beginning to work with Peter, Ross emailed the sisters: "You should really meet this friend of mine . . . I think you'd work well together." After the girls spent an evening chatting and singing with Peter in his London home, they almost immediately started working together. It's not surprising that Peter would respond positively to the sisters' musical attitude, as a lot of the records the pair gravitated toward while growing up, "we subsequently discovered that Peter produced," sister Charley explained: "James Taylor, Linda Ronstadt . . . that whole era of harmony singing; 'folkie-wokie,' as we call it." She laughed.

At the beginning of 2008, the sisters flew to LA to record with Peter and Nathaniel Kunkel at Conway Studios. Said Hattie: "It was very much rugs on the walls and on the floor, candles, and Peter standing in the middle of the room waving his arms," conducting the intimate quartet of musicians, including Charley on acoustic guitar and Hattie's evocative harp.

But the sessions were soon interrupted, as the sisters were hired as supporting players for beloved poet/singer/songwriter Leonard Cohen—becoming onstage harmonic muses for Cohen until his final performance in 2013. The album was finished piecemeal in between their worldwide tour commitments. On one occasion, Peter flew all the way from Australia, catching the girls in between shows in Europe, to record a steel guitar overdub; he drove straight to the studio, reclined on the couch with eyes closed, and, though jetlagged, continued to make coherent musical suggestions, "and then he would come up with amusing jokes while he appeared to be asleep." Hattie smiled. "He was sharp as a razor."

Their performance of Cohen's "If It Be Your Will" from a 2010 UK tour was included in the completed album, but other than that one cover, *Savages* was a collection of delicate, inventive original songs of love, loss, and longing, highlighted by the sisters' angelic harmonies and Peter's sensitive, uncluttered production touches. As Hattie said: "He gives a lot of courage in the studio about the simplest things being powerful."

Savages album cover.

Peter might add a few bars of mellotron flutes here or a dash of his own baritone guitar there; produce "Burn" with the crisp snap of a Ronstadt rocker, while agreeing with the sisters that "Dark Sky" be left starkly *a cappella*. Released on the sisters' own small label with no real promotion budget, *Savages* was not a commercial hit, but the album stands ready to share its magic with any listener who comes across it.

In between his "Memoir" shows, finishing *Savages*, and preproduction on a new tribute to Buddy Holly ("I've rarely known somebody so busy," Hattie marveled, "and hungry for inspiring projects"), an exciting new endeavor came by way of his old friend, composer Hans Zimmer.

"It seemed like we were friends from the moment we met," Zimmer explained to me, and he began to describe how Peter's wife saved his life: "I was working on a movie with a friend of Wendy's called Andrew Birkin." (This was *Burning Secret*, released in 1988.) "We were *so* low-budget that Wendy took pity on us and would come 'round to the studio and cook dinner for us—it was, maybe, the only square meal we ever got.

"I was basically 'the poor, starving musician,'" Zimmer confessed. "That I'm still alive has a lot to do with Wendy's cooking!"

Starving no longer, the busy Oscar-winning composer was relaxing after a meal, chatting with Peter, who explained that he was neither consulting for Sony nor supervising at Sanctuary any longer. Zimmer thought: "People have all this knowledge, all this stuff you *love*, you know, in their head—and nobody really seems to want it. . . . And I just said: '*I want it!*'

"It was *so* obvious to me," Zimmer said, immediately offering Peter the chance to consult for his company, Remote Control Productions, and work on major motion picture scores, songs, and soundtracks. One of his first assignments was for the *Sherlock Holmes: A Game of Shadows* album. "A lot of it was turning the music cues into workable album tracks," Peter recalled, plus he gave each track its title—a skill that Zimmer had been somewhat lax in: "He paid no attention to names, and at one point he was naming things depending on what he was doing at the time somebody *asked* him for the name." But that practice ended after Zimmer tuned to Classic FM one day while in London: "They play quite a lot of film score stuff," Peter explained, and when the stirring symphonic theme concluded, the composer was a tad embarrassed to hear the DJ announce: "That was Hans Zimmer's beautiful track: 'Budget Meeting.'" Peter, laughing, shared that relying on lines of dialogue to ultimately dictate the song titles was a *far* more sensible method.

Concurrent with his ongoing film work, Songmasters, a communications and marketing coalition, reached out to Peter for help with a project honoring the seventy-fifth anniversary of Buddy Holly's birth. First, an album was envisioned featuring Holly's songs interpreted by various artists. Peter was, of course, perfect for the job, having learned almost every Holly tune when first introduced to them by Gordon at Westminster.

Some artists—Ringo Starr, Brian Wilson, Jeff Lynne—tackled the material on their own. With other longtime friends—including Jackson Browne, Lyle Lovett, and Stevie Nicks—it gave Peter the opportunity to work with them in the studio for the first time. For Nicks, Peter suggested the ballad "Learning the Game," but she demurred: "I wanna do 'Not Fade Away'!" The track, coproduced with guitarist Waddy Wachtel, opens the collection *Listen to Me* with a passionate, rocking performance. It was former 10,000 Maniacs frontwoman Natalie Merchant who ultimately tackled "Learning the Game," infusing the song with a haunted weariness. And for something completely different, old friend Eric Idle—a fan, like Peter, of the comedy records Sir George Martin produced for Peter Sellers and Spike Milligan—presented a Pythonesque interpretation of "Raining in My Heart."

A definite highlight for Peter was producing Holly's "Peggy Sue" with the electronic pop band Cobra Starship. His daughter Victoria, formerly a film student at The Tisch School in New York, had joined the group in 2007, escaping academia much as her dad did in 1964—leaving King's College to pursue this rock'n'roll "foolishness." "When Victoria phoned up from NYU," Peter recalled, "and said, 'Oh, by the way, I've decided to quit school and join a band,' there was nothing I could say but, 'Oh!' You know? 'Cool!' Because to start suggesting it was a bad idea would *clearly* be historically untenable." What she thought would be a short lark—finally putting those dreaded piano lessons of her youth to *some* use—had turned into an unexpected career, with the band's last album, *Hot Mess*, making it into *Billboard*'s Top Ten upon release. "Maybe Peggy Sue could say a few words on her own behalf this time around," thought Peter, so after lead singer Gabe Saporta initiates the tune, Victoria steps to the microphone with a sassy sweetness and grabs one of the verses, announcing: "*I'm Peggy Sue/and I love you . . .*" turning Holly's declaration of love into a duet of devotion.

On Holly's birthday, September 7, 2011, the *Listen to Me* project continued—unveiling a star for Holly (next to The Beatles) on Hollywood's Walk of Fame in the morning, and later that evening the taping of a PBS special, where many of the artists from the tribute album performed live. Peter acted as both master of ceremonies and

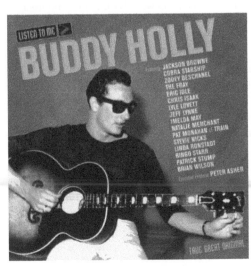

Listen to Me
album cover.

performer—sometimes as background singer, sometimes at center stage, as when he and Graham Nash duetted on Holly's obscure B-side "Take Your Time."

Nash, one of the greatest harmonizers of the rock era, said of Peter: "He knows musically what harmony's all about," and called him, next to Holly, "my *other* musical hero."

Dame Joan Sutherland was Nadine Loren's musical hero. At the age of nine, attending a concert by the operatic goddess, "I just tugged on my mom's arm," Loren recalled, "and said: 'I wanna sing like *that!*'" At age thirty-three, and after years of study, she wondered: "How do we package opera in a way that makes it more relatable, makes it more *fun?*" She had ultimately sung alongside such modern operatic giants as Andrea Bocelli, but was thinking back on her very first public performance as a kid in Germany, belting out "99 Luftballons." Looking to incorporate the expressive tonal colors of opera into the pop songs of her youth, she mentioned the idea to manager Barry Krost, who had partnered with Peter back in the eighties and was a mentor to Loren. He thought his old colleague might be able to help her realize this idea, and Peter was definitely game.

The resulting album, *Naked '80s*, reimagined tracks from that decade with some wonderful instrumental touches—a flamenco guitar dances throughout "Boys of Summer," for example, and a wild harmonica ignites "99 Luftballons." Loren uses her operatic range sparingly, employing it within a track as if another instrument. Covering Def Leppard's "Love Bites," her lead vocal—tender in the verses, impassioned in the chorus—is augmented with operatic vocalizations that fit into the gorgeous string arrangement as if substituting for a violin lead, later swirling around Larry Klein's fretless bass in a mid-song dreamy *pas de duex*.

"He makes the whole process so easy and comfortable," Loren said of Peter. "I really believe in the power of play; to give yourself the place to sound terrible and have terrible ideas"—she laughed—"because it's only by trying things that you real-

Naked '80s
album cover.

ize when something's a good idea or not." Peter, she said, supplied that place: "He made the process fun. And I know it was somewhat of a stressful time for him," she admitted, "but you would never have guessed it from what he brought to the table every day and the energy that he brought into the room."

Loren was referring to a cancer diagnosis that Peter received in late 2010. It was caught early, thankfully, and taken care of quickly and efficiently—as, of course, Peter would.

Also in 2010, Peter assisted Hans Zimmer with the music to the fourth film in the popular *Pirates of the Caribbean* series. Subtitled *On Stranger Tides*, its soundtrack would feature a vibrant, new musical element: the talents of the Mexican guitar duo Rodrigo y Gabriela, known for their amazing amalgam of Latin, rock, and jazz flavors presented with rhythmic power and dexterous precision.

"We clicked with Peter almost immediately," Gabriela Quintero said, as he guided the pair through the stranger tides of Zimmer's film world. They wouldn't be "scoring to picture," as more traditional composers might; Zimmer would share with the guitarists his themes and ideas, and Peter would produce their sessions and encourage their creativity, making sure the results would work within the composer's vision.

During those sessions, along with enjoying Peter's storytelling and sense of humor, "we understood he had a great sense of knowing when the best take was recorded," Rodrigo Sanchez recalled. "He was spot-on. He noticed all the things that only probably Gab and myself would have noticed."

The two guitarists had for years been toying with the idea of recording an album in Cuba, to inject their material with the island's rhythms. After their experience working on *Pirates*, they realized Peter was *the* producer to have by their side, "because he loves music," explained Gabriela, "he's a workaholic, and he likes what we do!" Their management team suggested working with a producer based in Cuba, but Rodrigo sensed that Peter's background producing rock music would be essential to the ultimate sound he was going for, as Peter "understood that we come from the rock side," Rodrigo explained, noting his and Gabriela's early years playing heavy metal.

Also essential was an arranger who understood different Latin rhythms, which is what they found in Alex Wilson. A British pianist/composer/arranger, Wilson is a salsa expert with a love of Cuban music, and he was happy to take on the project. Meeting up in Mexico City with Peter, Rodrigo, and Gabriela for preproduction, "we sat for three or four days," Wilson recalled. "Two guitars, a piano, and Peter making notes," detailing, for every song, what needed to be recorded and in what order—wanting, as usual, to be as meticulously prepared for the sessions as possible.

The studio and musicians were booked, and the quartet flew from Mexico City to Havana. Luckily possessing dual citizenship, "I used my British passport," said Peter, noting the US embargo still in place. "I figured if there was one occasion to choose *not* to be an American, this was probably it!"

The musicians hired were some of Havana's finest and were up to the task of turning Wilson's musical notations into performance pyrotechnics. Regardless of any communication problems—Peter does not speak Spanish—music seemed to be the universal language, much like Ronstadt's *Canciones di Mi Padre* sessions. "Although they didn't understand what he was saying," Rodrigo recalled, Peter "found a way to tell them how to react, how to do the right things according to what our original idea was—to make it a little more 'rockier,' instead of going 'all the way Latin.' He was great."

"The person that he is, you have to have a laser focus," said Wilson of Peter, "and sometimes you have to make brutally harsh decisions, as we all do if we want to ensure quality, and those weren't *too* many, but he did them in such a humane, gentle, and polite way. I was so impressed."

The differing rhythms and time signatures (often within the same tune) were complex, with Gabriela describing learning them all a "nightmare." But she praised Peter's "incredible ability to understand all these crazy rhythms. They're not the easiest things in the world. And to be able to have these 'atomic ears'"—she laughed—"to know perfectly who is out, who is in . . . out of tune, out of sync . . .

"That's why you get somebody like him, that brings everything up to a greater standard."

Once the Cuban sessions were wrapped, multiple layers of guitars were added in Rod and Gab's studio back in Mexico, including electric solos—a splash of Santana's sound here and a dose of Pink Floyd there. "There's always certain points in albums," Peter said, "where you kind of go: 'Let's stop and let's listen to everything and see what we need to do and how we're gonna do it.'" The decision was made to broaden the scope even further, inviting friends like sitarist Anoushka Shankar and the Palestinian oud players Le Trio Joubran to add more flavors to the mix. Eventually, sessions for the project were recorded in five different countries.

It was up to mixer Rafa Sardina to sonically weave it all into a seamless whole—to achieve a unity of sound with layer upon layer of instruments performing complex

Area 52
album cover.

and often lengthy compositions. "Incredible" is the word Gabriela used to describe Sardina's efforts, with every guitar lick, horn line, percussive roll, and piano flourish clearly defined and sitting neatly in place.

The fiery rhythms and rock attitude, the impeccable musicianship and swirling melodies—each piece takes you on a journey . . . and sitting still is simply futile. The album's title, *Area 52*, was a nod to the "alien" rhythms Rodrigo y Gabriela encountered in Cuba—a successful experiment for them and another fun challenge for Peter.

As *Area 52* wrapped production, Peter was, as usual, juggling a few other projects, including supervising sessions for the Australian group The McClymonts. The three sisters, a massively popular act in their native country, were recording in Nashville and Los Angeles in hopes of finally breaking through in the United States. Peter heard their demos and agreed to produce three tracks. "We were just over the moon," sister Brooke McClymont recalled, "because, I mean, he's a *legend!*

"He really brought out our harmonies," she said. "Those three songs, he brought them to *life!*" The track "Two Worlds Collide," written by all three sisters with Lindsay Rimes, certainly sounded hit-bound with its anthemic chorus and driving beat. "There were so many great players" that Peter procured, she recalled excitedly, including Dan Dugmore, Waddy Wachtel, and Jeff Alan Ross. "It was amazing!"

The album, also called *Two Worlds Collide*, was released in 2012 but failed to break the band in the States. "It *all* has to align," McClymont sighed, with tour plans abandoned as her pregnancy "kind of just halted everything." But back in their home country, the record ended up winning Best Country Album in Australia's ARIA Awards.

Peter was also helping to produce an album for *another* country music trio, composed of Gary Burr, Georgia Middleman, and Peter's old friend Kenny Loggins. They called themselves Blue Sky Riders. "They're all three amazing singers," Peter enthused, but the group had started to get concerned while planning their debut album: "We were worried that Kenny and I were gonna 'lock horns' in the studio," Burr explained, "and that would always put Georgia in a position of being 'The Vote,' and since Georgia and I are *married*, we thought that that was kind of unfair to Kenny.

"So we said, 'Why don't we bring in another guy to produce us, and he can be the guy who settles all the disputes?'" Names were discussed, Burr mentioned Peter, Loggins agreed he was a great choice, and, after seeing the band play live, Peter said: "I'm in."

Composing members who were all seasoned singers, songwriters, and producers, they were obviously well-prepared, but at one point, with extra time in the studio, the group decided to try a song that they hadn't already worked up: "I Get It."

"We played it," Burr recalled, "and Peter said, 'No—that's not how this song should go.'" He directed everyone to put down the instrument they were playing and pick up something else—someone moved to the conga drum, another picked up an unfamiliar guitar. "We just started fooling around with the song," Burr said, coming up with a completely different attitude and groove, "and it was terrific!" "Sometimes it's good to stop everything," Peter noted, "and start again from scratch."

"Peter's job was pretty much to restrain the horse from running away with the song," said Burr. "His point always was: 'The song is great—let the people hear the song. Does *that thing* that you wanna do, does that make people *hear* the song any clearer? Then what do you need it for?'" Unfortunately, after basic tracks were completed, Peter had other commitments and wasn't available for the overdub sessions. "That was when we piled on more stuff than we would have had Peter been in the room," Burr admitted, with Peter noting: "Kenny gets a bit complicated; he tends to want to overdub everything on everything."

When it came time to mix, Peter returned. Burr called the process "amazing. . . . A guy like that has every right to just say: 'You guys step out of the room. I'll mix this. I'll tell you what it's supposed to sound like.' But it was *very* democratic, and *everybody's* opinion was given worth and value." Peter brought Nathaniel Kunkel in to mix the album, and Burr called him "a genius," adding: "I want him to mix everything in my life!"

The album, *Finally Home*, was a solid, contemporary country showcase—full of heavenly harmonies and hook-laden tunes, with a touch of soul ("How's That Workin' for Ya") and even a pinch of prog ("As Luck Would Have It"). Unfortunately, lacking an expensive promotional campaign, it didn't reach a large audience. "It did as well as a self-released album does these days," Burr admitted, but fans of twenty-first-century country should search it out.

Not many are tasked to write a love song celebrating the romance between a lion and a jaguar, but Peter accepted the mission and was surprisingly rewarded with his first solo recording.

Finally Home album cover.

"We were in London," Peter recalled, "to work on some themes Hans had developed." Zimmer was composing the music for the latest DreamWorks animation project, *Madagascar 3: Europe's Most Wanted*, and while recording at AIR Studios, they received word from the film's creative team: For the scene where the lion falls in love with the jaguar, they suggested to "maybe put a song in there," according to Peter.

"Dave and I," he continued, "decided to go off and write one." Dave Stewart of The Eurythmics was part of the musical team assembled, and "that night, we had a couple of martinis," Peter confessed, "and sat down with our guitars and wrote the song." Peter came up with the opening line: *"Love always comes as a surprise"*— "which is the essence of what the song is supposed to be about," he explained—and it became the song's title. A quick demo was made, recorded on an iPhone, and played the next day for the film's executives, who liked it. "But we were very unconfident," Peter admitted. "Not that we didn't like it—we did," he said, but they were simply unsure the song would successfully survive the various layers of approval to be ultimately used. Back in LA the following week, he produced a track using mandolins and accordion to enhance his romantic waltz-time melody. Peter sang the lyrics himself, just to give the team an idea of how it would sound when finished. "Then there was a meeting about who should sing it in the movie," Peter remembered, "and it was Jeffrey Katzenberg who, halfway through the meeting, said, 'This sounds fine. Peter should just sing it.' Okay, you're the boss!"

Then CEO of DreamWorks, Katzenberg certainly *was* the boss, and Peter praised his "impeccable taste" in vocalists. The track's use in the film and its inclusion on the soundtrack album gave Peter, after fifty years of recorded work, his very first solo performance credit. The use of this "untried singer" didn't seem to hurt, as, to date, the film has earned almost three-quarters of a billion dollars, worldwide.

28

WAY BACK IN THE DAY

"I'd been writing songs for the banjo ever since I started playing it," comedian Steve Martin told me. Completely self-taught, Martin was always good at coming up with melodic chord progressions while employing the various picking styles he was able to glean off records. He incorporated the banjo into his stand-up comedy from the beginning, including early appearances at The Troubadour opening for Linda Ronstadt.

In October 2011, Martin attended a dinner party with Paul Simon and his wife, singer Edie Brickell—best known for her eighties hit "What I Am" with the band New Bohemians. As they were leaving, Martin recalled: "Edie turned to me and said, 'Do you want to write a song together?' And I'd never even *heard* of that! I didn't know how it was *done!*

"But to be polite"—Martin laughed—"I said, 'Sure!'"

They made one attempt to write face-to-face; it was unsuccessful. "I didn't really know what I was doing," Martin admitted, but before departing, he mentioned to Brickell: "I have these tunes I write for the banjo; let me send them to you." He'd record the piece onto his phone, then email the music file to Brickell. Once she had it, "I would put it on GarageBand," she said, "and then I would pick up my phone, and before I even *listened* to it, I would hit 'record' because, so often, the first melody and the first thoughts that come would be . . ." She paused, searching for the right words: ". . . so *authentic.*" While listening, a stream of consciousness would start: "I let the music inspire me and dictate what the song should be."

Steve, Peter explained, "was expecting her to write using the melody of the banjo piece, but she didn't; she wrote these *other* melodies!" The melodies were so strong that one would think it was *Steve* who'd come up with clever banjo accompaniments to *Edie's* lyrics. Brickell placed her stories in a real world of freeloaders and faithful friends, of hope and despair, of cats and dogs and sunshine and suppertime; she'd use words or phrases —"El Camino," "my creepy cousin"—that simply made her smile. Martin admitted, "I was blown away!"

Some months later, "I was having dinner with Steve," Peter remembered, "and he played me three or four" of these mp3 files of just banjo and voice. "I told him how much I liked them, and I thought they should make an album." It was only after Peter left that Steve began to consider the possibility that the legendary Peter Asher, though a friend, would seriously agree to produce the project. "That was sorta over-reaching"—he chuckled—"for these little, uh, '*tunes*.'"

Flying back to Los Angeles the next day, "I got an email from Steve saying: 'Do you want to produce the album?'" Peter immediately wrote back: "Yes, yes, yes!"

A week was spent at engineer Frank Filipetti's home studio outside New York City, first recording Martin's lightly stepping banjo, then Brickell's vocals—which had an easy swing with her light Texas drawl. By the end of those original sessions, Martin recalled Peter saying: "The one thing I believe is: This shouldn't be a bluegrass re-cord." Taking the basic tracks back to Los Angeles, Peter developed a detailed plan, dusting each song with a mixture of elements artfully chosen to reveal each song's whimsical beauty. Some tracks were arranged for string quartet accompaniment, while a couple added the extraordinary jazz bassist Esperanza Spaulding; a few have the fiddle and mandolin you might expect, but then, surprisingly, a small choir appears in one song like an eerie apparition. Peter added light percussion touches throughout—patting his thighs, for example, to lend rhythm to the album's title track, "Love Has Come for You."

"We were worried," Martin admitted, waiting to hear the results of Peter's efforts, as he and Brickell loved the simple rawness of unadorned banjo and voice. "But," he quickly added, "we needn't have been." The pair's performances were warmly clothed with Peter's tasteful choices, and upon hearing the rough mixes, Martin recalled feeling "flattered" by Peter's production. "We flipped out," Brickell laughed. "We loved it."

Love Has Come for You
album cover.

A beautiful, gentle slice of modern Americana, *Love Has Come for You* was a hit in folk and bluegrass circles upon its release in April 2013. That same month, the album *Save Rock and Roll* was released by the band Fall Out Boy. How Peter came to participate in *that* album—at the very last minute—is a story that begins with a phone call from Sir Elton John regarding another project entirely.

"He called me out of the blue," Peter remembered. "He likes doing that to people!" Elton explained that 2014 would mark the fortieth anniversary of his iconic album *Goodbye Yellow Brick Road*. As part of a proposed Deluxe Edition, his idea was to ask a handful of modern artists to reimagine songs from that collection in a new way. Would Peter help in producing a few? "I said 'Of course!'"

Peter and Elton began brainstorming which songs would best suit which artists, choosing the pop-punk band Fall Out Boy to tackle "Saturday Night's Alright for Fighting." The band felt honored to be asked, agreeing to participate, but the next day they phoned Peter back with a request of their own: Would Elton John return the favor and sing on the album the group was days away from finishing? "So I called Elton," recalled Peter, "and he said 'Yes,'" requesting that Peter supervise the session. He flew out to Atlanta the next day to produce Elton's vocal contribution, which added some gravitas to the album's title track. Mixed and mastered within days, *Save Rock and Roll* debuted at number-one in *Billboard*'s album chart the week of its release.

Superstar Ed Sheeran was another artist invited to participate in the *Goodbye Yellow Brick Road* project. He and Peter gave "Candle in the Wind" a spritely, acoustic feel with layers of background harmonies, a touch of violin, a mandolin, and a little percussion, courtesy (no surprise) of Peter. It might have lacked some of the solemnness of Elton's version, but in its place is a youthful innocence and simplicity—like Norma Jeane Baker herself.

Peter produced an electro-funk version of "Bennie and the Jets" with Miguel, adding Jason Bonham on drums and sampling Elton's original hit. He guided Imelda May toward delivering a swingin' rockabilly take on "Your Sister Can't Twist" and worked with The Band Perry for a countrified version of "Grey Seal." Other acts also participated, but the only artist that Elton insisted take part in the project was singer/songwriter John Grant, whose first solo LP, *Queen of Denmark*, was named 2010's Album of the Year by many music critics.

"Sweet Painted Lady"—lyricist Bernie Taupin's ode to prostitutes—was the track chosen for Grant. "I love that song. I love that whole album." Grant laughed, recalling how much *Goodbye Yellow Brick Road* was spun by his siblings while growing up in Michigan. For the few days he was in Los Angeles, instead of a hotel, Grant stayed with Peter and his wife, Wendy, in their Malibu home. Though he now had two critically acclaimed albums under his belt, he felt "pretty intimidated," he said, due to Peter's legendary stature. "He's worked with all those people, and I'm just some kid from some little town in Michigan," Grant confessed. "Like, how the fuck did I end up here with this guy . . . ?"

"But they were *so kind* to me," Grant said of the Ashers, "and treated me as if it were perfectly natural"—he laughed—"that I was there!"

Once in front of the microphone, Grant used his crooning baritone to good effect, and within a few takes, Peter was happy. Grant was not: "I hated my vocal. It's not that Peter didn't do a good job," he explained. "I'm just way too self-critical. But it was a great experience. It was fun to be around him." Despite his decades of success, Peter still remained, much to Grant's surprise, "humble."

"Which is a beautiful thing."

Martin and Brickell, meanwhile, had gone on the road to promote *Love Has Come for You*. One day, while traveling by bus, the pair began to share their love of musicals. When she was a kid, "my mom would sing songs from musicals," Brickell recalled. "The rhyming patters of those songs always caught my ear—so fun, so playful." As the bus rolled down the freeway, filled with the sounds of one memorable show tune after another, the thought came: "Hey—why don't *we* write a musical?" As Martin wondered what the subject might be, "Edie suggested, 'Maybe we can look at the songs we've already written and find something.'"

One track on their album happened to be based on a true story, and Edie recalled the song's origin: One of Steve's banjo pieces, for a change, did not bring lyrics immediately to mind—but one part of the tune *did* suggest a train whistle. "I thought: 'A train song? Well, why not give it a shot?'" Recalling the classic tune "The Orange Blossom Special," she noted, "That's such a beautiful title." Determined to find a similarly evocative name, she Googled: "*names of Southern trains*." "And the first one to catch my eye," Brickell said, "was the Iron Mountain. I thought: 'Oooh, *that* sounds nice and strong.' I clicked on it, and *right there* they tell you this *crazy* story!"

In 1902 Missouri, a farmer walks near the Iron Mountain railway just as the train crosses a bridge fifty feet above his head. Once it passes, he begins to hear the sound of a muffled baby's cry, eventually finding a suitcase tossed from the train that holds the bruised, but still living, child. "And then, when I see that the woman who raised him was named Sara Jane," continued Brickell, "and her name rhymed with 'train,' I said, 'Well, there ya go.'" She laughed. "Look no further!"

"Sara Jane and the Iron Mountain Baby" eventually occurred to Steve as the basis on which to build their proposed musical—their own backstory of *whose* baby and what eventually happened to both mother and son. They originally planned on incorporating many of the songs from their album into the show, but as the story came together and the character's lives developed, they largely wrote a new score—keeping only three tunes from their earlier efforts. "In any kind of creative situation," Carmen Cusack explained, "you know going in that you can't get too attached, 'cause it's a process."

Cusack was chosen to portray Alice—the show's lead character. "I remember walking into one of our first days of rehearsal, and the musicians were whispering," observed Cusack. "I thought they were in gaga land over Steve Martin, but no—it was Peter Asher that they were all starstruck over!" With a long résumé, including Fantine in *Les Misérables* on London's West End and Elphaba in the national touring company of *Wicked*, she was there to observe all the changes as the show went from its workshop stage in 2013 to its Broadway opening in 2016. "Peter was there from the beginning," she said. "He was very hands-on."

"I worked a lot on the background vocal arrangements," Peter noted, with the show's music director, Rob Berman, who was hired early on. As the orchestrations were prepared for the musicians tasked to perform Martin and Brickell's music onstage, Peter recognized a problem: "When the orchestrator first came in," Martin recalled, "he ignored the interstitial melody of the banjo." Peter had to explain that it wasn't simply a sequence of chords featuring only the singer's melody—the *banjo's* melody, the *riffs*, were a crucial part of the songs and needed to be retained in the arrangements.

Peter "was a *spirit-guider*," Martin enthused, "to keep *all* of us on the path." Carmen Cusack laughed, recalling her wizardry nickname for Peter: "Rock'n'Roll Gandalf."

Martin and Brickell's new songs included such delicately crafted tunes as "Always Will" and "What Could Be Better," but the one Cusack called her favorite was a song that Brickell thought up on her own: "I was sitting next to Peter," she remembered, "on a flight, when the idea for that song came to me. I got very excited—the first line, the melody, all came to me. And I turned to him and said, 'Do you like this?'" Brickell sang: "*Way back in the day/I would have gone with you.*"

"Peter's face said it all; the encouragement for me to continue allowed that song to flourish," Brickell said. "A moment of magic—and he was right there!"

"I don't have a ton of confidence when an idea first arrives," she confided, "and so it's just uplifting for somebody to *look* at you and give you that little nudge that you need."

When finished, "Way Back in the Day" certainly retained its magic—a gorgeous slice of melancholy with the singer recalling the "happy and carefree" person they once were. Martin didn't hesitate to call the song "fantastic" and "crucial" for the show.

By the time *Bright Star* held its world premiere in San Diego in September 2014, Peter, Steve, and Edie had decided to record a second album—one that would include "Way Back in the Day" and many more songs from the musical but, again, produced from scratch by Peter. Starting with the basic tracks of banjo and voice, Peter would then, as before, overdub everything, making the sonic choices that, as he would note, "frame the songs and present them in the best way."

But before recording began, there was that fateful phone call from the chief of staff at the British Consulate General's office . . .

"Are you alone?" the voice on the other end of the line asked. "Can you speak freely?"

Cautiously, Peter answered: "Uhhh, yes?"

"Well, I'm happy to inform you that Her Majesty the Queen has decided to offer you the rank of Commander of the Most Excellent Order of the British Empire."

Peter, sitting alone in his home office, was stunned, yet he calmly responded: "How extraordinary. Thank you."

The Honors in Britain are awards of merit given to citizens who have distinguished themselves and brought honor to the Empire. The lists are announced publicly at each New Year and on the queen's birthday in June. Most people are familiar with Knighthoods—with men styled "Sir," the female equivalent being "Dame"—but there are also Orders of the British Empire: commander, officer, and member. Peter's CBE honor placed him highest in this category, which particularly amazed him: "I don't know how that happened."

"I think the thing that the British government really appreciated and valued and wanted to recognize," former British consul general Chris O'Connor explained, "was the extent to which Peter had, for many years, helped the wider effort on building cultural connections between the UK and the US." The British Consulate in Los Angeles holds various yearly events—from "Brit Week," which promotes British innovation and creativity, to parties surrounding the BAFTA Awards, to any number of British-based initiatives—and Peter "was always actively, enthusiastically involved, coming and banging the drum, joining in and helping expand and amplify that message.

"It's not something that anybody *has* to do," O'Connor continued, but Peter always had, and with a "consistent commitment and enthusiasm." All that, added to his phenomenal music career, made Peter's nomination one they happily endorsed.

As the phone call continued, the chief of staff asked if he would formally accept the title, and Peter said yes immediately. "It *is* rare," O'Connor noted, for some to refuse being so honored, "but the system would prefer to avoid the embarrassment of that happening in the public glare." They would also prefer to avoid word of any of the queen's Honors leaking out before officially announcing the list themselves, so Peter was sworn to secrecy—only Wendy could be told. "We didn't even tell Victoria," confirmed Wendy, until after the list of honorees was made public weeks later.

"I used to always make fun of him," Wendy said, cracking jokes about Peter ever getting a medal: "Yeah, *that's* never gonna happen!"

On February 23, 2015, Peter, Wendy, and Victoria were driven through the gates of Buckingham Palace. "Once you're in," Peter recalled, "it's guards on the stairs and Beefeaters everywhere"—referring to the ceremonial guards dressed in Tudor-era scarlet and gold. "You go in and they separate you out; there's the audience or the guests, and then there's the OBEs and the MBEs in one waiting room, and the CBEs and the Knights and Dames in the other waiting room." There, honorees are given instructions on how to comport themselves during the ceremony. Tea is served—no alcohol, Peter noted.

"I thought it was gonna be all snobby and weird," Wendy assumed, but everyone "was really nice!" Because it was such a big day for Peter, they had arrived at the palace early ("I'm *never* early," noted Wendy), so she and Victoria scored seats in the front row.

Though the Honors come from Queen Elizabeth II, she's not always there to present them—any member of the Royal Family can be called upon to officiate the Investiture, and in Peter's case it was Prince William. Was he disappointed it wasn't

Her Majesty? "Not really," he said. "William's pretty cool, and he *is* the future king, so it was exciting." Once each honoree is called forward and their medal presented, there occurs a few brief seconds during which they have a somewhat private chat. With Peter honored for his services to the music business, Prince William asked the inevitable question: "How *is* the music business?"

"Terrible," Peter joked, "but the *music* is still good."

The Honor and the investiture ceremony "really did mean a lot to him," Wendy confided. "He's very English that way. It's just really too bad that his mother hadn't been around to see it." Margaret Asher, unfortunately, had passed away four years earlier.

The Honor is one thing—Peter proudly puts "CBE" after his name on *all* official correspondence—but, as Steve Martin told me: "He's the nicest cynic you'll ever meet." Upon showing me his medal, I read aloud the phrase emblazoned upon it: "*For God and the Empire.*"

"Thus committing my life to two nonexistent entities—that's what I particularly like about it." He laughed.

EPILOGUE

While some might take a break and bask in the royal glow of the queen's honor, over the next few years, Peter continued to immerse himself in varied musical adventures. *So Familiar*, the second Martin and Brickell album, was released toward the end of 2015 and became, as its predecessor, a hit in folk music circles. *Bright Star* finally opened on Broadway in the spring of 2016; it might not have won any Tony Awards (though it was nominated in five categories), but the show was given the Outer Critics Circle Award for Outstanding New Broadway Musical and a Drama Desk Award for Outstanding Music. Peter, as you would expect, produced the Original Broadway Cast Recording of the show, which topped the Folk Album charts and was nominated for a Grammy Award.

For Hans Zimmer, Peter took on the role of director, helping him stage a highly successful live show featuring music from over a dozen of his film scores. Along with overseeing the staging and pacing of the show—performed by an impressive orchestra, choir, and band—Peter also helped by scripting much of Zimmer's onstage commentary. "You always need someone who has your back," Zimmer said, "and Peter definitely had my back." Including a dazzling light show and intricate sound design, the tour was staged in various countries around the world for years.

In May 2017, Sirius XM Satellite Radio launched "The Beatles Channel" and engaged Peter to host a weekly hourlong radio show. Entitled *From Me to You*, the program features Peter as storyteller emeritus, playing songs by The Beatles and those who influenced them, charmingly digressing here and there for a personal reminiscence or offering facts about music in general, but always circling back to highlight the genius of his old friends.

Harkening back to his roots—playing small venues as part of a duo—Peter undertook a series of short tours: first paired with guitarist extraordinaire Albert Lee (onetime musical director for Peter's heroes The Everly Brothers), and later teaming up with Jeremy Clyde—one half of Chad and Jeremy, another duo from the British Invasion years. Friends before either made hit records, Clyde—a celebrated actor as well as singer—found that Peter had retained his comedic timing as they played up their friendly sixties rivalry between songs. "He *thinks* like an actor," Clyde said, which made working with him "a joy."

With all this, Peter still found time to perform his "Memoir" show in various countries, consult on a number of film soundtracks, *and* fully produce two recording projects between 2017 and 2021: *The Long-Awaited Album* by Steve Martin and the Steep Canyon Rangers (which hit number-one on the Bluegrass chart) and *Why Wait!*—a second (and also "long-awaited") album collaboration with Kate Taylor. Along with Jeff Alan Ross as musical director, Peter hired essentially the same band from *Sister Kate* fifty years earlier—Danny Kortchmar, Lee Sklar, and Russ Kunkel—who, after a half century, continue to deliver for Peter the deepest grooves this side of Muscle Shoals.

"I'm not going to write an autobiography, no."

Peter always seemed emphatically negative on that subject the few times I raised the issue. He *did* end up writing a book, *The Beatles: From A to Zed*, based on his radio show and published in 2019. Though sprinkled with stories from his history with The Fabs, it didn't dwell on his own extraordinary career to any real extent.

Somehow I felt the need to attempt to document *all* of Peter's achievements in one place, give those of us who are fans of his work more of a sense of how these productions came together, and try to paint the picture of a man who, after close to sixty years in the music business, still radiates an endless exuberance and a childlike joy at making music.

"I think in some ways," musician Donald Fagen explained, "although he's a very organized person (in an English sort of way), I think he's also basically a very childlike person—which makes it easy for me to get along with him, 'cause I don't do well with adults."

"You *play* music," Hans Zimmer observed. "You don't labor at it, you don't work at it, you *play* it. So the *playfulness* is vital. And of course, there's a playfulness about Peter."

The composer continued to marvel at his old friend's enthusiasm: "You know, sometimes I forget that I'm not dealing with a twenty-year-old who is just so excited about doing music—because he *IS* a twenty-year-old who's so excited about doing music!"

"Quite a unique specimen," is how James Taylor described his longtime friend—the man who discovered him, signed him, and for years produced and managed him. "And he also loves music—he just *loves* it, you know? It's a delight knowing him, and I really credit him with my being able to just sustain for as long as I did."

Peter might not be managing acts any longer, but he's not finished discovering new talent and helping them in the studio. He recently produced a couple of tracks for a talented young vocalist named Raquel Garcia, hoping it might help her land a record deal. "I think, at the end of the day, what it comes down to is his talent for discovering other talent. He's someone who can spot a diamond and, at the same time, put their ego aside and make something fabulous," Hans Zimmer noted. "He's more excited about the diamond than they themselves are—and, weirdly, that's what turned Peter into a diamond."

"I *am* available for work," Peter insisted, with no plans for retirement. As I write this (near the end of 2021), he's finishing up sessions with Susanna Hoffs, best known as lead singer for pop-rock band The Bangles. Asked about artists with whom he might like to work, he paused, noting there were many, but eventually named Holly Humberstone, Kasey Musgraves, and Brandy Clark.

"I actually talked to somebody at Warner Brothers," Peter revealed. "I said, 'Look, I'd love to produce Brandy Clark one day, if she'd like to make a change.' And they kinda went, 'No, well, she's already decided that she's doing this album with so-and-so'—somebody good, who I know.

"But they said, 'It's funny you should say that.'

"I said, 'Why?'

"He said, 'Well, we were talking on the phone one day, and she told me that one of her ambitions was to make an album as good as *Heart Like a Wheel*.'

"And I went: 'Well, *next* time somebody *says* that . . . !'" He laughed. "It is that thing where you have to keep going: How do I remind people I'm not deaf or dead?" Adding quietly: "Which are the only two real impediments . . ."

Please, feel free to pass this book on to anyone who needs reminding.

Peter Asher: "It's a relatively harmless career."

ACKNOWLEDGMENTS

This is my first attempt at writing a book, and I would not have succeeded were it not for the help of a huge number of people. I would like to acknowledge a few to which I owe a great deal of thanks . . .

Author Sheila Weller gave me an early push to keep going, as did author Harvey Kubernik. My old friend, writer Matt Hurwitz, always offered encouragement, as did Don Wrege and George (not the) Martin—two friends from my college days who were always ready to read chapters and offer, not only invaluable critiques, but their love and support.

My eternal thanks to everyone who spoke with me in person, or on the phone, or sent an email recounting their adventures with Peter. Of course, you don't get in touch with over two hundred entertainers and show business folk without various managers and publicists clearing the way, and I'm indebted to you all (too numerous to list here, unfortunately). A handful of interviews ended up being drastically reduced or edited out entirely, but they were always important in helping to broaden my understanding of Peter's life and career.

A big thanks to Keith "Avo" Avison, who managed to hang on to hundreds of negatives from his days with Peter and Gordon and simply mailed them all to me (they're in Peter's hands now).

That you're reading this is due in no small part to my literary agent, Barbara Hogenson—for this project to ever see the light of day, she was essential. And thanks to the folks at Backbeat Books for their faith in what I was attempting to do.

And to my biggest fan, Kathleen Forrest—because of you, I won't ever have to stay in a world without love.

Finally: "Fond thanks to Peter Asher—cool and thoughtful throughout."

David Jacks
April 2022

INDEX